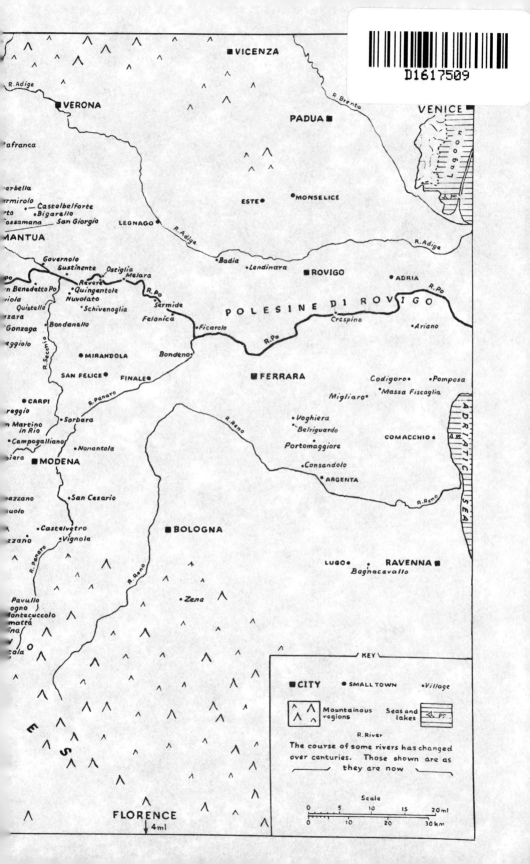

■VICENZA

R.Adige

■VERONA

PADUA ■

VENICE ■

R.Brenta

Lagoon

'afranca

'erbella

'rmirolo — •Castelbelforte
'to •Bigarello
'ossamana •San Giorgio

LEGNAGO •

R.Adige

ESTE •

•MONSELICE

•Badia

R.Adige

■MANTUA

•Governolo
•Sustinente
•Ostiglia
•Revere •Melara
n Benedetto Po •Quingentole
'iola •Nuvolato
Quistello •Schivenoglia
•zzara
•Gonzaga •Bondanello
•eggiolo

•Lendinara

■ROVIGO

•ADRIA

R.Po

P O L E S I N E   D I   R O V I G O

R.Po

•Crespino

•Ariano

R.Po

•Sermide

•Felonica

•Ficarolo

•Bondeno

R.Secchia

•MIRANDOLA

•SAN FELICE •FINALE •

■FERRARA

•Codigoro •Pomposa

•Migliaro •Massa Fiscaglia

R.Panaro

•CARPI
'reggio
'n Martino •Sorbara
in Rio
•Campogalliano

•Voghiera
•Belriguardo
•Portomaggiore

COMACCHIO

A
D
R
I
A
T
I
C

S
E
A

•Nonantola

■MODENA

R.Reno

•Consandolo

•ARGENTA

'azzano •San Cesario
'uolo

•Castelvetro
'zzano •Vignola

■BOLOGNA

R.Panaro

R.Reno

LUGO •   •RAVENNA ■
•Bagnacavallo

Pavullo
'ogno
'ontecuccolo
'mattà
'ina
'cola

•Zena

O

E

S

FLORENCE
↓4ml

Clean Hands and Rough Justice

STUDIES IN MEDIEVAL AND EARLY MODERN CIVILIZATION
Marvin B. Becker, General Editor

Charity and Children in Renaissance Florence:
The Ospedale degli Innocenti, 1410–1536
  Philip Gavitt

Humanism in Crisis: The Decline of the French Renaissance
  Philippe Desan, editor

Upon My Husband's Death: Widows in the Literatures
and Histories of Medieval Europe
  Louise Mirrer, editor

The Crannied Wall: Women, Religious, and the Arts
in Early Modern Europe
  Craig A. Monson, editor

Wife and Widow in Medieval England
  Sue Sheridan Walker, editor

The Rhetorics of Life-Writing in Early Modern Europe: Forms of
Biography from Cassandra Fedele to Louis XIV
  Thomas F. Mayer and D. R. Woolf, editors

Defining Dominion: The Discourses of Magic and Witchcraft in
Early Modern France and Germany
  Gerhild Scholz Williams

Women, Jews, and Muslims in the Texts
of Reconquest Castile
  Louise Mirrer

The Culture of Merit: Nobility, Royal Service, and the Making of
Absolute Monarchy in France, 1600–1789
  Jay M. Smith

Clean Hands and Rough Justice: An Investigating Magistrate
in Renaissance Italy
  David S. Chambers and Trevor Dean

Clean Hands and Rough Justice

An Investigating Magistrate
in Renaissance Italy

David S. Chambers and Trevor Dean

Ann Arbor

THE UNIVERSITY OF MICHIGAN PRESS

Copyright © by the University of Michigan 1997
All rights reserved
Published in the United States of America by
The University of Michigan Press
Manufactured in the United States of America
⊗ Printed on acid-free paper

2000   1999   1998   1997   4   3   2   1

A CIP catalog record for this book is available from the British Library

Library of Congress Cataloging-in-Publication Data

Chambers, David (David Sanderson)
  Clean hands and rough justice : an investigating magistrate in
Renaissance Italy / David S. Chambers and Trevor Dean.
    p.   cm. — (Studies in medieval and early modern civilization)
  Includes bibliographical references and index.
  ISBN 0-472-10748-8 (alk. paper)
    1. Cusadro, Geremia, 1453–1536.   2. Judges—Italy—Biography.
3. Podesta—Italy—Biography.   4. Criminal justice, Administration
of—Italy—History—16th century.   5. Italy—Politics and
government—1268–1559.   I. Dean, Trevor.   II. Title.   III. Series.
KKH110.C87C46   1997
347.45'014'092—dc21   96-45861
                                                            CIP

Preface

This book first took shape as a joint project after each of us had, quite independently, presented papers on Beltramino Cusadri at the seminar in Italian History, 1250–1550, at the Institute of Historical Research in London. Trevor Dean had for some time been working on crime and justice in the Este state, with a focus on Beltramino Cusadri; David Chambers had been pursuing over a number of years various aspects of Gonzaga rule in Mantua. Nicolai Rubinstein suggested a collaboration, and both authors gratefully acknowledge this.

Many debts have been incurred in the long course of completing this study. Trevor Dean wishes principally to thank the British Academy, which, through a Postdoctoral Research Fellowship and a number of travel grants, funded the main stages of his research; and the Leverhulme Trust, which funded its final phase. Seminar audiences—in London, Guildford, Oxford, Cornell, and Verona—have heard of Beltramino Cusadri from one or the other of the authors, and both of them thank those audiences for their comments. Trevor Dean is grateful to Roehampton Institute London for a semester of sabbatical leave that allowed the writing to be completed; David Chambers is grateful as ever to the Library and to his colleagues at the Warburg Institute. Philip Jones read some chapters in early drafts, and Sam Cohn generously read through the whole typescript: both are thanked for their time and valuable suggestions. The authors are also grateful to Boris Weltman, who drew the map, and to Rodolfo Signorini for his help in tracing and checking some documents and for arranging for a photograph to be made. Finally, this book would not have been possible without the courteous openness of northern Italian archives and libraries: their staff's ready help has been deeply appreciated.

Although this book is a genuine collaboration, in that each author commented on and added to the other's texts, David Chambers was principally responsible for chapters 2, 3, 4, and 7, and the epilogue, while

Trevor Dean was the principal author of chapters 1, 5, and 6, and the conclusion. The introduction was written jointly.

Permissions to reproduce material as plates has been granted by the Ministero per i Beni Culturali e Ambientali (Soprintendenza per i beni artistici e storici di Mantova, Prot. no. 71/11F/3C, for the photograph of the *stemma* of G. Ginori; and Archivio di Stato, Mantua, Prot. no. 4887/V/9, for the reproduction of the documents in AG, b. 2413, fols. 783v, 785r) and by the Comune di Ferrara (Biblioteca comunale ariostea, Ferrara, Prot. no. 001258, for the reproduction of the illustration in MS Cl. I, 404).

Contents

Abbreviations

AG	ASMn, Archivio Gonzaga
AMMo	*Atti e memorie della Deputazione di storia patria per le provincie modenesi*
AMRo	*Atti e memorie della Deputazione di storia patria per la Romagna*
AN	ASMn, Archivio notarile
ASBo	Archivio di Stato, Bologna
ASCMo	Archivio storico del comune, Modena
ASE	ASMo, Archivio segreto estense
ASFe	Archivio di Stato, Ferrara
ASMn	Archivio di Stato, Mantua
ASMo	Archivio di Stato, Modena
ASRe	Archivio di Stato, Reggio-Emilia
b.	*busta*, "file"
BCFe	Biblioteca comunale ariostea, Ferrara
BCCr	Biblioteca comunale, Crema
BCMn	Biblioteca comunale, Mantua
BL	British Library, London
Cam. duc.	ASMo, Camera ducale
CS	ASE, La casa e lo stato
DBI	*Dizionario biografico degli italiani* (Rome, 1960–)
LD	ASE, Cancelleria, Leggi e decreti
RdS	ASE, Cancelleria, Rettori dello stato
reg.	register

Clean Hands and Rough Justice

Introduction

Law and order, crime and punishment in the Renaissance principality have not been much investigated.[1] Historical interest has continued to focus more on the ruling families' courts or on their domestic lives and their sponsorship of education and the arts; most work on crime and justice has been, and continues to be, concentrated on Venice and Florence, or at most Tuscany.[2] This lack of study remains true of many institutional aspects of the Renaissance principality. Giorgio Chittolini has noted the absence of satisfactory research on the bureaucracy of the Sforza dukes of Milan—on the provenance of officials, their social origin, their mentalities and culture, their attitude toward office, their ambitions and careers.[3] In an outline history of the Este state, Marini, intent on not

---

1. But see E. Verga, "Le sentenze criminali dei podestà milanesi, 1385–1429," *Archivio storico lombardo*, 3d ser., 16 (1901); G.S. Pene Vidari, "Sulla criminalità e sui banni del comune di Ivrea nei primi anni della dominazione sabauda (1313–1347)," *Bollettino storico-bibliografico subalpino* 68 (1970); W. Gundersheimer, "Crime and Punishment in Ferrara, 1440–1500," in *Violence and Civil Disorder in Italian Cities, 1200–1500*, ed. L. Martines (Berkeley, 1972); G. Bonfiglio Dosio, "Criminalità ed emarginazione a Brescia nel primo Quattrocento," *Archivio storico italiano* 136 (1978); R. Comba, "Il progetto di una società coercitivamente cristiana: Gli Statuti di Amedeo VIII di Savoia," *Rivista storica italiana* 103 (1991). And see the bibliographical surveys for Umbria (by M. Vallerani) and Piedmont (by F. Panero), in *Ricerche storiche* 19–20 (1989–90). For law, see M.G. di Renzo Villata, "Scienza giuridica e legislazione nell'età sforzesca," in *Gli Sforza a Milano e in Lombardia e i loro rapporti con gli stati italiani ed europei (1450–1535)* (Milan, 1982); G. Chittolini and D. Willoweit, eds., *Statuti città territori in Italia e Germania tra Medioevo ed Età moderna*, Annali dell'istituto storico italo-germanico, Quaderno 30 (Bologna, 1991).
2. See the general survey of A. Zorzi, "Giustizia criminale e criminalità nell'Italia del tardo medioevo: Studi e prospettive di ricerca," *Società e storia* 46 (1989); and the bibliography in idem, "Tradizioni storiografiche e studi recenti sulla giustizia nell'Italia del rinascimento," *Cheiron* 8 (1991): 61–78.
3. G. Chittolini, "L'onore dell'officiale," *Quaderni milanesi* 17–18 (1989): 6–7; and see idem, "Su alcuni aspetti dello stato di Federico," in *Federico di Montefeltro: Lo stato, le arti, la cultura*, ed. G. Cerboni Baiardi, G. Chittolini, and P. Floriani (Rome, 1986), 61.

writing a history of the cultural "golden age" ("il secolo d'oro: per chi?"),[4] wished to direct attention away from Ferrarese cultural glitter toward the whole state and all sectors within it; but he found that the groundwork had simply not been done, and he was forced to rely on outdated general works and conjecture. At Mantua even such a critical stance as Marini's has yet to be adopted.

Within the broad area of crime and justice, policing—the provision of personnel and resources to prevent and detect crime and disorder—has received least attention. Most historians of Italian justice have remained focused on the judicial process and on the records it produced (trial records, lists of fines or punishments). They have dealt with the history of judicial institutions, their powers, personnel, and activity,[5] and on types of crimes or criminals as viewed through institutional records (laws, decrees, judicial records), sometimes combined with literary or moralistic material, but with a pronounced taste for "deviants" and "marginals."[6] Within this genre, there have been increasingly sophisticated surveys of the activity of courts in given cities or regions over given periods,[7] with

---

This has been said to be even more true of Florence: A. Zorzi, "Giusdicenti e operatori di giustizia nello stato territoriale fiorentino del XV secolo," *Ricerche storiche* 19 (1989): 517.

4. L. Marini, *Lo stato estense* (Turin, 1987), 22.

5. G. Antonelli, "La magistratura degli Otto di Guardia a Firenze," *Archivio storico italiano* 112 (1954); J. Brackett, *Criminal Justice and Crime in Late Renaissance Florence, 1537–1609* (Cambridge, 1992).

6. M. Rocke, "Il controllo dell'omosessualità a Firenze nel XV secolo: Gli Ufficiali di notte," *Quaderni storici* 66 (1987); P.H. Labalme, "Sodomy and Venetian Justice in the Renaissance," *Tijdschrift voor rechtsgeschiedenis* 52 (1984); G. Ruggiero, *The Boundaries of Eros: Sexual Crime and Sexuality in Renaissance Venice* (New York, 1985); M.S. Mazzi, "Il mondo della prostituzione nella Firenze tardo medievale," *Ricerche storiche* 14 (1984); D.R. Lesnick, "Insults and Threats in Medieval Todi," *Journal of Medieval History* 17 (1991); C. Caduff, "I 'pubblici latrones' nella città e nel contado di Firenze a metà Trecento," *Ricerche storiche* 18 (1988); G. Cherubini, "Appunti sul brigantaggio in Italia alla fine del Medioevo," in *Studi di storia medievale e moderna per Ernesto Sestan* (Florence, 1980); E. Artifoni, "I ribaldi: Immagini e istituzioni della marginalità nel tardo Medioevo piemontese," in *Piemonte medievale: Forme del potere e della società* (Turin, 1985); C. Klapisch-Zuber, "The Medieval Italian Mattinata," *Journal of Family History* 5 (1980); G. Ruggiero, *Violence in Early Renaissance Venice* (New Brunswick, 1980).

7. Pene Vidari, "Criminalità di Ivrea"; Bonfiglio Dosio, "Criminalità ed emarginazione a Brescia"; S. Cohn, "Criminality and the State in Renaissance Florence, 1344–1466," *Journal of Social History* 14 (1980); P. Roque Ferrer, "L'infrazione della legge a Cagliari dal 1340 al 1380," *Quaderni sardi di storia* 5 (1985–86); D.J. Osheim, "Countrymen and the Law in Late Medieval Tuscany," *Speculum* 64 (1989); A. Ryder, "The Incidence of Crime in Sicily in the Mid-Fifteenth Century: The Evidence from Composition Records," in *Crime, Society, and the Law in Renaissance Italy*, ed. T. Dean and K.J.P. Lowe (Cambridge, 1994).

special attention paid to the social or political framework of analysis, that is, to the relationship between judicial institutions and sociopolitical realities.[8] There have also been studies of specific moments in the judicial process,[9] of individual criminal "careers,"[10] and, of course, of punishment.[11] But few have focused on the structure, size, powers, and methods of police, and those few have still tended merely to count numbers and define categories.[12]

This lack of study of criminal justice in the Renaissance principality is not for want of source material. For law and order in the Este and Gonzaga states, there are the statutes of the cities;[13] there are long series of decrees that include pardons and privileges,[14] as well as registers of proclamations *(gride)*,[15] the enactments whereby the prince added to or altered the law. In Mantua there are the continuous—but not entirely complete—records of sentences in the court of the podestà and his subordinate judges from 1416 to 1464;[16] in Reggio there is a similarly lacunous series of the podestà's criminal trials.[17] There are the records of appointments, again incomplete, of judicial officers.[18] In Modena, Fer-

8. Cohn, "Criminality and the State"; A. Zorzi, "L'amministrazione della giustizia penale nella repubblica fiorentina: Aspetti e problemi," *Archivio storico italiano* 533 (1987), on which see the criticism of T. Kuehn, *Speculum* 65 (1990): 243–44; C. Povolo, "Contributi e ricerche in corso sull'amministrazione della giustizia nella repubblica di Venezia in età moderna," *Quaderni storici* 44 (1980).

9. D. Romano, "*Quod sibi fiat gratia:* Adjustment of Penalties and the Exercise of Influence in Early Renaissance Venice," *Journal of Medieval and Renaissance Studies* 13 (1983).

10. G. Cecchini, "Ghino di Tacco," *Archivio storico italiano,* 115 (1957); G. Pinto, "Un vagabondo, ladro e truffatore nella Toscana della seconda metà del '300: Sandro di Vanni detto Pescione," *Ricerche storiche,* n.s., 4 (1974).

11. Gundersheimer, "Crime and Punishment."

12. W.M. Bowsky, "The Medieval Commune and Internal Violence: Police Power and Public Safety in Siena, 1287–1355," *American Historical Review* 73 (1967); H. Manikowska, "Polizia e servizi d'ordine a Firenze nella seconda metà del XIV secolo," *Ricerche storiche* 16 (1986); idem, "'Accorr'uomo': Il popolo nell'amministrazione della giustizia a Firenze durante il XV secolo," *Ricerche storiche* 18 (1988); E. Pavan, "Recherches sur la nuit vénitienne à la fin du Moyen Age," *Journal of Medieval History* 7 (1981).

13. *Statuta Ferrariae* (Ferrara, 1476); *Statuta Mantuae,* in BCMn, MS 775, and (slightly later) AG, b. 2003; see M. Vaini, "Gli statuti di Francesco Gonzaga IV Capitano. Prime ricerche," *Atti e memorie dell'Accademia virgiliana di Mantova,* n.s., 56 (1988).

14. AG, Libri dei decreti, 3–32 (1416–1500); LD, ser. A, B, and C.

15. AG, b. 2038–39, Gride, fasc. 1–9; ASE, Cancelleria, Gridario.

16. AG, b. 3452–53.

17. ASRe, Comune, Curie della città.

18. AG, Libri delle patenti, 1–4 (1407–1516); LD (especially A 6).

rara, and Reggio, there are registers of communal deliberations, which include a variety of judicial business.[19] In addition to these administrative records, there exist many registers of outgoing correspondence (for the Gonzaga from 1443, for the Este from 1360),[20] and there survive, particularly from the 1450s onward (in both archives) large and miscellaneous collections of incoming correspondence relating to the cities and their subject lands, much of it letters from law officials.[21] On these this study is largely based. Finally, there are the chronicles, both printed and unprinted, which, in the manner of such writings, pay great attention to particular types of crimes and punishments.[22]

As a pair of contrasting, yet similar, principalities, Mantua and Ferrara have special points of interest as a case study. Both were ruled by long-lasting dynasties, implanted, the Este in 1240, the Gonzaga in 1328. Both families ruled cities that enjoyed little commercial or industrial fame and whose populations, though growing in the fifteenth century, could not compare in size to those of Milan or Venice. Both were in the second rank of Italian powers and were variously pressed and courted by their more powerful neighbors. The rulers of both looked to strengthen their international positions by, for example, offering themselves as condottieri or contracting prestigious marriages (Ludovico Gonzaga married Barbara of Brandenburg in 1433; Ercole d'Este married Eleonora d'Aragona, daughter of the king of Naples, in 1473). Both families made special contributions to the chivalric culture of fifteenth-century Italy, while also participating in Renaissance-humanistic cultural developments, in education (Guarino da Verona at Ferrara, Vittorino da Feltre at Mantua), the visual arts (Pisanello, Mantegna), and theater (the revival of classical comedy in Ferrara). Though there were periods of tension between these two neighboring rulers, there were also bonds that brought them together: Leonello d'Este married Margherita Gonzaga in 1447, and

---

19. ASCMo, Vacchette; ASRe, Comune, Provvigioni; Archivio storico del comune di Ferrara, Deliberazioni dei dodici savi.

20. AG, b. 2882–2909 (1443–1500); LD.

21. AG, b. 2390–2455 (1450s–1500); ASE, Rettori dello stato.

22. B. Zambotti, *Diario ferrarese dall'anno 1476 sino al 1504,* ed. G. Pardi, in *Rerum italicarum scriptores,* 2d ed., vol. 24, pt. 7 (Bologna, 1934–37); *Diario ferrarese dall'anno 1409 sino al 1502,* ed. G. Pardi, in ibid (Bologna, 1928–33); Ugo Caleffini, "Cronaca ferrarese," Biblioteca apostolica vaticana, MS Chigi I.I.4. Schivenoglia's untitled chronicle is in BCMn, MS 1019; an abbreviated edition was published by C. D'Arco, "Cronaca di Mantova di Andrea Schivenoglia dal 1445 al 1484," in *Raccolta di cronisti e documenti storici lombardi,* ed. G. Müller, vol. 2 (1857; repr., Mantua, 1976); a complete edition is being prepared by R. Signorini, to appear in the series "Fonti per la storia di Mantova."

Francesco Gonzaga married Isabella d'Este in 1480; the Gonzaga were frequent visitors to Ferrara in the second half of the fifteenth century (for festivals, horse races, theater), and official personnel circulated between the two states (see app. 2). One such official forms the center of our attention in this book.

However, there were also differences, of size and complexity. Gonzaga territory, containing only the one city, of some importance as a local commercial center, consisted of an unhilly region of scattered rural settlements and fortresses, set in rich agricultural land, woodland, floodland, and marsh, bisected by a major waterway, the Po, and various minor rivers. Its frontiers with Venetian, Ferrarese, and other neighboring dominions were easily crossed, facilitating the passage in or out of criminal elements, and it contained no highland refuges or significant areas of legal immunity of any sort. The Cavalcabò family had surrendered to the Gonzaga their rights over Viadana and other castles in the direction of Cremona and Parma in 1420; the da Persico had renounced Sabbioneta in 1435; the Torelli counts of Guastalla seem in general to have been complaisant neighbors; the Ippoliti, with their tiny imperial fief of Gazoldo, surrounded on all sides by Mantuan territory, were quite content to be counted among the elite of the Gonzaga court.[23] Even the great monastic lordship of San Benedetto Polirone, south of the Po, had become very largely subject to Gonzaga control by the early fifteenth century. Thus the *marchesato* of Mantua, divided into rural vicariates— apart from a few subordinate *podestarie* (Canneto, Ostiglia, Sermide, Viadana)—was relatively simple in its structure of administrative control. Above all, it was not threatened by any significant forces of opposition or by any network of rival families aspiring to replace the regime, though some complications arose through subdivisions among the Gonzaga themselves in the course of the fifteenth century. As the seat of professional condottieri and of lesser military captains, Mantua was at some risk from brawling soldiers (*armigeri* or *provvisonati* and their servants occur quite often in the records of trial for assault in public places), but in general it might seem a relatively stable and governable region where criminal violence was not in fact endemic.

23. L. Mazzoldi, *Mantova: La storia*, vol. 2 (Mantua, 1960), 1–6 and nn. 46–47; A. Cavalcabò, "Le vicende storiche di Viadana," *Bollettino storico cremonese* 18 (1952–53), *estratto*, 49–52; M. Vaini, *Ricerche gonzaghesche* (Florence, 1994), chap. 5 ("Il comitato"). Surviving correspondence from Guastalla (AG, b. 1390) and Gazoldo (AG, b. 1795, 1797) does not suggest frequent clashes over matters of jurisdiction, but see A. Luzio, *L'Archivio Gonzaga* (Verona, 1922), 2:251–52, where Gazoldo is described as a "nido di banditi."

By contrast, the Este state was more complex, comprising three main cities, as well as numerous secondary districts or centers (Garfagnana, Polesine di Rovigo, Finale), some even with their own bishoprics (Adria, Comacchio). This state encompassed the pastoral economies of the Apennines, the rich agricultural plains, and coastal communities dependent on fishing, salt making, and river transport. Though Ferrarese law and governmental practice did tend to spread into these other areas (often at the request of subject communities, not at the order of the prince),[24] the jurisdictional map was quite fragmented. Most of the Ferrarese *contado* formed a jurisdictional unit: it was all subject to Ferrarese statute law; there were no *podestarie* or rural lordships with criminal jurisdiction. However, at its edge we find even small settlements with their own statutes.[25] At Modena and Reggio, the geographical space ruled by civic statutes and jurisdiction was narrower. These cities had their own statutes and commanded a subject territory, but their provinces contained many places with their own law books, their own fully powered podesta, or their own lords. These cities had but small command over their territories. In the language of the time, they had little "obedience," as they were fond of complaining to the prince: in 1425 the commune of Modena complained that "in every well-governed city, such as Bologna or Ferrara, the whole *contado* obeys the city," but Modena, "because no castle anywhere obeys it, is desolated and without the means to sustain itself."[26] Instead, many of the castles obeyed local aristocratic families, who appointed their own officials and had direct links, personal, fiscal, military, and legal, with the Este. This lack of rural obedience to the cities was most clearly seen on the feast days of their patron saints: whereas the Este promoted the St. George's Day procession in Ferrara, requiring attendance from representatives of communities outside Ferrarese territory (as from Comacchio, Lugo, Bagnacavallo, Finale, and so on),[27] they had refused to allow Modena to enforce offerings from the *contado* to its patron, San Gimignano,[28] while the San Prospero proces-

---

24. See Comba, "Gli Statuti di Amedeo VIII," 37.

25. "Statuti di Massafiscaglia," ed. P. Antolini, *Atti e memorie della Deputazione ferrarese di storia patria* 5 (1893); *Statuta Pomposiae annis MCCXCV et MCCCXXXVIII–LXXXIII*, ed. A. Samaritani (Rovigo, 1958); *Statuti di Lendinara del 1321*, ed. M. Pozza (Rome, 1984).

26. LD, B IV, fol. 129v; T. Dean, *Land and Power in Late Medieval Ferrara: The Rule of the Este, 1350–1450* (Cambridge, 1987), 152.

27. ASFe, Archivio storico del comune, Libro delle commissioni 1457–71, fol. 9v.

28. ASCMo, Lettere, Niccolò III d'Este to the *savi*, 22 Jan. 1437.

sion at Reggio was a sad affair indeed, attended by representatives from only two or three country places.[29]

The judicial system in the Gonzaga and Este states, as in most other Italian cities and states, was based on a collection of statutes going back to the thirteenth century, and it centered on the ancient office of the podesta and on the several judges and policing officials subordinate to him. The podesta, necessarily a noncitizen, was appointed for a term of six months in the first instance, with the possibility of renewal. Regulations governing this office, which predated the regimes of both the Gonzaga and the Este, comprised a book of the civic statutes.[30] In Mantua they were incorporated, with only minor changes, in a revised version of the statutes promulgated in 1404.[31] In 1444 some new modifications were made concerning the office:[32] the podesta's entourage was required to consist of two knights, a constable, twenty foot soldiers, four domestic servants, eight horses accompanied by two squires, and one cook; the salary for six months was to be 2,415 lire.

By the early fifteenth century, the podesta of Mantua, though still a prestigious figure, had become subject in almost every way to the Gonzaga lordship *(signoria)*. A decree said to have been issued in 1401 even laid down that it was the duty of the podesta and other officials simply to act on whatever the signore decided.[33] While such a craven role may not always have been what occurred in practice, it is clear that there was an almost continuous extension of a complementary or controlling higher judicial authority, stemming from the will of the signore. A strong current of suprajudicial authority was in progress, by which the signore could give direct orders to arrest and imprison, to charge, interrogate, and torture, to prescribe sentence and punishment, even to withhold the right of appeal/petition. Since the duties of peacekeeping and the dispensation of justice were the very essence of signorial authority, all this could

---

29. ASRe, Provvigioni, reg. 98, fols. 194v–5, 250v; reg. 100, fols. 97r–v, etc. Cf. G. Chittolini, "Civic Religion and the Countryside in Late Medieval Italy," in *City and Countryside in Late Medieval and Renaissance Italy: Essays Presented to Philip Jones*, ed. T. Dean and C. Wickham (London, 1990).

30. C. D'Arco, *Studi municipio di Mantova intorno al* (Mantua, 1871), 51–61, for the earlier statutes concerning the podesta's jurisdiction; idem, vol. 6 (Mantua, 1874) for a discursive list of holders of the office. See also app. 2.

31. See intro n. 13.

32. AG, Lib. pat. 2, fols. 2r–v.

33. "quod potestates etc. . . . teneantur facere, attendere et observare quicquid ipse dominus Franciscus capitaneus dixerit, mandaverit et receperit quocumque modo quo placuerit eidem domino Francisco": D'Arco, *Studi,* 6:9.

conveniently, even conscientiously, be presented as a Solomonic performance of sacred duty by the ruler rather than as the exercise of arbitrary power and violation of statutory law. Should the lord not be available or inclined to carry out such duties, the so-called Council of Justice (Consiglio di Giustizia), composed of his own nominees, could, in an increasing number of ways as the century progressed, act on his behalf.[34]

Mantua's judicial administration consisted of the civil and criminal law courts presided over by the podesta and his subordinates, which he appointed, and by several specialist courts presided over by judges separately appointed by the Gonzaga ruler (the *capitano,* from 1433 the *marchese*). The most important of the latter category was the judge of appeals and fiscal matters *(iudex appellationum et datiorum)* who, like the podesta, had to be a foreigner; others included a judge of wills and testaments and a judge of the riverbanks *(iudex aggerum)*. The podesta's jurisdiction was first and foremost in civil disputes, the *ius suum cuique tribuens,* over which he presided at the Bench of the Eagle; his criminal jurisdiction, if less dignified intellectually, was nevertheless more formidable, and in this capacity he presided at the Bench of Hell *(banco dell'inferno)*.[35] The sessions of these and other courts took place in the great *salone* of the Palazzo della Ragione. No functional description of this building survives (cf. the description of the Palazzo della Ragione in Padua by Giovanni da Nono),[36] and only a few fragments of its mural decorations remain visible today,[37] but this hall (much smaller than that in Padua) probably had similar painted images from which the *banchi* took their names. The senior assistant of the podesta, known as his *vicarius,* had to be a doctor of law and could also hear cases at the Bench of the Eagle, which was served by the largest number (nine) of the twenty-seven notaries of the palace. The second judge *(iudex malleficiorum)* was authorized to hear criminal proceedings at the Bench of Hell and had to be at least a licentiate in law. The third judge heard lesser civil disputes

34. C. Mozzarelli, *Mantova e i Gonzaga dal 1382 al 1707* (Turin, 1987), 25; repr. from *Storia d'Italia,* ed. G. Galasso, vol. 17 (Turin 1979); also on the "consilium domini" and the "consiglio di giustizia" see idem, "Il senato di Mantova: origini e funzioni," in *Mantova e i Gonzaga nella civiltà del rinascimento* (Mantova, 1977), 66–68.

35. See statutes, BCMn, MS 775, fols. 7v–10r, and Vaini, "Gli statuti," 199.

36. The "visio Egidii Regis Patavinae," in G. Fabris, "La cronaca di Giovanni da Nono," *Bollettino del Museo civico di Padova,* n.s., 10–11 (1934–39): 15–16.

37. Some are earlier than the rebuilding of c. 1250, but details of the crucifixion, patriarchs, saints, etc. on one wall may have been part of the "Paradiso": see G. Paccagnini, *Mantova: Le arti,* 1 (Mantua, 1960) 140–44, 256.

(up to the value of twenty-five lire), sat at the Bench of Paradise *(banco del paradiso)*, and was required to be merely a civil law jurist *(iurisperitus)*. The other judges—those not attached to the podesta—also had their emblematic *dischi*: the griffon for the judge of appeals, the elephant for the judge of riverbanks and dikes, St. Michael for the judge of wills.

A similar structure was to be found in Ferrara, though almost nothing of the medieval Palazzo della Ragione there survives.[38] The major judicial offices were the civic *podesterie*—that of Ferrara carried a salary of 105 lire per month and required a staff of sixteen (two judges, a knight, a constable, nine catchpolls *[berroeri]*, and three servants). At Modena and Reggio, the podesta, the city captain, and the ducal *massaro* (revenue officer) formed a three-man *reggimento* that governed the city. Around the civic podesta were a cluster of others: at Ferrara a sindic-general and an appeals judge; at Modena and Reggio an appeals judge and a *capitano del divieto;* at all cities a range of officials for food supply, watercourses, passports, roads and bridges, and so forth, who had power to impose administrative fines. Each city, and some of the smaller towns, had or came to have a squad of guards on the piazza, under a constable or captain. Secondary centers of the Este state, such as Argenta or Rovigo, had a military captain, who had charge of the keys, gates, and bridges and commanded the castle garrison, but who was also supposed to support other officials in the collection of taxes; and a judicial official with both civil and criminal jurisdiction. Podestas in villages commanding a rural district might have full jurisdiction, as well as additional responsibilities (inspecting and maintaining dikes and watercourses, halting smuggling, checking border defenses), but in the Ferrarese *contado* they mostly had limited civil and no criminal jurisdiction (save in relation to criminal damage *[danni dati]*, arms carrying, blasphemy, and gambling). For some regions of the state—the Garfagnana, Este territory in the Romagna—there were commissioners, above the town and village podestas, who had full and general *arbitrium* to do all that they thought necessary and useful to the public good.[39]

Men chosen to serve as podestas tended to come either from the noble or professional elites of the main cities of the state or from a judicial elite that circulated among the cities of north and central Italy. In this, Ferrara

38. L.N. Cittadella, *Notizie relative a Ferrara per la maggior parte inedite* (Ferrara, 1864), 333–34. For Modena, see T. Sandonini, "Del palazzo comunale di Modena," *AMMo*, 4th ser., 9 (1899): 97–103, 107–8.

39. LD, B 5, passim.

and Mantua resembled Milan but differed from Florence and Venice, which reserved the office of podesta in subject cities for their own citizens.[40] In the major cities, however, such office seems to have become more an honorable prize for aristocrats, to such an extent as to impede its effective functioning. Dissatisfaction arose from the pressure governments came under from patrons and brokers to appoint their protégés and from the ceremoniousness of podestarial entries and exits. Evidence for this comes in the efforts made in the later fifteenth century, across northern Italy, and common to princely and republican states, to reduce the costs of the judicial structure inherited from the communal city-state. Florence abolished the office of podesta altogether, substituting citizen committees; at Mantua the *podestaria* was downgraded to a vice-podestaria for a long period, and semipermanent judicial officers were also appointed.[41] Other cities (Ferrara, Bologna) legislated to resist the pressure to award outgoing podestas "the usual insignia," as signs of gratitude for good service.[42] The reason given in Ferrara in 1467 was to remove an occasion for rancor and dispute between podestas. More plainly admitted in 1470 was a desire to cut costs. Together these efforts suggest that increased competitiveness for judicial posts (and for the profits they brought) did not result in greater effectiveness.

This competitiveness would also explain the desire of podestas for insignia—to leave their own on display, to take with them the commune's—as evidence of good service. Among those *palazzi del podestà* that survive in Italian cities (and even small towns),[43] the external walls often still bear the coats of arms of their late-medieval podestas. These are usually sculpted in stone, but those of Florentines tend to stand out for being in glazed and polychrome terra-cotta. Gabriele Ginori's coat of arms (plate 3) seems to be an especially elaborate example of the genre, showing not only his own arms but also those of the Medici and Florence, as well as those of his employers, the Este and Gonzaga (he served

40. Zorzi, "Giusdicenti," 521–22.

41. Zorzi, "L'amministrazione della giustizia penale nella repubblica fiorentina," 426–46; for Mantua, see chap. 3.

42. ASFe, Archivio storico del comune, Libro delle provvigioni statutarie 1457–91, fols. 7v–8v (1467), 11v–12, 13 (1470); *Statuta Ferrarie,* fols. 205v–6v, 209r–v, 210r–v; ASBo, Comune, Governo, Libri partitorum, reg. 1, fols. 45v, 77 (1452), 152 (1454). See, for Pavia, F. Fossati, "Nuove spigolature d'archivio," *Archivio storico lombardo,* 8th ser., 7 (1957): 390–91.

43. See, e.g., L. Borgia, *Gli stemmi del Palazzo d'Arnolfo di San Giovanni Valdarno* (Florence, 1986).

as podesta in Ferrara, Mantua, and Reggio: see app. 2).[44] It was perhaps this sort of thing that city governments found rather tiresome. In other respects, Ginori was typical of the way that podestas came to be appointed. He was a partisan of the Medici in Florence and acted for Lorenzo as an "unofficial envoy and informer" during his terms of office in northern Italian cities.[45] When podesta in Reggio, he proposed to exalt "the glorious Medici family and yourself," he informed Lorenzo, by putting the Medici arms, as well as his own, on the facade of the podesta's palace there (as he later did also at Mantua). In return, Lorenzo wrote many letters of recommendation on his behalf, securing offices or extensions to office and assisting in sindications (reviews of judicial officials). Princes, however, found it irritating to be so inundated with requests from patrons to consider their protégés for office; they disliked having major offices in their states booked up for years in advance with other rulers' favorites. In self-defense, they devised secret signs, placed on letters of recommendation, that told their recipients which letters could be disregarded.[46] In time they also reacted against the whole system of patronage, as we shall see.

The procedural norms and sentences for criminal trials were pre-scribed by city statutes. The podesta and the criminal judge could take action against individuals ex officio, by inquisition, in cases of homicide, violent assault, robbery, theft, arson, abduction or rape of females, sodomy and other "offenses against nature," blasphemy, sacrilege, offenses against clergy, conspiracy and treason *(laesa maiestas),* and any offense carrying, on conviction, a money penalty higher than one hun-dred lire.[47] At the less serious level, denunciations, particularly for minor acts of disorder and violence, might be made through the *capitano del divieto* or his deputy. For all the graver crimes in the preceding list (to

44. See the heraldic analysis by G. Malacarne, "La stemma del podestà di Mantova Gabriel Ginori: un magistrato del XV secolo," *Civiltà mantovana,* 30 (1995): 39–55, point-ing out the errors in the shields apparently meant to refer to the Este and the Papacy. The square at the base (right) illustrates Ginori emblems.

45. For this description and the discussion that follows, see F.W. Kent, "*Ottimati* fam-ilies in Florentine Politics and Society, 1427–1530: The Rucellai, Capponi, and Ginori" (Ph.D. diss., University of London, 1971), 338–42; idem, *Household and Lineage in Renaissance Florence: The Family Life of the Capponi, Ginori, and Rucellai* (Princeton, 1977), 162, 177, 213, 218; L. Passerini, *Genealogia e storia della famiglia Ginori* (Florence, 1876), 12–13.

46. V. Ilardi, "Crosses and Carets: Renaissance Patronage and Coded Letters of Rec-ommendation," *American Historical Review* 92 (1987): 1127–28.

47. BCMn, MS 775, lib. I, cap. xxi, fol. 12; *Statuta Ferrarie,* fol. 82v.

which, for Mantua, magic and incantation should be added), suspects could be subjected to torture in order to extract information and confession,[48] though it was laid down that torture should be inflicted in a manner appropriate and moderate, according to the quality of the person accused—at the discretion of the judge.[49]

As in many other places, imprisonment was not prescribed in the Mantuan statutes as a retributive punishment;[50] at least in theory, it was simply a means of securing the persons of suspect individuals who were awaiting investigation or trial or who had yet to pay their fines or costs. In reality, imprisonment on these grounds could sometimes last for years, and there seem to have been cases (perhaps after remission of the death sentence) where it lasted for life.[51] The statutory penalties on conviction were monetary, corporal, or sometimes both. A variety of death sentences and a range of mutilations were prescribed; for some lesser offenses either the pillory or the instrument of torture normally used in interrogation, the rope hoist, was used. Atrocious exemplary penalties were laid down for conspiracy and treason. Beheading and a fine of one thousand lire, in addition to confiscation of all or part of property, were the statutory punishments for homicide.[52] These penalties could also apply to rape and to "offenses against nature," such as incest and sodomy (though burning was the prescribed form of punishment).[53] Method of decapitation varied among Italian cities: in some—including, it seems, Mantua—the executioner wielded a mighty mallet that pressed a primitive guillotine *(mannaia)* down on the neck of the victim, who was

48. BCMn, MS 775, lib. I, cap. xxviii, fol. 14.

49. BCMn, MS 775, lib. I, cap. xxv, fol. 15.; *Statuta Ferrarie*, fol. 87v; *Statuta civitatis Mutine* (Modena, 1487), fol. 91 (III.6). See also L. Camerali, *La tortura a Mantova e altri scritti* (Mantua, 1974), which includes some discussion of criminality in Mantua in the later sixteenth century.

50. But see T. Dean, "Criminal Justice in Mid-Fifteenth-Century Bologna," in *Crime, Society, and the Law in Renaissance Italy*, ed. T. Dean and K. Lowe (Cambridge, 1994), 28.

51. E.g., the podesta Giambattista da Castello wrote in 1483 (*sic*, but probably 1493) concerning a prisoner in the tower, "dove sono consueti stare quelli che sono carcerati per la vita": A. Bertolotti, *Prigioni e prigionieri in Mantova dal secolo XIII al XIX* (1888; repr., Bologna, 1976), 17. In 1498 Giacomo da Capua wrote to Marquis Francesco Gonzaga regarding the recapture of some escaped prisoners, "tuti loro erano per la vita carcerati": AG, b. 2451, fol. 234 (8 Mar. 1498). (On Giacomo da Capua, see chap. 7 nn. 77–82.) See also Dean, "Criminal Justice in Bologna," 28.

52. BCMn, MS 775, lib. I, cap. xlv, fol. 21v; *Statuta Ferrarie*, fol. 94v; *Statuta Mutine*, fol. 97v (III.45).

53. BCMn, MS 775, lib. I, cap. xli, fols. 16v–17; *Statuta Ferrarie*, fol. 99v; *Statuta Mutine*, fol. 99 (III.57).

outstretched on a raised platform;[54] in others, including Ferrara, the executioner used an ax.[55] Hanging was prescribed for theft when aggravated by violence (e.g., highway robbery), for stealing property worth more than twenty-five lire (Mantua) or ten lire (Ferrara), and for a third offense, even of petty theft.[56] There was some experimentation with methods of hanging in Ferrara: convicts were more frequently hanged at the windows of the Palazzo della Ragione,[57] and a wooden platform and trapdoor were added to the outside of that building for the purpose. For sodomy, incest, and other "offenses against nature," burning alive (in Ferrara, after strangulation) was prescribed.[58] Assaults causing injury or bloodshed could lead to sentences of dismemberment (of one or both arms, feet, eyes, or ears), but the well-to-do were usually able to commute such penalty into a monetary fine. Perjury or false testimony could be punished by cutting out the offender's tongue.[59] Blasphemy, usually in the form of swearing against the Madonna or a saint, carried a monetary penalty of ten lire in Mantua (fines were graded in Ferrara—fifty lire for the Virgin Mary, twenty-five lire for other saints—as too in Modena),[60]

---

54. For drawings of *mannaie* in late-fifteenth-century Neapolitan chronicles, see F. Cognasso, *L'Italia nel rinascimento* (Turin, 1966), 2:657–58; A. Zorzi, "La giustizia a Firenze in età Laurenziana," in *Lorenzo il Magnifico*, ed. F. Cardini (Rome, 1992), 32–33. A more primitive version is illustrated in the (mainly destroyed) fresco by Mantegna of "The Execution of St. James," in the Church of the Eremitani, Padua. See also the description of a Mantuan *mannaia* used in the execution, on 25 Sept. 1540, of two officials found guilty of corruption: A. Luzio, "Una ghigliottina rudimentale nel Cinquecento," *Gazzetta di Mantova*, 12 Mar. 1899.

55. See plate 4, reproduced in color in *Palazzo Paradiso e la biblioteca ariostea*, ed. A. Chiappini (Rome, 1993), 15. From the position of the illustration in the manuscript, it would appear to represent the beheading, to be followed by the quartering, of Albertino Boschetti and his accomplices for treasonable plotting in 1506. On Albertino Boschetti, see chap. 5.

56. BCMn, MS 775, lib. I, cap. liii, fols. 19v–20; *Statuta Ferrarie*, fols. 102v–3; *Statuta Mutine*, fol. 98 (III. 51).

57. This practice was not, as Zorzi maintains, a Florentine invention, improvised following the Pazzi conspiracy and then transmitted to other cities, for it is recorded in Ferrara already in 1476: A. Zorzi, "The Judicial System in Florence," in Dean and Lowe, *Crime, Law, and Society*, 56–57; Zambotti, *Diario*, 8. It is recorded earlier elsewhere; e.g., see A.A. Bernardy, "Dall'archivio governativo della repubblica di San Marino. Il carteggio della reggenza: 1413–1465," *Atti e memorie della Deputazione di storia patria per le Marche*, n.s., 8 (1912): 153 (1443).

58. BCMn, MS 775, lib. I, cap. xli, fol. 17; *Statuta Ferrarie*, fol. 98v; *Statuta Mutine*, fol. 99 (III.57).

59. BCMn, MS 775, lib. I, cap. l, fols. 18v–19, and cap. lxxxviii, fol. 26v; *Statuta Ferrarie*, fol. 101v; *Statuta Mutine*, fol. 98v (III.55).

60. *Statuta Ferrarie*, fol. 93v; *Statuta Mutine*, fol. 94 (III.26).

but at Mantua failure to pay within fifteen days meant a day's exposure
at the pillory *(berlina)* with the tongue held in a device called the *giova*.
Another penalty, for blaspheming any saint, was the fine or a dipping in
the lake in a basket *(corbella)*, though no recorded use of such a device
has come to light. Defacing an image of God or the Madonna could be
punished by loss of a hand.[61] This was also the penalty for forgery,
though forging documents could also mean the loss of an eye.[62] In practice, sentences varied quite widely, as will be shown, and there was a
measure of discretion left to the judge in some crimes.

It is precisely this discretionary area that the present study opens up
for examination, for the study is based on the career of one official, Beltramino Cusadri da Crema, who served first the Gonzaga, then the Este,
at key moments of judicial change, when enforcement of the statutes was
systematically overridden by other considerations. Our study is without
precedent, for it presents a fifteenth-century official through his own
voluminous correspondence with his princely employers.[63] Obviously
such a source presents peculiar problems for the historian: official letters
do not tell the whole truth but shape it so as to justify conduct taken or
proposed. That rhetorical shaping itself is partly the object of study here.
However, letters do reveal a side of the judicial process usually held away
from the historian: unlike the trial record, which gives the public history
of indictment and sentence, letters show us the inner workings of judicial
attitudes and methods (such as torture). Beltramino's story—both for the
problems it threw up and for the forceful manner in which he reported on
them—is fascinating enough; but it may also be used to illuminate many
other aspects of these two states, from the character of officialdom and
the political structure, to fiscal history and economic policy, during
difficult years of crisis and transition.

Study of criminal justice thus cannot exist outside the historiography
of the state.[64] Persistent, of course, is the view that equates the modern

---

61. BCMn, MS 775, lib. I, cap. xl, fol. 16v.

62. Ibid., I.xl, fol. 18v.

63. The only parallel is G.P. Massetto, *Un magistrato e una città nella Lombardia spagnola: Giulio Claro pretore a Cremona* (Milan, 1985), which examines Claro's tenure of the
office of podesta 1560–61, but with the emphasis more on "watching the great jurist at
work . . . , coming to grips with the thousand practical problems of the law in action" (viii).

64. E. Fasano Guarini, "Gli stati dell'Italia centro-settentrionale tra Quattro e Cinquecento: Continuità e trasformazioni," *Società e storia* 21 (1983); C. Povolo, "Aspetti e problemi dell'amministrazione della giustizia penale nella repubblica di Venezia: Secoli
XVI–XVII," in *Stato, società e giustizia nella repubblica veneta (sec. XV–XVIII)*, ed. G.

state with centralization (concentration of power, limitation of local autonomy, development of capital cities and courts) and with bureaucracy (which, as government by office, is thought to mean the creation of both official systems and official memory). Such a view also places the transition from the medieval to the modern state in the Renaissance period. Objections to this old-fashioned interpretation have been made since the 1960s. It is too dependent on the image and policy announced by the ruler. It is too dependent on legislation and central institutions. It pays too little attention to the realities of government, especially in the territories and at the geographical periphery of the state: there other power centers and forces opposed to centralization persisted into the sixteenth century, and "the state" was no more than a pair of officials with a small garrison and staff. In one strong historiographical stream, these local "realities," untouched by the state, have taken center stage and have prompted the study of local communities, networks of noble power (factions, *parentele,* clienteles), and the court (as a zone of personal, non-bureaucratic government), as if the state could be written out of the story.[65] At the same time, in other quarters, there has been a continuing stress on the mid and later sixteenth century for truly significant developments in state power, though this is perhaps merely a manifestation of the rigid and continuing academic division between medievalists and early modernists. Such historians give privileged place to "massive" interventions by sixteenth-century monarchs and central governments, thus reducing previous, similar interventions to mere "prefigurings." In the sixteenth century, to such historians, new legislation becomes Great New Laws, law is "rationalized" and procedure "streamlined," criminals are punished without regard to social rank, and judicial venality is brought to an end. If it is conceded that medieval governments strove in the same directions, the argument is that only in the sixteenth century were those goals achieved.

Between postponing the modernization of the state and denying the

---

Cozzi (Rome, 1980), 155; J.-C. Maire Vigueur, "Justice et politique dans l'Italie communale de la seconde moitié du XIIIe siècle: L'exemple de Pérouse," *Académie des inscriptions et belles-lettres, Comptes rendus,* 1986, 312.

65. See, e.g., O. Raggio, *Faide e parentele: Lo stato genovese visto dalla Fontanabuona* (Turin, 1990). For this trend, see most recently G. Chittolini, "Il 'privato,' il 'pubblico,' lo Stato," in *Origini dello Stato: Processi di formazione statale in Italia fra medioevo ed età moderna,* ed. G. Chittolini, A. Molho, and P. Schiera (Bologna, 1994), 554–64. See also D. M. Bueno de Mesquita, "The Place of Despotism in Italian Politics," in *Europe in the Late Middle Ages,* ed. J. Hale, R. Highfield, and B. Smalley (London, 1965), 324.

state altogether has arisen a third way: Chittolini's composite, regional state. Chittolini has argued forcefully against the antistatists,[66] while also distinguishing his vision from that of the modernizers. Chittolini's regional state, located in the late fourteenth and fifteenth centuries, is neither medieval-particularist nor modern-centralist[67] but combines state power with that of semi-independent social bodies and groups ("corpi e ceti"). Princely power, for Chittolini, was based on a de facto accord between the prince and these social groups (cities, communities, aristocracies, factions, and so on): they recognized the prince's sovereignty and authority in necessary matters (war, justice, public order, finance), while retaining rights of legitimate self-government, often on the basis of written accords (e.g., *capitoli* of surrender, feudal investitures). The characteristics of such states are distinct from those of the modern "absolute" state: "They are characterized by a strong pluralism of bodies, classes and political centers within the state, each holding authority and powers; they are characterized by the central government's limited capacity and will to intervene . . . They are states that amply recognize privileges, immunities, exemptions."[68] In developing this model, Chittolini has investigated the role and function in the state of fiefs and feudatories, separated territories, small towns, officialdom, and statute law.[69]

Chittolini's study of statutes and of the experience of Sforza officials can connect consideration of the state with our study of Beltramino Cusadri. In both cases, Chittolini stresses the enduring power of local institutions. Even in regional states, in which one city or ruler dominated several other cities, the attachment of subject cities to their old statutes remained tenacious. Subject-citizens saw their statutes as both the "product and symbol of old autonomy" and as a means to protect what remained of that autonomy. Despite the trends to superimpose legislation by prince or capital city over local laws or to limit the subject city's right to make new law, Chittolini has stressed the remarkable survival of local statute law and the slowness of its decay.[70] The Sienese government

---

66. G. Chittolini, "Stati padani, 'Stato del rinascimento': Problemi di ricerca," in *Persistenze feudali e autonomie comunitative in stati urbani fra Cinque e Settecento,* ed. G. Tocci (Bologna, 1988); idem, "Il 'privato,' il 'pubblico,' lo Stato," 573–74.

67. J.S. Grubb, *Firstborn of Venice: Vicenza in the Early Renaissance State* (Baltimore, 1988), xiv.

68. Chittolini, "Il 'privato,' il 'pubblico,' lo Stato," 567–69.

69. Chittolini, "L'onore dell'officiale."

70. G. Chittolini, "Statuti e autonomie urbane: Introduzione," in Chittolini and Willoweit, *Statuti città territori,* 21–25, 40–41

expressed a general view when it proclaimed that "without the statutes, no state ('republica') can be properly governed."[71] Good governance and respect for statute law were identified.

Similarly, Milanese officials were often enjoined by the duke to take a stern and vigorous attitude toward wrongdoing, but cities and aristocrats, faced with officials' efforts to expand the scope of ducal action, responded with fierce defense of their privileges: cities and aristocrats saw their rights and honor being unjustifiably and presumptuously threatened and trampled on; officials in turn were alarmed for ducal rights and honor. Hence there was frequent, systematic tension between officials and social bodies, ranging from coolness, dilatoriness, and non-cooperation; through hostility, insolence, and defiance; to intimidation, assault, and murder. But for most practical purposes (arresting criminals and bandits, halting smuggling) officials needed the collaboration of the locality, while remaining dependent also on the locality for their salary and for some of their staff. Without collaboration, an official could not penetrate the "thick, solid network of solidarity and connivance that united the members of a community, the members of a faction, . . . or which bound together a feudatory and his men, a 'gentleman' and his clients."[72] As the duke listened to the complaints of aristocrats, citizens, and communities and conceded to their wishes by canceling his officials' sentences, releasing their detainees, and lightening their punishments, officials were weakened and humiliated, abandoned by the duke who had previously spurred them to firm and energetic action. Thus, Chittolini concludes, the zealous official could be more dangerous than useful—disrupting local order, turning every incident into a question of state—while the best official knew the limits of ducal power, eschewed exemplary action, and respected local families and the local power structure, even at the risk of incurring accusations of weakness, inactivity, or injustice.

However, one of the criticisms made of Chittolini's regional state is that it presents the contractual balance between the prince and the cities, aristocracies, and rural communities as something stable and unchanging, rather than as the object of a dynamic process, modified by external factors or by the development of relations between the various centers of

---

71. M. Ascheri, "Statuti, legislazione e sovranità: il caso di Siena," in Chittolini and Willoweit, *Statuti città territori*, 182.

72. Chittolini, "L'onore dell'officiale," 15.

power.[73] Our study of Beltramino therefore serves as a test of Chittolini's interpretation, by taking account of dynamic action by the prince. What happened when the prince decided on a truly energetic campaign of official action against crime and disorder, or when he decided that local statute law was no longer indispensable to good government but an impediment to it? What was the outcome when the local communities and aristocracies faced a tenacious law enforcer who refused to adapt to local conditions? Could the prince sustain such insistence on respect for his laws and his officials against the power of elites entrenched both in the localities and at court? A study of one judge, in his various posts in two different states, provides an ideal testing ground for the variable of personality, as against structure, in interpreting the princely state. Beltramino Cusadri did not change; but he did work in two different places, at two different times, under two different princes, and those differences explain his successes and failures.

73. Fasano Guarini, "Gli stati," 630; but see more recently Chittolini, "Il 'privato,', il 'pubblico,' lo Stato," 580: "Le istituzioni riflettono il mutare delle forze politiche . . ."

1

The Challenge of Crime
in the Este State

The study of late-medieval judicial records has revealed a significant gap in our understanding of medieval criminality: for all that trial records tell us about types of prosecuted crime or the course and outcome of prosecution, they usually remain exasperatingly silent on the origin of the assaults, brawls, and homicides that pack out so monotonously the judicial registers. Why did interpersonal violence take place? To understand the contexts and origins from which crimes of violence arose, we have to look at other sources, not the trial record, but the record of legislation and policing. It is here, in the record of the way that contemporaries themselves analyzed social evils, that we can approach the situations and relations that were perceived as habitually productive of "scandals and inconveniences," to use the words of many enactments. It may of course be that legislators and judges were mistaken or were consciously or unconsciously sensitive to the actions of certain groups in society, but as prosecutions were also made under such misconceptions or biases, it is necessary first to understand the judicial-legislative mind. This chapter focuses on the territories ruled by the Este dukes, Borso (1450–71) and his brother, Ercole (1471–1505), and will investigate the sources of crime, the trend of legislation, and the character of judicial officialdom and of corruption. As will become apparent, some features were common to other states, in particular Gonzaga Mantua, though their incidence and intensity could vary with short- or medium-term social and economic changes. For this reason talk of crime as endemic is unsatisfactory.

According to city statutes, major causes of interpersonal violence were often prostitution and gambling, and this is borne out by the correspondence between the dukes of Ferrara and their judicial officials in the city and countryside. Male gatherings were seen as a prime context of disorder. "From public and private gambling are borne blasphemies, thefts, woundings, homicides and many other disorders," declared Ercole d'Este in a proclamation in 1496.[1] The many "evils" arising from gambling led to the extension in 1471 of Ferrarese bans and penalties to the separate town of Adria.[2] The appearance of prostitutes in rural areas generated disorder because of the congregation of men, with brawls and disturbances, and led to pressure for their expulsion.[3] Trouble at rural fairs was ordinarily expected: "there is never a fair at Pavullo at which many robberies and homicides are not committed," wrote the Modenese *anziani* to the duke.[4] Those of the duke's subjects who were allowed to carry weapons could not have them at *feste,* because of "the perils that usually arise from weapons where there is a gathering of people."[5] Youth groups—celebrating May Day or conducting charivaris *(mattinate)*—caused problems of nocturnal disorder, including assault and homicide.[6] It was explicitly to satisfy the youth that masking at Carnival was authorized,[7] but masking, which combined the twin evils of anonymity and license, was also subject to prohibition and penalty, "to avoid the scandals that easily happen from going masked."[8] In the early sixteenth century, the duke learned that "the majority of disorders, brawls, and disturbances" arising at Minozzo, in Modenese territory, "originate in

---

1. ASE, Cancelleria, Gridario, Gride manoscritte, 1, 1 Apr. 1496; likewise a later decree: Gridario, B, Registri di gride, b. 1, vol. 1, fol. 291 (1566).

2. LD, C 3, fol. 60 (20 June 1471).

3. RdS, Ferrara, b. 19, Massari, comune et homines, 28 May 1462; RdS, Ferrara, b. 46, letters of A. Cavalluzzi, 12 July 1464.

4. "il non si fa mai alcuna de dicte fere che non se gli commeta de molti robarie e homicidii": RdS, Modena, b. 1a, *savi* to Ercole d'Este, 25 July 1498. Because of these disorders, the market was transferred to Fanano: ibid.; ASE, Minutario, Lettere sciolte, b. 4, 30 July 1498; *Cronaca modenese di Tommasino de' Bianchi,* ed. C. Borghi (Parma, 1862), 1:12. For violence at the markets at Sassuolo and Montefiorino, see LD, C 5, fol. 2 (3 Jan. 1478); LD, C 14, fol. 144 (20 Aug. 1506).

5. LD, C 4, fol. 17 (25 Jan. 1476).

6. For concern with *mattinata,* see RdS, Reggio, b. 1, 6 July 1496; RdS, Reggio, b. 153, *Anziani,* 6 July 1496; RdS, Ferrara, b. 56, Roberto Drugi to Borso d'Este, 13 June 1462. For a fight among youths going out to plant the may on the night of St. James, see ibid., Lanzalotto Costabili to Borso, 31 May, 1 and 5 June 1454. For other May Day violence, see Cam. duc., Mandati, vol. 39, fol. 36 (18 Mar. 1499). See also Massetto, *Un magistrato,* 220–24.

7. Zambotti, *Diario,* 58, 71, 171.

8. "per evitare li scandali che facilmente potriano accadere in quella nostra cita per andare in maschara": LD, C 11, fol. 156 (6 Jan. 1496); LD, C 11, fol. 13 (12 Feb. 1493); RdS, Reggio, b. 153, *Anziani,* 28 Jan. 1495; ASRe, Provvigioni, reg. 98, fol. 113 (Dec. 1488). See also Gundersheimer, "Crime and Punishment," 121. For masked violence at Carnival, see Zambotti, *Diario,* 72, 85, 86, 100, etc.

dances held on saints' days, which should be sanctified in other ways."[9] Public sermons, too, and dynastic celebrations, in attracting and enflaming men (and women), could lead to attacks on Jews, which the prince was anxious to forestall.[10]

Of more private sources of violence, we might expect property disputes to have featured prominently, but only two forms of property significantly appear in the reports of podestas: brides and benefices. As a source of violence, marriage seems the more frequent, whether it be attempts to negotiate marriage,[11] the unhappy outcome of forced marriage,[12] parental reaction to clandestine union,[13] physical violence arising from nonpayment of dowry,[14] or crimes of passion resulting from adultery.[15] Conflict over benefices produced violent occupation of churches, raiding on the properties attached to the cure, assaults on rivals, and, as we shall see, deadly feuds among families.[16] Was it the case that, whereas disputes over land were now conducted in the law courts, disputes over brides and benefices issued in violence because of the increased difficulty of arranging marriage[17] and because of increased patrician dependence on ecclesiastical revenues?[18]

Above all, though, it was arms carrying, when associated with private enmity *(inimicitia)*, that most concerned judges and princes as a source of violence (and, as we shall see, as an obstacle to judicial action). Local edicts prohibiting the carrying of weapons and refreshing the penalties

9. LD, C 14, fol. 3 (4 Mar. 1506).

10. Ercole d'Este feared anti-Semitic disorder in Modena in celebrations if his wife bore a son: LD, C 4, fol. 110 (16 June 1476); RdS, Reggio, b. 112, 28 July 1473. See also Tommasino de' Bianchi, in *Cronaca Tommasino de' Bianchi*, 1:49–50; T. Torri, "'Allegrezze' e feste pubbliche: Modena fra '400 e '500," *Quaderni storici* 79 (1992): 215, 218, 223–24; Venturi, "Relazioni," 335–36. Jacopino de' Bianchi attributed the 1476 disorders specifically to "li zoveni": *Cronaca Tommasino de' Bianchi*, 1:27–29.

11. The Paladini family "molested" Ugolino Marascone, because they wanted to "put" a girl into his family by marriage, to such an extent that Ugolino was granted an arms license: LD, C 10, fols. 222 (24 Aug. 1487), 296–97 (21 Feb. 1488).

12. RdS, Ferrara, b. 46, letters of Albertino Giocoli, 11 Feb. 1454.

13. Dean, "Criminal Justice in Mid-Fifteenth-Century Bologna," 34.

14. LD, C 10, fol. 312 (1 Apr. 1488).

15. RdS, Reggio, b. 1, *Cancellieri, 5,* 7, and 30 June 1494.

16. RdS, Reggiano, Castelnovo ne' Monti, Tommaso Arienti to Ercole d'Este, 16 and 30 Oct. 1494, 22 Jan. 1495; LD, C 10, fol. 26; LD, C 14, fols. 108, 306–7.

17. A. Molho, *Marriage Alliance in Late Medieval Florence* (Cambridge, Mass., 1994), 214–30.

18. R. Bizzocchi, "La dissoluzione di un clan familiare: I Buondelmonti di Firenze nei secoli XV e XVI," *Archivio storico italiano* 140 (1982): 30–31.

were a frequent resort,[19] and strict assertion was made of the prince's "regalian" monopoly on the granting of licenses to carry arms.[20] But neither of these measures offered more than a temporary cure, for the prince continued to approve licenses in large numbers: during the course of 1472 thirty-two licenses were issued to citizens of Modena and Reggio, covering 120 individuals and other unnamed *consorti* and *attinentes;*[21] a similar number was issued in 1473.[22] By 1482 it was reckoned that there were two hundred licenses in the city of Reggio alone, which was "a cause of disorder of the whole city";[23] it was alleged in 1490 that there were over five hundred arms licenses in Ferrara.[24] Despite the large numbers, licenses were not issued indiscriminately: a request was usually scrutinized by superior officials and could be refused;[25] licenses did not cover fairs, markets, and holy days;[26] and periodic reviews were undertaken.[27] One report on a request implies that licenses were not given to those with a record of involvement in fights and brawls.[28] The ideal was certainly to afford protection to the innocent and to victims in their daily lives against their more powerful enemies; but licenses were easily misused and were often retained long after the original cause had been removed.[29]

Most licenses to carry arms were issued "on account of enmity." *Inimicitia*, often coupled with hatred *(odio)* or war *(guerra)*, is not in itself vendetta, which more usually involved an exchange of specific injuries; nor did it necessarily have the extensions over time and throughout a family clan that are associated with feud. Enmities were sustained hatreds, and they could erupt between individuals, within and between

---

19. RdS, Ferrara, b. 40, *Diversi,* 27 Jan. 1500: Comacchio; RdS, Reggio, b. 2, Lippo Boccamaiori to Ercole d'Este, 24 Oct. 1482; LD, C 5, fol. 53 (26 Mar. 1478: Rovigo); LD, C 10, fol. 258 (12 Nov. 1487: Adria); CS, b. 131 (8 Mar. 1471: Ferrara); ASE, Gridario, Gride manoscritte, 1, 2 Jan. 1491 and 4 Apr. 1492 (Ferrara); ASCMo, Vacchetta 1487–88, fol. 73 (24 May).

20. LD, C 4, fol. 79 (7 May 1476); RdS, Ferrara, b. 41, 21 Feb. 1491.

21. LD, C 3, fols. 90ff.

22. Ibid., fols. 107ff.: 34 licenses covering 121 named individuals and others without number.

23. RdS, Reggio, b. 2, Lippo Boccamaiori to Ercole d'Este, 24 Oct. 1482.

24. RdS, Ferrara, b. 1, Gregorio Zampante to Ercole d'Este, 31 Jan. 1490.

25. RdS, Modena, b. 1a, Reggimento, 8 Apr. 1473 and 10 Mar. 1479; RdS, Ferrara, b. 1, Gabriele Ginori to Eleonora d'Aragona, 23 Aug. 1488; LD, C 3, fols. 77ff.

26. Ibid.

27. LD, C 4, fol. 21 (27 Jan. 1476); LD, C 10, fol. 156 (2 May 1487).

28. RdS, Ferrara, b. 1, 23 Aug. 1488.

29. LD, C 10, fol. 156 (2 May 1487).

families, between whole villages, and across borders. They could arise suddenly and be quickly pacified, or they could develop into feuds, involving whole, extended families and including episodes of blood vengeance. Stifling enmities as they arose could be a hard and precarious labor for a local judge. Events at Massafiscaglia in 1454 serve as an example: the podesta had to deal with an explosive conflict between the Tamoni and da Go families, following Zapelin da Go's wounding of Ognibene Tamoni; thrusting his way through the Tamoni as they beat, arms in hand, at the doors of the da Go house, he had to issue penal orders to get them to disperse, detain them until they gave promises not to offend, then interview the original attacker and negotiate peace.[30] The need was for prompt action while enmities were in their beginnings, and this could lead the prince to bypass the local judiciary in favor of men who had "good familiarity" with the area and who were respected by the adversaries.[31] However, extrajudicial pacification brought its own risks: as the Bolognese government averred during efforts to settle an enmity on its border with Modena, when justice does not take its course, anger easily arises, encouraging and legitimating private attempts to take vendetta for injuries, such that pacification settles nothing and generates more disorder.[32] Even in their beginnings, such pacifications needed patience and fortitiude, and all the more so when they had a more extended development, as in the town of Sassuolo in 1487: "the enmities have many heads and depend on many principals," the duke declared in listing the reasons for an aborted pacification.[33] In such cases, as one podesta reported in 1486, the enmity between two families could involve most of the rest of the town.[34]

Much of the correspondence between the dukes and their judges is filled with problems such as these, but judges were also especially exercised in dealing with two types of criminal: the ill-famed and the bullies. In the eyes of the authorities, at least, public reputation was lost by association with the world of taverns and gaming tables, gamblers, pimps and

---

30. RdS, Ferrara, b. 45a, Benedetto Giacobelli to Borso d'Este, 19 Aug. and 19 and 22 Oct. 1454.

31. LD, C 10, fols. 139, 142–43 (8 and 10 Apr. 1487).

32. Archivio di Stato, Bologna, Lettere del comune, vol. 5, fols. 90v–91 (17 Dec. 1492), 93 (18 Jan. 1493).

33. "perche queste inimicitie hano multi capi et dependono da multi principali": LD, C 10, fols. 194–96 (22 June 1487).

34. RdS, Ferrara, b. 13, Lodovico Lardi to Eleonora d'Aragona, 23 July 1486; similarly RdS, Modena, b. 2c, Demetrio Vistarino to Ercole d'Este, 6 Apr. 1498.

prostitutes, and petty thieves and their receivers. Sources are quite clear in identifying these groups as the ill-famed, subject to suspicion and judicial maltreatment (they were explicitly excluded from controls on the torture of suspects).[35] A typical infamous career may be that of a confessed thief reported in 1494: he began as a child by begging and gambling, then took to robbing and gambling, and finally progressed to pimping, robbing, and gambling.[36] Other activities that brought the suspicion of ill-fame were habitual going abroad at night (and correspondingly not being seen during the day) and seeming to have plenty, living better than others, without owning or earning any wealth.[37] Conviction for crime also brought infamy, which neither pardon nor pacification could completely erase: hence there are occasional petitions to the duke for full rehabilitation to "honors, status, and repute" and for "removing the stain of ignominy" that came from a criminal conviction.[38] The words used to denote the ill-famed—*ribaldi, cattivi, tristi, giotti, giottoni*—emphasized their separation from the respectable (and respectful) society of *uomini da bene*. Such characters were especially associated with insolent and disobedient behavior, with theft and highway robbery, and with nocturnal disturbances. They congregated wherever there seemed to be some protection from the judicial apparatus: on borders, in the hills, and in the houses and households of officials and noblemen (see chap. 5).

In this they seem to differ from the more independent local bullies: for example, the smuggler of Adriano who always wore a sword, "that he appeared to be the lord of Adriano," and did not fear the local judiciary or the prince's decrees;[39] the "scandalous, dangerous, and disobedient man," also of Adriano, who had no fear and went around armed, with a brother and a cousin, singing derisive songs, such that they seemed to be lords of the area;[40] the man at Mellara who "does not want to have a

35. Dean, "Criminal Justice in Mid-Fifteenth-Century Bologna," 21.
36. RdS, Reggio, b. 112, Paolo Prosperi to Ercole d'Este, 10 June 1494.
37. RdS, Ferrara, b. 32, Alberto della Grana to Borso d'Este, 10 Apr. 1454; ibid., b. 41, Bernardo Salati to Borso d'Este, 13 Aug. 1454.
38. LD, B 1, fol. 159 (15 Mar. 1393); LD, B 6, fol. 97 (1 Apr. 1449). Cf. *Statuta comunis Vincentiae* (Vicenza, 1490), 88v, where those convicted of crimes of violence, short of homicide, are not therefore to be considered "infamous."
39. "va sempre con la spada al lato che para signore d'Adriano e non stima ne capitani ne cride": RdS, Ferrara, b. 12, Tommaso de' Grassi to Borso d'Este, 28 Dec. 1463.
40. Ibid., 8 May 1464.

superior in this place who is not obsequious to him," who armed his servants and laborers and "does law in his own way with arms against some poor men and to make himself feared in this area";[41] or, finally, the Pardi brothers at Cisarana, who, with their *parenti,* were said to be "continually keeping the poor community of Cisarana in fire and flame, wanting to lord it over everyone and to enjoy others' property by force and threats, and in spite of all the others of the community who do not dare to stand up to them."[42] Judges' reports on such men emphasize both their fearlessness ("they fear neither God nor me" is a typical formulation) and their social pretension (they acted like lords or gentlemen).[43] Nothing better illustrates the role of local judges in maintaining existing social and political structures: the judges' main aim and weapon was to create and increase fear of themselves and of the prince. In their eyes the fear of punishment was the best deterrent of criminal activity: the fearless were those who refused to accept the sort of social and political order sought by the duke and his local representatives, refusing to give them respect or obedience. In such refusal we can of course see heroic resistance to the state and its demands;[44] we can also see the state intervening in local society to support the *uomini da bene,* the prince's friends and servants.[45]

When the fearless were already in the ascendant, the podesta faced even greater difficulties: the podesta of Felina, in the Reggian hills, at one point complained of being calumniated by one Antonio Cavichiolo, "who hates me because I did not tolerate his devouring of the commune with his accomplices, as he is wont to"; so Antonio mobilized his faction and relatives *(parentella)* to complain. Antonio, the podesta reported, was the sort of man who, through his large *parentella,* got the local community to pay all his expenses, "under cover of doing the common

<hr/>

41. "non voria havere superiore in questo luocho se non obsequente a lui, il me ha in odio e studia reportar me quoquomodo il puo . . . non cessa far portare l'arme ad altri suoi lavorenti bandegiati de mantoana. Et gia conduxit mercede qua de Veronexe soldati e bandegiati in desprecio de l'officio e fecesse la ragione ad sua posta cum le arme contra alcuni poveri homini e anche per farsi temer in questo paexe": RdS, Ferrara, b. 46, Galvano Calcagni to Borso d'Este, 19 Feb. 1470.
42. LD, C 13, fol. 65 (15 May 1498).
43. Cf. Chittolini, "L'onore dell'officiale," 31–33, 36.
44. G. Pinto, "Controllo politico e ordine pubblico nei primi vicariati fiorentini: Gli 'Atti criminali degli ufficiali forensi'," *Quaderni storici* 49 (1982).
45. Dean, *Land and Power in Late Medieval Ferrara,* 154; Chittolini, "L'onore dell'officiale," 17.

good," and against whom little can be done, "because the evil can do more than the good, as in many of these mountain places."[46]

Bands of *giotti* and would-be local bosses were not, of course, the only problems that judges complained of in their endeavor to maintain law and order. Difficulties in establishing their own authority were combined with intractable social structures and deficiencies in the judicial system to make the criminal side of judges' work seem (conveniently perhaps) nigh impossible. In rural areas, podestas had only the local male inhabitants to call on in order to make arrests and to hold suspects. However, not only were these often insufficient,[47] but peasant solidarity, articulated through family relationships, as well as class, impeded the arrest and holding of suspects. Local responsibility to pursue and apprehend malefactors was still insisted on, and negligence in this was penalized in law and (less often) punished in fact.[48] At Adriano in 1454 the podesta reported that no secret assembly of men could be made for the purpose of surprising and arresting criminals, because "all are peasants and *parenti* and they stick together"; the only sure method, he thought, was to employ a *giotto* to trick them, but even that failed.[49] The podesta of Bondeno in the same year faced the same difficulty of making arrests of thieves, "because of the *parentadi* that they have, as they are forewarned by them of everything that is being planned against them."[50] Suspects can never be taken when local *contadini* are ordered to the task, wrote the podesta of Bon-

---

46. ". . . ser Antonio Cavichiolo quale me nemico capitale, non per mio manchamento ma solo perche al mio tempo non ho voluto patire che il faza le manziarie in questo comune como il soleva cum alcuni altri soi complici, e per questo ha spinti questi tali quale sono de sua factione e parentella a dire male de mi . . . et che quello ser Antonio e quello como quello che ha il parenta pur asai grande che li spinzi e chi li fa bolzoni e fara de continuo e loro anche voluntera pigliano questa provintia per pagare le lore colte cum queste andare e stare e triumfare suso le hostarie ale spese deli altri sota spetia de dire et fare il bene del comune. Et bene la brigata se ne avede ma non ge pono provedere perche piu posono li maligni che li boni, como accade in piu de quisti luogi montanari": RdS, Reggiano, Felina, Bernardino Respagiari, 3 May 1494.

47. RdS, Ferrara, b. 41, Marco da Badia to Eleonora d'Aragona, 14 Sept. 1478; ibid., b. 45a, Francesco Caligi to Ercole d'Este, 5 Mar. 1499.

48. ASE, Minutario, Lettere sciolte, b. 3, 29 Nov. 1489; RdS, Reggio, b. 173, 20 Aug. 1485; LD, A 1, fol. 39 (12 June 1365). See also H. Manikowska, "'Accorr'uomo.'"

49. "Vi signifiho come qui seria difficille cossa haverlli perche qui non e possibille mai potere fare choadunazione de zente secretamente che non se sapesse per fare simile execu- tione, che tuti son villani et parenti et tengono l'uno con l'altro": RdS, Ferrara, b. 12, Bar- tolomeo "de Blado" to Borso d'Este, 9 Mar. 1454.

50. "non me pare avere lo modo de averli per li parentadi che anno li quali son avixati da loro de zascaduna cosa che contra loro se tratano": RdS, Ferrara, b. 19, Bartolomeo Ovetari to Borso d'Este, 29 June 1454.

deno in 1483, "because all the peasants in this place are either *parenti* or *compadri*."[51] These *parentadi*, though dividing whole communities when in conflict, could also unite them in passive resistance to the podesta. The podesta had to beware of raising up whole communities against himself, as he needed the cooperation of local men to apprehend and detain suspects or known criminals.[52] This situation could have severe repercussions on the quality of justice: Ercole's commissioner-general in the Romagna in 1471 advised not proceeding in a murder inquiry, because the seven wounds given to the victim could each have been made by men from seven different families; because of these families' numerous followings, "great scandals" could arise.[53]

As the podesta of Adriano hoped, the only solution some podestas could see was the employment of men from outside the locality, whether they be thieves set to catch thieves, for example, or men-at-arms, *fanti*, sent from the city (though these categories are not mutually exclusive, as we shall see). A recurrent refrain in podestas' letters is the admission of personal insufficiency, of the need for additional manpower and stronger, more secure prisons.[54] The podesta of Comacchio, faced with the difficulty of making arrests, asked for some *fanti* in 1464, to make the obedient obey and "with such terror that they will be obedient in the future."[55] Thirty years later, the podesta there, in similar circumstances, asked for the *bargello* (rural law enforcer) to be sent, "otherwise, as all these *malabiati* are *parenti* and *compagni*, we can do nothing."[56] In 1499, the podesta of Massafiscaglia insisted that without the *bargello* it would not be possible to arrest some *giotti* sheltering in the bishop of Cervia's house in the village, for the local men, "though they come with arms, will not take anyone."[57] The podesta of Portomaggiore, in recognizing that the *bargello* could not be everywhere at once, suggested that a *bargello* in every village was needed, because of the number of *giotti* and thieves going around at night.[58] It was said that at Comacchio "they

---

51. "sel se ha a fare per li contadini comandati, mai se poterano pigliare dicti brazoli perche tuti li contadini in questo luoco sono o parenti o compadri": ibid., Francesco Maria Montachiesi to Francesco Nasello, 25 Aug. 1483.

52. RdS, Ferrara, b. 32, Pietro da Ponte to Eleonora d'Aragona, 1 Apr. 1479.

53. LD, C 3, fol. 76 insert (16 Sept. 1471).

54. See Bueno de Mesquita, "The Place of Despotism," 324; Chittolini, "L'onore dell'officiale"; Povolo, "Aspetti e problemi," 209.

55. RdS, Ferrara, b. 35, letters of Carlo Galluzzi, 24 Oct. 1464.

56. Ibid., Giacomo Perondoli to Eleonora d'Aragona, 26 Aug. 1492.

57. RdS, Ferrara, b. 45a, Francesco Caligi to Ercole d'Este, 5 Mar. 1499.

58. RdS, Ferrara b. 56, Roberto Drugi to Borso d'Este, 13 June 1462.

don't fear fines," and the podesta, unable even to distrain on property because of the power of *parenti*, sought the dispatch of some *fanti* to lend some "terror" to his authority.[59] But even reinforcement from the center could go disappointingly wrong: when he asked for some *fanti* to arrest a group of roving robbers, the podesta of Mellara added, "but I would want them to come secretly, so that the thing goes other than in the usual fashion, because, according to what I understand, when similar cases have occurred, the smoke has been seen from as far as Ficarolo."[60] As these demands imply, the manpower to effect arrests was much greater in the city, but even there podestas encountered resistance. In Ferrara in 1470 the podesta noted the habitual violence used against his staff whenever they brought prisoners in, often forcing them to let prisoners go.[61] And in the city, the range of those seeking to rescue prisoners was much greater: they included not just *parenti* but also groups of clerics, courtiers and their servants, and students and their rectors, who sought to liberate their clients and colleagues.[62] It was not just noblemen who sought to intimidate podestas and constables.[63]

The greatest admissions of inadequacy do seem to come from the *contado*. Letters to the duke penned by the podesta of Argenta, a small town between Ferrara and Ravenna, provide some extreme examples of this. Already in 1483, the podesta there complained of his inability to command obedience, urged the forcible removal to Ferrara of some "arrogant malefactors," and tried to delay the issue of some ducal pardons, so as to reestablish his own shambling authority: "alone I cannot exercise this office as obedience is not given to me, and I lack the force and the means to make the ill-behaved obey . . . Please send someone to help me."[64] In 1485, it seems that the house assigned to the podesta was in

---

59. RdS, Ferrara b. 35, Carlo Galuzzi to Borso d'Este, 24 Oct. 1464.

60. "ma voria havessero cervello in zucha et venisseno secretamente acio la cosa seguisse altramente che a modo usato, perche secundo intendo quando e accaduto simile caso, fina dal Figarolo si e sentito il fumo": RdS, Ferrara, b. 46, letters of Alberto Cavalluzzi, 8 Nov. 1464. See also Bueno de Mesquita, "The Place of Despotism," 324: "There seem to have been few troops to spare for the fight against crime, and when they were used for the purpose they often came back empty-handed."

61. RdS, Ferrara, b. 1, Luchino da Savona to Borso d'Este, 30 July 1470.

62. RdS, Ferrara b. 1, Scipione Roberti to Borso d'Este, 13 June 1469; ASE, Consigli, b. 1a, 13 Aug. 1466.

63. Cf. Povolo, "Aspetti e problemi," 208.

64. "da mi solo non posso fare questo officio per non mi essere prestato obedientia et mancharme la forza et el modo de fare obedire li mali costumati . . . supplico a v. Ex. mi voglia . . . mandarme per utile de v. S. et mia conservatione qualche uno che mi adiuti a fare

ruins.[65] In 1486, the then podesta wrote of his difficulty in arranging a pacification between two families (the Quieti and Veterani).[66]

Such officials had a clear explanation for the disobedience and disrespect they daily faced. One of them made the point succinctly, commenting that the *tristi* and *cattivi* "have no respect for your lordship or your officials, which arises from their never being punished and from your lordship's excessive clemency."[67] This view is confirmed by an earlier podesta, who notes that these "arrogant men have never been punished for their faults and were reared without restraint."[68] Such a diagnosis of disorder and criminality was a common one among judges. They invariably believed that fear and punishment corrected disorders and deterred crime, and conversely that crime and disorder resulted from slack discipline. The necessity of instilling fear justified conduct: the podesta of Ferrara in 1470 admitted that he might on occasion exceed his statutory powers in making arrests, but only "to a good end," "to greater fear."[69] Belief in fear was equaled only by belief in exemplary punishment: if only one "eminent thief" could be taken, asserted the podesta of Adriano in 1454, "all his peers" would leave the area.[70] A tumult in Carpineti against the *capitano del divieto* of Reggio was attributed by the governors of the city to a failure to punish an earlier assault on the same official.[71] Contrary to the civic monopoly on capital punishment, the local hanging of thieves and murderers, in their villages, was sometimes authorized so as to concentrate the example and the fear it inspired where they were most needed.[72] However, local execution could have an effect contrary to that intended, intensifying the passions

---

questo offitio": RdS, Ferrara, b. 13, letters of "Mazonus de Valisneria," 7, 16, and 17 June 1483.

65. Ibid., Lodovico Lardi to Eleonora d'Aragona, 6 Oct. 1485.

66. Ibid., 23 and 25 July 1486.

67. "parendomi che questi talli non habiano reverentia alcuna a la v. S. ne a soi offitialli, la quale cosa procede per non essere mai puniti li tristi e cattivi e questo per tropo clementia di v. S.": ibid., Filippo Bardelli to Ercole d'Este, 30 Oct. 1490.

68. Ibid., "Mazonus de Valisneria," 16 June 1483.

69. "se qualche volta io excedesse a maiore timore li ordini delli statuti in pigliar qualcuno . . . ne do adviso volonteri a quella, perche nol faria salvo a buon fine": RdS, Ferrara, b. 1, Luchino da Savona to Borso d'Este, 30 Apr. 1470.

70. RdS, Ferrara, b. 12, Bartolomeo "de Blado" to Borso d'Este, 4 Sept. 1454.

71. RdS, Reggio, b. 2, *Capitani,* 2 Nov. 1494.

72. RdS, Reggiano, Castelnovo ne' Monti, b. 1, Paolo da Roma to Eleonora d'Aragona, 28 May 1485.

of the condemned man's *parenti,* to the point of threatening his victim's relatives.[73]

Officials thus defined their self-image in terms of the fear and obedience they inspired, hence they were sensitive to local pretenders using fear for private, and therefore (in official eyes) illegitimate, purposes.[74] But it is obvious from their letters that many judges had little of the formidable about them, and that local inhabitants had difficulty in perceiving them as representatives of the prince or the state. "Who do you think you are?" demanded one man when ordered by the podesta of Mellara to lay down his weapons.[75] "I shit on you . . . this is the honor I do you," shouted another.[76] Insolence and threats were commonly directed at officials, who persuaded themselves, and tried to persuade the prince, that these insults were injurious to him and his "estate," as much as to themselves personally.[77]

It is quite clear that many men who took judicial office had no aptitude or taste for the type of work involved: dealing promptly and boldly with armed gatherings and village feuds; facing down challenges and insults from local braggarts; pursuing delinquents and bandits against the opposition of local families. Ludovico Ariosto was not alone in taking such office out of financial need, while coming to recognize that he was completely unsuited to the work (*Satire* 4). The satirical poet Antonio Cammelli noted two types of podesta: one made from pike bones, broom twigs, and marsh grass, who had no expertise in assaying men's faults; the other made from bats' wings, crocodile blood, and plague water, who valued human blood so highly that he taught other judges how to be butchers.[78] Between these extremes of weakness and ferocity, there were, it seems, few who could deal firmly yet gently with policing matters.

---

73. LD, C 5, fols. 70–71 (19 Apr. 1478).

74. Chittolini, "L'onore dell'officiale," 10.

75. The podesta was threatened, "fina a dirmi chio mi credeva essere et se io era piu che visconte de questo loco": RdS, Ferrara, b. 46, Alberto Cavalluzzi to marquis of Mantua, 23 Jan. 1464.

76. After being fined for repeated invective directed at the podesta's lieutenant ("Io tene incaco"), Pietro Contrari persisted, arms in hand, against advice to behave more soberly, and, "me fece uno manegato dicendo tuo questo e lo honore che io te fazo . . . io voglio stare qui al tuo despecto cum le mie arme": RdS, Ferrara, b. 19, podesta's lieutenant to Ercole d'Este, 26 Nov. 1479. See also Chittolini, "L'onore dell'officiale," 19–21.

77. RdS, Ferrara, b. 19, Giovanni Condulmer to Ercole d'Este, 11 Nov. 1479. See also Chittolini, "L'onore dell'officiale," 26 n. 44, 34.

78. A. Cappelli and S. Ferrari, eds., *Rime edite ed inedite di Antonio Cammelli detto il Pistoia* (Livorno, 1884), 127–28.

Was there more to this problem than mere personal incapacity? Was there also a structural failure in the way men were selected for office? Did the system allow the accumulation of experience or specialization in judicial matters? These are precisely the questions that may be raised from the surviving lists of official appointments in the Este state from the 1450s, as recorded in a unique register giving both duties and salaries and the names of successive officeholders between 1451 and 1457.[79] Excluding the *podesterie* of the major cities and their appeals judges, who were almost always foreign lawyers or noblemen, some sixty offices with some form of judicial authority were held in these years by only 180 men. Since the term of all offices was six months in the first instance, this shows at first sight a high level of confirmation or circulation in office: some men were confirmed in office for three or four successive terms; others (but fewer) held many different offices. However, the majority (over one hundred) held only one office (even if for several successive terms), and the vast majority no more than two. This meant that there was only a small core of more frequent holders of judicial office: twenty men held between three and six offices. With three exceptions,[80] they all came from within Este territory and were either members of old Ferrarese or Reggian noble families (Boiardi, Costabili), "foreign" nobles who had in the previous century moved to Ferrara and into Este service (Ariosti, Condulmer, Fontana), or notables and lawyers from Ferrara and Modena (e.g., Giovanni Bertazzi and Antonio Calora). Roughly half of the twenty were settled in Ferrara or had Ferrarese citizenship. Similar concentration of judicial office holding has been found in the Florentine state.[81] In addition to this slight accumulation of judicial experience, recruitment from the major subject cities, Modena and Reggio, was narrow, implying that there was little integration of local elites into a unified state. There is little evidence of an officeholding circuit here. Two objections may be made to this conclusion: first, we may need to look more widely across northern Italy for the circulation of officials, as the circuit or circuits perhaps existed at a level beyond that of individual states; second, we may also need to look at nonjudicial offices, as it is likely that men moved from judicial to financial, military, or court positions. But the former objection would reinforce, not weaken, the argument that little

79. LD, A 6.
80. Tommaso "de Panzaticis" (Panciatichi?), Giovanni "de Dyrachio," and Antonio Sandri da Montagnana.
81. Zorzi, "Giusdicenti," 531.

integration occurred, while the latter does not alter the suggestion that few officials acquired continuous experience of judicial matters.

The incapacity of officials for the tasks set them is also suggested by evidence from later decades. In April 1470, the podesta of Ferrara observed that in other cities he knew, cities marked by factional strife, he had not been surprised at the many "insolences" and armed assaults committed, "because these were to the purpose of their factiousness," but that he had been surprised to find these things in Ferrara.[82] In this observation we find a hint, maybe, that Borso d'Este, for all his public display of affection for justice, had achieved neither the stability nor the order commonly expected of principalities. Possible confirmation of this comes in the hundreds of old, still-pending cases discovered by the new podesta in 1470.[83] A few years later comes evidence that the criminal judges available to the duke had for several years failed to meet the problems put to them: the duchess Eleonora confessed that, during Ercole's absences commanding allied forces in Tuscany in the Pazzi War, she had had to deal with many criminal complaints (especially of forgery and perjury, but also of other crimes) but had not found a judge who could act on them satisfactorily. She reminded Ercole that he needed a "valent'homo" in criminal matters: she had recommended a hundred times "Messer Augustino" when he was alive;[84] and now she had heard of one "Messer Francesco Lucano," of whom she wrote, "from what I have heard he is of an alert mind, thoroughly prudent and well-experienced in these atrocious criminal matters."[85]

---

82. "Qualche volta siando me trovato in citade di parte, non me sono maravigliato di molte insolencie, insulti facti cum arme, percussione e morte occorse perche glerano alle partialita loro conveniente, ma occorrando tanti insulti e percussione publice apensate in questa cita pacifica de v. Ex. come per lo mio tempo ho veduto, me ne maraviglio e doglo": RdS, Ferrara, b. 1, Luchino da Savona to Borso d'Este, 30 Apr. 1470.

83. Ibid., 30 July 1470. For a similar problem in the Venetian Terraferma in the seventeenth century, see Povolo, "Aspetti e problemi," 187.

84. Agostino Bonfranceschi (1437–79), who distinguished himself for severity toward rebels and traitors in Ferrara in the 1470s; see A.I. Pini, "Bonfranceschi Agostino," *DBI* 12 (1970): 32–33. Zambotti did not share Eleonora's high opinion, attributing Bonfranceschi's unshriven death to God's judgment "per la soa mala conscientia et infinite sceleritade": *Diario,* 62.

85. "Doppo che v. Ex fu in campo il mi e accaduto haver querela de molte cosse criminose, maxime de falsita e de instrumenti falsi et de testimoni falsi et altri piu malefitii criminali de piu sorte, a la intelligentia dei quali seben gli ho proposto mo uno cognitore mo un altro, tamen io non ho mai trovato chi mi satisfacia . . . Et certo v. Ex. ha desaio qui de uno valenthomo che fusse de questa sorte che in criminalibus havesse una bona cognitione et cum prudentia sapesse cavare le machie de li panni altrui. Io ho ben commendato cento

Problems also arose with the staff that podestas were supposed to bring with them. Noting that the city was swarming with thieves and robbers, the commune of Ferrara in 1473 decided to end the practice by which the podesta hired his own subordinate judges, at salaries that he set and paid; it took to itself the power to choose and hire these judges, setting their salaries at a uniform level.[86] "Many times it has happened that these judges have not been very learned or expert or self-disciplined, perhaps through not receiving their due from the podestas, who, to avoid spending much, hire any men they can," explained the head of the communal council.[87] Here the commune makes a clear connection between levels of crime and method of appointment: allowing the podesta to hire his own judges and to negotiate their salaries left him too much temptation to economize on experience and ability, especially in the criminal court, so as to increase his own profits, while allowing unpunished criminality to flourish. By taking the power of appointment into its own hands and standardizing salaries, the commune was making a stand against the free play of the market in judicial office, in the interest, as it said, of the res publica.

Low levels of competence naturally bred high levels of complaint. Just as judges faced difficulties making arrests, so too every subsequent phase of criminal procedure, from custody to punishment, could generate obstacles for such men. Jails were insecure and easily broken: in the cities they would be sounder constructions, but in Ferrara in 1470 prisoners broke out using only their bare hands, as a result of which the prison governor resigned, admitting that he was too old and physically unfit for the job.[88] In the countryside there was even less provision for holding men securely: "here nothing is kept under lock and key," wrote the podesta of

volte il quondam Messer Augustino perche secondo mi in questo cognitione criminale il ni era bon maestro et bon praticho. Sentendo mi de la fama de misser Francesco Lucano, de la sua vaglia et de la sua condictione, e, per quanto mi e dicto, che l'e de vivo inzegno et tuto prudente e ben maniroso a queste cosse atroce de maleficii, concludo chel suppleria molto-ben al bisogno qui in simile cosse": CS, b. 131, 9 Aug. 1479.

86. ASFe, Archivio storico del comune, Libro delle provvigioni statutarie 1457–91, fols. 16v–17.

87. Ibid., Libro delle commissioni ducali 1476–81, fol. 42 (10 June 1477). Cf. Zorzi, "Giusdicenti," 539–40.

88. ASE, Archivio militare, b. 2, Capitano delle carceri, 13 July 1470. Cf. Povolo, "Aspetti e problemi," 218–19.

Ficarolo in 1462,[89] and prisoners had to be left at inns, awaiting transfer to the city.[90]

Whenever the podesta's staff brought someone in, he was subject to lobbying from *parenti* and patrons.[91] When university students were arrested, the rector, accompanied by students and doctors, made clamorous descent on the podesta's office to demand their release.[92] At trial, perjury was allegedly common: "the *giotti* buy each other . . . and would take thousands of false oaths for a penny."[93] Witnesses lied.[94] When these methods failed, petition could be made to the duke for pardon, but judges doubted the truthfulness of petitions: "everyone lies in petitioning in order to obtain your excellency's pardon," declared the stern Ferrarese captain of justice in 1491.[95] A petition against a murder sentence in Frignano in 1488 was found to be full of lies.[96] The podesta of Massafiscaglia in 1454 had to deal with a petition to the prince that told a totally different version of the crime and inculpated him of favoring thieves.[97]

Sometimes the fault lay not in the podesta's ability to command but in local statutes that, in judges' eyes, seriously hampered their effective power. Suspects' awareness and use of loopholes allowed them to slip through a podesta's fingers. At Bondeno, blasphemy and arms carrying flourished because accusers were not remunerated and had to swear out their accusations in the presence of the accused;[98] at Argenta a "bestial" statute contrary, it was asserted, to usage in the rest of Italy gave suspects time to flee by requiring the podesta to summon them, before interrogation, to receive a copy of the charges.[99] Such examples suggest a consis-

89. "qui non se serra niente con chiave": RdS, Ferrara, b. 43, Giacomo Gentili to Borso d'Este, 5 May 1462.

90. RdS, Ferrara, b. 32, Alberto della Grana to Borso d'Este, 28 Feb. 1454.

91. RdS, Modena, b. 2c, podesta to Eleonora d'Aragona, Apr. 1487.

92. RdS, Ferrara, b. 1, letters of Scipione Roberti, 13 June 1469, and Gregorio Zampante, s.d. 1490.

93. "li giuti si copereno l'uno l'altro e toriano mille sagramenti falsi per uno dinaro": RdS, Ferrara, b. 35, Giacomo Perondoli to Eleonora d'Aragona, 26 Aug. 1492.

94. LD, C 10, fols. 283–84 (20 Jan. 1488), 340 (20 June 1488); similarly RdS, Ferrara, b. 1, G. Zampante to Ercole d'Este, s.d.

95. "tuti supplicano il falso per havere gratia da v. Ex.": ASE, Archivio militare, b. 2, Capitani di giustizia, 15 July 1491; RdS, Ferrara, b. 1, Gregorio Zampante to Ercole d'Este, s.d.

96. LD, C 10, fols. 283–84, 340.

97. RdS, Ferrara, b. 45a, Benedetto Giacobelli to Borso d'Este, 13 June 1454.

98. RdS, Ferrara, b. 19, Bartolomeo Ovetari to Borso d'Este, 4 Aug. 1454.

99. RdS, Ferrara, b. 13, Bartolomeo Pioli to Ercole d'Este, 3 Mar. 1491.

tent need to clear the course of criminal trial of obstacles, such as the reluctance of witnesses to testify or rules of procedure that, while ensuring openness, also allowed delay or absconding.

Among the most prominent of these obstacles was the church. Criminous clerks, benefit of clergy, and sanctuary were, of course, among the chief points of conflict between secular governments and local churches throughout the high and later Middle Ages. Although the Italian communes had, in the thirteenth century, challenged the church in many areas, these seem not to have been among them.[100] This was no longer the case in the late-medieval principalities. In the 1450s, for example, Francesco Sforza, unsatisfied with the bishop of Milan's judicial inaction against a clerical arsonist, installed one of his own councillors as an associate judge to oversee the trial.[101] Secular concern in Ferrara at clerical immunities was sufficient in the late 1480s for the duke to press the pope for concessions in this area: in 1470 the sacristy of the Ferrarese cathedral had been described as a "receptacle for all thieves and rogues";[102] by 1480 Ercole had reached an agreement with the bishop of Ferrara that those who fled into churches after having committed offenses incurring corporal penalty would no longer be safe from arrest there;[103] in 1478 the governors of Modena sought ducal action to restrain priests from attacking the podesta's staff with the intention of releasing a prisoner;[104] and in 1487 Ercole registered his astonishment that the bishop of Modena should claim as a cleric one who had neither tonsure nor habit and who pursued secular occupations.[105] However, it was only in the following decade that firmer legislative action was taken to deal with this problem (see chap. 5).

These were not, however, the only motives inspiring legislation. The accumulating modification of the criminal law reveals much about the aims, methods, and reasoning of the prince and his judicial advisers. This

---

100. Jones, "Communes and Despots," 80, 83, 90; L.A. Botteghi, "Clero e comune in Padova nel secolo XIII," *Nuovo archivio veneto*, n.s., 9 (1905): 262–63. But see, to the contrary, *Statuti di Bologna dall'anno 1245 all'anno 1267*, ed. L. Frati (Bologna, 1869–77), 3:277.

101. F. Fossati, "Noterelle viscontee-sforzesche," *Archivio storico lombardo*, 8th ser., 4 (1953): 222; see also Comba, "Gli Statuti di Amedeo VIII," 54.

102. ASE, Consigli, b. 1a, 10 May 1470.

103. ASFe, Libro delle commissioni, fol. 103v (28 May 1480).

104. LD, C 5, fol. 36 (28 Feb. 1478).

105. LD, C 10, fol. 234.

process has rarely been traced in detail,[106] but it can be followed, for Modena, in the "provisions" annexed to the Modenese statutes of 1420 and printed, with the statutes, in 1487. In general, these provisions reveal a continuous endeavor to supplement and adjust the criminal law in order to deal with contemporary problems. In 1404 Niccolò III d'Este had authorized the podesta to vary and augment statutory penalties, on the grounds that "experience teaches that many crimes are committed that require harsher punishment than the law provides"; and when this discretionary power was omitted from the revised statutes in 1420, Niccolò insisted on its retention.[107] In 1426 the ceiling for fines for disobedience to officials was raised from twenty soldi to twenty-five lire;[108] and later, in response to a case of resistance to arrest, Borso d'Este decreed that the penalty incurred for such acts should henceforth be the amputation of both hands and perpetual imprisonment, a penalty that the commune protested against as "not a little hard," given that "equity requires that the penalty should not exceed the crime."[109] In 1437 two local practices were the object of the lord's censure: the delay in implementing sentences caused by appeals, which were therefore forbidden in serious criminal cases; and extortions flourishing in the countryside through the sale or subletting of the rural small-claims court (*danni dati*).[110] Conversely in 1442, it was the "audacity" of peasants in confronting citizens that was seen as needing restraint.[111] Pressure for allowing criminal appeals had to be resisted again in 1449.[112] In 1454 much more specific penalties were ordained for abduction and clandestine marriage.[113] The year 1457 brought a decree to facilitate the extradition of bandits from the territories of the nobility,[114] while in 1459 a *capitano del divieto* was instituted for the *contado,* with specific powers against smuggling, arms carrying,

---

106. G.M. Varanini, "Gli statuti delle città della Terraferma veneta nel Quattrocento," in Chittolini and Willoweit, *Statuti città territori,* 248–51, 266–69, 289–95; I. Lazzarini, "Il diritto urbano in una signoria cittadina: Gli statuti mantovani dai Bonacolsi ai Gonzaga (1313–1404)," in ibid., 402–8.

107. *Statuta civitatis Mutine* (Modena, 1487), fols. 175r–v (BL copy); Leonello d'Este renewed this power in 1446: ibid., 182.

108. Ibid., fol. 175v.

109. Ibid., fols. 194r–v.

110. Ibid., fols. 176v, 179v.

111. Ibid., fol. 182v.

112. Ibid., fols. 187v–188.

113. Ibid., fol. 197.

114. Ibid., fols. 198v–199.

banditry, and abduction.[115] In 1461 steps were taken to ensure the secrecy of accusations of blasphemy and gambling.[116] The ability of suspects to hide the truth and to frustrate trial, under a statute requiring the podesta, before trial, to release details of prosecution evidence, led in 1476 to such publication being made discretionary, not obligatory.[117] The 1470s saw the duke issuing enactments to curtail the expenses of imprisonment, legal action, and collection of fines, to ensure proper selection of auditors (sindicators) of *contado* officials, and to end the corrupt "customs" of allowing defense witnesses and counsel in criminal cases and of selling judicial office.[118] Throughout this legislative activity, there would seem to be a number of trends: the sharpening of powers and penalties; the movement toward greater secrecy; the reining in of extortionate practices; and the abolition of "customs" or statutes that allowed crimes to go unpunished or that frustrated trials through undue acquittal. The explicit rationale of new enactments is, however, narrow: that punishment deters;[119] that fear was the only weapon against the "disobedient and reprobate";[120] that officials should be able to exercise their offices without obstacle;[121] and that unpunished crime encouraged other people to worse deeds.[122]

A very similar picture—in outline if not in detail—results from the enactments *(provvigioni)* amending the Ferrarese statute book of 1456.[123] A new tribunal was created to deal with peasant complaints against debt collectors ("exactors");[124] an existing tribunal to punish notarial fraud was reformed.[125] Existing offenses were widened: the scope of *danni dati* was extended to gardens and orchards in the city and

---

115. Ibid., fols. 202v–204.

116. Ibid., fol. 204v.

117. Ibid., fol. 205.

118. Ibid., fols. 207, 209r–v, 212v.

119. Ibid., fol. 175.

120. Ibid., fol. 175v.

121. Ibid., fol. 194.

122. Ibid., fol. 212v.

123. ASFe, Archivio storico del comune, Libro delle provvigioni. The volume was compiled in 1476 at Ercole's order and was subsequently added to: ASFe, Libro delle commissioni, fol. 16v.

124. ASFe, Libro delle provvigioni, fol. 1 (1457); *Statuta Ferrarie* (Ferrara, 1476), fols. 200r–v (BL copy and numeration).

125. ASFe, Libro delle provvigioni, fols. 26r–v (1475), 62v–63 (1479); *Statuta Ferrarie,* fols. 221–22.

its suburbs.[126] New penalties were appointed for new offenses: for gambling with certain foodstuffs;[127] for smearing doors or walls at night or for indecent painting on them;[128] for women covering their heads and faces in public, which allowed dishonest women to mix with honest virgins and daughters of nobles, "infecting" and "corrupting" them.[129] New procedures were created for treason trials, in the wake of Niccolò d'Este's attempted coup of 1476,[130] and for the prosecution of clandestine marriage.[131] Almost every stage of criminal trial was subject to some revision, from the immediate inventorying of a suspect's property (to prevent dispersal), to increased penalties for impeding implementation of sentence.[132] Above all, these enactments endeavored to stop lawyers from obstructing criminal trials. In no criminal trial was a defense lawyer to be allowed audience (even to prove innocence) unless the accused had appeared in person and entered custody.[133] The accused person's right to reject a judge suspected of partiality was restricted.[134] Submitting appeals at every stage of trial—which had the effect of rendering trials "immortal"—was banned in 1477; five years later there were second thoughts, as "by this the road opens to unjust judges,"[135] but the complete prohibition on appealing from sentence was firmly restated.[136] The duke and his legal advisors were thus fighting on two fronts: the need for "new remedies to correct delinquents"[137] resulted in the creation of new offenses and the extension of old ones, in the construction of new tribunals and the increase of old penalties; the need to halt the evasion of punishment through lawyerly obstructions or through resistance resulted in stricter, less open procedure.

Just as the prince was active in reforming the law, so too he pressed his officials to conform to his expectations. The prince was not always sym-

---

126. ASFe, Libro delle provvigioni, fols. 9v–10 (1468). For other regulations of *danni dati*, see ibid., fols. 47v–48v, 66v, 68v; *Statuta Ferrarie*, fols. 206v–8.

127. ASFe, Libro delle provvigioni, fol. 2v (1460); *Statuta Ferrarie*, fol. 201.

128. ASFe, Libro delle provvigioni, 27v–8 (1475); *Statuta Ferrarie*, fol. 222v. See also Dean, "Criminal Justice in Mid-Fifteenth-Century Bologna," 32.

129. ASFe, Libro delle provvigioni, fols. 31v–32v (1476); *Statuta Ferrarie*, 225v–26.

130. ASFe, Libro delle provvigioni, fols. 44v–45 (1479).

131. Ibid., fol. 45v.

132. Ibid., fols. 32v, 70; *Statuta Ferrarie*, fol. 226v.

133. ASFe, Libro delle provvigioni, fol. 66 (1480).

134. Ibid., fols. 6r–v (1463), 25v (1475); *Statuta Ferrarie*, fols. 204v, 220v–21.

135. ASFe, Libro delle provvigioni, fols. 40–41, 70r–v; *Statuta Ferrarie*, fol. 223v.

136. ASFe, Libro delle provvigioni, fols. 16r–v (1473); *Statuta Ferrarie*, 213v.

137. ASFe, Libro delle provvigioni, fol. 9.

pathetic to his officials' inadequacies. He expected his officials to have a commanding personal presence, to take control of situations and not to need specific ducal decrees to do it for them. Officials had powers to issue penal commands, the duke reminded the captain of Nonantola in 1471, and should use them to disperse crowds.[138] Ercole wanted officials who were awake and alert: "These are things where we want you to set to work to punish these rogues without waiting for us to wake you up," he told the governors of Modena in 1486–87, following an act of violence between two families.[139] Dissatisfied with daily news of disorders at Castelvetro and Levizzano in 1476, Ercole rebuked his noble governor there: "You must reform well and promptly and govern these places in a different way . . . We tell you to take good care and thought to their government, so that it does not seem that these places are in the hands of people who are asleep."[140]

When Ercole kept receiving complaints of bandits in the Reggian hills but heard no news of action by his officials in the city, he wrote strictly to them: "You are men of worth who should know how to do better than this."[141] The emphasis on acting "virilely" was several times drummed out: "conduct yourself so virilely that we know you are a man who is in office," Ercole commanded the podesta of Ferrara in 1476.[142] What was meant by virility? Contemporary usage in the late fifteenth century (as in the late thirteenth)[143] associated virility with fighting, with public, fearless, and frontal assault on the enemy.[144] The virile official was not sus-

---

138. LD, C 3, fols. 24–25.

139. LD, C 10, fol. 122.

140. LD, C 4, fol. 75.

141. "Voi seti homini de tale vaglia che saperesti fare mazore cossa che questa": LD, C 10, fol. 203 (30 June 1487).

142. "Governative si virilmente che conosciamo siati un homo che sii in officio": LD, C 4, fol. 96; similarly ASE, Minutario, Lettere sciolte, b. 3, 6 Aug. 1493.

143. *Cronica fratris Salimbene de Adam ordinis minorum*, ed. O. Holder-Egger, Monumenta Germaniae historica, Scriptores, vol. 23 (Hannover, 1905–13), 127 ("viriliter . . . agressus est hostes"), 376 ("viriliter dimicando fuit occisus"), 632 ("viriliter fecerunt insultum contra adversam partem sicut leones consurgentes ad predam"), and 24, 29, 60, 193, 378, 473, 480, 490, 528, 637.

144. "inimicis nostris non tergivertus sed pocius viriliter debellando": LD, A 3, fol. 241 (27 Dec. 1400); "lassa el guerir viril l'aspro ferir / del suo nimico poiche in terra iace": *Seraphino aquilano opere nuovemente ricorrette* (Venice, 1548), sonnet 161; "ab inimicorum processibus viriliter defensare": A. Gianandrea, "Della signoria di Francesco Sforza nella Marca," *Archivio storico italiano*, 5th ser., 2 (1888): 307; Sforza the condottiere led his men alone from the front, "virilmente": A. Minuti, *Vita di Muzio Attendolo Sforza*, ed. G. Porro Lambertenghi, *Miscellanea di storia italiana* 7 (1869): 206–7. Cf. Chittolini, "L'onore dell'officiale," 11, who associates virility instead with honor.

pectable of favoring rather than punishing delinquents;[145] he kept a good company of men, performed his duties "gaiardamente," "senza alcun respecto,"[146] and did not try to walk away from threats to his life.[147]

Furthermore, the imperative metaphors used to rouse officials to action mostly have the smack of dominant masculinity: "keep them under the bridle as much as you can";[148] "put so many dogs on their trail that these ribalds fall into your nets";[149] "dig out the evil weeds from our land";[150] "knock the stains out of his cloth."[151] The rounding up of criminals was thus conceived as mastering a willful horse, hunting game, weeding a tare-strewn field, or cleaning soiled fabric. The metaphors connect, of course, to other symbolic representations of power: to the equestrian statue, so much in vogue in the fifteenth century, in which the ruler's or captain's command of his horse was identified with his command of men,[152] or to the depiction of the prince with his hunting dogs.

However, the oppression involved in keeping the garden of state free of weeds was manifested in reports from Finale in 1480. Three letters from the podesta make intensive use of the metaphors of sowing and gardening to justify his handling of one Peregrino Bazaliero, whom he had expelled from the local governing council.[153] According to the podesta, Ercole had appointed him to "extirpate and remove the grass from the good grain," and Peregrino, "born of bad seed, a malevolent instigator of discords," was a "bad weed" preventing Ercole's sweet garden from resting in "peace and joy." Peregrino's main offense seems to have been in giving

---

145. ASE, Minutario, Lettere sciolte, b. 3, 6 Aug. 1493.

146. LD, C 13, fols. 48, 100 (27 Apr., 3 July 1498); Bueno de Mesquita, "The Place of Despotism," 325.

147. G.B. Venturi, "Relazioni dei governatori estensi di Reggio al duca Ercole I in Ferrara (1482–99)," *AMMo*, 3d ser., 2 (1883–84): 246.

148. "tieni sotto el freno piu che tu poi": LD, C 10, fol. 3 (5 Jan. 1486); RdS, Ferrara, b. 32, letter of Pietro da Ponte, 5 Apr. 1479.

149. "mettiati tanti cani a le poste che questi ribaldi . . . caschino nel vostre rete": LD, C 10, fol. 204; see also ibid., fol. 333. See E. Muir's presentation of vengeance killers as hunting dogs: *Mad Blood Stirring: Vendetta and Factions in Friuli during the Renaissance* (Baltimore, 1993), 215ff., 222–33.

150. "cavare le male herbe de quella nostra terra": LD, C 10, fol. 241 (11 Oct. 1487); ASRe, Comune, Carteggio del reggimento, b. 561, 5 Feb. 1483. Cf. "levar via il loio dal bon frumento": RdS, Finale, b. 1, Ludovico Mazzanti to Eleonora d'Aragona, 27 Sept. 1480.

151. "cavati le machie di pani de questui": LD, C 10, fols. 36, 90; CS, b. 131, 9 Aug. 1479. See also Bernardy, "Dall'archivio governativo della repubblica di San Marino," 167.

152. See. W.J. Connell, "Il commissario e lo stato territoriale fiorentino," *Ricerche storiche* 18 (1988): 612.

153. RdS, Finale, b. 1, Ludovico Mazzanti to Ercole d'Este and Eleonora d'Aragona, 12 Aug., 31 Aug., and 27 Sept. 1480.

favor to peasants indebted to the commune of Finale, in alleging "with his evil oratory ['male suasione'] that the people are robbed . . . by those who govern this commune," and in winning the confidence of the common people, "who believe anything." Whatever the truth of these allegations, such dissent was not tolerated: Ercole wanted local councils to govern unanimously, "for the good and profit of the community"; actions like those of Peregrino were interpreted as the pursuit of private "appetite." It was the gardener-duke who decided which plants should grow; and what was good for those plants was good for the whole garden.

Such metaphors are also revealing not only because they imply the application of physical force, even cruelty, to a wild, untrained nature but also because they suggest the instrumentality of that action—a horse had to be bridled to move in the desired direction, a field had to be weeded if useful crops were to grow. So what was the "proper" use to which society had to be directed through the disciplining of its wilder elements? "Angel order" is what Ercole d'Este asked for.[154] He wanted his officials to govern "in such a way that men can say they continuously have in their mouths the sweet milk" of the duke and his house.[155] He wanted a world without discord or argumentativeness,[156] in which people were well behaved toward officials.[157] He expected his officials to "aim at the same target" and not to quarrel among themselves.[158] He desired that "each of his subjects should live virtuously and attend to his own business, his trade or craft, and that his officials should be respected and obeyed."[159] Moreover, the duke believed in the exemplarity of official action. In one case, the duke rejected advice to permit only "sim-

---

154. Complaining of foreigners hunting in the *campagna* around Crespino, Ercole told the podesta there that he wanted it put into "ordine di angeli": LD, C 10, fol. 341 (11 June 1488).

155. "havendovi nui mandato a quella parte . . . governarli iustamente, amorevolmente et sanctamente in maniera che potesseno dire havere del continuo in bocha el dolce lacte de Nui e de la casa nostra": LD, C 3, fol. 117 (13 Jan. 1475: Ercole d'Este to commissioner in Garfagnana).

156. Concerning dispute over a benefice in the Garfagnana, Ercole wrote: "et diremo pur questo che la discordia de loro homini e casone de tuti quisti mali . . . solo per essere li homini male dacordio insieme . . . dove doveriano essere uniti e tirare tuti ad un fine . . . Ma loro si voleno regere per suo capo e fare questione . . . et stare suso le punte et si tagliano l'aqua adosso loro stessi et poi voriano che nui reconzassemo tute le cosse malfacte quando le hano guaste": LD, C 4, fol. 39 (14 Mar. 1476).

157. RdS, Modena, b. 1a, Reggimento, 28 Nov. 1495.

158. "doveresti trare ad uno bersaio et intendervi insieme et havere in mente che tuti dui siti li per nui": LD, C 3, fol. 54 (2 June 1471: Ercole d'Este to podesta of Montefiorino).

159. ASFe, Libro delle provvigioni, fol. 32v (3 Mar. 1476).

ulated show of rigor" when the prosecution of all those involved in a murder might create local difficulties for the podesta: this would give a bad example, and there was a duty to give breath and comfort to those who wished to see justice done.[160] The force of example was one that Ercole hammered out in a long complaint to Reggio of the number of pardons he was being asked to approve: give an example to those of your sons who live well and who do not expect to be pardoned for serious offenses.[161]

Ercole's expectations thus seem to be entirely conventional and predictable: combining the traditional goals of medieval government, peace and concord, with a sense of ultimate religious purpose and of the parental duties of those in authority (giving breath and milk to subjects, even at personal risk). The prince, his family, and his officials were to be mother and father to their subjects; their duty was to protect those who wanted to live decently (*ben vivere*), to preserve them from the dangers of robbery and rape, intimidation and violence.

> It is understood that many are exercised in gaining pardons for those who every night and many times have violated and forced monasteries and nuns, for those who rob and cheat, for those who threaten this one and that one, for those who carry arms in the piazza and throughout the city to the despite and in the sight of officials and of those who want to *ben vivere,* for those who beat and wound others on the piazza and in the law courts, for those who last Thursday night . . . entered a house of the best citizens . . . and sought to force their daughters in the presence of their mother because the father was away.[162]

---

160. "vedemo chel seria un mal exempio a fare altramente et se bene non si pigliasseno adesso tutti septe, per non mettere tanta carne al fuoco, il non e chel non fusse molto ben facto haverni dui o cussi . . . Il che piu presto daria respiratione et conforto a tuti quelli nostri homini vedendo fare ragione et punire li malfactori che non faria il non li procedere, se bene in principio si facesse qualche simulata demostratione de rigorosita come racordati": LD, C 3, fol. 76 insert (16 Sept. 1471).

161. ASRe, Carteggio, b. 561, Ercole d'Este (?) to *reggimento*, s.d. (1470s?).

162. "El se intende che molti sono pratichati per fare gratia a quilli che ogne nocte et tante volte hanno violato e forzato monasteri et sore, a quilli che robano et abarano mo uno mo uno altro, a quili che menazano mo a questo mo a quello, a quili che portano al despecto et conspecto de li officiali et de quelli che voleno ben vivere le arme per la piazza et per tuta la cita, a quili che hanno dato dele bote e ferisseno altri suso la piaza et nel palazo de la raxon, a quilli che pur zobia passata di nocte . . . introno in uno logo et in una casa de li migliori citadini . . . et . . . volsene forzare le figliole in presentia de la madre, perche el padre era absente": ibid.

Officials were thus expected to supply the authority and protection of the absent father: but the protection they were to offer amounted to enforcing respect for established institutions and persons—monasteries, property, public spaces, law courts, and the houses and womenfolk of "the better sort."

The provision of justice was not merely an operation in safeguarding the "better sort" and their property; it also had important financial roles, both for officials and for the princely state. The prince's revenue office had an interest in the fines imposed either as a result of sentence or summarily following penal commands; officials had an interest in fees levied for their services from criminals and their local communities (the costs of arrest, escort, and custody were charged to the accused or to his locality). Such a system created conflicts between justice and financial interest. The more cash-productive sector of the judicial system seems to have been not the fines imposed following trial for crimes of violence but the summary levying of fines for offenses such as arms carrying, blasphemy, gambling, disobedience, and insolence. Judicial fines, though laboriously listed in registers, brought in only modest sums.[163] By contrast, summary fines could be high both individually—enough to push poor men into destitution[164]—and collectively.[165] They could also be levied in what might be seen as an arbitrary fashion. A petitioner from Adria rehearsed the following story: he was at the barber's having his hair washed, when a messenger arrived from the local podesta commanding his immediate appearance before him; the petitioner replied that he would go when he was washed, but for this disobedience he was fined ten ducats and immediately summoned again; once more he replied that he would go when his hair was toweled, and for this the podesta fined him a further twenty-five ducats. This was not an example of disobedience, the petitioner reasoned to the duke, but only one of official anger.[166]

It was in this area, of summary orders and fines, that conflict arose. For example, collection of fines for arms carrying at Lendinara was dis-

163. Dean and Lowe, "Writing the History of Crime," 7; R. Roia, "L'amministrazione finanziaria del comune di Ancona nel secolo XV," *Atti e memorie della Deputazione di storia patria per le Marche,* 4th ser., 1 (1924): 169.
164. Cam. duc., Mandati, vol. 30, fol. 135 (30 Aug. 1488).
165. E.g., offenders could be fined twenty-five ducats for disobedience (RdS, Ferrara, b. 35, 20 June 1464) and 150 lire for arms carrying (ASCMo, Vacchetta 1487–88, fol. 38; similarly RdS, Ferrara, b. 43, s.d.; RdS, Reggiano, Toano, Georgio da Toano to Ercole d'Este, 28 Mar. 1493).
166. Cam. duc., Mandati, vol. 31, fol. 24v.

puted between the local podesta and the central revenue office; likewise, fines for gambling were disputed at Crespino.[167] However, there were various levels to summary jurisdiction. Though only some of those were criminal, they all contributed to maintenance of the "angel order" desired by the duke. At one level was the enforcement of reserved access to natural resources. This could be harsh. Unlicensed boar hunting carried fines of fifty ducats.[168] Fishermen found to be "stealing" fish from ducal lakes were said to need "not the hand of mercy but that of justice."[169] The ducal estate steward at Belriguardo imposed flat-rate fines, of forty soldi or ten lire, on tenants for illicit hay making, vine cutting, or pond fishing or for failing to clear out the stables and to bring straw under cover.[170] Similarly, the *maestro di campagna,* who had the power to fine country folk for transgressions of hunting laws, was adjudged by Eleonora, as he resisted audit by declaring to have kept no records, to be "a good *maestro di campagna,* but . . . a better maestro for his own profit than for that of others."[171]

The profitability of such jurisdiction generated rivalries. Some characteristic problems are revealed in letters from the Reggian *capitano del divieto,* who among other things policed the city's food-supply regulations. "This office is stripped of its emoluments," he complained in 1483, for two reasons: first, because he is unable to levy any fines (out of which he was paid), "because every man carries weapons, sometimes thirty, forty, or fifty people together, as if they were going to war"; second, because the salt office in Reggio claimed the right itself to levy fees associated with the salt levy. "It having been your intention," he wrote to the duke, "to give me this office to succor my need, I am sure you will want to provide that I may have the terms and emoluments that my predecessors had." He added, "if my predecessor did not levy your lordship's revenues, perhaps he did not have my need." So the captain asked the duke to provide that he may do his job according to its specification "or, if your excellency agrees, ensure that the *contadini* of this area should pay, as they deserve it on account of the great homicides, 'assassinations,' and ribaldries that they commit continuously."[172] Three significant themes

---

167. LD, C 5, fol. 14 (23 Jan. 1478); RdS, Ferrara, b. 41, Bernardo Salati to Borso d'Este, 14 Nov. 1454.

168. Cam. duc., Mandati, vol. 32, fol. 124v (8 June 1493).

169. ASE, Carteggio di referendari, b. 166, Aug. 1462.

170. Cam. duc., Mandati, vol. 32, fols. 134, 143v, 194, 207, 212, 217v.

171. CS, b. 131, 10 May 1479, quoted in Chiappini, "Eleanora d'Aragona," 42.

172. RdS, Reggio, b. 152, Capitano del divieto, 29 Aug. 1483. Cf. Venturi, "Relazioni," 323–24; Massetto, *Un magistrato,* 33–37.

are evident here: the competition among officials for income-generating activity (the salt-levy fees had been "the best emolument of this office"), the varying need of officials for income, and the displacement of costs onto despised *contadini*.[173]

Letters from other officials reinforce these features. Some officials were clearly dependent on income from office: "if ever I needed your excellency's favor, this is the year," began one podesta in pleading for renewal of appointment;[174] "the expenses are heavy, and the salary is small," reasoned the podesta of Ferrara in 1472 in arguing to employ one fewer constable but to keep his pay.[175] The *capitano del divieto* of Reggio at one point coolly stated that his intentions in taking office were personal gain and advancement in Este service.[176] Noting that crops were flowing out of the duchy contrary to the prohibition of export, he identified both the usual route and the reason (lack of punishment), and he proposed that he be granted summary powers to deal with smugglers, in which case he and his companions would be prepared to go out and guard day and night, exposing themselves to cold, hunger, and thirst, provided that their share of fines was not taken from them and could be had without argument.[177] In this way, a genuine public interest—a halt to defrauding of the revenue and to the fattening of foreigners at local expense[178]—was linked to an expansion of summary jurisdiction to the evident profit of officials.

The most contested of the summary jurisdictions was possibly that over the carrying of weapons. Possession of the power to confiscate weapons and to levy fines was a source of conflict between the captain and podesta of Reggio,[179] for example, and between the Ferrarese captain of justice and the ducal revenue office.[180] But whereas their disputes were couched in terms of effectiveness in improving the quality of

---

173. Cf. Jones, *Malatesta,* 329–30.

174. "Se may io hebi bisogno de la gratia de la v. Ex. . . . questo e l'anno"; because the podesta had divided joint property with his brother and because a storm had destroyed his crops, he asks, "cum le mane zunte," that Borso "non mi lassi disoperato," as it would be "la mia totale disfactione": RdS, Ferrara, b. 45a, Benedetto Giacobelli, 18 Dec. 1454.

175. "perche le spese sono grave e lo emolumento e salario e picolo": RdS, Ferrara, b. 1, Marcantonio Scalamonti to Ercole d'Este, 18 Sept. 1472.

176. RdS, Reggio, b. 152, 16 Feb. 1494.

177. Ibid., 3 Dec. 1494.

178. "ingrassare li forasteri": ibid., 4 Feb. 1495.

179. ASRe, Carteggio, b. 561, 26 Nov. 1486; see also Massetto, *Un magistrato,* 183–85.

180. RdS, Ferrara, b. 1, Gregorio Zampante to Ercole d'Este, 31 Jan. 1490.

policing and public order, elsewhere the abuse of such power for financial gain had to be confronted more directly. In 1484 Ercole had to rein in the prosecution of arms carrying by the *capitano del divieto* of Reggio;[181] in the Frignano in 1487 it was ordered that future prosecution be based only on direct discovery or proof by a witness, not, as in the past, on secret accusation, by which "they [accusers] strike at the innocent rich rather than punish the delinquent poor";[182] and in Modena in 1488 there was concern that expansion of the powers of the *capitano del divieto* to fine *contadini* for arms carrying would open the way to extortion.[183]

However, there were limits to the profitability of judicial office. On the one hand, the imposition of obedience and order reduced judicial income: the notary in the Ferrarese criminal court complained in 1491 of loss of income "as not many crimes are being committed out of fear of the captain of justice" (the chillingly effective Gregorio Zampante).[184] On the other hand, the podesta had to strike a delicate balance between making a satisfactory income and alienating the local population. This is clear in letters from the podesta of Codigoro in 1479: he could not live on the simple salary (so he claimed) and needed the emoluments of office, principally the fines for arms carrying,[185] but when he was ordered to prosecute a large number for this offense, he found that local cooperation vanished—witnesses said they knew nothing, men refused to assist in making arrests. The podesta was sure of the cause: "for these convictions I have become so hated by some that they would not fear any evil provided they could do me harm."[186] The same limit, he argued, applied to those who brought accusations, "because if they were not certain of earning their third [of fines], they would not expose themselves to the risks of enmities."[187]

---

181. ASRe, Carteggio, b. 561, 19 Mar. 1484.
182. "piu tosto offendono li richi innocenti cha castigino li tristi delinquenti": LD, C 10, fol. 139 (8 Apr. 1487).
183. ASCMo, Vacchetta 1487–88, fol. 73.
184. "per non se fare molti malefitii per terrore del Magnifico Capitanio del Justitia": Cam. duc., Mandati, vol. 30, fol. 161v (12 Dec. 1491). On Zampante, see chap. 5.
185. RdS, Ferrara, b. 32, Pietro da Ponte to Ercole d'Este, 11 May 1479.
186. "per queste condemnason facte son devegnuto a tanto odio di alchuni che non extimariano male alchuno pur me potesseno far dispiacere": ibid., 1 Apr. 1479. See also Chittolini, "L'onore dell'officiale," 22–23.
187. "peroche donde non sapesseno de guadagnar il loro terzo non se exponeriano al pericolo dele inimicitie": RdS, Ferrara, b. 32, 11 May 1479.

Violent and nonviolent clashes among officials and their staffs seem to have been related to their competition for revenue. In such a context, officials readily informed against their colleagues. When the new captain of the piazza of Ferrara saw himself being frozen out of the system for collecting fines and payments, he complained that "this will be my ruin . . . for I shall not be able to find a *compagno* to stay with me, especially having paid more for this office than the others."[188] The trading of insult was also speedily reported to the duke: "I did not get my office through whores as you did," one official had told another; "he greeted me as if I were his disobedient ass, his subordinate or vassal," reported another official.[189] Such comments perhaps reflect both questionable methods of appointment and uncertainties of official hierarchy.

More violent conflict was common toward the end of the century, with fights, assaults, and injuries between competing agencies—the captain of justice and the podesta, for example, or the podesta and the captain of the piazza.[190] Sometimes the immediate source of such conflict was the employment by one judge of *giotti*, whom other officials then sought to arrest and prosecute. In 1485 the vicar of the podesta of Reggio wrote to the duchess that a criminal had become a servant of the captain of the *cittadella* and was threatening and assaulting lesser officials whenever moves were made to denounce his crimes.[191] It was one of his own servants, arrested for theft, whom the *capitano del divieto* of Reggio tried to release by force from the hands of the podesta in 1495.[192] In the same year there was a report that the captain of the *cittadella* was letting his *fanti* out at night to "do things,"[193] and in 1498 one of the captain's men was arrested for theft: the *cittadella* should not be a shield for thieves, the podesta angrily remarked.[194] Podestas were not always averse to the employment of such men: in 1473 "hatred" had arisen between the podesta of Reggio and the constable of the piazza there over competition to hire as servants some rogues who had recently arrived in

---

188. ASE, Archivio militare, b. 2, 30 Jan. 1493.
189. ASE, Minutario, Lettere sciolte, b. 4, 17 Dec. 1496; RdS, Reggiano, Carpineti, b. 1, Feltrino da Bismantova to Ercole d'Este, 3 June 1494.
190. RdS, Ferrara, b. 1, Antonio Gazoli to Ercole d'Este, 13 Jan. 1491; RdS, Reggio, b. 2, Antonio Sandei to Ercole d'Este, 17 Aug. 1473; ibid., b. 112, vicar of podesta to Ercole d'Este, 14 Nov. 1495, and Alberto da Montecatino, 16 Apr. 1497; ibid., b. 152, Niccolò Ariosti to Eleonora d'Aragona, 22 Nov. 1482.
191. RdS, Reggio, b. 112, 18 June 1485.
192. Ibid., vicar of podesta to Ercole d'Este, 14 Nov. 1495.
193. RdS, Reggio, b. 152, Giovanni Manfredi to Ercole d'Este, 17 Mar. 1495.
194. Ibid., 21 Apr. 1498.

48   *Clean Hands and Rough Justice*

the city—this hatred erupted in a nocturnal confrontation in which two of the podesta's men died.[195] Officials needed such men to be effective and to instill fear; and the milieu of professional soldiery, police constabulary, and general roguery was a fluid and composite one.

The line between effectiveness—in judicial and financial terms—and corruption was thus a fine one. Officials accused their colleagues of unacceptable conduct, not merely, one may suppose, because they were in competition, but also because they drew that line in different places. Deciding in these circumstances what were the forms and incidence of corruption is a thorny task, but the reports or corrections of explicitly corrupt behavior evident in the letters and registers fall into four main types. First come reports of simple "exorbitant" profiteering, through the imposition of fees and fines and the confiscation of property. Notaries and other officials levied fees and costs contrary to statutory limitations—for example, taking the costs of custody from suspects who had proved their innocence.[196] In 1491 the podesta of Ferrara complained that when the captain of justice's constable arrested anyone, he charged one ducat for himself and one teston for his servant, whereas the podesta's own knight charged only two soldi, with one soldo for each *fante*; the podesta also complained that the constable was making arrests, contrary to the statutes, "for every crime, however small, even if insulting words are used."[197] Similarly, some podestas tried to levy huge fines for arms carrying, and prison governors overcharged for custody.[198]

Second, there are allegations of more extensive and deliberate misuse of the judicial apparatus for private gain, as in the case of the podesta of Finale who took pledges from men suspected of smuggling and later required them to pay the costs even though they turned out to be innocent,[199] or as in the case of the judicial commissioner in Comacchio who was reportedly scouring the area in 1500, "more for gain than to punish thieves and criminals with the law," taking *uomini da bene* and releasing

195. RdS, Reggio, b. 2, Antonio Sandei to Ercole d'Este, 17 Aug. 1473.
196. ASCMo, Carte sciolte, b. 1, *capitula* of 1498; ASCMo, Vacchetta 1491, fol. 11 (1 Mar.). For the general issue, see A. Zorzi, "I fiorentini e gli uffici pubblici nel primo Quattrocento: Concorrenza, abusi, illegalità," *Quaderni storici* 66 (1987): 738–43.
197. "vedendo che per ogne delicto, quamvis picolo etiam se per alcuni seranno dite parole iniuriose, tuti se pilgiano, contra li statuti, condescendo per so utile a le volgie de Messer Gregorio": RdS, Ferrara, b. 1, Antonio Gazoli to Eleonora d'Aragona, 22 July 1491.
198. Cam. duc., Mandati, vol. 30, fols. 62v–63 (23 June 1486/5 Jan. 1491); LD, C 11, fol. 4 (21 Jan. 1493: letter to podesta of Castelnovo); *Statuta Mutine*, fol. 207.
199. LD, C 11, fol. 113 (26 Jan. 1495).

them only after payment had been made.[200] Into the same category would fall the "subletting" of judicial office and of specific duties that podestas found tedious.[201] Such subcontractors, Ercole learned, were "in almost constant negotiation to have such office, in order to do and direct things more in their own way," to the damage of the ducal revenue office, the public interest *(republica)*, and private persons, because of the number of crimes that went unpunished.[202]

Third, officials reported that some podestas tolerated malicious or exploitative use of the judicial apparatus by others: for example, anti-Semitic calumnies[203] or the use of accusations to harass opponents.[204] Finally, also identified as corrupt *(corruptelae)* were local judicial "customs" that allowed acquittals to flourish: for example, in Modenese criminal trials, the permission given to third parties to appear as "excuser or as a person of the people," bringing in justifications and witnesses to excuse the criminal act, while the suspect did not personally appear as required by law;[205] or the Reggian statute allowing committal of lighter crimes to judicial counsel—Niccolò III d'Este declared it absurd that power in criminal matters should thus be transferred from judges whom he had chosen to private persons he did not even know.[206]

Related to explicit "corruptions," were the informal networks created by podestas to connect themselves to members of local elites. The wives of officials seem to have been important agents here. Podestas were forbidden by law from entering any relationship (for example, matrimony) with local inhabitants that might betoken obligation, and, strictly speaking, they were not supposed to be accompanied by their wives. However, in 1487 the podesta of Reggio married a local heiress, contrary to the statutes.[207] Earlier in the 1480s, Niccolò Ariosti, while captain of the *cittadella* of Reggio, had married a daughter from an important civic family, and members of another such family acted as godparents to his children by her.[208] The baptismal records of another prominent Reggian

200. RdS, Ferrara, b. 32, letter of Francesco Maria Grotti, 11 Apr. 1500.
201. RdS, Ferrara, b. 56, 7 Aug. 1454.
202. *Statuta Mutine,* fol. 212v (19 Feb. 1480); see ibid., fol. 179v (3 Apr. 1437) for an earlier example. For an example of subcontracting, see Zambotti, *Diario,* 199.
203. LD, B IV, fols. 22v (1420), 215v (1432).
204. LD, C 10, fol. 239 (10 Oct. 1487).
205. *Statuta Mutine,* fol. 212v (11 Oct. 1479).
206. LD, B IV, fol. 97v (1 Nov. 1423).
207. ASE, Minutario, Lettere sciolte, b. 3, 22 Nov. 1487.
208. M. Catalano, *Vita di Ludovico Ariosto* (Geneva, 1930), 1:26, 39–40.

family reveal the frequent presence at such ceremonies of members of the *reggimento*, and, on one occasion, the wife of the podesta was present.[209] Such association with local families was sufficiently common in northern Italy for a cautionary tale to be penned by Giovanni Conversini.[210]

Such customs, when combined with the "subletting" of office and the pressure for allowing criminal appeals, would seem to constitute a persistent trend for judicial power to pass out of the hands of public officials installed by the prince and be reclaimed by members of the local community (not, it should be assumed, in the interests of that community). Sometimes the duke was content to concede to this pressure: at his accession in 1471 Ercole approved the petition of the Modenese college of notaries, which had the effect of strengthening or restoring its positions of control (and abuse)[211] within the civic administration, especially over the rural small-claims court *(danni dati)*; earlier in the century, Niccolò III d'Este had granted to the inhabitants of Migliaro the office of notary to the podesta there, so that they might appoint whomever they liked, but at a cost of one hundred ducats per annum.[212] Local communes were also more likely to prefer custom to statute. In 1494 the commune of Modena ordered custom, not statute law, to be followed in the rural court, so as to avoid intensifying burdens on the already "exhausted" peasants.[213] Similarly, when a new podesta arrived in Mellara in 1464, the first thing he tried to do was read the local statutes, but he was told that there were none, only "ancient customs," "which cannot be seen and, as I understand, are such as the mind of the notary here chooses."[214] Were podestas who allowed themselves to be guided by local leaders praised for their conduct in office, while those who stood by the letter of the public law stirred up complaint at their actions?

209. BL, Add. MS 22,345, "Cronaca originale di Reggio di Giovanni Fontanella," fols. 2–4v.

210. V. Zaccaria, "Il *Memorandarum rerum liber* di Giovanni di Conversino da Ravenna," *Atti dell'Istituto veneto di scienze, lettere ed arti* 106 (1947–48): 237.

211. In 1497 Ercole broke the hold of the college of notaries on notarial office in the criminal court and appointed a foreign notary, because of Modenese notaries' "mala deportamenta" in office: ASCMo, Vacchetta 1496–97, fols. 63 (3 Feb. 1497), 65 (20 Feb.), 102r–v (18 Dec.). For similar problems, and similar central-state action, in the Venetian Terraferma in the sixteenth century, see Povolo, "Aspetti e problemi," 192–96.

212. ASCMo, Carte sciolte, b. 1, 1471; LD, B III, fol. 186 (23 May 1405).

213. ASCMo, Vacchetta 1491, fols. 25r–v (17 May).

214. "Mi fu risposto che non havevano ne mai hebero statuto ne ordine, ma che se gubernano cum loro consuetudine antique che non se vedeno, le quale come comprendo sono tale quanto cape lo intellecto del notaro": RdS, Ferrara, b. 46, letter of Alberto Cavalluzzi, 20 Jan. 1464.

There was a formal forum in which complaint at official misconduct could be voiced and investigated: the end-of-term review (sindication) to which all judicial officials were subject. But there were serious flaws in the operation of this system. For many officials the investigation was routine and perfunctory, with no real complaint entered or investigated.[215] At Modena, the rules governing the selection of sindicators were in 1446 acknowledged not to be observed.[216] Sindication could be accelerated or anticipated to suit officials' convenience.[217] There was an apparently quickening trend for rural communities to petition the duke for sindication of outgoing podestas to be waived, either because there was (allegedly) no complaint to be heard or because the overburdened community needed to be spared an unnecessary expense.[218] But the partisan falseness of the assertion that no one wished to complain is laid open in at least one case: from Castelnovo ne' Monti in 1493 came a petition from "the men and persons of the *podesteria* of Castelnovo who want to complain." This asserted that the opinions of over twenty people who had just grievance had been ignored by those who had written to the duke praising the conduct of the outgoing podesta and asking for sindication to be waived. These petitioners did not want their grievances simply referred to the new podesta, for "ten out of twelve of our complaints are such that he too will want to do" as the old podesta had decided: "we have a proverb here in the hills," they explained, "that one wolf does not eat another."[219]

---

215. Dean and Lowe, "Writing the History of Crime in the Renaissance," 9; Jones, *Malatesta*, 322; Zambotti, *Diario*, 263; Connell, "Il commissario," 609–10; Massetto, *Un magistrato*, 352.

216. *Statuta Mutine*, fol. 183v; see, for similar complaint, ibid., fol. 207.

217. ASRe, Carteggio, b. 561, 5 Mar. 1482, 12 Dec. 1487, 15 May 1495.

218. LD, C 4, fols. 114 (19 June 1476), 120 (24 June 1476); LD, C 5, fols. 81 (30 Apr. 1478), 88 (14 May 1478), 92 (19 May 1478), 105 (13 June 1478); RdS, Reggiano, Castellarano, 1481; RdS, Ferrara, b. 32, Smiraldo de Pisis to Ercole d'Este, 21 Dec. 1490; RdS, Reggiano, Castelnovo ne' Monti, 2 Feb. 1493; LD, C 11, fols. 5 (29 Jan. 1493), 14 (17 Feb. 1493), 141 (23 June 1495); RdS, Ferrara, b. 40, commune of Comacchio to Ercole d'Este, 21 Dec. 1494; ASE, Minutario, Lettere sciolte, b. 4, 2 July 1496; LD, C 13, fols. 67 (16 May 1498), 76 (28 May 1498). See also ASCMo, Lettere, Niccolò III d'Este to *savi*, 10 June 1432, rejecting a request to waive sindication; and A. Ryder, *The Kingdom of Naples under Alfonso the Magnanimous* (Oxford, 1976), 158–59, where it is the king who resists requests in parliament for judges to be subject to annual sindication.

219. "Ad nui non pare essere licito chel podesta novo sia quello che iudichi sopra le nostre querelle, per quello che de le dodexe le dexe sono de tale natura che lui etiam se volesse reservare de potere fare come havesse dicto Alexandro et per questo iudicaria come in causa propria, non diremo miga a caricho de epso Messer lo podesta futuro, ma per uno proverbiale parlare se dice in montagna che uno lupo non mangia del altro": RdS, Reggiano,

When not protected by local allies, podestas who had overstepped the mark could be subjected to comprehensive assault on the record of their behavior in office. Documentation of such sindications is rare, but one report that does survive, from San Felice, reveals the extent and variety both of official corruption and of local response to an unpopular podesta.[220] The official concerned was the Ferrarese nobleman Bartolomeo Trotti, who served as podesta of San Felice in the early 1480s. He had already shown, while podesta of Finale a few years before, a tendency to take up a critical position as regards the local "richi et potenti et capi di parte,"[221] and in this perhaps lies the origin of the wave of complaint against him at San Felice. The sindicator's report is divided into two sections. First come the general charges, routinely made in all sindications: illicit trade, absence without leave, negligence, bribery, inactivity, and so on. Having examined witnesses, the sindicator found all of these general charges proved, in addition to a further charge of forgery of a ducal letter purporting to extend Trotti's term of office for several years. The most serious of Trotti's offenses, apart from forgery, were trading in grain and wine, "such that he has made infinite profits"; appropriating fines (especially the "many moneys" he collected for blasphemy and arms carrying); failing to punish malefactors or to hand down sentences, especially for criminal damage *(danni dati)*; and taking bribes to deny justice to creditors and to release debtors from prison. We should note that Trotti was not completely inactive: the list is an interesting combination of too much justice in some areas and too little in others.

The sindicator then moved on to consider the claims of individuals for repayment, damages, and compensation. There were forty of these claims, from all sections of local society: from a neighboring gentleman, for grain and beans that Trotti had allegedly taken by force from his granary; from two local priests, for unlawful arrest and seizure of property; from local Jewish moneylenders, for debts and seizures; from local barbers and notaries and from many other local inhabitants; and finally from the local commune and the ducal revenue office, for losses and frauds. These claims fall into four main types. First come claims for dam-

---

Castelnovo ne' Monti, b. 1, 10 Mar. 1493. For a similar complaint at the waiving of sindication, see LD, C 13, fols. 91, 96 (June 1498). For the wolf metaphor, see also Zorzi, "I fiorentini e gli uffci pubblici," 743.

220. RdS, San Felice, b. 1, Bartolomeo Trotti, with archival dating of 1485. For the discussion that follows, see Zorzi, "I fiorentini e gli uffci pubblici."

221. RdS, Finale, b. 1, Trotti to Eleonora d'Aragona, 19 Oct. 1479.

ages arising from unjustified imprisonment or distraint. If we are to believe the complainants, Trotti had been in the habit of imprisoning men in the castle without cause and then demanding money for their release. Claimants demanded ten, twenty-five, fifty, or even two hundred ducats' compensation for the injury to their reputations, in addition to sums in costs and lost earnings. Others demanded the repayment of money Trotti had taken from them, so they might recover their livestock that he had impounded or their belongings that he had seized and pawned to Jews. Second come allegations of denial of justice (failing to summon defendants in civil suits, failing to prosecute a murderer). Third, we have acts of sheer official excess: detaining and insulting a man who had refused to lend a cart; billetting four of his *fanti* on a local inhabitant for dinner; seeking to have his own business partner killed; threatening to evict the tenant miller; having his *fanti* knock off his horse a man who had been slow in paying a promised bribe. Last come a group of creditors and suppliers, who had provided Trotti with grain and other foodstuffs, hay, wood, cloth, and clothing. Present also as objects of complaint were Trotti's wife, to whose protection he seems to have detailed some of the castle guard, and the nearby Trotti family estate (he forced at least one man to work there).

We should not believe every word of these complaints. The sindicator himself certainly did not, as several he found not proven, while against others he noted that "the witnesses have been corrupted to testify falsely." Moreover, in all cases, he severely reduced the claims for damages: his tariff for the monetary value of injured reputation did not rise above a handful of lire. In addition, it is easy to see how official acts that in this case were presented as bribery, unlawful arrest, or seizure of property would in other cases be seen simply as the ordinary and accepted activity of a podesta collecting his fees, making arrests for questioning, and impounding property to ensure payment of fines. Trotti, it is clear, had made some mistakes, but he must also have so alienated the local establishment that they allowed his forceful ways to be interpreted as illegality, not efficiency.

Usually sindication occurred quietly and routinely, without generating any such comment or complaint.[222] What lay behind this silence has been revealed by Andrea Zorzi:[223] podestas would ensure local sympathies by

---

222. See regular appointment of sindicators in LD, B 1, passim.
223. Zorzi, "Giusdicenti," 535–38.

holding dinners for local councillors and other "cittadini di stima," by executing at least one bandit during their term of office, or by putting in hand repairs to public buildings. Such podestas liked to think that they preserved and augmented their own "honor" by such actions (and so too they have persuaded the historian), but it is more apparent that they were making sure of leaving office with their profits intact and free from challenge.

Just as podestas made a show of public-mindedness in order to emerge with "honor" from sindication, so too the prince's brusque impatience with the whole process is occasionally revealed. In 1487 both duke and duchess denounced the dishonest whipping up of complaints against the outgoing captain of Camporeggiano (Garfagnana): the whole thing, they stormed, was got up by three or four *caporali,* who incite other men—at no risk to themselves—to file claims "out of emotion and anger." Ercole wanted justice to be done, but he did not want the "crying up of injuries and anger." "We have great loathing," the duke's agent was told, "for those who step outside the law against our officials, as often happens in sindications . . . The sooner you finish it, the happier we shall be, even if you have to honey over some harshness."[224]

It was not altogether unusual for podestas to come to the defense of local communities against the demands and pressures from the center of the princely state. Some podestas seem to have been genuinely shocked by the poverty of the rural areas where they held office. Letters to the duke from podestas of Bondeno, on the Po between Ferrara and Mantua, are notable for this: "in this place there is such poverty and such poor men, and I was never in a place where there was so much misery as there is here," observed Giacomo Boiardi in 1464.[225] The features and effects of that poverty may be pieced together from reports of other podestas and officials there. "There are many in this place who have neither bread nor flour nor corn in their house," reported the podesta in 1454, and a similar lack of basic foodstuffs was noted ten years later.[226] There was a

---

224. "havemo in odio assai quando altri se move fora de li termini de ragione contra li officiali nostri, come accade per le piu volte ne li sindicati . . . quanto piu presto la terminareti, tanto piu ne restaremo contenta, etiam mettendo del zurare et del mele suso qualche dureza": LD, C 10, fol. 161 (10 May 1487).

225. "in questa terra e tanta povertade e tanti poveri homini . . . et mai non fui in luogo dove fusse tanta miseria quanta e qui": RdS, Ferrara, b. 19, Giacomo Boiardi to Borso d'Este, 5 Mar. 1464.

226. "Advisando la v. S. che in questa terra glie sono molti che non hanno ni pane ne farina ni frumento in casa": ibid., Massari, comune et homines, 28 Oct. 1454, 7 Jan. 1464.

resistance to public works and burdens (such as food requisitioning),[227] repeated petitioning for tax relief,[228] and an inability and unwillingness to make a collective gift to the duke on the marriage of his son.[229] There was almost total illiteracy,[230] smuggling,[231] emigration,[232] and debt-induced sales of land.[233] Elements of this picture were noted elsewhere too. The inadequacy of crops in the autumn or of grain stocks at the end of the winter was remarked on at Massafiscaglia and Mellara[234] and led the podesta at Mellara to take the Ferrarese grain office to task for doctoring the estimates of supplies, which enabled it to insist on the transfer of available stocks to Ferrara.[235] The "great poverty and misery" of the men of Isola pomposiana led them to offer only three calves as a wedding gift to Alfonso d'Este in 1491, and the podesta urged Alfonso's father to accept these in good heart and pardon the men if the gift was small and inappropriate.[236]

The plea of peasant poverty was often raised by podestas against the too frequent visitations of public-debt collectors *(exactores)* from the city. The podesta of Mellara described a typical scene: the *bargello* and his men arrived with an order from the city council to levy some tax arrears: immediately they wanted lodgings and feed for their horses and expenses for themselves; they spoke with "words as ignominious and gestures as insulting as could be used, then they eventually took pledges from two men, who complained that they had not previously been requested to pay and do not believe that they owe." "From the great rush and noise that the *bargello*'s men make, it ought to be some terrible business," remarked the podesta, but he added that it "resolves into the dis-

227. Ibid., Bartolomeo Ovetari to Borso d'Este, 29 Aug. 1454; Antonio Zeno Ovetari to Borso d'Este, 8–9 Dec. 1454; podesta to Borso d'Este, 25 June 1462.

228. Ibid., Massari, comune et homines, 20 Jan. 1464, 1 Dec. 1483.

229. Ibid., Antonio Zucheta to Ercole d'Este, 25 Jan. 1491.

230. The local commune hired a grammar teacher "perche in questo castello non se ritrova essere se non pochi che sapiano legire et quili pochi anche sano male legire": ibid., Massari, comune et homines, 15 June 1494.

231. Ibid., letters of Bartolomeo Ovetari, 26 Sept. 1454, and Giacomo Boiardi, 3 Feb. 1464.

232. Ibid., Antonio Zeno Ovetari to Borso d'Este, 13 Dec. 1454.

233. Ibid., Giacomo Boiardi to Borso d'Este, 5 Mar. 1464.

234. RdS, Ferrara, b. 45a, Benedetto Giacobelli to Borso d'Este, 31 Jan. 1454, and Giovanni Bertazzi to Eleonora d'Aragona, 22 Oct. 1479; RdS, Ferrara, b. 46, Albertino Giocoli to Borso d'Este, 1 Mar. 1454.

235. RdS, Ferrara, b. 46, Albertino Giocoli to Borso d'Este, 13 Mar. 1454.

236. RdS, Ferrara, b. 32, "Rainaldus a Canali" to Ercole d'Este, 26 Jan. 1491.

training of two poor men for old taxes . . . This seems even more strange and cruel given that, not having yet harvested anything this year to eat, for themselves and their children, they have to meet these expenses."[237] A similar scene was reported from Toano a few years later, when the Reggian *capitano del divieto* arrived with an "asserted list of fines": the local podesta, not being shown the list, suspected that the captain was levying fictitious fines or at least ones already collected by his predecessor.[238] Ercole d'Este found the number of complaints of extortion by "exactors" and by the *capitano del divieto* in the *contado* "stupendous";[239] even ducal pardons were not respected, being overridden by the exactor's keenness to collect.[240] No wonder then, that Borso d'Este, on visiting Modena in 1470, had been swamped with such complaints.[241]

It would be exaggerated, therefore, to cast the prince and his officials as unheeding oppressors: both could be sensitive to excess. There were always two sides to any complaint, and the prince did not favor the unqualified strengthening of official power. Indeed, when we review the response of princely government to forms of crime and violence, to the personal and other inadequacies of judicial officials (especially in the *contado*), and to corruption and abuse of office, it is obvious how high-minded the prince was: arms carrying as a source of woundings and homicide prompted restrictive proclamations; the spread of new forms of gambling was halted by legislation and action; much legislative activity focused on official extortion. However, most legislation dealt with judicial procedures and responses to them (resistance to arrest, impeding execution, and so on) or with the spread of existing offenses (gambling, thieving, prostitution), while ducal action might seem limited to dictating fresh proclamations and writing enjoinders to officials to virile combat against wrongdoing. How much percipience and resourcefulness was there to address what judicial officers themselves recognized as the main problems: that incapable officials inspired no fear, that constables and

---

237. "per lo grande impeto e rumore facevano epsi del barisello dovesse essere qualche terribile facenda," but "se risolvesse in pignorare dui povereti per conto de colte vechie . . . Qual cossa parendo piu che strania e crudele che non havendo prima ricolto questo anno cossa alchuna da manzare per loro et per li fioli, gli bisogno fare tale spesa": RdS, Ferrara, b. 46, lieutenant to Ercole d'Este, 13 Mar. 1490.

238. RdS, Reggiano, Toano, Giovanni Superchi to Ercole d'Este, 24 Mar. 1493.

239. LD, C 10, fols. 271–72 (14 Dec. 1487).

240. Ibid., fol. 281 (14 Jan. 1488).

241. RdS, Modena, b. 1a, Reggimento, 17 Oct. 1470.

fanti were insufficient in number, that terror needed to be intensified? And how far were these problems exacerbated by competition for office, sale of office, and administrative cost cutting? In Ferrara, solutions to these problems were attempted in the 1490s: the permanent appointment of feared, foreign crime fighters; the multiplication of armed *fanti* to assist them; and the wholesale disregarding, not just revision, of statute law. With these measures, the Estensi followed the Gonzaga into an era of "deep judicial change," in which the more concentrated power of the prince laid a controlling network on the gentler justice of local privileged autonomy.[242]

---

242. R. Muchembled, *Le temps des supplices: De l'obéissance sous les rois absolus, XV–XVIIIe siècles* (Paris, 1992), 71–75.

2

Crime and Punishment in Gonzaga Mantua

The long mid-fifteenth century in Mantua, meaning the reigns of Marquis Ludovico Gonzaga (1444–78) and of his son Marquis Federico (1478–84), is the setting for most of the discussion in this and subsequent chapters, but there needs to be some overlap at either end of that forty-year period. Some initial reference must be made to the government of Ludovico's father, Gianfrancesco Gonzaga, who had become captain of Mantua at the age of twelve in 1407 and marquis in 1433. The first years of Gianfrancesco's reign coincided with the early operation of the new statutes of Mantua according to the already mentioned revision, which his father had entrusted to a leading Bolognese jurist, Rafaelle Fulgioso, and which in many respects reinforced signorial authority. But another event—comparable to what happened seven years later in Padua—may seem to represent the decline of ancient civic legality even more tangibly than these statutory changes. This was the burning in 1413 of one of the palaces of the commune—not, apparently, the seat of the Mantuan law courts, the Palazzo della Ragione, which was also in disrepair, but the adjacent palace of the podesta, part of the block of earlier communal buildings that included the repository for court and notarial records.[1]

In 1430, at least some amends were made by a controlled experiment in testing public opinion by selective consultation, a rare event under a signorial government.[2] Dissatisfaction was expressed with the adminis-

---

1. S. Davari, *I Palazzi dell'antico comune di Mantova e gli incendi da essi subiti* (1888; repr., Mantua, 1974), 11–12; P. Gazzola, *Il Palazzo del Podestà a Mantova* (Mantua, 1973), 46–48.

2. AG, b. 2002. Discussed by U. Nicolini, "Principe e cittadini: Una consultazione popolare del 1430 nella Mantova dei Gonzaga," in *Mantova e i Gonzaga nella civiltà del rinascimento,* (Mantua, 1977), 35–46. For the text of the twenty-two submissions, see M.A. Grignani et al., eds., *Mantova 1430: Pareri a Gian Francesco Gonzaga per il governo* (Mantua, 1990).

tration of justice as with many other aspects of the Gonzaga regime, and some of the complaints reflect a set of problems different from those we have just encountered in the Este state. In addition to requests for building repairs to the commune's decrepit palace or palaces, there was a demand for the full complement of judges to be employed, supported by the argument that the expense of their salaries would quickly be outweighed by the increased revenue from fines and the common benefit from more rapid hearings in place of interminable delays.[3] Of particular interest is the point that a podesta should again be appointed, as prescribed by the statutes, rather than a vice-podesta, a substitute presumably less prestigious and costly.[4] In fact, the overall picture was of justice badly served—its seat a neglected ruin, its officials reduced in number and dignity. Similarly, in a summary of proposals "circa justiciam ministrandam," drawn up in the name of one Andrea Gonzaga, it was requested that the palace be restored, that the podesta be reinstated with all his *famiglia,* that cases be heard within the prescribed time limits, that a judge of appeals be appointed each year, that the captain not intervene in judicial matters "except in a matter of great weight," and that the podesta or vice-podesta not belong to the marquis's Council of Justice or hold office for longer than one year.[5] All this seems to suggest that in the recent past the state had suffered a combination of inertia, cost cutting, and high-handed signorial intervention in defiance of the statutes.

Unfortunately there is no direct evidence of Gianfrancesco's response to these complaints or of why he held this consultation at that particular time.[6] An expectation of the imperial title of marquis might have had something to do with it; this would add little to the substance of Gonzaga authority, which already had a dual source, as captain (by acclamation) and imperial vicar; nevertheless it did confer a higher dignity and respectability. Gianfrancesco, perhaps stimulated by the humanist schoolmaster Vittorino da Feltre, might have been seeking at last to make

3. Grignani et al., *Mantova 1430,* 134–35 (Niccolò de Antis): "exequutiones criminalium annuatim facte ascendent multo plus quam sit summa 600 ducatos."

4. Ibid., 160–61 (anon.): "che lo palazo sia facto per la rasone segundo lo primo stato . . . ch'el seria bene aconzar el dicto palazo . . . che lo officio de la podestaria cum tuta la sua femeglia sia reintegrato come soliva esser."

5. Ibid., 166. "Council" at this date may imply the vaguely defined "Consilium Domini" rather than the incipient "Consiglio di Giustizia" (see intro. n. 34).

6. Concerning another *consulta,* at the end of the fifteenth century, see the end of chap. 7.

his regime look less like the shabby autocracy of a mercenary warlord and more like an imperial principality benevolently governed under its laws. The documentary sources from the time of Gianfrancesco are much more sparse than they are for his son Ludovico, but at least it can be proved that the office of vice-podesta had been extant in 1429[7] and as late as March 1432,[8] when a new statute redefining aspects of the civil-law jurisdiction of the podesta—as such—was issued.[9] Although the name of the incumbent for 1432–33 has not come to light, by 1434 there was again a full-fledged podesta in office, whose term seems to have been extended for a second year.[10] The point is of interest here, considering what was to happen between 1467 and 1481, when there was again a vice-podesta and when Beltramino Cusadri, the central figure in the present study, dominated the Mantuan judiciary. In the interim, or until 1467, vice-podestas were just temporary replacements for a serving podesta, as in 1451, for example, or—for rather longer—in 1455–56, when the regime was inconvenienced by the twice postponed arrival of the new podesta, Manno Donati, a Florentine grandee. Manno's arrogance had not impressed Ludovico Gonzaga favorably when he asked for part of his salary in advance and proposed for *giudice del maleficio* a protégé of his own who did not fulfill the Mantuan requirements for the job.[11]

The Gonzaga archives are much less rich in judicial records than in correspondence, but they contain some records of sentences and acquittals in the court of the podesta and of the *giudice del maleficio* from the early fifteenth century up to 1464.[12] These lists inform us, therefore,

---

7. E.g., AG, Lib. decr. 4, fol. 12v, 19 Mar. 1429 (decree postponing for a month "condemnationes seu conciones . . . de presente mense martii per d. vicepotestatem Mantue et eius curia").

8. AG, b. 3452, fol. 201r: "Infrascripti sunt condempnandi per spectabillem famosumque legum doctorem Madium de Madiis vice-podestatem Mantue" (heading of list, 14 Mar. 1432).

9. D'Arco, *Studi,* 6:139–40.

10. See app. 2 for a list of podestas. According to D'Arco, *Studi,* 6:63: "Gli storici ed i documenti non accennano alcuno che fosse stato podestà in Mantova dall'anno 1422 al 1433."

11. "non è usanza de pagare li potestati inanti tracto che ancor non è finito de pagar el predecessore vostro . . . respondemo che essendo questo uno de li boni et degni officii che sia a questa parte, non me pare per alcun modo de farlo, né derogare ad alcuno suo ordine": AG, b. 2885, lib. 26, fol. 19r, Marquis L. Gonzaga to Manno Donati (5 Apr. 1455).

12. AG, b. 3452–53. In b. 3452 (up to 1449) the sheets have been numbered consecutively, as cited in the subsequent footnotes; in b. 3453 (from 1450 to 1464) they have not.

about the period immediately preceding that with which this book is most concerned. The earlier section, the lists from Gianfrancesco's time, contains many gaps, and in the present context it is of less importance than the documentation from 1444 onward, on which the following discussion will concentrate. The two decades from 1444 to 1464 cover the last nine months of Gianfrancesco's lifetime and the first twenty years of his son Ludovico's rule as marquis. Information from this span of time is presented in this chapter in the form of analytical tables, a method that cannot be attempted at all for the period after 1464, when the available source material consists mainly of letters.

The lists in question survive as unbound but sometimes sewn-together sheets, apparently copied from lost registers by notaries of the podesta's court. They record the public announcement of sentences made every few weeks from the *arengario* above the piazza. The main snag, which admittedly destroys some of the value of a quantitative analysis, is their incompleteness. Sometimes as many as six months are missing from a single year, and even in the fullest years there is no way of knowing whether every occasion in the month is included. Nevertheless, with the period of twenty years being split into four periods of five years (within which coverage by months will be indicated), some worthwhile overall findings may emerge. Certainly these lists are a valuable source of information about the varieties of offense allegedly committed and about the proportion between types of offense; they also reveal a lot about punishment. Moreover—and although the number of persons involved may seem few by comparison with numbers from Milan or Florence—they are a rich quarry for details about ordinary people. One of the striking facts to emerge is that many of those put on trial were not residents of Mantua itself. The majority—on average at least four-fifths of the total—came from the numerous rural communities of the *marchesato*.

A fair inference is that what we have in the lists is preponderantly a record of rural, rather than urban, crime, though some cautionary points need to be made. For instance, an accused person, even if described as resident somewhere in the *dominio*, might have been visiting the city for the day when his or her[13] alleged offense was committed: the actual scene of an insult, assault, or theft or the site of a violated property is seldom specified. Like the foreigners whose names occur—Italians from neighboring states; Germans, usually described as cloth workers or soldiers;

13. I hope to discuss female criminality in Mantua in another place.

and a few northern French or Flemish tapestry weavers[14]—some offenders may have been very recent immigrants to the city or only temporary residents. The question is, should a crime be classified as rural or urban according to the place where it occurred or the place where the perpetrator came from?

Despite these difficulties, it seems fairly evident that most prosecuted crimes were happening outside the walls of Mantua and were committed by people with few or no claims to urban civility. It is also important to bear in mind that the reign of Marquis Ludovico Gonzaga saw an unprecedented—if impermanent—geographical expansion of the *marchesato*. Ludovico's direct control spanned a much extended dominion, particularly over territories west of the river Oglio, thanks to his father's assimilation by 1420 of the Cavalcabò *signoria* of Viadana, to the disgrace, exile, and death (1456) of his brother Carlo, and to the deaths without heirs of his brothers Gianlucido (1448) and Alessandro (1466), all of whom had held sizable lordships within the *dominio*.[15] This may help to explain why, on average, only about one-fifth of all the recorded sentences of the podesta of Mantua were imposed on persons described as inhabitants of the city.

Accused persons might be denounced to the court of the Mantuan podesta by private accusers, by the podesta's own officials (knight and constable), or by other agents of the marquis and the city of Mantua, such as the *sindico* (fiscal auditor) of the commune. A long-term holder of the last-named office was Giacomo da Palazzo, already an active prosecutor in the 1440s; throughout the 1460s and 1470s he emerges as one of the most zealous and probably most dreaded figures in Ludovico Gonzaga's administration.[16] Until 1446, but not thereafter, the prosecutor for minor offenses was quite often a *capitano di contrada*, the spokesman for one of the twenty subdistricts into which the city's four quarters were

---

14. Germans are identified as "teutonicus" or "de Alamanea"; in October 1460 "Johannes de Roseo de Picardia," a tapestry weaver working for the marquis, was condemned *in contumacia* to be beheaded for mortally wounding one Martionus, and another Picard, called Johannes, was to be fined for punching the same victim: AG, b. 3453.

15. On the recent assimilation of lesser signori and the expansion of Gonzaga dominion, as well as some of the implications, see Mazzoldi, *Mantova*, 2:4–5, 12; Vaini, *Ricerche gonzaghesche*, chap. 5 ("Il comitato").

16. E.g., in July 1447 the accusation against a man who helped a miscreant to escape was brought "per Jacobum de pallazo sindicum comunis Mantue": AG, b. 3452, fol. 476r. Schivenoglia the chronicler names him as "sendico" under the heading "Alchuny officially," compiled in the later 1460s: BCMn, MS 1019, fol. 54v. On this office see Vaini, *Ricerche gonzaghesche*, 14.

divided. But it was the *capitano del divieto* (*capitaneus ad vetita* or *vetitorum*) who was most often named as the accuser on charges against public order and morality. His main function was that of police inspector and revenue officer, with a particular duty to control the transporting of agricultural products, animals, and other goods, to catch tax evaders and smugglers. However, he also seems to have had a special line in reporting the utterance of blasphemous oaths, gambling, unlicensed carrying of weapons, or doing work and trading on Christian holidays. The same man might hold the office of *capitano del divieto* for many years, as did Matteo da Vicenza, whose name occurs in the lists from 1447 to 1455; Giovanni da Cremona, who appears from then until 1458; and Giorgio da Vicenza, who takes over until the end of the series in 1464. The *capitano del divieto* might be substituted in the work of accusation by full- or part-time assistants—individuals described variously as his proctor, associate *(socius)*, or secretary *(canzelarius)*.

The police work of the *capitano del divieto* extended over the *dominio* as well as the city, and this ubiquity may help to explain the rather spasmodic or random occurrence of accusations brought in his name on the official lists of sentences. It is interesting that a second *capitano*—with jurisdiction beyond the Po *(ultra Padum)* is found in 1458–59 in the person of Federigo Negri, who continued to operate in the following years as colleague and auxiliary. More serious criminal charges in the *dominio* would, however, often be referred to the podesta of Mantua by local magistrates. Before 1444, that is, in the time of Marquis Gianfrancesco Gonzaga, letters of referral from a rural podesta or vicar are sometimes mentioned in the records of sentences; after about 1450, in the time of Marquis Ludovico, the originals of such letters quite often survive. For instance, the vicar of Bigarello wrote on 1 March 1460 that an assistant of the *capitano del divieto* had delivered to him one Bartolomeo da Parma, in whose house a large amount of contraband corn and salted meat had been found. Bartolomeo was now being consigned to the podesta of Mantua.[17] Sometimes the local authorities were ordered from above to transfer their more serious cases. In July 1458 the vicar of Revere, Gianmaria Rodiano, wrote that he was obeying an order to hand over Andrea Zato, a self-confessed murderer, to the knight of the podesta of Mantua; he would be brought to the city by an armed guard of eight men from Revere.[18] Alternatively, the podesta himself might be put

---

17. AG, b. 2394.
18. AG, b. 2398, fol. 132.

under pressure should the marquis's order for such a transferral be disregarded. In August 1458 Bernardo Maggi informed Ludovico that the vicar of Cavriana had done nothing about delivering up one Zohanne Francesco, son of Paride da Ceresara; more information was required about his alleged offense, and the podesta insisted he was doing his utmost to satisfy the marquis's desire for delinquents to be punished.[19]

In the majority of cases accused persons failed to present themselves for trial. Presumably they had already fled from Mantuan territory and were therefore judged guilty, deserving punishments of maximum severity should they ever return. Thus, during the years 1460–62 sentences were pronounced *in contumacia* in about two-thirds to three-fourths of all recorded cases; there are indications that this was about the average proportion in previous years, too, though as many as four-fifths were sentenced contumaciously in 1456. (In tables 1 and 2 the first figure shown within each section, the number of persons judged guilty, includes the contumacious; immediately below is shown the number of these among each total who were *in contumacia*). The overwhelming majority of acquittals are found in cases where the accused person was physically present, either voluntarily or because he or she had been arrested and held in prison. It could happen that for the same offense those who presented themselves for trial were acquitted and those who did not do so were condemned to mutilation or death.[20] The risks of surrendering your person must have seemed so great, however, that even with evidence to prove innocence, flight and banishment would often seem the better choice.

In additional ways the lists of sentences make unsatisfactory evidence, because even in cases where the accused had been present for investigation, trial, and sentencing, there is no information about appeals and acts of grace on the part of the marquis—though a perusal of the *Libri dei decreti* can sometimes bring facts of this sort to light. Only occasionally is a positive notice included that the sentence had been carried out, that is, that a monetary fine had been wholly or partially collected and a cor-

---

19. AG, b. 2390, fol. 318 (16 Aug. 1458). This letter is written in Beltramino's hand (see n. 86, and chap. 3, n. 28); its tone (". . . conosco esser intention de la Illu. S. V. che i delinquenti siano puniti") is also unmistakable.

20. E.g., in a case in November 1447, two brothers whose victim died of the battering he received at their hands received contumaciously the statutory death penalty and a fine of one thousand ducats, but their father, who had also laid about him, wounding with bloodshed the dead man's brother, presented himself for trial and was acquitted (AG, b. 3452, fol. 480r).

TABLE 1. Sentences in the Mantuan podesta's court, 1448–63

	Years (and months)			
Offenses	1444–48 (45)	1449–53 (43)	1454–58 (49)	1459–63 (55)
Homicide				
Guilty	61	63	61	76
Contumacious	57	55	57	59
Acquitted	5	3	5	7
Robbery & theft[a]				
Guilty	82	67	121	138
Contumacious	73	37	78	52
Acquitted	51	25	6	20
Jailbreak[b]				
Guilty	10	45	91	85
Contumacious	7	7	45	6
Acquitted	—	1	—	2
Fraud[c]				
Guilty	5	22	29	18
Contumacious	8	15	18	8
Acquitted	23	4	11	12
Assault[d]				
Guilty	431	371	398	423
Contumacious	339	327	365	379
Acquitted	121	91	70	99
Verbal insult[e]				
Guilty	79	99	168	206
Contumacious	71	88	161	186
Acquitted	40	27	9	26
Carrying weapons				
Guilty	12	82	71	81
Contumacious	11	72	64	63
Acquitted	17	15	6	3
Impeding justice[f]				
Guilty	44	48	12	52
Contumacious	39	45	9	45
Acquitted	1	5	4	44
Damage to property[g]				
Guilty	109	179	298	278
Contumacious	82	169	259	252
Acquitted	75	62	50	65
Sexual assault[h]				
Guilty	32	11	50	41
Contumacious	15	9	24	32
Acquitted	9	6	5	7
Blasphemy				
Guilty	19	19	49	65
Contumacious	5	16	44	54
Acquitted	4	8	1	11

TABLE 1—*Continued*

	Years (and months)			
Offenses	1444–48 (45)	1449–53 (43)	1454–58 (49)	1459–63 (55)
Gambling[i]				
Guilty	3	85	46	24
Contumacious	1	72	34	23
Acquitted	2	27	1	1
Working on holidays				
Guilty	15	10	33	11
Contumacious	10	9	30	11
Acquitted	4	4	—	1
Other[j]				
Guilty	8	26	35	17
Contumacious	7	21	34	17
Acquitted	4	3	—	1

[a]Includes offenses varying from petty theft by a first offender (punishable by a modest money penalty or whipping) and less petty theft by a first or second offender (punishable by a substantial money penalty or mutilation) to recurrent theft and major robbery with violence (punishable by hanging).

[b]Includes attempted, planned, and assisted escapes from custody, as well as successful ones.

[c]Includes giving false testimony, making or circulating counterfeit coin, forging legal documents, claiming false identity, and using fraudulent weights and measures.

[d]Includes the whole range of physical assault and battery, short of causing death. Bloodshed, major injury, or intention to do mortal harm would aggravate the severity of the sentence.

[e]Slanderous and indecent words often accompanied physical assault but could also constitute a charge on its own.

[f]Includes physical assault or insult to law officers and their assistants, as well as aiding malefactors and failing to respond to the hue and cry against or to arrest a fugitive malefactor.

[g]Unlawful entry on private property with the intention or achievement of malicious damage.

[h]Includes rape (or attempted rape), abduction, or assisting such acts, as well as incest, sodomy, bigamous marriage, and so on.

[i]Offenses are sometimes cited as "de ludo" but can be specified as dice or other games of hazard.

[j]Miscellaneous.

poral mutilation or capital execution performed. Finally, the lists fall short of giving an overall picture of criminality in Mantua and its territory because they only relate to cases in which suspects had been named and charged, whether or not they were present for trial and sentencing. Probably no suspects at all were charged for the majority of crimes, which would have gone undetected. Policing was obviously very inadequate, even within the city; the odds against running into the podesta's night patrol squad must have been quite high. For this reason the penalties were severe for those convicted of not helping to raise the hue and cry against malefactors or of helping them to evade capture. For instance, in October 1448 heavy fines of forty lire each were imposed, *in contumacia*,

TABLE 2.   Sentences in the Mantuan podesta's court, 1460–62

Offenses	Years		
	1460	1461	1462
Homicide			
Guilty	21	13	26
Contumacious	17	13	21
Acquitted	—	2	4
Robbery & theft			
Guilty	67	10	20
Contumacious	21	2	12
Acquitted	2	4	4
Jailbreak			
Guilty	67	2	3
Contumacious	60	—	2
Acquitted	—	—	—
Fraud			
Guilty	1	2	11
Contumacious	—	1	6
Acquitted	—	1	4
Assault			
Guilty	76	113	93
Contumacious	66	107	77
Acquitted	24	9	34
Verbal insult			
Guilty	29	57	58
Contumacious	27	57	49
Acquitted	3	3	7
Carrying weapons			
Guilty	22	30	13
Contumacious	21	30	13
Acquitted	—	—	1
Impeding justice			
Guilty	11	12	25
Contumacious	10	9	25
Acquitted	—	—	9
Damage to property			
Guilty	49	77	97
Contumacious	40	75	89
Acquitted	11	9	15
Sexual assault			
Guilty	16	3	8
Contumacious	13	2	6
Acquitted	4	2	3
Blasphemy			
Guilty	20	9	9
Contumacious	17	9	8
Acquitted	1	—	2

TABLE 2—*Continued*

Offenses	Years		
	1460	1461	1462
Gambling			
Guilty	3	7	2
Contumacious	3	7	2
Acquitted	—	—	—
Working on holidays			
Guilty	15	4	—
Contumacious	1	4	—
Acquitted	—	—	—
Other			
Guilty	3	6	5
Contumacious	3	3	5
Acquitted	—	—	—

on three men who had not hastened to ring the church bells of San Giorgio (near Mantua) and secure an assailant whose victim had died after being struck on the head with a bar or pole *(stanga)*.[21]

Those tried for major crimes seldom received an acquittal, though it did occasionally happen. In rape cases, for instance, the eternal problems arose of possible consent by the victim-witness or lack of any corroboratory evidence. In February 1444 the prisoner Bono, of San Benedetto, confessed to violating and sodomizing his sister Zeliola and was sentenced to death by burning, but a year later Giovanni Marteleti, accused of the sodomitical rape of Margarita, a maidservant, escaped with an arbitrary fine of three hundred lire.[22] Even a Florentine vagrant ("Jacobus de Florentia vagabundus") was acquitted in 1446 for want of evidence that he had violated a certain Paola.[23] And in a rather circumstantial case in August 1456, the verdict was also acquittal for want of evidence; the accused, "Brexianus de Perchazino" (who had presented himself for trial) had allegedly broken into the house and then the bed of a married woman called Ysabeta, wife of Marco del Zano "de Foxato," raped her, and wounded her in the arm.[24] Ad hoc or *ad arbitrium* variation in punishment is not often found, but in a particularly shocking case

21. AG, b. 3452, fol. 501r.
22. Ibid., fols. 404v, 430r.
23. Ibid., fol. 456v.
24. AG, b. 3453.

of double murder in October 1448—two women had had their throats cut—the podesta sentenced the contumacious suspect, "Johannes Picenenus" of Naples, to be tied to an ass's tail and dragged to the scene of the crime before his beheading.[25]

Despite the many reservations to bear in mind, it seems nevertheless worth making a numerical breakdown of information from the lists, taking the inclusive twenty-year period from 1444 to 1463 and dividing it into four spans of five years each (see table 1). The information accumulated over each five-year period should be enough to signal any notable changes, allowing for some variations in the number of months for which sentences are recorded in any one year: in 1451, for example, there are only five months, but this was exceptionally low; nine months would be nearer the average. Admittedly, the fourth and last period, 1459–63, contains a notably larger total of months than the others do, but as the number of recorded occasions for proclaiming sentences varies a lot within the months, even they are not wholly satisfactory as units of measurement. In 1461, for example, sentences during some months are recorded twice in the lists, usually in the first and last weeks, but in other months of the same year they are only recorded once. The last three months of 1463 are missing, and only four months, which are not consecutive and which comprise the lowest total of all, survive from 1464. To avoid serious distortion, this fragmentary evidence from the final year of our time span has not been included. Late 1463 and early 1464 was an abnormal time in any case, because of the outbreak of plague and the enactment of emergency measures: as a long letter from Giacomo da Palazzo explains, the podesta had to move out of town, though his assistant judges stayed there; "transgressors and delinquents," particularly thieves and night prowlers, could expect little mercy.[26] Strict quarantine was imposed, and special powers were held by a military governor, or *collaterale*.

Various general inferences may be drawn from a reading of these lists of sentences. Action against certain offenses seems to have been pressed with greater vigor at different times, perhaps on the initiative of the individual podesta or of the other officials involved in bringing charges and inflicting sentences. Initiatives on the part of the marquis also seem to have fluctuated. Perhaps a greater resolution and severity may have been aroused by some soul-stirring event, such as the visit of a charismatic

---

25. AG, b. 3452, fol. 501v.
26. AG, b. 2399, Giacomo da Palazzo to Marquis L. Gonzaga, Bozolo (31 Oct. 1463).

preacher. After the visit of the papal court and other dignitaries to organize a crusade in 1459, the marquis may have been inspired to enforce higher moral standards on his subjects to impress the outside world. Accusations of blasphemous swearing rise conspicuously, for example, in 1458–60, though it was in 1458 that the total was highest (fifty-three perpetrators were found guilty, of whom twenty-five were listed as contumacious). Sometimes there is an unusual cluster of sexual "offenses against nature," as happened in 1444. Was there perhaps a special witch-hunt for sexual crimes at that time, toward the end of Marquis Gianfrancesco Gonzaga's reign (he died on 23 September 1444)—a campaign to purge lax morality influenced by San Bernardino's last preaching campaign in Lombard cities in 1442? Several of the cases of incest from February and March 1444 have already been mentioned; a brother and sister confessed to copulating frequently and having had a child,[27] as did a father and daughter.[28] In May of the same year there was the case of one Giacomino who had sodomized his eight-year-old niece, Caterina, and was sentenced to be burnt in the place of public execution ("in locum iusticie").[29] Since Giacomino had outraged nature on at least three counts and his person was secured in prison, the possibility is high that this sentence was in fact carried out. Sentences for sodomy are very rare in these Mantuan lists, and sodomy between males is not recorded at all, though this should not of course be taken to mean it did not occur: a case is in fact mentioned in a letter in 1465.[30] To be burnt alive ("igne cremetur") was a rare death sentence, usually reserved for incest and sodomy, though it was once imposed in a rape case which did not involve either of these additional offenses, in February 1435.[31] But punishment for convicted rapists could vary from one extreme to the other, and even incest might be punished by something less than death; an adolescent girl called Maria, made pregnant by her brother—she gave birth to a daughter in prison—was sentenced to a whipping and the pillory in 1445, a relatively merciful penalty on account of the youth of both parties (whether the brother also suffered punishment is not recorded).[32]

---

27. AG, b. 3452, fol. 404v.

28. Ibid., fol. 406r.

29. Ibid., fol. 409v.

30. Bartolomeo Ferioli was accused of committing sodomy with a boy, according to a letter of 2 July 1465 (AG, b. 2404, Revere).

31. AG, b. 3452, fol. 254v.

32. Ibid., fol. 435v.

Beheading was the most common form of death sentence in Mantua. It was usually for homicide, but it was occasionally imposed for other offenses, such as abduction and rape. And in 1461 there was one sentence of beheading for sacrilegious theft (whereas in May 1446 the sentence for a similar crime had been—interestingly—life imprisonment).[33] While aggravated forms of this mode of execution might be prescribed for political charges, rather surprisingly, on 2 May 1461, a certain Antonio Tubeta (or Trombetta), who had stabbed Federico Gonzaga, Ludovico's eldest son and heir, and drawn blood, was condemned to just a conventional beheading; it was lucky for him that Federico had escaped death thanks to his thick surcoat *(turcha)*.[34] (Nevertheless, Trombeta, who was probably insane, had been beaten up after the crime by bystanders and may have been put on the rope hoist—Barbara of Brandenburg reported that the podesta asked if she required this—before he was tried and condemned.)[35] Hangings for robbery seem comparatively rare. Perhaps oddest of all is a lone sentence for suicide: in July 1456 one Franceschino, formerly of Suzzara, was found guilty ("contumax quia mortuus") of throwing himself in a ditch and remaining there until he drowned; the penalty, which presumably was meant as a deterrent to others, was the confiscation of half of his goods.[36] Cases of perjury often seem to have been dismissed for want of proof, but forgers of documents were less lucky, as presumably the accusation always rested on tangible evidence: in May 1462 a notary, Biagio, the son of Niccolò de' Grassi, was sentenced to a fine of five hundred lire or else loss of his right hand and eye, but in any case he was to be paraded around the town and put in the pillory with a miter of infamy on his head.

One of the most difficult facts to determine, and one on which the lists cast only a little light, is how many sentences, particularly the more savage ones, were carried out in practice. In a study of the comparable records of sentences given in the podesta's court in Milan from 1385 to 1429, it was reckoned that very few at all of the capital sentences were performed, and that in a great many cases the duke's grace was

33. ". . . ad perpetuos carceres": ibid., fol. 453r.
34. AG, b. 3453. There are letters from Barbara of Brandenburg to the marquis concerning this case, dated 18, 19, and 21 Apr. 1461 (AG, b. 2096bis, fols. 640–43). According to her (18 Apr.), while Federico was at play, "Trombeta prese esso Federico per il pecto dicendo 'ha, traditore!' e detegli de la cortella ch'el havea in mane pur nel pecto."
35. "Antonio è stato ferito e mal tractato da molti. El potestate me havea mandato a dire se voleva che lo metesse a la corda": ibid., (18 Apr.).
36. AG, b. 3453.

granted.[37] A rather similar, though not quite so lenient, picture has been given for Ferrara, where it has been calculated from the "Libro dei giustiziati," which (unlike the Mantuan records) lists sentences that were implemented, that there were on average only three capital executions a year between 1460 and 1501; excluding death sentences for political crimes, the highest totals were eleven executions in 1454 and seven in 1458.[38] In contrast, a recent study concerning another nearby region, Brescia and its *contado* in 1411–17, during the brief *signoria* of Pandolfo Malatesta, suggests that the option of a pecuniary penalty was usually chosen not only in minor cases, such as blasphemous swearing, but even for homicide, and that there were no gracious pardons at all.[39]

The nature of the evidence in Mantua permits no numerical certainty, but occasional memoranda in the lists provide proof of some sentences being carried out. For instance, on 16 March 1451 there is a marginal note that Bartolomeo da Lodi, a former servant of the podesta's constable, was hanged for robbery;[40] on 26 February 1453 there is similar note[41] concerning the beheading of Agostino da Valcamonica, servant to Domenico da Volterra, whom he had been found guilty of murdering; and in August 1453 another execution for murder is noted.[42] In the case of "Laurentius de Ungaris" of Bondinello, convicted at the end of May 1460 of drowning his wife,[43] beheading followed two weeks later, upon rejection of his appeal. Likewise, on 11 December 1460 the hanging of a thief, "Guerinus de Gorno" from Bergamo, was recorded.[44]

Table 3 is based on these comparatively rare entries recording the actual carrying out of capital or corporal punishments. They certainly seem to be too few and far between to provide plausibly an inclusive total. Besides the lacunae in the lists, which must be borne in mind, there are the many contumacious offenders, some of whom might eventually have been captured and punished. There are also the cases where persons

---

37. See Verga, "Sentenze criminali," 120–24 (on grace and suspension of sentences) and 130 (for a table enumerating prosecutions, executions, etc.). Verga maintained that only two out of fifty-three capital sentences for homicide were carried out.

38. Gundersheimer, "Crime and Punishment," 110–12.

39. Bonfiglio Dosio, "Criminalità ed emarginazione."

40. "condemnatur ad furchas et fiet executionem": AG, b. 3453.

41. "Executio eidem sententie": ibid.

42. "Executio amputationis capitis quondam Ludovici de Zabarellis da Pisa": ibid.

43. "sofocavit in canale Situle Johaninam eius uxorem": ibid.

44. "hec est quedam executio . . . quia alias fuit condemnatus . . . ideo furcis suspendatur": ibid.

held in prison had received sentences of death or mutilation redeemable on payment of a sum of money (sometimes a very large sum) within a fixed term, usually not more than two weeks. One rare exception to the usual silence of the lists about the payment of money penalties occurs in December 1445, when it was recorded that a convicted thief who had failed to pay the fine of twenty-five ducats should be whipped and placed in the pillory.[45] Blasphemous swearing was a crime that could be purged for a fairly low cash payment, though multiple swearing could run up a higher bill. Giovanni Greco, who was held in prison in 1448, was sentenced to pay forty-five ducats for cursing the Virgin Mary as well as swearing by St. Anthony and All Saints; even so, he was relatively lucky, as he was also accused of slashing an image of the Virgin, and this could have led to the amputation of a hand.[46] With the standard fine set at only ten lire for taking a saint's name in vain, it should have been possible for many offenders to avoid the horror of a day in the pillory with their

TABLE 3.   Recorded executions and corporal punishments in Mantua, 1444–63

Offenses	Years			
	1444–48	1449–53	1454–58	1459–63
Homicide Beheadings	5	4	3	13
Robbery & theft				
Hangings	3	2	1	10
Mutilations	—	—	8	5
Whippings	1	2	2	1
Perjury & fraud				
Mutilation & pillory	1	4	9	2
Hangings	3	2	1	10
Sexual assault				
Burnings	5	—	—	1
Beheadings	1	1	—	2
Mutilations	—	—	1	—
Whippings	—	—	—	1
Blasphemy				
Pillory	—	—	—	—
Insult to authority				
Beheading	—	—	—	2
Sacrilege				
Beheading	—	—	—	1

45. AG, b. 3452, fol. 442r.
46. Ibid., fol. 498r.

tongues in the *giova;* and many were not convicted at all if the allegation depended on a single witness—it says something for Mantuan justice that a Jew accused of a blasphemous oath was acquitted in 1445.[47]

Nevertheless, the money penalties were high for many offenses, and it is likely that many convicted persons were quite unable to muster in time the cash required to save their bodies from punishment. It was bad enough for relatively well-to-do people, like the two millers of Viadana found guilty of smuggling or evading tax in 1463: one of them had a benevolent father, who offered to pay everything to get him out of prison (where it was feared he might otherwise die), though the local podesta was still unwilling to release him without the marquis's approval;[48] the other, sentenced to a fine of 370 lire, which he protested he could not raise, was told that he would stay in prison until he did so.[49] But how could any cash at all have been raised by people like Bastiano and Silvestro, two so-called vagabonds from Venice, who were sentenced in Mantua in 1460 to lose an eye each and be whipped and banished for stealing a *spalliera* (a "dorser," or tapestry, for bench backs) from the marquis's brother Alessandro Gonzaga? Another thief, one Paolo of Vicenza, whose petty but habitual offenses had led to a total bill in fines of nine hundred lire in December 1457, was also perhaps in difficulty; and nonpayment meant that on each count he would lose a member—two eyes and two ears—as well as have to endure a whipping.[50] In September 1448 Tommaso da Salerno, the former servant of a soldier *(armigerius)* of the marquis, was handed over for whipping because he had failed to pay.[51] In 1456 it was specifically noted in the cases of two convicted thieves that the time limit for payment had passed; thus, in June one of the thieves, Agostino Galucci of Bologna, lost an eye,[52] and in August the other, Giovanni Anselmo, a priest's servant, lost an ear.[53]

Some convicted criminals may have obtained a gracious pardon or reduction or postponement of payment, but many must have languished in jail or had to submit to judicial butchery. The repellant role of public

47. AG, b. 3452, fol. 435v.

48. AG, b. 2400, fols. 549, 551, Giovanni Malatesta, podesta of Viadana, to Marquis L. Gonzaga (15 and 17 Mar. 1463).

49. Ibid., fol. 592, "Johannes Bolzonus molinarius" to Marquis Ludovico Gonzaga, Viadana (21 Apr. 1463).

50. AG, b. 3453.

51. AG, b. 3452, fol. 500r.

52. "fiet executio quia eruitur oculus sibi": AG, b. 3453.

53. "crastina die fiet executio": ibid.

executioner—*ministero di giustizia* or *manigoldo*—was evidently a full-time job, with the workweek divided between city and *dominio*. The holder was closely guarded and sometimes, if not always, was himself a convicted criminal; for instance a thief who had tried to break through a wall of the podesta's room where he was held was sentenced to two years' service as executioner in March 1455.[54]

The figures from tables 1 and 2 seem to suggest that during the last five-year period violent crime was increasing—sentences for homicide rise very markedly,[55] as do those for the more serious cases of robbery and for most sorts of assault. Meanwhile, both interrogations and sentences were becoming harsher. These points are borne out also from other sources. An example is provided by the orders that Marquis Ludovico Gonzaga gave to the podesta in June 1460 about interrogating a nighttime housebreaker arrested and imprisoned by the *capitano del divieto*. The house in question belonged to the prominent and wealthy Mantuan merchant Giovanfilippo da Concoreggio, and Ludovico was evidently outraged; "if there should be any statute or decree inhibiting you from using torture to make him talk," he wrote, "we give you *pieno arbitrio* to disregard it."[56] The number of sentences of death or mutilation are notably higher in these years than formerly, and it is no cause for wonder that on 28 February 1461, by proclamation, the confraternity that accompanied the condemned to the place of execution and afterward took their corpses to be buried were given exemption from all communal impositions.[57]

Escapers or would-be escapers from prison received very harsh sentences. On different occasions in 1460 no less than twenty-nine sentences of beheading were imposed on contumacious, or successful, escapees from prison, and others who did not get away were condemned to muti-

---

54. ". . . quod sit magister iusticie comunis Mantue per bienniam": ibid. See also Bertolotti, *Prigioni e prigionieri*, 31–32, where the author quotes a letter of 25 Jan. 1485 that promises loan of the executioner *(maestro de la justicia)*—under strong guard so that he will not flee—to hang a robber at Guastalla.

55. In fact, in 1463 the trend seems to have gone into reverse, with only six cases of homicide recorded, but from just the four months recorded in 1464 there were eleven cases.

56. ". . . se'l vi parese che qualche statuto, leze o decreto vi fosse contrario et che per vigore de quelle non potesti metter a la tortura, per questa nostra littera signata de nostra propria mane vi concedemo et daghemovene pieno arbitrio, vogliando faciate dare al guardiano lì da le presone": AG, b. 2885, lib. 31, fol. 65v, Marquis L. Gonzaga to the podesta of Mantua, Cavriana (22 June 1460).

57. AG, Lib. decr. 14, fol. 190r (28 Feb. 1461). Nineteen members of this fraternity (the *fratres scoparum nigrarum*) are named.

lation. According to the podesta Giacomo Cesarini, writing on 13 February, seven persons—all poor men ("tutti sono poveri"), he noted, perhaps with a trace of compassion—were awaiting amputation of a hand for their part in one attempted breakout. However, Cesarini thought it would be equally effective as an exemplary punishment to change this sentence to a few jerks on the rope hoist.[58] Cesarini's proposal to use the rope-hoist as a punishment for would-be jail breakers was in fact upheld in later years,[59] but more savage sentences were the order of the day in the early 1460s. Strange to say, he may have got the figures wrong, since only four persons are listed as condemned to amputation of a hand in February 1460, though perhaps the other three had remained from an earlier bid to escape; there were eight more unsuccessful escapees due to be mutilated in December.[60] It is likely they all suffered this penalty, since jail breaking was regarded as a major defiance of authority. It was not a new problem. For instance, 1456 had been a particularly lax year for prison security. Two prisoners had successfully escaped in January and May, and another had failed in the attempt in February. Fifteen got out in November (all were condemned to beheading should they ever be caught) and seven more in December. Not surprisingly, the jailer, Bartolomeo Borelli, also fled, and he was sentenced contumaciously to have his right hand and tongue cut out.

In January 1461 Domenico of Venice, sentenced for theft, was whipped and deprived of both ears. In February of that year Tomà of Asola was hanged for robbery according to a loose page inserted among the list of sentences for that month,[61] Niccolò Bonesio (who had committed twenty-six previous thefts) was hanged,[62] and Bonamento da Villafranca had an ear cut off for theft. In May 1461 Giovanni Michele Buzacho confessed and was sentenced to be hanged for using defamatory words against the vicar of Bigarello; there is no note confirming execution, but it is perfectly probable that the sentence was carried out in this case too. Prosecutions of persons who impeded or even assaulted officers when trying to carry out their duties increased, as did those of persons

58. ". . . saria buono ad terrorem delli altri alterare altrove in mutazione della mano qualche tratto di corda . . . pure quanto comanda la Vostra Signoria si facia": AG, b. 2395, fol. 301.

59. AG, b. 2897, lib. 100, fol. 88v, letter of Marquis Federico Gonzaga (26 Sept. 1480), cited in chap. 4, n. 11.

60. AG, b. 3453.

61. "fiat executio contra dictum Thomam ad furcas": ibid.

62. "in exequtione sentencie furtis laqueo suspendatur": ibid.

who had been slow or negligent to detain malefactors. Officials who abused their powers were also being brought to book: Cristoforo of Milan was accused of corrupt dealing in October 1460 and February 1461; Biagio, an assistant of the *capitano del divieto,* was convicted of assault in November 1461. An attempt to corrupt the podesta himself was made by a Mantuan tailor, but whether whatever he offered was too paltry to be of interest or the integrity of the podesta (probably Giacomo Cesarini) was unassailable, he failed and was condemned in July 1460 to a fine of forty gold ducats.

In 1462 there was an even higher total number of capital and corporal sentences than in any of the three previous years. Again, absolute proof of death sentences being carried out is limited. "Martinus Petroni de Bressana," inhabitant of Fossamana (a small village east of the city) was sentenced to beheading on 31 May for the abduction and rape of a woman, and this punishment certainly took place.[63] In December, Martino son of Bartolitio (who confessed and was imprisoned) was beheaded for murdering his two daughters,[64] and "Marchinus Bertolucii de Bredellis," safely imprisoned, was beheaded for murdering his wife.[65] The robber Francesco Viviani, son of a building mason, was hanged in May,[66] and—also in May—Todeschino, a former servant of Bartolomeo da Gonzaga, was almost certainly beheaded for an unspecified offense in the past (he had presumably been arrested and found to have a contumacious sentence on his head);[67] the unsuccessful jail breaker "Blasius Bucius," sentenced to loss of a hand, probably had to undergo this punishment. Execution is also likely in some other cases. In January, one Recchio was held in jail when convicted of murder, so unless the marquis intervened to spare him (which is somewhat unlikely), he presumably lost his head. The case of the notary Biagio de' Grassi, condemned to mutilation and ignominy, has already been mentioned, and in August a jailed lawyer from Verona, "magister Bartholomeus de Arduinis," was condemned to lose his right hand and tongue and stand mitered in the pillory for false testimony. In June Caterina, wife of Antonio "de Burgo," was whipped for theft;[68] in July one Antonio, son of Antonello, held in prison, was to

---

63. "nunc vero pro exequtione amputetur ei caput": ibid.
64. "executio in amputatione capitis": ibid.
65. "executio in amputatione capitis": ibid.
66. "nunc vero pro executione": ibid.
67. "pronuntiatur dictam sententiam": ibid.
68. "Exequtio/nunc vero fustigetur quia non solvit penam": ibid.

be decapitated for the murder of a German ("Johannes Teutonicus"); and in December Giovanni da Ferrara, having confessed his crime, was sentenced to beheading for putting counterfeit Venetian coins into circulation.

Thus the total of judicial deaths in 1462 (not counting the mutilations, which might also have resulted in early death) could have been as many as eight. Bartolomeo, son of Manfredo Boccamaggiori, was contumacious and presumably escaped the beheading to which he was sentenced on 16 October for the incestuous rape of his niece Francesca; others condemned *in contumacia* include in January one Maffeo (to be hanged for highway robbery), in March three homicides to be beheaded, two more in April and May, and as many as eleven persons condemned on 26 June to be hanged above the piazza for insulting the *capitaneus vetitorum* (the *capitano del divieto*). Although public hanging in the piazza had been the penalty for obstructing the podesta or his staff since a *grida* of 1454,[69] the *capitano del divieto* was a lesser official; it would seem that any defiance of authority was now being treated as a major crime. In July four contumacious homicides were sentenced to beheading and two bearers of false testimony were to lose their tongues and right hands and to stand mitered in the pillory—the fact that these two were soldiers *(provvisionati)* makes the point that under Ludovico, in contrast to his successors, no military immunity was allowed. In August there were five contumacious homicides to be beheaded and a receiver of stolen property to be hanged; one homicide was to be beheaded in September, one in both October and November, and two in December, while another receiver of stolen property was sentenced to hanging in October.[70] Counting in all of these, the number of capital and corporal sentences for the year rises to a quite formidable total.

There may be some grounds, therefore, for inferring that the middle years of the reign of Marquis Ludovico Gonzaga saw increasing official concern about crime and moral disorder (gambling and swearing were also more frequently punished), leading to more habitual use of harsh exemplary penalties. This is evident during the final five-year span of the records of sentences under study (1458–62) and continues during the incompletely recorded years of 1463–64. Alarm—and the need for severity—were expressed not only in Mantua itself but also in the *dominio*.

---

69. AG, b. 2038–39, Gride, fasc. 5, fol. 10v.
70. Ibid.

Early in 1462 Ludovico de la Torre, podesta of Sermide, wrote indignantly of the need to restore order there and of the many thefts committed,[71] claiming that as well as needing a man "to do the necessary things" like tying up and hoisting suspects under interrogation,[72] he also wanted a stipendiary knight and a servant: his authority needed strengthening. This provincial podesta readily condemned to death thieves who had confessed to recurrent offenses, because crime was flourishing undeterred.[73] In June 1462 he announced his intention to hang or—as the Mantuan statutes prescribed—behead another robber who had abducted a small child *(putta)*. He wished to send his knight to escort the executioner from Mantua.[74] He mentioned this or another exemplary hanging that took place on 5 July 1462 and his order that the victim's body be left on the gallows for several days or until its bad odor made the air dangerous.[75] He was still at it in November 1462, when he declared that there were more thieves than honest men around ("in questi confini dubito che non sia più ladri che homini") and that terrible examples were needed ("grandissime e terribilissime demonstratione"). He begged that the executioner should be sent every time he asked for him.[76]

Likewise, at the other end of the *dominio*, Giovanni Malatesta, podesta of Viadana, wrote in October 1461 asking for the executioner to be sent as there was a confessed robber due for dispatch.[77] He complained in a letter of 9 March 1463 that too often in the past grace had been bestowed on malefactors, three out of four getting off, as a result of which every day there were more offenders;[78] on 4 August he announced that because of the increase in nighttime robberies and other crimes he

---

71. ". . . molti e desonesti furti,": AG, b. 2397, fol. 1051 (letter of 16 Feb. 1462).

72. ". . . né ho chi a lo examine facia quello se deve como è ligare, tirare sula corda e far l'altre cosse necessarie": ibid.

73. AG, b. 2397, fols. 1055, 1062 (letters of 13 Mar. and 23 Apr. 1462).

74. Ibid., fol. 1069 (letter of 12 June 1462).

75. Ibid., fol. 1077.

76. ". . . supplico se digni comandare che lo ministro de la iusticia ad ogni mia richiesta mi sia dato": ibid., fol. 1105 (letter of 13 Nov. 1462).

77. "Ritrovo che Jacomo da Lodesano, che ho qui per ladro, ha confessato tanti furti che secondo el statuto qui merita la morte; et essendo passato el termine che gli ho dato, dignasse la Vostra Signoria scrivesse al podestà di Mantua che potesse havere el maiestro de la iusticia lunedì e martedì proximo": AG, b. 2396, fol. 960, Giovanni Malatesta to Marquis L. Gonzaga, Viadana (30 Oct. 1461).

78. "Ricordando ancora la Vra Si. si degna fa oportunamente fargie bona provisione aziò che li malfatori non rimangano como anno fato per lo passato, che di quatro li tri non si po fare rasone perché li fano le gracie, et qui ogni dì si abunde più tristi e cativi": AG, b. 2400, fol. 549.

had decided to reissue an edict threatening that anyone out of doors one hour after sunset could receive six months in jail and a fine. He had already arrested four men found cavorting at night in strange attire with a prostitute.[79] Soldiers and law officers were marked down for harsh treatment if they were convicted; in September 1463 the rare sentence of burning alive was pronounced in Mantua on a soldier, Giovanni of Milan, *in contumacia*; this was for sodomy, aggravated by robbery and verbal insult. In 1464 Gaspare "teotonicus," *capitano del divieto,* was found guilty of raping a certain Maria from Luzzara; he was condemned to lose his right hand and foot unless he paid the huge fine of one thousand lire. In July 1464 there were three sentences of beheading for homicide, a rapist was sentenced to have his right hand amputated, and a man who wounded a Mantuan noble was condemned to lose his right ear. Admittedly, these were all contumacious cases, whereas many of those who presented themselves for trial were acquitted, including one man accused of perjury and another held on a charge of theft. The pattern is not, therefore, wholly consistent, either then or at other times: why, for example, in November 1462, was Andrea Pegorini contumaciously sentenced for rape—after denunciation by the victim's uncle—not to mutilation or worse but to the relatively unusual penalty of a fine of ten lire and six months imprisonment? In September 1464 no capital or corporal sentences were imposed at all, and over one-third of all cases heard were dismissed—most of them, however, for relatively minor offenses.

It should be remembered that assault and injury to persons and property, verbal abuse, and the implied threat of carrying arms or otherwise endangering public order were punished according to a tariff of fines that could be increased according to time and place, as happened in the case of six youths of Nuvolara in March 1456 who faced fines of three hundred ducats for singing *mattinate* and attacking the house and person of Donato Barberio. But they might also be diminished on appeal, as in one case in February 1458 that demonstrates the workings of the marquis's Council, who lowered the fine of twenty-five ducats to which Niccolò Gattico had been sentenced for injurious words against his accuser to five *lire in pizzoli*.[80]

To a striking extent the marquis used his *arbitrium* and intervened in individual cases or even dictated sentences. There is no doubt that active

79. ". . . per li molti excessi, furti et malificii se cometiano la nocte": ibid., fol. 556.
80. AG, b. 2390, fol. 224.

participation in matters of justice was a deliberate policy, and the enhanced role of the marquis's Council as a council of justice (seemingly just what the protesters of 1430 had not wanted) confirms this, even if the Council had only a delegated form of the signorial authority and in the beginning was limited to handling civil disputes and cases concerning foreigners.[81]

Throughout this period podestas often went out of their way to seek instructions from the marquis. Fulco Ariosto wrote on 28 July 1453 about the case of Bartolomeo da Marmirolo, who had been subjected to the rope hoist, as demanded by the marquis, and then had confessed to the robbery of which he was accused. However, the victim insisted that he had been unaware of a recent proclamation that made his crime punishable by hanging. Fulco pointed out that in any case Bartolomeo's thefts were subject to punishment at the podesta's discretion, which did not extend to death but could include the loss of an eye or a hand. He was also writing to find out from the local officials whether Bartolomeo had committed other crimes, in which case the sentencing would be more straightforward (presumably he would impose a death sentence).[82] Bernardo Maggi wrote on 27 May 1458 acknowledging the marquis's instruction not to proceed against two persons under investigation;[83] on 17 August he reported that he and his deputy ("vicarius": Beltramino Cusadri) had, as commissioned by the marquis, examined with torture a certain Pino and Gabriele, both servants, but had found nothing culpable;[84] he later asked the marquis what should be done in the case of some persons arrested after the third bell at night.[85] However, he went ahead without seeking special instructions in a case of sexual misconduct defying prison regulations, though on 23 November 1458 the marquis was asking him about it. While the other prisoners were at mass, Giacomo dalle Bredelle had managed to have *coniunctum carnale* with a female prisoner called Margarita, and she had become pregnant. This irregular happening was thanks to the assistant jailer, one Mandello, who (according to Giacomo) had himself often slept with Margarita, and his motive in bringing her and Giacomo together—they claimed to have been lovers previously—was to divert suspicion from himself. Nevertheless, "I have

---

81. Mozzarelli, *Mantova e i Gonzaga,* 25, 29.
82. AG, b. 2390, fol. 198.
83. Ibid., fol. 315.
84. Ibid., fol. 319. See n. 86.
85. Ibid., fol. 321 (20 Aug. 1458).

condemned him [Giacomo] to amputation of the left hand, according to the statutes of the city," the podesta dryly informed Ludovico;[86] Giacomo wanted to appeal against this sentence, and the podesta now asked if the marquis wished to intervene with an act of grace?

While there is no shortage of letters from Marquis Ludovico Gonzaga to document his active intervention in criminal prosecutions, there is also evidence that in some cases sentences were set aside by his special acts of grace. These remissions are often recorded among the registers of decrees, though they are sometimes dated so long after the original sentences—as in Milan[87]—that they raise more questions. Do they imply long periods of imprisonment while a sentence was suspended pending appeal, banishment or contumacious exile followed eventually by relaxation of the sentence, or simply—in acknowledgment that the condemned person had already suffered punishment—removal of the moral stain, a lifting of social ignominy, and the offender's formal restoration of status to his or her family, probably in return for a hefty fee?

In the latter half of 1460 there were several such cases. Francesco di Turricella, who had received the statutory sentence for murder (decapitation and a fine of one thousand lire) on 29 November 1452, was absolved;[88] so was Desiderato da Riparolo, who had been sentenced to a fine of two thousand lire for not pursuing a murderer or raising the alarm even longer ago, in 1444.[89] Also annulled was the sentence of beheading passed nearly thirty years earlier on Giovanantonio Andrea of Mantua for raping a virgin, Filippa de Sorbis, whom he had then stabbed to death with a knife; in any case, he had escaped execution thanks to an amnesty celebrating the Emperor Sigismund's visit in March 1433.[90] Often, however, the delay was a matter of only two or three years, as in the case of Niccolò of Parma, whose full sentence for homicide, handed down on July 1458, was lifted on 30 August 1460.[91]

Even before Ludovico Gonzaga decided to move in a new direction,

---

86. Ibid., fol. ". . . e tio, havuta la spontanea soa confession, segondo gli ordeni de la raxon e di statuti de questa alma cità de la Ill.ma S. V., lo comdennato in l'amputation de la mane sinistra" (ibid., fol. 322). This letter (like the one at n. 19) is—significantly—in the hand of Beltramino, the podesta's *vicarius* (see chap. 3 n. 28).

87. Verga ("Sentenze criminali," 109) notes that the sentence of a woman condemned in 1385 for poisoning her husband was canceled by ducal letter ten years later.

88. AG, Lib. decr. 14, fol. 146v (30 Aug. 1460).

89. Ibid., fol. 148v (18 Sept. 1460).

90. Ibid., fol. 157r (6 Nov. 1460).

91. Ibid., fol. 146v.

abolishing the office of podesta in December 1466, he had experimented
by selecting as podesta an individual who was virtually Mantuan by
adoption and who therefore might be more compliant than an overbearing figure from, say, Tuscany or the Romagna. Gianfrancesco Soardi was
appointed to serve from May 1466. A nobleman from Bergamo and a
poet, Soardi had long been a prominent figure in the Gonzaga court; a
former pupil of Vittorino da Feltre, he had also been tutor to one of the
marquis's sons. Furthermore he had had some magisterial experience in a
foreign city, having served as *capitano del popolo* in Florence in
1456–57.[92] He also had experience in Mantua's provincial jurisdiction:
he was podesta of Ostiglia in 1458.[93] A few letters that survive from
Soardi during his term as podesta of Mantua suggest that he very readily
referred himself to the marquis for instructions as to what he should do.
Writing on 11 August he discussed the case of Pasqua, wife of one
Girardo, and their son aged eleven, accused of stealing twelve lire, which
he had then given to his mother. In response to Marquis Ludovico's order
that he must find out the truth, Soardi had had Pasqua and the boy
hoisted on the rope; the latter confessed, but Pasqua continued to deny it.
Soardi asked Ludovico what he should do next.[94] More decisively, on 25
September he informed the marquis that he had condemned three jail
breakers to have one hand each amputated unless Ludovico was opposed
to this punishment.[95]

Ludovico Gonzaga was no doubt sincere in requiring a man of
integrity and sound legal learning, close to his own ear, to do the job of
podesta; years later, in 1478, he claimed that he had been weary of
receiving endless requests for the office so that it was always booked very
far ahead in conferment of favor.[96] There are, we have seen, positive indications that crimes, particularly violent crimes, were on the increase in
Mantua in the late 1450s and early 1460s; the marquis, in agonies of
rheumatic gout, and concerned for the state of his soul as well as for the
prestige of the city, may well have regarded it as a matter of conscience
for him as a just ruler to take firm action. In the early 1460s—after the
visit of the papal court—Ludovico took action to make judicial adminis-

92. D.S. Chambers, "Cardinal Francesco Gonzaga in Florence," in *Florence and Italy: Renaissance Studies in Honour of Nicolai Rubinstein,* ed. P. Denley and C. Elam (London, 1988), 242.
93. AG, b. 2392 (Ostiglia) (letter of 7 Apr. 1458).
94. AG, b. 2405, letters of 1 Mar. and 11 Aug. 1466.
95. ". . . se altro non haverò in contrario": ibid., 25 Sept. 1466.
96. AG, b. 2895, lib. 87, fol. 32v (letter of 31 July 1478), cited in chap. 4, n. 134.

tration more expeditious and efficient,[97] and to improve its physical setting. Repairs went ahead on the civic palaces, including the palace of the podesta, and the surrounding road surfaces were improved.[98] These measures expressed signorial rather than municipal authority, as did Ludovico's concern about who should hold judicial office—and how they should discharge it—in these refurbished premises. Whether or not he took advice from members of his entourage—Giacomo da Palazzo, for example, would have been a likely advocate of hard men and tough measures—it is clear that he was on the lookout for new methods and more effective solutions.

97. For instance, a statute of 7 May 1462 laid down that before criminal sentences were publicly announced they must be recorded in writing (cl. 13) and appeals in criminal cases must be made within fifteen days of the sentence (cl. 23): AG, b. 2003, fols. 235r–v.

98. Albertinus de Pavexiis wrote to Marquis L. Gonzaga, 8 May 1461: "la piaza del broleto è fornita de salegare: anchor e domane se fornirà fra l'una porta e l'altra del pallazo brusato [i.e. the burnt palace: see n. 1] e li scalini de la piaza de la masseria" AG, b. 2395, fol. 386. See also E. Marani, "Architettura," in *Mantova: Le Arti*, ed. E. Marani and C. Perina (Mantua, 1961), 2, 81–82; Gazzola, *Il palazzo del podestà*, 50, 70.

3

Beltramino's Origins and Early Career in Mantua

Beltramino Cusadri, destined to be the right-hand man in law-and-order enforcement for two of the foremost ruling dynasties in northern Italy, came from a family prominent in the affairs of Crema, a minor city of central Lombardy that in 1449 had passed under the rule of Venice. Not much is known about Beltramino's early life. His father, named Pantale-one after one of Crema's patron saints, was born allegedly in 1406 and had one daughter and four sons, of whom Beltramino was the youngest.[1] There is no certainty that this birth date for Pantaleone is accurate, and it would make him a very young father of so many children; Beltramino— as evidence in this chapter will make clear—cannot have been born later than 1424–25. Pantaleone had been active in undermining the local *sig-noria* of Giorgio Benzoni in Crema, making secret overtures to the Vis-conti of Milan in 1422;[2] he was in a key position as castellan of the cas-tle of Crema.[3] Thereafter a favored supporter of the Visconti regime,[4] from 1449 onward Pantaleone collaborated closely with the Venetian

---

1. BCCr, "Codice Zurla" (genealogies of leading Cremaschi, compiled in the seven-teenth century), fol. 93r. Pantaleone, his grandfather Amato, his father Bonino, his chil-dren, and their progeny are noted in this genealogy, but no birthdates after Pantaleone's are given.

2. P. Terno, *Della historia di Crema,* ed. M. Verga and C. Verga (Crema, 1964), 179–84. Pietro Terno (b. 1476) is a good source, although vague on chronology: he outlines Beltramino's careeer (229–30) and mentions as an exiled Benzoni supporter (184) his own grandfather, who would have known Pantaleone and his sons. See also C. Verga, *Pietro Terni* (Crema, 1964), 11–22. Most of Pietro's chronicle (the autograph MS is privately owned) was written by 1551; Alemanio Fino, who pirated it for his own works, reported in a letter of 1 September 1566 that it had been shown to him about two years before by Pietro's son Giambattista (ibid., 22 n. 64).

3. "1422–5: Pacta Pantaleonis de Cuxatris olim castellani castri terre Creme," *Inventari e regesti dell'Archivio di Stato in Milano,* vol. 1, *I registri viscontei* (Milan, 1915), 128.

4. G. Vittani, ed., *Inventari e regesti dell'Archivio di Stato in Milano,* vol. 2, *Gli atti can-celareschi viscontei* (Milan, 1919–20), 85, 92.

87

governors, as did his sons. He was sent on an embassy of congratulation to Venice in November 1449, confirming the terms of submission; already a member of the city's Council of One Hundred, he was appointed as one of ten deputies to advise the podesta in February 1450.[5] A notary by profession, Pantaleone was a strong candidate, only narrowly outvoted, for the office of chancellor of Crema in January 1452.[6] During the 1450s he and his sons[7] and various other members of the Cusadri family are frequently recorded in the registers of the commune as members of the Council of One Hundred, as deputies to advise the Venetian podesta, or as other short-term officeholders or candidates for office. One of Beltramino's elder brothers, Giovanni, was a physician, and already in January 1450 he had been appointed the city's medical officer;[8] Beltramino himself soon became equally valued for his legal expertise.

At the first appearance of Beltramino's name in the civic registers he is already described as a doctor of laws (i.e., of both civil and canon law). The little that has come to light about his student life is, first, that he studied at Pavia—as might have been expected, seeing that Pavia, with its first-rate law school, is not at all far from Crema—and, second, that while he was a student there in 1446, about twenty-one years old, he was indicted for homicide, the victim being a fellow law student, one Pietro Alemani.[9] It would appear that Beltramino had fled and been judged contumacious, so that the possessions he left behind, consisting of his books (all the recorded titles are Roman civil law texts) were confiscated. This episode—particularly murky in the light of Beltramino's later professions of integrity as a prosecutor and judge—remains unexplained. It may be

---

5. BCCr, Archivio storico II, reg. 1, fols. 1r, 2r, 5r (page numbers of these registers are transliterated from roman to arabic numerals here and in subsequent citations); Terno (*Historia,* 205) names him on the embassy.

6. BCCr, Archivio storico II, reg. 1, fol. 93v. I could not find registers of Pantaleone's notarial *acta* in the Archivio Storico at Lodi, which does hold registers of his fellow notary Giacomo Rabatta, the successful candidate for appointment as chancellor.

7. The "Codice Zurla" names the eldest as Giacomo, who went to live at Lodi and died in 1484, followed by Giovanni and Guido. Their sister was called Giovanna.

8. BCCr, Archivio storico II, reg. 1, fol. 8r. Other members of the family active in civic affairs included Bartolomeo, elected to the Council of One Hundred in August 1450 (ibid., fol. 30v) and Jacobus, son of Agostino Cusadri (ibid., fol. 100v). Bonino (passim) was presumably not Beltramino's grandfather but another of that name.

9. *Codice diplomatico dell'università di Pavia,* vol. 2, pt. 2, "1441–50" (Pavia, 1915), 489–92, no. 634 (15 June 1446) from Archivio notarile, Pavia, *Atti* of Giovanni Mangano. The *giudice del maleficio* is named as Giovanni Bruno.

presumed that he was later cleared of involvement in the murder or at least pardoned and allowed to return to complete his doctorate, although no record of such an act of ducal grace has come to light. It is suggestive that one of his prosecutors, the ducal vicar and *locotenente,* Stefano Zampi, was a jurist from Mantua, who in later years worked with him there. Just conceivably, Stefano was so impressed by Beltramino's potential within the legal profession that he helped to clear his name in Pavia. It is also tempting to speculate whether, if he was innocent, Beltramino obtained from the experience a modicum of sympathy for victims of false accusation or some scruple about starting investigative proceedings on poor evidence, or whether, if he was guilty, he remained for the rest of his life a supreme hypocrite, despising as rogues less smart than himself those whom he judged and condemned.

In Crema Beltramino's public career had begun by 3 September 1451, when he was appointed in place of his father as one of the ten deputies, or *savi,* to advise the podesta.[10] From January to August 1452 he served with two others as a financial auditor, or *sindico,* of the commune[11] and was one of the ten deputies to the podesta.[12] In May 1452 he was nominated to be an ambassador to Venice but was voted down;[13] however, he may have been sent there on a mission in November of the same year concerning the proposed appointment of a new commander for the Venetian army,[14] and there is more certainty of his appointment in January 1453 to consult the Venetian military commander Gentile Leonessa.[15] From January to May 1453 Beltramino is recorded as a member of the Council of One Hundred in place of his brother Giacomo and as a deputy,[16] and in October and November he served again as a deputy to the podesta in place of Tommaso Benzoni.[17] In December 1453 he was elected ambassador to Venice, to negotiate about the property of Ghibelline (i.e., pro-Milanese) exiles from Crema; these negotiations were still in progress in October 1454, when the Council of Ten referred their

---

10. "Beltraminus Cusatrus loco Johannis [sic] patris sui" (BCCr, Archivio storico II, reg. 1, fol. 83r).

11. Ibid., fols. 98r, 104r, 128r–132v.

12. Ibid., fols. 101r, 104r, 109r, 130r–131v.

13. Ibid., fols. 123v–124r.

14. Terno, *Historia,* 212.

15. BCCr, Archivio storico II, reg. 1, fol. 170r.

16. Ibid., fols. 170r, 174v, 181r, 185r, 187v, 188r; reg. 2, fols. 3v–9r passim, 16v, 17v, 18r, 22v, 24r.

17. Ibid., fols. 29r, 31r–34r passim.

proposals back to Crema.[18] On the strength of this mission, he had been rewarded in April 1454 with some property near Crema.[19] Some suspicion about his conduct had arisen, however, for although he was again elected as a deputy to the podesta in June 1454,[20] the Council of One Hundred voted to revoke his property donation the following November, on the grounds that he had negotiated beyond his commission and to his own profit.[21] This may cast another shadow on Beltramino's integrity. Pantaleone Cusadri had died in October,[22] and Beltramino continued to play a prominent part in the affairs of Crema during the next two or three years; he was an "adiuncto" (substitute) in the Council of One Hundred from July to November 1455,[23] an orator to Venice in October and December 1455, one of the ten deputies to the podesta for most of 1456, a member of the Council of One Hundred up to December 1456, and again (as "adiuncto") one of the deputies to the podesta in February 1457.[24]

What brought Beltramino to Mantua? Some autobiographical verses written in the early 1530s by his son Geremia, whose own date of birth was 1453 (so it can be inferred that Beltramino was married by then) records that as a boy Geremia had seen Pope Pius II.[25] In other words, his father was in Mantua at the time of the papal Diet in 1459: Pius II arrived at Mantua on 27 May of that year.[26] This may be the truth but not the whole truth, for it transpires from a Mantuan decree of 1461[27] that already in 1458 Beltramino had received a judicial appointment in Mantua, to act as the podesta's vicar or senior assistant judge in civil cases "at the Bench of the Eagle" *(ad banchum aquilae).*[28] He presumably owed

---

18. BCCr, Archivio storico II, reg. 2, fols. 35r–36r; Terno, *Historia,* 215.

19. Ibid., fol. 48r; see Archivio di Stato, Venice, Senato, Terra, reg. 3, fols. 112r–117v, for a record of agreements on various matters with ambassadors from Crema on 13 May 1454.

20. BCCr, Archivio storico II, reg. 2, fol. 49r.

21. Ibid., fols. 73r, 80r.

22. Pantaleone was replaced as a deputy on account of his death, on 19 October: ibid. fol. 67.

23. Ibid., fols. 105r, 109r, 115r–116r, 119r, 122v, 127v.

24. Ibid., fols. 123r–v, 130r, 143r–144v, 148v, 150v, 155r, 162r, 167v, 177r.

25. BCFe, MS Cl. II, 357, "Hieremie Cusatri cremensis seu mantuani carmina" (cf. *DBI,* ` ad vocem*), fol. 26: "Mantua cum tua sunt primum mihi moenia visa / Vidi pontificis tunc puer ora Pii / Hic didici lingue tum prima elementa latine . . ."

26. G.B. Picotti, *La dieta di Mantova e la politica de' veneziani* (Venice, 1912), 111.

27. AG, Lib. decr. 19, fol. 195r (28 Mar. 1461).

28. On this court see Vaini, "Gli statuti di Francesco Gonzaga," 199; BCMn, MS 775, lib. 1, cap. 6. For evidence of Beltramino's collaboration with Maggi, see chap. 2 nn. 19, 84, 86.

his nomination for this job to the serving podesta in Mantua, Bernardo Maggi of Brescia, who (as we have seen) even delegated to Beltramino the writing of some letters in his own name. Maggi might have heard about his ability from the Venetian authorities in Crema or Brescia, though Marquis Ludovico Gonzaga might also have come across Beltramino in the course of negotiations during or after the Milanese War or might have been told about him by one of his legal experts, such as Stefano Zampi.[29] As the podesta's vicar, Beltramino served in Mantua with merit in 1458, according to the decree already mentioned. His year's term of service may have just overlapped with the beginnings of the papal Diet, bearing out Geremia's recollection, or (if it had expired) he might have either stayed on for a few months or returned to Mantua in the hope of new opportunities.

By July 1459 Beltramino was back in Crema, and he served for the rest of the year as a member of the Council of One Hundred in place of his brother Guido.[30] At the end of December he was elected in his own right as member of the Council of One Hundred, to serve in 1460;[31] on 1 January 1460 he was also appointed as consul of the merchants,[32] and in February he was appointed as deputy to the podesta, again substituting Guido.[33] Beltramino was a deputy (in his own right) from June until October and is also recorded in the Council of One Hundred;[34] he was still a member of the One Hundred in January 1461.[35] But the Mantuan decree, previously mentioned, had laid down on 28 March 1461 that, provided the statutory interval of two years had elapsed, he should be readmitted to his previous post, to serve now as vicar to the podesta Raynerio Almerici of Pesaro. This means that Beltramino returned to spend another year in Mantua, although he was given permission to go to Crema for two weeks in July 1461.[36] He was evidently back in Crema

---

29. Zampi, who had been involved in the prosecuting, and maybe the absolving, of Beltramino in 1444 (see n. 9), in April 1460 escorted protonotary Francesco Gonzaga, Ludovico's second son, to Pavia (D.S. Chambers, *A Renaissance Cardinal and His Worldly Goods* (London, 1992), 50–51 n. 6). The chronicler Andrea Schivenoglia noted him as "Stevano zudexe di Zampi: el padre de questi vene da Cremona" (BCMn, MS 1019, fol. 2r).

30. BCCr, Archivio storico II, reg. 3, fols. 80v, 82r, 83r, 86v, 87v, 92r, 94v.

31. Ibid., fols. 98v, 99r.

32. Ibid., fols. 100r–v.

33. Ibid., fols. 103r, 106r.

34. Ibid., fols. 117r–132v passim.

35. Ibid., fol. 137v.

36. AG, Lib. decr. 14, fol. 222v.

by July 1462, when he was among the three ambassadors, "aves et nobiles Cremae," appointed to congratulate Cristoforo Moro upon his election as Doge of Venice;[37] this embassy set off on 13 August.[38] On 29 August 1462 Beltramino's wife—her name has not emerged from this or later references—was given permission to transport a bed from Mantua to Crema,[39] though it seems that her ambitious husband did not intend to stay long in his native city, for on 21 September he was agitating for reimbursement of the expenses of his recent Venetian trip because he was about to leave for "distant southern parts where he would remain for a good while."[40] The authorities in Crema were still deliberating four months later whether to pay him what he claimed.[41] Whether he did travel south to some unknown destination in the winter of 1463–64— perhaps he had been offered a short-term judicial appointment in the kingdom of Naples or the papal state—is unknown.

However, Beltramino's credit with Marquis Ludovico Gonzaga was such that it was not long before he held another post in Mantua, this time as judge of appeals and fiscal matters *(iudex appellationum et datiorum)*, an office that, as previously mentioned, was independent of the podesta. It is from this time that the earliest examples of his letters to Marquis Ludovico Gonzaga survive, written in tightly upright, scrupulously tidy and exact handwriting—an example of it is provided in plate 1—that itself speaks volumes about his character. The earliest letter, containing also the first evidence of his appointment, is dated 28 June 1463; Beltramino wrote from Venice, where he had gone to defend a claim of his own, appealing against the government's confiscation of some property, presumably the same property near Crema that he had been granted in 1454 and then deprived of.[42] He asked for leave to stay longer, even if it meant he would be too late to take up his appointment in Mantua on the right day in August and could only begin in September. Incidentally, he complained about the expenditure of time and honor that the procedures of Venetian justice entailed; this anticipated some critical reflections about Venice that he was to make on a visit in July 1477.[43]

---

37. BCCr, Archivio storico II, reg. 4, fol. 4v (11 July 1462).

38. Ibid., fols. 10v–11r.

39. AG, Lib. decr. 15, fol. 63r.

40. "ad partes longinquas meridionales ibi moraturus bono spatio": BCCr, Archivio storico II, reg. 4, fol. 12r.

41. Ibid., fols. 26r–v (31 Dec. 1462, 5 Jan. 1463).

42. AG, b. 1431bis, fol. 521.

43. See chap. 4.

Equally characteristic was the way in which Beltramino lost no time in drawing attention to his own diligence and concern for what was legally correct. In January 1464 it emerges from a letter he wrote to the marquis from the parish of San Silvestro in Curtatone, a village to the west of Mantua, that he was based there on account of the plague scare and quarantine regulations.[44] He pointed out that as this place was so near the city and the marquis's residence of Belgioioso, he could have easy access and carry on with his judicial duties. However, unfortunately there had been a few deaths from plague at Curtatone, so it too was under a strict cordon and all movement of persons was forbidden. He needed to review the appeals of some convicted persons held in prison in Mantua and also to pursue cases against suspected evaders of customs duty, fraudsters, and unauthorized bird catchers. He asked if the marquis would like him to come to the city for a few hours on two days of the week. Beltramino strikes precisely that note of professional zeal combined with deference that may help to account for his success in building up a confidential relationship with Ludovico. He evidently was allowed into Mantua, because a week later he wrote from there asking Ludovico's advice whether he should consent to the postponement of a hearing for three or four days (on grounds of bad weather) in a dispute between the inhabitants of Rodigo and the marquis's vicar there, Giacomo dei Balestrieri,[45] to which the marquis replied with an emphatic negative.[46] Still at Curtatone in March, Beltramino wrote in an even more meticulous vein, asking for clarification on a point of law. The *capitano del divieto* had accused some persons of illegally driving cattle and sheep between one vicariate and another. Beltramino was unsure whether the *capitano* was in the right; he could not find a clear ruling either in the statutes or in recent proclamations and ordinances, nor could the *maestro dell'entrate* or other experts enlighten him.[47] The point seems to have turned on the drovers' purpose and the age of the livestock; unlicensed transport to different pastures was an offense, but taking four year olds to slaughter and salting was not.[48] Beltramino wrote again that

44. AG, b. 2402 (filed under Curtatone, but dated "in burgo turrium Sancti Silvestri die 20 januarii 1464" and signed "servus Beltraminus de Crema, Iudex apellationum et datiorum Mantue").
45. AG, b. 2401 (Mantua, 26 Jan. 1464).
46. AG, b. 2899, lib. 50, fols. 31v, 34r (Goito, 27 and 29 Jan. 1464).
47. AG, b. 2402 (Curtatone), Beltramino to Marquis L. Gonzaga, San Silvestro (16 Mar. 1464).
48. AG, b. 2887, lib. 43, fol. 92r, Marquis L. Gonzaga to Beltramino (17 Mar. 1464).

he was still uncertain about the penalties; he enclosed the text of the proclamation, but he had also been shown some letters on the subject from the marquis. The accused were getting restive, he noted, but he would take his time and come to see Ludovico in person.[49] Perhaps it was a token of the marquis's confidence in him that Beltramino was given leave to visit Crema in June, during which time any cases pending were to be suspended until his return;[50] this was repeated in August 1464, but by then Beltramino was described as the former judge of appeals,[51] so his term of office must have expired.

Evidently Beltramino continued to practice in Mantua as an advocate or a legal consultant and made himself readily available to the marquis for any miscellaneous services required of him. The confidence he had inspired is shown by his employment on special missions in the spring of 1465 to find out what he could about the plans of Bartolomeo Colleoni, the famous *condottiere* from Bergamo who was captain-general of the Venetian army. Colleoni wrote from his castle at Malpaga, agreeing to meet Beltramino in Brescia, and Beltramino went there more than once, reporting back to the marquis.[52] The business was highly secret, and Beltramino's own letters are very cryptic. It is not always clear where he was writing from, though it would seem that a letter of 10 April was from Crema; "I had better not stay here or I shall be too far away," he wrote, mentioning that a character he calls "the friend" *[l'amico]* had gone to Brescia.[53] A letter of 20 April was certainly dated from Crema.[54] This enigmatic correspondence continues into May.[55] Among the matters in hand was an appointment to an ecclesiastical benefice, because Beltramino wrote on 23 April that he had yet to speak to a certain prior and remarked—perhaps with a twist of irony, but perhaps out of sheer earnest piety—"God governs in ecclesiastical matters, and when he

49. AG, b. 2402 (Curtatone), Beltramino to Marquis L. Gonzaga, San Silvestro (21 Mar. 1464).

50. AG, Lib. decr. 15, fol. 210v (9 June 1464).

51. "olim iudex datiorum et appellationum": ibid., fol. 223v (2 Aug. 1464).

52. AG, b. 1599, B. Colleoni to Beltramino (9, 19, and 24 Apr. 1465).

53. AG, b. 1431bis, fol. 538 (Beltramino left a blank space for the provenance of the letter; a late-nineteenth-century archivist wrote "Crema" at the top).

54. Ibid., fol. 585.

55. In a letter of 5 May, Beltramino reported news he had heard from Venice and Malpaga; there is a letter from Colleoni to Beltramino dated at Malpaga on 4 May 1465, and there are further letters from Beltramino to Ludovico dated at Brescia on 8, 10, and 11 May 1465: AG, b. 1599.

thinks the time is right he will inspire the pope to order the prior to confer the benefice."[56] One of the most interesting points to emerge is that Beltramino declared that he did not intend to claim his expenses, so dedicated to the marquis did he profess to be.[57] He had learned a lesson, perhaps, from the way his claims for ambassadorial expenses had been ill received in the past by the authorities of Crema. Meanwhile, Beltramino's legal practice evidently continued to flourish; in order to revisit Crema in the autumn of 1465, he again secured a decree that no cases in which he was involved as advocate, judge, or consultant should be heard in Mantua during his absence.[58]

In the summer of 1466 Beltramino appears from the records to have been acting in tandem with none other than Stefano Zampi, the senior Mantuan jurist who knew that Beltramino had been indicted for homicide when he was a student at Pavia. They were going together to hear a case at Canneto and were excused any legal duties in Mantua.[59] In August it was again decreed that while Beltramino was away in Crema, any legal cases in which he was involved should be suspended.[60]

The handful of letters from Beltramino already quoted are enough to indicate what made him so indispensable to the Gonzaga regime. Professionally qualified and able, he nevertheless was prompt to show deference to the word of the signore in judicial matters, and the reward he sought was low.[61] In less than ten years he had built for himself in Mantua a remarkable prominence as a nonnative career lawyer. Even his relatives helped him by making themselves useful. His physician brother, Giovanni, had come to treat the marquis's wife, Barbara of Brandenburg, in 1463[62] and wrote to the marquis in November 1466, sending some medicine and information that had come to his ears in Vicenza about

---

56. ". . . non posso altramente saper la caxone salvo che le cosse ecclesiastice Dio li governa, e quando a lui parerà inspirarà lo papa che comandi a lo priore che conferisca il beneficio": AG, b. 1431bis, fol. 539.

57. ". . . più caro mi serà l'accepti il mio bon servir e lo spendere ch'io fazo, perché ad ogni modo spendo quello de soa Signoria quando spendo dal mio": AG, b. 2404, Beltramino to Marsilio Andreasi, no provenance given, but perhaps from Crema (1 May 1465).

58. AG, Lib. decr. 15, fol. 336v (28 Sept. 1465).

59. Ibid., 16, fol. 57r: this leave was extended for twenty days from 27 July (ibid., fol. 61v). Zampi continued to be an active legal practitioner in Mantua during Beltramino's heyday; other short absences were granted him in November 1468 (AG, Lib. decr. 16, fol. 245r) and February 1469 (AG, Lib. decr. 17, fol. 8v).

60. AG, Lib. decr. 16, fol. 64v (18 Aug. backdated to 9 Aug. 1466).

61. See nn. 57, 66, also chap. 4, chap. 6, and epilogue.

62. D'Arco, *Studi*, 6:73.

Florentine political troubles.[63] Giovanni treated both the marquis and his daughter Dorotea in 1467.[64] Meanwhile Guido, another of the Cusadri brothers, had married a Mantuan noblewoman of the Cavriani family, who provided him with a house in the parish of San Silvestro, perhaps the same house at Curtatone to which Beltramino had evacuated himself during the winter of 1463–64.[65]

The decisive point in Beltramino's career came at the end of 1466, when Marquis Ludovico Gonzaga nominated him to the highest magistracy in Mantua on extraordinary terms: on 24 December he was appointed to serve as vice-podesta beginning on 1 January 1467 with a salary of 200 lire per month.[66] This was a return to Gianfrancesco Gonzaga's practice, which—as was mentioned at the beginning of the previous chapter—seems to have been abandoned under pressure in the early 1430s, as an abuse that contravened the statutes. After his accession as marquis, in December 1444 Ludovico had confirmed that he would appoint a podesta (*ad pristinum vocabulum*) not a vice-podesta, with a salary of 2415 lire for his six-month term. Since then the office of vice-podesta had come to mean just a temporary replacement or deputy for an incapacitated or absent podesta, a locum tenens like Niccolò Chieregati, who had stood in for his cousin the podesta Chieregino Chieregati in 1465.[67] Now it again meant a full and regular substitution for the office itself. Beltramino was charged with virtually all the podesta's same duties and staff (two knights, a constable with fifteen *famulos*, two domestic servants, and a page), but for half the salary and without a *vicarius* or deputy judge. Although he was appointed to serve from 1 January 1467 for an initial term of six months, his term would be renewed not only once (as prescribed for the podesta) but five times, so that in the end he served for three consecutive years without interruption.

---

63. AG, b. 1431bis, fol. 640.

64. AG, b. 2406, G. Cusadri to Barbara of Brandenburg, Goito, 10 Oct. 1467.

65. "Messer Beltramin, Guy di Achasadry [sic] fradely da Crema. Questo messer Beltramin sie vice podestado, e Guy tolse una dona di Chapriany, che ge ha dato una chaxa da San Silvestro e una posissione a Goida [Goito?]. Questi viveno de questo a Mantua": BCMn, MS 1019, fol. 5v.

66. AG, Lib. pat. 2, fol. 14v, quoted in R. Signorini, *"Opus hoc tenue": La Camera dipinta di Andrea Mantegna* (Mantua, 1985), 297 n. 447.

67. Ludovico's affirmation of December 1444 is in AG, Lib. pat., 2, fol. 2r; for the temporary vice-podesta see the letter signed "N. Chieregatus vincentinus eques et doctor Mantueque eiusque marchionatus vicepotestas," to Niccolò d'Este, Mantua, 6 July 1465: AG, b. 2401. Since 26 May he had deputized for Chieregino, who had had to go to the Roman curia.

What was the purpose of such a measure on the part of Ludovico Gonzaga, that paragon among Italian princes, who had been educated in classical literature and moral values in the famous school of Vittorino da Feltre? Ludovico certainly had a virtuous conscience and a sense of the prince's paramount duty to dispense justice. His explanation in the first decree appointing Beltramino is that he wanted Mantua to be governed healthily ("salubriter") and by the wisest men available. His lawful right to overturn fundamental statutes concerning the podestaship derived from his plenitude of power as an imperial vicar and captain of the city. As an example of this, he often suspended or replaced miscellaneous laws by means of proclamations, but such lesser tinkering was a recognized feature of executive power, common under republican as well as signorial regimes. The reintroduction of the vice-podesta was something more. Yet it would be too simple to see the abolition of the podesta as part of a long-term scheme to extend autocracy, going back to a program of government that Ludovico's father had followed but then modified; equally, it does not make much sense as an expression of Ludovico's would-be imperial vision of himself as a new Trajan.[68] Ludovico probably did not think in such terms at all, though some of these elements might figure in his overall view of the Mantuan scene, if he felt, as he professed to do, moral concern about the weaknesses of the administration in detecting and punishing criminals and offenders against public order and decency. Perhaps it was part of the same paternalistic concern that, at much the same time, was prompting him to intervene in ecclesiastical appointments and building programs and to preside over the amalgamation of the city's guilds and hospitals and the introduction of other urban improvements.

If Ludovico saw himself at the end of 1466 as acting only as befitted a virtuous prince—in the defense of life, property, and morals—it is clear he meant to keep a tight hold on the judiciary by appointing Beltramino as vice-podesta. He could rely on Beltramino for rigor and rectitude, as well as for compliance or even—in the last resort—subservience. In other words, the marquis could place more confidence in him than he could in an unknown and unpredictable podesta from some distant place. Indeed, even though Beltramino's provenance from Crema was explicitly professed and universally known, by the winter of 1466 he had been resident in Mantua for most of over eight years: thus he could hardly have

68. See G. Mulazzani, "La fonte letteraria della 'Camera degli Sposi' di Mantegna," *Arte lombarda*, n.s., 50 (1978): 33–46.

appeared eligible for the more prestigious title of podesta, which required its holder to be a foreigner. By appointing him vice-podesta Ludovico deftly maneuvered his own man and confidential servant into the presidency of Mantuan justice. There was no attempt, however, to conceal the fact that the appointment was justified not only on Beltramino's record of integrity in office previously but on the *arbitrium* and *plenitudo potestatis* of the marquis. These points were also stressed in the successive renewals for consecutive six-month terms. For the fourth term, authorized in the summer of 1468, Beltramino was even praised for his moderation;[69] for the fifth term, dated 3 January 1469, Beltramino's "singular integrity and most diligent care" were specially emphasized;[70] and on 1 July 1469, for the sixth (and final) term, it was laid down that "the prince's duty is to adorn the city with such outstanding men."[71]

Some years later, in 1477, the marquis explained his motive rather differently, claiming that his appointment of Beltramino had been one of mere convenience in order to circumvent the clamor of outside recommendations and applications for the job of podesta.[72] He now admitted that from this point of view the experiment had failed, since advance bookings for the vice-podesta's office were equally high, extending nine years ahead to 1486. (Incidentally, none of the vice-podestas who followed Beltramino from 1470 onward were extended for more than one extra six-month term.)

However, Ludovico's explanation seems a bit disingenuous or at least economical with the truth. The new office of the vice-podesta had not been seen in such an innocent light in Beltramino's day. Schivenoglia wrote that "it deprived Mantua of some of its honor," that part of the marquis's purpose was to cut costs, to reduce the chief magistrate's entourage and their salaries; moreover, he added significantly that Ludovico's nominee, Beltramino, was a "tyrannical man."[73] Much more

---

69. See AG, Lib. pat. 2, fols. 15r and 15v for letters of reappointment dated 1 July 1467 (the December 1467 renewal is missing) and 7 July 1468.

70. Ibid., fol. 16r.

71. Ibid.

72. Commenting on Girolamo Riario and Gianfrancesco Gonzaga's recommendation of one Ludovico Paulucio to be vice-podesta, the marquis wrote: "come sapeti nui mutassemo quello officio de potestaria in vicepotestaria solamente per tante richieste ce ne erano facte et per le molte promesse ce era stato necessario farne, ma hora siamo a questo medesmo de la vice-potestaria, la qual se trova promessa per tuto lo anno 1486": AG, b. 2103, Marquis L. Gonzaga to Barbara of Brandenburg, Milan, 5 Mar. 1477.

73. "Recordanza che de l'anno 1467 fo tolto via uno pocho de honore che avia la città de Mantoa. Mantoa avìa podestà com vicharii e zudexi; destà, el qualo avìa nome messer

to Schivenoglia's taste, evidently, was the last podesta, Gianfrancesco Soardi, that courtly Bergamask nobleman and part-time poet, an obvious contrast to the professional lawyer and careerist Beltramino Cusadri.[74]

The chronicler was right about the financial motive. Ludovico was insolvent in the mid-1460s and needed to raise credit and new sources of revenue wherever he could. A stronger and more controlled judicial administration might be expected to bring in more income from fines and confiscations. Moreover, not only was there a huge saving on the salary, but the running costs of the office would be appreciably lower, at least while Beltramino held it (to begin with, there would be no traveling expenses from some distant city).

Writing on 6 February 1467,[75] after a month in office, Beltramino expressed to Ludovico his sense of the honor paid to him and assured the marquis of his unfaltering commitment to perfection in all things. As an example of this, he mentioned that he had been checking the qualifications of his assistant judge in criminal cases (giudice del maleficio) and had found that he claimed to have a doctorate of law from Parma, which was not one of the universities approved for the purpose in the Mantuan statutes.[76] This man claimed that he had received a special dispensation from Marquis Ludovico, but Beltramino declared that personally he did not regard such an exception as valid. He added that he could easily find a substitute judge within four days, though he would of course defer to the marquis if he felt strongly about the matter. Ludovico replied the next day that he was very grateful to Beltramino for pointing out the disqualification and that he too always wanted to adhere to the correct rules; in fact Beltramino may have been wrong on this point of law, as this statutory rule applied to the first assistant judge or *vicarius*, whose office had been suppressed.[77] Evidently Beltramino had resolved to lose no time as a new broom. And it seems more than a coincidence that

---

Beltramino da Crema ed era homo tiranno e si avìa asay asay manche provixione che non avìa i potestati passaty et cetera": BCMn, MS 1019, fol. 49r, quoted in Signorini, *"Opus hoc tenue,"* 297 n. 447.

74. About Soardi, Schivenoglia wrote, "luy foe el derdano [= ultimo] podestà de Mantoa sino a qui, ma luy hè piaxevolle con la bella spoxa e cortexe . . .": BCMn, MS 1019, fol. 55v. On the importance of the podesta's wife, see chap. 1.

75. AG, b. 2405, fol. 506. For the text, see app. 1.

76. The approved universities were those of Bologna, Padua, Pavia, Perugia, Montpellier, Orleans, and Toulouse: BCMn, MS 775, lib. I, cap. 6 (fols. 7v–8r).

77. "et piacene el parere vostro perché anche nuy volemo che li ordini et statuti nostri se servino": AG, b. 2890, lib. 59, fol. 10r. The statutes are specific about the academic qualifications of the *vicarius*, but not of the *iudex malleficiorum* (BCMn, MS 775, caps. VI,

within his first week in office a proclamation drastically tightened the penalties for the familiar offenses against public order of singing in the streets *tortelli o matinate*—lewd songs usually in mockery of elderly or unmarried couples cohabiting—or going out after the third bell without a torch or in disguise. "This city," it was rehearsed, "used to be in such a [peaceful] state that one never heard the slightest suggestion of such scandals: now nowhere is safe, neither churches, the [prince's] court, nor any other place." Offenders, regardless of social rank, would henceforth incur the huge fine of one thousand ducats, would suffer confiscation of all their property if they could not raise this sum, or else would be hanged on the beam at the Porta di Guardia, with no excuses allowed in mitigation.[78] Beltramino had tried to force the pace in his first month, but he was permitted to take a week's absence from 11 February 1467 because he had been rather unwell.[79]

Although no extant register survives of the cases tried in the vice-podesta's court during Beltramino's tenure, evidence can be brought together from correspondence, official decrees, and proclamations, all of which seem to point to a rigorous tightening-up on law and order, a partnership in severity between himself and the marquis. In June 1467 the vicar of Redondesco was exhorted to do everything possible in a murder hunt; he was told that it was necessary to fight against murderers and assassins everywhere, to cleanse and make safe the country ("netegiare e segurare el paese nostro").[80] In the same spirit, on 3 September 1467 much more severe penalties were announced for publicly molesting Jews.[81] In August 1467 Beltramino wrote twice to Ludovico about what may seem a rather more petty matter, a theft of pears from Guidone da Bagno's orchard at Revere: but the da Bagno were a noble family and this fact was probably what counted most. Only two of the three pear stealers had been caught, and one had taken sanctuary in the church at Sustinente and then escaped into Veronese territory. Beltramino had had the

---

XVIII, fols. 7v–8r, 11v). Moreover, the Marquis' letter of appointment to Beltramino had only required "unum bonum et expertum iudicem legum doctorem vel saltem licentiatum ad malificia et unum alium iudicem" (AG, Lib. pat. 2, fol. 14v).

78. ". . . questa sua citade soleva essere in tale consuetudine che mai non se senteva una minimo di questi scandali . . . adesso non è securo giesie, la corte sua, ni niuno altro loco": AG, Gride, fasc. 6, fol. 3v (5 Jan. 1467). A proclamation of 5 August 1469 confirmed these penalties: ibid., fol. 5v.

79. "stetit et fuit aliquantulum infirmus": AG, Lib. decr. 16, fol. 123v.

80. AG, b. 2890, lib. 59, fol. 49r.

81. AG, Gride, fasc. 5, fol. 4r.

unsuccessful pursuers arrested as well as the less fortunate culprits; two of the trio turned out to be soldiers in the service of Ludovico's son-in-law Francesco Secco, and the third was a cobbler from Revere. As the value of the stolen pears did not reach the minimum prescribed by the statutes to incur a serious penalty, Beltramino proposed doubling their estimated value.[82] It is clear that Beltramino wanted the threats to petty thieves and those who walked about at night without lights or in disguise to be strictly enforced. On 29 September of the same year he reported that the night patrol squad of his knight (*lo cavalero con la famiglia*) had arrested two suspect youths, unarmed but wearing unfamiliar livery, with their tunics inside out. They claimed just to be on the lookout for women to pick up ("diconno esser andati li per femine"), but Beltramino asked the marquis for his opinion in this case.[83]

An even more ruthless campaign against theft and willful damage to property was launched in 1468, probably with the added purpose of enforcing order at a time when plague quarantine regulations were in force; the marquis's government moved right out of Mantua from April to September of that year.[84] Lawlessness in the countryside was stressed in the reports of local officials; the vicar of Luzzara complained in May about the excessive number of *giotti*,[85] and the vicar of Roverbella likewise deplored the spate of robberies and cover-ups.[86] Even so, local officials may sometimes have been to blame, because of their wariness of policing initiatives by central authority: Villichino, the *deputato al divieto* had complained from Luzzara in February 1468 that he was prevented from carrying out the vice-podesta's orders to make an arrest in the territory of Gonzaga because the vicar would not provide him with a posse of six or eight men for the purpose unless he gave details.[87] One central enactment meant to reduce the common offense of stealing wood was to impose heavy monetary penalties on those who stole and cut it. A letter from the marquis to the vicar of Quistello on 14 June 1468 acknowledged receipt of a ducat's fine from one offender,[88] but by Octo-

---

82. AG, b. 2405, fol. 508, Beltramino to Marquis L. Gonzaga, Mantua (10 Aug. 1467), signed "servus fidelissimus Beltraminus de Crema vice-potestas Mantue"; and fol. 509 (25 Aug. 1467). For the text of the latter, see app. 1.

83. Ibid., fol. 510.

84. For a note recording this, see AG, b. 2890, lib. 59, fol. 84r.

85. AG, b. 2408, letter of 16 May 1468.

86. Ibid., letter of 27 June 1468.

87. Ibid., letter of 16 Feb. 1468.

88. AG, b. 2890, lib. 60, fols. 67r, 71r.

ber the penalty was four ducats for every log.[89] Meanwhile, a proclamation of 16 July 1468 had prescribed draconian penalties for theft, on the grounds of the frequency and increase of this crime.[90] Stealing any item worth more than a pair of shoes valued at thirteen soldi was henceforth to be punished by hanging. There was a special tariff of severe punishment for robbers of vineyards and orchards. Every stolen bunch of grapes or head of corn ("uno grapo," "uno covo de formento") would earn a hoist and drop on the rope; if thieves operated in a gang of ten or more, each member of the gang would be hanged. There is direct evidence that Beltramino was concerned about the drafting of this proclamation. He wrote on 10 July to the marquis that he had seen the first version and written some additional clauses, to take into account a recent case, to make clear that the same penalties should apply to those who stole from vines after the grape harvesting had begun, and to reward informers with half of the fine collected (unless they were fellow culprits, in which case they would not be absolved but would get a lighter penalty).[91] The swingeing new penalties for what may seem rather petty crimes were no doubt a boon to irascible urban proprietors or those with a grudge against their neighbors; the most famous example in Mantua was the court painter Andrea Mantegna, who on 27 July 1468 denounced the gardener in charge of the property *(logeta)* next to his house, just outside one of the western gates to the city;[92] this complaint was drawn to Beltramino's attention by the marquis.[93]

The *grida* against theft and damage in gardens and orchards was proclaimed throughout the *dominio;* instructions to vicars and podestas even included a macabre order to have a gallows and rope hoist erected in each locality, to frighten the population into obedience. This is apparent from the letters written by officials to express compliance. Thus the podesta of Ostiglia wrote on 17 July that he was already taking action

89. Ibid., lib. 59, fol. 86r, letter to the vicar of Quistello (7 Oct. 1468).

90. "la frequentia de furti che ogni zorno ze cometteno . . .": AG, Gride, fasc.6, fol. 4v.

91. The marquis wrote on 8 July authorizing Beltramino to draw up the *grida* as instructed (AG, b. 2890, lib. 61, fol. 3v); Beltramino wrote from Borgoforte, "ho fatto una aditione ad essa crida" (AG, b. 2407). In a letter of 11 July, Ludovico thanked Beltramino enthusiastically for the additional clause permitting the accuser to claim half the fine: AG, b. 2890, lib. 61, fol. 6r.

92. Mantegna's letter appears in P. Kristeller, *Andrea Mantegna* (Berlin, 1902), dok. 40, 525–26.

93. AG, 2890, lib. 61, fols. 23v and 24r, letters of 1 Aug. to Mantegna and to Beltramino.

and having a gallows and rope hoist set up;[94] on 19 July Marsilio Gatego told the marquis that he had convoked everyone in his vicariate of Belforte, everyone who cared about *ben vivere,* and announced the measures to suppress these frequent thefts and destruction, and he promised to have the required equipment made; the vicar of Governolo also promised to set up a gallows.[95] On 20 July the vicars of Bigarello, Ceresara, and Castelluchio gave similar assurances;[96] so did the vicars of Reggiolo and Revere.[97] The vicar of Quistello, Bartolomeo Montaldo, wrote on 21 July that he was ordering the proclamation to be made in public places and from house to house; a gallows would be set up on the highest ground in front of the castle, and a rope hoist would be prepared.[98] On the same day, the vicars of Bozzolo, Marcaria, and Sabbioneta wrote in similar terms.[99] It seems clear that Beltramino and the marquis were determined at this point to cow the countryside, even if it seems unlikely that capital punishment could have been carried out on a large scale throughout the *dominio* when there was normally only one executioner, based in Mantua. In practice the vicar of Quistello was rather diffident when faced by night raids on pear trees and by armed prowlers, and in a letter of 3 August he asked for advice.[100] On the next day, the marquis bluntly replied that if, as he said, he did not understand these judicial matters, he should refer himself to the vice-podesta (i.e., Beltramino) or just send to the latter under guard any man arrested with a weapon on his person.[101] But other rural magistrates professed to be all set, at least to get their rope hoists working; Malatesta da Gonzaga, the vicar of Marcaria, wrote on 5 September 1468 that one Zampetro who had picked and eaten a bunch of grapes would certainly have been given two jerks had he not managed to escape.[102]

Whether the stronger impetus came from Marquis Ludovico or from Beltramino is hard to say. Unfortunately we do not always have both

---

94. AG, b. 2408.

95. Ibid.

96. Ibid.; Bertolotti, *Prigioni e prigionieri,* 18, prints the letter of Malatesta da Fano, vicar of Castelluchio, 20 July 1468: "ho fatto una cidella cum la corda et stringa et per poter dar di squassi a quelli che contrafarà dicta crida."

97. AG, b. 2409, fols. 84, 129.

98. "parechiare la corda cum la stringa e la cidella per squassare li malfatori": AG, b. 2409, fol. 47.

99. AG, b. 2408; b. 2409, fol. 245.

100. AG, b. 2409, fol. 48.

101. AG, b. 2890, lib. 61, fol. 27v.

102. AG, b. 2408.

sides of the correspondence between them in particular cases, and many affairs may have been settled by word of mouth. On the one hand, it appears that if Ludovico often did defer to Beltramino's opinion, he cherished the idea that judgment was ultimately reserved to himself. On the other hand, Beltramino was no stooge or puppet; even if he addressed himself to the marquis in deferential tones, he laid down his own opinion forcefully at the same time as he asked for Ludovico's. It is sometimes difficult to tell which of them was more successful in manipulating the mind of the other.

The case of one Raimondo, "servant of Cornatello" (his alleged crime is uncertain), illustrates the tension that prevailed. Beltramino could detect no guilt in this man and reported he would have had him released had he not been imprisoned by command of the marquis. Ludovico did not care for this imputation and wrote to the vice-podesta on 17 September 1467, "it is not our intention that anyone should receive injustice; make your inquiries, tell us whether he should be condemned or absolved, and having heard your opinion we will tell you what we wish."[103]

As in the case of Raimondo, often it was Ludovico himself who issued the order to apprehend some suspected malefactor and who showed impatience with judicial norms and the restraints on summary proceedings. He could also insist that no favor be shown. When a member of his household was charged for punching a Jew in the face in the presence of an official, Ludovico ordered Beltramino to render justice indifferently.[104] In another case, about which he wrote on 3 July 1469, he reproached Beltramino for being too lenient;[105] the case concerned a young man arrested for taking part in a fray, and a defense under statute law had been allowed rather than punishment in accordance with recent proclamations.

Sometimes the marquis seems to have relaxed his punitive vigilance

---

103. ". . . non esser nostra intentione che iniusticia se faza ad alcuno . . . vogliamo ne advisati come sta il facto suo, et se in esso è culpa alcuna o non, et s'el vi pare deba essere dampnato o absolto; ne faremo adviso de quello voremo": AG, b. 2890, lib. 58, fol. 16v.

104. ". . . la intentione nostra è che vui faciati rasone senza guardar in fronte a persona. Del acto usato per Ludovico da Gonzaga in dar del pugno suxo el volto al zudeo da Marcharia, et in presentia del officiale nostro, vogliamo che senza havere rispecto che esso Ludovico sia de la casa nostra vui procedate in questa facenda e faciati rasone": AG, b. 2891, lib. 63, fol. 11, Marquis L. Gonzaga to Beltramino (25 Oct. 1468).

105. "ve ne siate passato molto lezermente": AG, b. 2891, lib. 63, fol. 45v (3 July 1469).

with a degree of clemency. He occasionally allowed a composition for money; for instance he let off a rapist, who had subsequently married his victim, provided that he paid a fine of twenty-five ducats.[106] Sometimes he gave way to personal intercession. In September 1467, for instance, he ordered that a suspected thief should be released, but only to please his pious daughter Susanna, who had interceded.[107] During Beltramino's tenure as vice-podesta, as in the past, there were instances of very long-standing sentences being overturned; for instance, on 23 March 1469 Paolo Questario of Saviola was absolved of the sentence of hanging imposed in 1460 for stealing twenty-four *braccie* of fabric.[108] But there were also a number of cases in Beltramino's own period as vice-podesta when accused persons he or his assistant judges had found guilty and sentenced were absolved by Ludovico's special acts of grace. Some of the sentences lifted were for minor civil offenses like verbal abuse, but others were more serious. For instance, on 14 January 1468 the marquis set aside a fine of two hundred lire imposed by the vice-podesta's court on 28 November 1467 on "Maffeo," a tapestry maker of Mantua, for assaulting the nobleman Federico Gonzaga (presumably Ludovico's eldest son and heir) by hitting him on the head with a stone, drawing blood.[109] In January 1469 he absolved Domenico Gratia of Bigarello from having an ear cut off (the sentence of the court the previous November) even if he failed to pay fifteen lire for stealing a bedcover and a pair of sheets.[110] But the marquis was more concerned for retribution or else cash profit a few months later, when he wrote to the podesta of Canneto about the fate of a thief: "If you let him off with no punishment, it will be a temptation to steal again. We would be more pleased to see him hanged than to let him go. Still, if he pays a fine of a hundred ducats and compensation for the thefts, we will allow him our grace." Ludovico added even more cynically that if the man did not have this money (as was most probably the case), perhaps others at Canneto would be moved by compassion to make the payment on his behalf.[111]

Perhaps as Beltramino's term as vice-podesta approached its end, the marquis felt it would be wise to distance himself slightly. Surprisingly, on

---

106. AG, b. 2890, lib. 59, fol. 64r, letter to Giacomo da Palazzo (11 Aug. 1467).
107. AG, b. 2890, fol. 6v.
108. AG, Lib. decr. 17, fol. 25r.
109. Ibid., Lib. decr. 16, fol. 203v.
110. Ibid., Lib. decr. 17, fol. 3r.
111. AG, b. 2890, lib. 62, fol. 95r.

6 December 1469 Cristofolo Fasolo was let off a fine of ten ducats and the loss of his left eye—the sentence of the court in 1468—for having attacked a member of Beltramino's own entourage ("Laurentium dictum Stercum"), both of whose hands he had knifed, causing much blood to flow.[112] On 13 January 1470—shortly after Beltramino's retirement—Antonio Copino, who had been condemned for blasphemy, was let off the statutory sentence pronounced on 29 July 1469 to stand at the pillory with his tongue fixed to the *giova* if he failed to pay the prescribed fine.[113]

With Beltramino, the main consideration was to apply the law and the authorized supplementary laws correctly. It would be wrong to see him as the sort of hard judge who in his zeal to convict and condemn would curtail or disregard proper and lengthy inquiries and procedures. If he could not obtain proof—not even by confession, which under the prevailing wisdom was a highly acceptable form of proof—he would acquit. In October 1467 he defended himself against the complaints of "Zohanne dai Texuti," who had formally accused one Girolamo da Perugia of wounding him. Beltramino reported that Zohanne had never been able to produce any witnesses, that he thought Zohanne was a liar, and that he had ordered Zohanne to pay the costs of the case. Girolamo had not been formally absolved of the crime, but there was simply no evidence against him. "It is not justice that is lacking, but proof," Beltramino wrote to the marquis on 24 October 1467, adding rather sententiously, "as Your Lordship knows, all our justice rests upon proven facts."[114] This did not go down very well; Ludovico replied two days later that he knew perfectly well what Beltramino's duty was as a judge, but that he did not wish the case to be dropped on account of some subterfuge; he had seen for himself Zohanne's wounded head.[115]

In the case of a robbed and murdered courier in July 1468, when the victim was found buried near a tavern at Bondanello, Beltramino went to the scene to make inquiries for himself. He arrested the innkeeper and interrogated many others. He later claimed that, having noticed that one of the people he interrogated, a peasant called Cavalaro, was agitated and spoke in a tremulous way, "I knew him to be the one who had taken

---

112. Ibid., fol. 96r.
113. Ibid., fol. 105v.
114. "como sa la Vostra Illustre Signoria, tutto el nostro iudicare sta sule prove fatte": AG, b. 2405.
115. AG, b. 2890, lib. 58, fol. 52v.

the money" (Beltramino evidently regarded the signs of fear itself as enough to incriminate a suspect). Cavalaro at once confessed that he had taken the purse. But he claimed to have buried it for safekeeping and to have found the money missing when he dug up the purse; Beltramino was in a quandary, reporting that this Cavalaro turned out to be "the best and poorest man in all these villages."[116] He wrote more decisively to Ludovico a few days later, "I have always thought that to make an example to others, whoever finds courier's letters . . . should be under grave suspicion. I arrested that man at Bondanello for having hidden the letters and then I learned that the courier's cloak and boots had been given to him for burying the corpse."[117]

Ludovico no doubt respected Beltramino for his assured judgments and knowledge of law, but when offenses against his own officials occurred or when the clergy were detected in criminal acts or offering sanctuary, the marquis was implacable. In July 1468 Beltramino wrote that he had taken note of what Ludovico had written concerning "excesses" committed against the vicar (secular governor) of Poleto by one Antonio Crescendino. Beltramino had ordered the arrest of all men and women who were engaged in subversive acts against the vicar; they would be punished, in accordance with the proclamation, by hanging.[118]

In November 1469 another murder case aroused Ludovico's righteous anger to a new pitch of disregard for normal process of law. First, a proclamation on 1 November ordered that anyone with information about Domenico Feriolo, denounced for the murder of one Andrea (known as Cristofano) Messeta, should immediately inform the marquis or the vice-podesta, with a promise of a reward of twenty-five ducats; on 4 November the reward was raised to fifty ducats, and anyone caught sheltering Domenico was promised the same punishment as the villain himself.[119] Then the marquis issued some extraordinary directives to Beltramino. Having congratulated the vice-podesta on Feriolo's arrest, although he had managed to escape from his captors and take sanctuary with the conventual friars of San Francesco, Ludovico ordered that he should be dragged out under a heavy guard—"let the friars protest as much as they like that I shall be excommunicated"—and that as soon as

116. AG, b. 2408, letter of Beltramino, 14 July 1468.
117. Ibid., letter of Beltramino, Borgoforte, 17 July 1468.
118. Ibid., letter of Beltramino, Borgoforte, 3 July 1468.
119. AG, Gride, fasc. 6, fol. 6r.

possible Beltramino should get to work on him.[120] Ludovico was always contemptuous of the rights of sanctuary for fugitives from the law; he had for instance written to the podesta of Sermide, on 23 August 1468, that a forger of coins should be sent under heavy guard to Mantua and on no account be allowed anywhere near a church, in case he tried to take refuge in it.[121] Only a few years later, when a tailor who had murdered his wife took refuge in the Church of San Bernabà, he tried to use his influence in Rome to forbid sanctuary altogether for criminals on the run.[122] In the case of Feriolo, the marquis was quite recklessly forceful on this issue. Prejudging the case entirely, he declared: "we had as much pleasure at the news of Feriolo's capture as desire of his punishment. There is no case for his defense under the statutes—and anyway, the statutes of Mantua are no book of legal wisdom for all the world." Not content with making this high-handed statement, Ludovico even added the ominous principle that jurists should use the laws as they needed them.[123] On the next day, he wrote to his wife, Barbara of Brandenburg: "If others do not judge this to be a case of murder, we do, and in no way will we let this malefactor escape punishment . . . we will be podesta, knight, and executioner."[124] Beltramino worked quickly and had obtained a confession from Feriolo by the following day. Sending his congratulations, Ludovico assured him he could disregard any statute he wished.[125] Only a week later, on 15 November, the marquis wrote to Beltramino from Goito, "we are a man whose nature is to love justice,"[126]

---

120. ". . . vogliamo che lo dobiati pur cavare da San Francesco e condurlo a la presone sotto bona guardia et comenciare a tocharlo e farli rasone, lasando protestare li fratri quanto vogliono che se saremo scommunicati . . .": AG, b. 2891, lib. 65, fol. 5v (letter of 7 Nov. 1469).

121. AG, b. 2890, lib. 61, fol. 51r.

122. Ludovico Gonzaga urged Giovanni Arrivabene to ask his brother Giovanpietro, Cardinal Francesco Gonzaga's secretary, "che per Dio se vedessse se per qualche via o modo se potesse provedere che le giesie no fossero speloncho de assasini et ladri": AG, b. 2892, lib. 69, fol. 42r (3 Oct. 1471). See also chap. 6.

123. "li statuti di Mantua non sono quelli che debano dare leze a tuto il mondo . . . la natura di iuristi è di tirare le leze in qua et in là, como gli piace, vui non dovete star per questo": AG, b. 2891, lib. 65, fol. 6v (letter of 8 Nov. 1469).

124. "vogliamo sia punito, e s'el vice potesta non lo vorà fare, nui veniremo a Mantua e saremo potestade, cavallero e manigoldo": ibid., fol. 7v (letter to Barbara of Brandenburg of 9 Nov. 1469).

125. ". . . ve diamo piena licentia de passare ogni statuto secondo ne parirà richiedere questo acerbo e detestabile caso": ibid., fol. 8r (letter of 9 Nov. 1469).

126. "nui siamo uno homo che da natura amamo la rasone": ibid., fol. 11v (15 Nov. 1469).

yet the following day he issued a decree announcing that under no circumstances would he entertain an appeal from Domenico Feriolo, against whom the vice-podesta was to proceed with maximum severity on the following Saturday.[127] In contrast, on 14 December, the marquis ordered that charges against Bartolomeo Feriolo, for instigating his brother to commit murder, were to be dropped.[128]

There were those who complained at Beltramino's actions. Already in 1468, a resourceful prisoner on remand, one Matteo da Formica, had obtained a stay in the investigatory proceedings against him, during which time he and his lawyer had put together countercharges against Beltramino and his assistant judge. This had done Matteo no good at all, for Marquis Ludovico predictably gave Beltramino full support, dismissing the dossier against him as simply a device of the defense lawyers to gain time.[129] At the same time, he reassured the vice-podesta that he had proceeded in what was only a juridical—that is, proper—manner, and he instructed the judge to go ahead summarily.[130] Some time later Beltramino himself set to work on his detractor, and on 20 October he wrote that he had had Matteo hoisted on the rope. As this failed to reveal anything, Beltramino observed disapprovingly that Matteo did not seem to fear the rope at all: he had even fallen asleep while suspended—Beltramino thought Matteo had perhaps had a spell cast on him or had eaten some devilish thing—so he was to undergo the alternative torment of the *stanghetta*,[131] a sort of vice attached to the foot. It does not emerge whether in the end Beltramino broke down this man who had been foolhardy enough to try and turn the tables on him. Nevertheless, some of the dirt thrown at Beltramino may have stuck, enough to serve as a warning to the marquis.

---

127. AG, Lib. decr. 17, fol. 89r.

128. Ibid., fol. 98v.

129. "Te mandiamo questo libro recusatorio che ha producto Matheo Formicha contra el vicepodestà nostro et suo iudice . . . Crediamo perhò [le suspitioni?] siano più tosto per fugire et prolungare el iuditio che per altra casone"; on 1 September he thanked Giacomo for returning it: AG, b. 2890, lib. 61, fols. 59r–60r, letters to Giacomo da Palazzo (31 Aug. and 1 Sept. 1468).

130. Letter to Beltramino, 1 Sept. 1468: "non habiati proceduto se non iuridicamente" (ibid., fol. 60r) and to the judge of appeals: "fareste debiate procedere summariamente" (ibid.).

131. AG, b. 2410, fol. 39; for the text, see app. 1. For another case of a supposed spell ("diverse sorte di bullettini de incanti contra la tortura") that had anesthetized the torment or sent the victim to sleep, see the letter of 2 May 1499 in Bertolotti, *Prigioni e prigionieri*, 18–19; see also chaps. 6 and 7.

A few weeks after Beltramino's sixth consecutive term of office as vice-podesta expired, at the end of December 1469, someone vandalized a votive image of the Madonna that bore his coat of arms and that presumably he had dedicated; an enormous reward was offered for any information about this act of blasphemy.[132] However, the offense was more probably intended as an insult toward Beltramino himself, that "tyrannical man" who had done so well for himself in Mantua. Resentment may have been generated not least by the project to build a new palace for the vice-podesta, allegedly started in March 1469, though it may be that what was planned was only some alterations and improvements to the old podesta's palace; in any case, almost a year after Beltramino's resignation, it was reported that little progress had been made, despite much money being spent.[133] By this time Beltramino's main family home seems to have been at Saviola, about twelve miles south of Mantua on the further side of the Po. He must have acquired this property by May 1468, when he notified the marquis that his family was there[134] and that he was proposing to join them; it is not clear how many of his children were already born and growing up at this point, though an infant daughter's health had been causing concern.[135] Saviola was very convenient while the plague quarantine was in force. Beltramino assured the marquis that he would come to the castle of Borgoforte every day to keep in touch with administration: meanwhile he asked permission that, despite his own absence, the *giudice del maleficio* (who remained in Mantua and was scared stiff of catching the plague) should be allowed to interrogate accused persons with the use of torture.[136] There is no evidence that his settling with his family in Mantuan territory and acquiring property was a source of grievance or accusation against Beltramino at this stage.

---

132. ". . . essendo la nocte passata deturpata et guasta o sia imbratata una nostra donna cum le arme de sp. messer Beltramino olim vice potestate de Mantua": AG, Gride, fasc. 6, fol. 6v (19 Jan. 1470).

133. "Primo al palaço novo del vici podestà . . . pare che de marzo 1469 in qua . . . glie sono spexi de opera de maestri muratori, marangoni et bracenti libre 1930, che è una gran suma de robi e de denari al pochissimo lavorero che s'è facto": AG, b. 2410, fol. 522, letter of Ludovico de Cipata, Mantua (12 Nov. 1470).

134. " . . . Sav[iola al dì] la da Po, dove è la mia famiglia": AG, b. 2410, fol. 42.

135. In a letter to the *collaterale,* Carlo Agnelli, on 17 April 1468, the marquis mentions the need of medical attention for "quella putta de Beltramino": AG, b. 2890, lib. 60, fol. 3r. The reference is perhaps to Beltramino's daughter Candida.

136. A letter from the marquis dated 17 May 1468 mentions that all hearings had been suspended because of the plague scare: ibid., fol. 40r.

More significantly, the defacement of Beltramino's Madonna coincided with the time of his sindication (the statutory investigation of an outgoing magistrate's alleged miscarriages of justice),[137] and the act of desecration might well have been provoked by rumors of a cover-up. One of the sindicators appointed was Giacomo da Palazzo, who had already once before been involved in suppressing criticism of Beltramino.[138] The outcome, after a ten-day postponement,[139] was announced on 24 January 1470; Beltramino and his assistant judges were cleared of any imputations raised against them, though there was a list added of about twenty cases in which fines slightly above the statutory norm had been imposed, including two cases that were more serious because they involved penal mutilation. In the worst case, Gerardo of San Ruffino, sentenced as a rapist to have both a hand and a foot cut off, had been permitted to redeem this by paying one thousand lire within fifteen days, for which, it was noted, there was no legal precedent.[140] All the indications—confirmed by Beltramino himself years later[141]—are that the marquis had intervened to ensure that the inquiry was minimal in scope and that no damaging repercussions should ensue from it, on the grounds of Beltramino's overall record of distinguished and loyal service. Even if his term as vice-podesta had ended, in 1470 his star was still in the ascendant.

137. Sindication of the podesta is prescribed in BCMn, MS 775, lib. I, cap. xvi, fols. 10–11. See also chap. 1 n. 222.

138. See n. 129.

139. AG, Lib. decr. 17, fol. 104v (postponement, 13 Jan. 1470).

140. Ibid., fol. 108r (24 Jan. 1470).

141. See the concluding part of chap. 4, where Beltramino's letter of 10 Dec. 1484 is cited.

4

Beltramino's Later Career in Mantua
and His Downfall

Why did Marquis Ludovico Gonzaga eventually cease extending Beltramino's tenure as vice-podesta? Perhaps he felt there was a potential danger to the regime, given Beltramino's reputation for severity, should his protégé stay in office beyond the already unprecedented term of three years. So from 1 January 1470 Mantua had a new vice-podesta, Giovanni Calzavachi from Parma. Nevertheless Beltramino was soon established in a fresh role, making him in effect Ludovico's permanent legal pundit and extraordinary judicial commissary.

Having stepped down and survived his sindication, Beltramino did not retire from the scene for long. Whether or not he returned temporarily to Crema,[1] he was soon needed by the marquis of Mantua for a variety of tasks requiring discretion and legal expertise. Already in June 1470 Ludovico commissioned him together with Giacomo da Palazzo to inspect land boundaries at Sermide and Revere and to meet Borso d'Este's commissioners there; before they had completed that job, he was requiring them to investigate illegal pasturing at Quistello and Bondanello and willful planting of willow trees by the monks of San Benedetto Polirone.[2] On 1 September 1470 Beltramino was instructed to look at excavations in progress in Veronese territory, because of the resulting threat to river waters or streams in the Mantuan *dominio*.[3] In fact, for health reasons, and because he was so busy giving advice to Ludovico, who was staying at Gonzaga, Beltramino's departure for

1. The communal registers of Crema (BCCr, Archivio storico II) for 1470, which might have shed some light on this, are missing.
2. AG, 2891, lib. 65, fol. 60v, Marquis L. Gonzaga to Beltramino, Gonzaga (19 June 1470); AG, b. 2411, Beltramino to Marquis L. Gonzaga, Sermide, reporting on progress, 21 June 1470.
3. AG, b. 1593, instructions to Beltramino, 1 Sept. 1470.

Verona had to be postponed.[4] Soon he was appointed a member of the Council of Justice and given the title of auditor. He was already so described before the end of September 1470;[5] subsequently he usually signed his letters "doctor et Auditor." Thus Ludovico retained, or even intensified, his radical experiment in Mantuan criminal jurisdiction, now employing Beltramino as a sort of director of prosecutions, his special consultant and supernumerary chief investigator.

Beltramino's supramagisterial role, not to mention his presence at investigatory hearings and depositions, must have been intimidating not only for the accused persons brought before him but also for his successors in the vice-podesta's office, most of whom do not seem to have possessed force of personality equivalent to his own. There was a steady flow of letters to the marquis and to successive vice-podestas in Beltramino's forbidding autograph, many of them bearing the seal impression of an antique gem (see plate 2) and representing a bearded and aggressive male profile that can conceivably be identified as Hercules—surely a very appropriate figure for Beltramino to identify himself with.[6]

Successive vice-podestas habitually referred to the marquis for opinions and rulings or received abrupt orders—as did Antonio da Montecatini, for instance, vice-podesta in 1471, when he was urged that a convicted man should wear the miter of infamy and be relieved of his ears on the following Saturday, even though payment of the fine, which at least saved him from losing a hand as well, had been guaranteed by his relatives.[7] Beltramino may have been prompting Ludovico in such cases, just as he probably played a leading role in the founding of a college of doctors and advocates, a boost for the Mantuan legal profession; and another initiative that may well have been Beltramino's is the choice of the first title to be printed in Mantua at the press of Petrus Adam de Michaelibus in 1472—the compilation about criminal law, *Tractatus maleficiorum*, by

---

4. AG, b. 2891, lib. 66, fol. 24r, Marquis L. Gonzaga to Beltramino, Gonzaga (23 Sept. 1470).

5. E.g., "el spectabile Beltramino nostro auditore è occupato qua per alcune nostre faccende": ibid., fol. 27v, Marquis L. Gonzaga to the judge of appeals, Gonzaga (27 Sept. 1470).

6. We have to thank Rodolfo Signorini for drawing attention to the article by Charles Davis, "'Colossum Facere Ausus Est', L'Apoteosi d'Ercole e il colosso padovano dell'Ammannnati," *Psicon* 6 (Jan.–Mar. 1976): 39 and fig. 15, which shows a very similar profile on a supposed Hercules medal in the British Museum. However, Luke Syson of the Coins and Medals Dept. finds the Hercules identification wholly unconvincing.

7. AG, 2891, lib. 68, fol. 95r (17 Mar. 1472).

the fourteenth-century jurist Angelus de Gambilonibus.[8] In May of 1471 it was Beltramino, so the marquis informed the vice-podesta, who had been asked to draft a revision to the statutes prescribing the severest punishments for jail breakers or those who assisted them. Instead of hand amputation for such accomplices, Ludovico preferred the penal use of Beltramino's favorite interrogating torture: three hoists and drops of the rope.[9] Ludovico's modification was upheld nine years later by his son Federico in reply to a query from the serving vice-podesta;[10] it should be done in public, Federico ordered, but the jerking should not be too violent, as the purpose was "terror rather than punishment."[11]

In 1473 a practice was noted that had been criticized back in 1430: that the vice-podesta was coming to meetings of the council (presumably the Council of Justice is intended) and joining in their deliberations, rather than the councillors coming respectfully to consult the podesta; so much dignity had been lost, that the vice-podesta was sometimes seen conferring with members of the Council, walking up and down in the piazza.[12] It is likely that the dominant figure on the Council was Beltramino, so this again suggests that his power was perpetuated.

Predictably, Beltramino played a prominent role in investigating and judging cases of political conspiracy and attempted assassination. Here the political situation of Ferrara impinged particularly on Mantua, since Niccolò d'Este, a nephew of the marquis, lived in exile there and was under constant suspicion of conspiring to seize power in Ferrara, as well as being himself the quarry of hit men in the pay of Borso or Ercole d'Este. Suspicious travelers might therefore be detained for questioning, and Beltramino's report in November 1471 about his examination of one Todeschino offers a precise documentation of his methods and assumptions. Todeschino had made a curiously roundabout journey from Ferrara to Mantua; he claimed that he was on his way to take up an offer of

8. Mozzarelli, "Il Senato di Mantova," 72; D.E. Rhodes, "A Bibliography of Mantua 1472–98," *La Bibliofilia* 52 (1955): 175.

9. AG, b. 2891, lib. 66, fols. 88v, 91r, letters to the vice-podesta (28 Feb. and 1 May 1471).

10. AG, b. 2424, fol. 130, Almerico degli Almerici to Marquis F. Gonzaga (26 Sept. 1480).

11. "vogliamo però se li usa discretione darli questi tracti, quali siano dati lezermente . . . più presto ad terrorem che a punitione": AG, b. 2897, lib. 100, fol. 88v, Marquis F. Gonzaga to Almerico degli Almerici (26 Sept. 1480). See also Bertolotti, *Prigioni e prigionieri*, 35.

12. AG, b. 2416, fol. 62, Giacomo da Palazzo to Marquis L. Gonzaga, Mantua (21 Aug. 1473).

employment from the duke of Milan. He was arrested in a Mantuan tavern frequented by Germans, and Beltramino pointed out to him that he had not taken a normal route to Milan. Further interrogation took place in the castle of Cavriana, in the presence of local officials (the vicar and castellan), and Beltramino emphasized that the prisoner was given very extended warnings and—following the standard practice of interrogators—alternately kind and rough words before being led to the rope hoist. There, when he was suspended high up but divulging nothing, some distinctly irregular things occurred. The operator of the rope let it drop by mistake, so that the victim crashed down to the floor. He was not too badly hurt, Beltramino commented dryly, just a bit stunned. Water was thrown in his face and he was hoisted up again, but he still said nothing different from before. Finally Beltramino sent him back to his cell, with the threat of more of the same on the next day; meanwhile, he reported all this to the marquis and asked for instructions.[13] A few weeks later Beltramino had greater success to report after some other suspects had been cross-examined; one of them, Cesaro Prondo, began to talk even before he was put on the rope hoist.[14] The outcome was that Beltramino obtained from Cesaro a ratified statement, in a crowded courtroom, of the further admissions exacted under torture and of his plan to murder Niccolò d'Este. He repeated what he had told his confessor, that before his arrest, he had already decided to throw away the poison, not to administer it. He was granted three days for his defense but said he wanted no advocates and "deserved a thousand deaths."[15] Beltramino must have found this a highly satisfactory outcome and a thorough vindication of his techniques. Federico Gonzaga and his cousin Niccolò d'Este wanted to press a further charge of theft, since some silver was missing; Beltramino declared that if they so desired they could do this, but he himself saw no point since the main charge had been sustained. Cesaro then received his exemplary punishment: he was dragged through the piazza by an ass, hanged at the Porta della Guardia, cut down, and

---

13. AG b. 2412, fol. 307, Beltramino to Marquis L. Gonzaga, Cavriana (21 Nov. 1471); for the text, see app. 1.

14. AG, b. 2413, fol. 394, Beltramino to Marquis L. Gonzaga, Mantua (11 Dec. 1471).

15. "Heri al tardo Cesaro ratificò tuto quello se contene nela inquisitione, siando il pallazo tuto pieno di gente. Ma volse se agiongesse al fine de la inquisitione come l'avia ditto al confessore, ch'el voleva butare via quello veneno. Gli fu dato il termino di tre giorni a fare sue diffexe et offertogli advocati e procuratori come è de usanza. Lui rispoxe che non voleva advocati, e ch'el meritava mile morte . . .": ibid., fol. 394.

quartered; his remains were exposed at the gates, while his head, stuck on a lance, was shown from a tower.[16]

Beltramino was also active in more ordinary cases, in which his methods were no less inflexible. For instance, in July 1472 Beltramino attempted, together with the vice-podesta and another judge, to extract a confession from a suspected murderer called Ludovico da Montalto. Four jerks on the rope achieved nothing. Beltramino wrote: "to us it seemed he was lying: tomorrow we will repeat it to the maximum we know he can bear. It seems he fears the rope little; if so, we will change the torture."[17] This they did a few days later, using a sort of vice (the "stanghetta senza dadi e poi con li dadi"), but finally even Beltramino had to give up. Meanwhile, to his regret, they could not repeat the rope hoist on another suspect, because his spine was already damaged.[18] Beltramino was scrupulous about having a doctor present and desisting if there was any risk of the victim dying and implicating his interrogators in homicide.

The embarrassment of a death in the presence of prosecutors and judges is shown by the case of Tomeo Bellabarba in 1477. The vice-podesta, Francesco Stefani da Mercatello, had written to tell the marquis that after Tomeo and his accomplice (who had been threatened to keep silent) were twice subjected to the rope hoist, Tomeo had confessed to being the main instigator and perpetrator in the murder of one Cristofano.[19] Several weeks passed, then the vice-podesta wrote in some trepidation to the marquis that Tomeo had appeared very pale and then collapsed when brought to confirm this confession before the judge. He had been placed on a bed and bathed with water, but he had expired. What should be done? The vice-podesta insisted that Tomeo had never tried to retract his confession to the murder of which he was accused, but that he had refused to eat. He noted that it was deeply regrettable that Tomeo had not received the death he deserved, although he might still be hanged as a corpse. Beltramino clarified that the first session of Tomeo's torture had consisted of two hoists and drops on the rope, the second of five, but Tomeo had seemed robust and healthy.[20] In this unusual case, Marquis

---

16. Schivenoglia in BCMn, MS 1019, fol. 68r.

17. AG, b. 2413, fol. 785, letter from Beltramino (9 July 1472).

18. ". . . gli sonno rotto doi ponti sotto la sena, e pericoloso seria a molestarlo altramente, segondo il iuditio del medico": ibid., fol. 784, letter from Beltramino (14 July 1472).

19. AG, b. 2418, letter of 23 May 1477.

20. ". . . del caso me n'è doluto et dole fino a l'anima per non havere possuto farli la morte che meritava": ibid., letter of 10 June 1477.

Ludovico was very prompt to express concern. He wanted to hear the likeliest explanation for the cause of death and implied that Beltramino had been a bit evasive on this point: had he died because of the upset state of his stomach or fear or what?[21] Beltramino meanwhile had Tomeo's corpse hanged by one foot at the site of his crime.[22]

Another of Beltramino's gruesome interrogations—one that had to be aborted—was in the case of Zohanne Antonio Zamperlino; the crime of which he had been accused is not specified in Beltramino's report of the interrogation, but it was a relatively minor matter. Beltramino ordered him to be raised slightly on the rope, but not far, because he was very fat. "I referred to some other misdeeds of his, which he denied," Beltramino wrote, "then he was lowered some way but began to gasp for breath; he was brought to the ground, but when raised again he again lost his breath because he is so fat."[23] Even Beltramino seems to have had enough of this interrogation and to have concluded that the charge was not worth pursuing. He justified this rather characteristically on the grounds that the penalty, even if a confession was obtained as proof, would not be more than fifty lire, pointing out regretfully that it had proved impossible to use the rope on him, and admitting about the alternative instrument of torture, "with the *stang[h]etta* they rarely confess." Having made his own views plain, he asked the marquis for his opinion,[24] adding as a masterstroke that according to the prison warden the accused had been spitting blood every day. Clearly Beltramino wanted nothing more to do with this case.

Sometimes it seems Ludovico used Beltramino as the direct medium of his arbitrary will. In March 1473 there is a significant letter from the serving vice-podesta, Archimede Suardi, about the delay in execution of one Antonio known as Baluchante, after the time permitted for his appeal had expired. Beltramino had been to see the vice-podesta and had briefly expressed, allegedly on behalf of Marquis Ludovico, dissatisfac-

---

21. AG, b. 2894, lib. 83, fol. 43r, letter to Beltramino, Goito (10 June 1477).

22. "ho facto menare Tomeo al loco del commesso asascinamento et lì lo facto apicare per uno pieio": AG, b. 2418, letter of 11 June 1477.

23. ". . . lo fece condure a la corda e levatolo alquanto ma basso, perché l'è grosso, è la più grassa cossa mai non vitti . . . io narrandogli alcuni altri soi manchamenti che haveva intexi quasi in simele caso, sempre negò, unde fo relaxato per doi braza; ma tanta è la graseza che gli stringea l'artarie del'anelito ch'el se soffocava, e fo messo a terra . . .": AG, b. 2416, fol. 194, Beltramino to Marquis L. Gonzaga, Mantua (8 Feb. 1473).

24. ". . . vedando la impossibilitate di darli la corda e che per il dare di la stangetta raro se confessa, e che la pena del delicto non passa cinquanta libre . . . parse de consultare la V.I.S.": ibid.

tion that the sentence had not been carried out. On 26 March Archimede reported their meeting and justified himself in a letter to the marquis.[25] He explained that the condemned man's lawyers had begged for a further delay, since he had assumed he would be released and had not had time to put either his affairs or his soul in order; the *guardiano* of the convent of San Francesco had also begged for a delay, and so had Ludovico's wife, Barbara of Brandenburg. Thus, wrote Archimede, "considering the desperation of this poor man," he had postponed the execution until the Saturday of the following week, at the same time as many other sentences were due to be carried out. Archimede apologized if he had acted against the intentions of Ludovico, who, he added, was known to be so benign and just; the vice-podesta declared: "I am not cold-blooded or harsh by nature . . . in the meantime, if this good Balucante is still alive, perhaps it is the will of Heaven." It is difficult to imagine Beltramino writing in this tone or approving of it.

In another case, in the same year, the reluctance of both the vice-podesta and the executioner to go ahead drew even more vehement anger from the marquis. It is a particularly interesting case because it confirms earlier indications[26] that Ludovico was adamant—more so than his successors—in punishing armed men on his payroll who assaulted civilians or who impeded the podesta and his officials in the course of their duties. Thus in July 1473 he wrote to the vice-podesta that he was outraged at the presumption of Diomede da Gonzaga against members of the podesta's entourage. He and his servant should be arrested, and if the vice-podesta needed any help, the marquis assured him that his son Federico Gonzaga would provide a posse of *provvisionati*.[27] On the next day, he duly congratulated the vice-podesta and his *giudice del maleficio* for the capture of Diomede[28] but was less satisfied with their treatment of Diomede's woman servant. What part she had taken in the assault is unclear, but Ludovico insisted that she as well as Diomede must be punished and that she should be examined under torture.[29] A month later it seems that although a sentence of death had been imposed on her, the executioner had declined to carry it out. In two letters to the vice-podesta Ludovico berated the executioner as a poltroon, adding that, should he

25. AG, b. 2416, fol. 217.
26. E.g., AG, b. 2892, lib. 70, fols. 32v, 80v (letters of 3 July and 18 Sept. 1472).
27. AG, b. 2892, lib. 72, fol. 61r.
28. Ibid., fol. 63v.
29. Ibid., fol. 70r (27 July).

persist, the woman would be pardoned and would be made to hang him instead—he deserved the gallows anyway because he had once slashed an image of the Virgin.[30] This serves as a reminder that executioners bore additional horror, being felons themselves.

A quite unfamiliar aspect of Ludovico Gonzaga begins to take shape from these and other episodes, showing an irascible urgency about the carrying out of judicial killings and mutilations. A few more examples will serve to underline this side of his character as a ruler. For instance, in the spring of 1472 he actively hastened the passage to the gallows of a horse dealer from Reggiolo. On 16 April he wrote from Gonzaga (which is quite close to Reggiolo, where the man had been arrested by the governor, or *vicario*), requesting the vice-podesta in Mantua to interrogate his victim, if necessary with the rope hoist. On 18 April he added briskly: "our intention is to have him hanged on Monday. Tomorrow please send our executioner *[el manegoldo]* to Reggiolo."[31] On 20 April he notified the *vicario* of Reggiolo that although the executioner *(maestro di iusticia)* had arrived, he should not hang the condemned man until the following Tuesday.[32] Ludovico was furious in July 1472 when he learned that one Bartolomeo dal Pozzo had not had his hand cut off.[33] In January 1475 he was equally adamant that three men held in the lockup at Revere should be executed for whatever offense it was they had been condemned (unspecified in the correspondence) and of which they claimed to be innocent. In their petition for clemency dated 7 January, when they had been told what their fate would be, they protested, "we are human beings, not dogs or wild beasts, who committed no crime and do not deserve the horrible death by hanging."[34] The commissary in this matter was none other than Beltramino's old associate, the jurist Stefano Zampi, whose hesitation to proceed was vehemently overruled; he finally assured the marquis on 10 January that the executioner had arrived to hang them and that on the following day their corpses would be hanged again on the public highway.[35] Ludovico could be equally insistent about mutilations;

---

30. "quello poltrono del maistro di iusticia"; "quello poltrono manigoldo": ibid., lib. 73, fols. 30v, 31v, Ludovico to the vice-podesta (30 Aug.)

31. AG, b. 2892, lib. 70, fols. 10v, 12v.

32. Ibid., fol. 14v.

33. AG, b. 2892, lib. 70, fol. 54v.

34. AG, b. 2417; quoted without reference to context in Bertolotti, *Prigioni e prigionieri*, 25.

35. Ibid., letters of Stefano Zampi, Revere, 2, 7, and 10 Jan. 1475.

in December 1477 he expressly ordered that two robbers should respectively lose an eye and an ear.[36]

Perhaps it was because of suspicions that the serving vice-podesta or other officers of the law harbored irresolution or weakness that Ludovico sometimes instructed his man of iron, Beltramino, to proceed regardless, and officials in the rural *dominio* also appreciated that Beltramino enjoyed special authority. The evidence is in letters that survive only at random (for example, there is virtually nothing surviving about such matters from the year 1474), but there is enough to be suggestive. The vicar of Rodigo, Giovangiorgio da Concorregio, wrote on 22 June 1475 that he was acting vigorously on his instructions to hunt down malefactors who damaged property; he intended to send three or four *giottoni* to the prison in Mantua to be examined by the vice-podesta or expertly examined by Beltramino.[37] In August 1475 Ludovico wrote directly to Beltramino thanking him for his opinion concerning the execution of one Pedrone; Beltramino had written on the previous day that he found the evidence of five witnesses absolutely sufficient, even though according to the statutes there was a right of appeal.[38] Ludovico replied: "We have decided to delay no longer, because we know him very well and know that he has committed innumerable crimes, for which he deserves death. Next Saturday he will be hanged on the gallows, then taken to Quistello by boat and hanged there again, as you will write to the vicar there. Bring the mandate with you and we will sign it, and the vice-podesta shall make the arrangements for this execution."[39] As a mandate issued by Beltramino could authorize execution, it could also authorize arrest and indefinite detention; in September 1475 Ludovico Cipata protested that for six months he had been kept in prison on Beltramino's order because of a wrongful denunciation for assault on the part of a physician called Tommaso; the Council of Justice had heard the case and he was on the point of being released when a new mandate came from Beltramino to keep him in jail.[40]

---

36. AG, b. 2895, lib. 85, fol. 80v.

37. ". . . overo per meser Beltramino siano examinati sutilmente e fato quanto vol raxone": AG, b. 2417.

38. AG, b. 2416, fol. 716, Beltramino to Marquis L. Gonzaga (22 Aug. 1475).

39. AG, b. 2893, lib. 79, fol. 71r, letters to Beltramino and to the vicar of Quistello, Borgoforte (23 Aug. 1475).

40. AG, b. 2416, fols. 1101–4, Cipata's letters (19, 25, and 27 Sept. and 21 Oct. 1475). On 19 September he wrote "ex carceribus Mantue": "E le sey mesy che messer Beltramino me fece meter in pregione per una querella fece uno maestro Tomaso medico a torto che lo

As well as performing his duties as auditor and councillor, Beltramino had gone on being entrusted with special missions either within the Mantuan dominion or abroad. In the autumn of 1471 he was sent to Rome for a month or so—presumably to congratulate Pope Sixtus IV on his accession.[41] On his way, Beltramino stopped at Siena in late September,[42] and he was recalled from Rome in November,[43] when he brought back a presentation copy of Platina's *De principe* for the dedicatee, Federico Gonzaga.[44] Probably Beltramino read this text, which contains passages about magistrates in a prince's service (particularly the office of "urbanus praetor") that closely correspond to the image that he cultivated for himself: "good, modest, continent, just, strong, prudent, and abstemious."[45]

As was evident already in the summer of 1470, Beltramino was credited with a special expertise in disputes concerning the exploitation of natural resources, whether land or water, and boundaries; by the following year he is even described as "commissarius aquarum."[46] Among Beltramino's recurrent commissions were those relating to territorial and aquatic rights at Sermide on the Ferrarese border and at Canneto on the Brescian or Venetian border. These areas he repeatedly visited. He was again at Sermide in January 1471,[47] and he was there in February 1473 at the request of Cardinal Francesco Gonzaga;[48] he was also there in August and September 1477, surveying and measuring boundaries in order to come to a new agreement with the duke of Ferrara over pas-

---

haveva asaltato, e quella sie visto in palazo de ragione, e revista per li magnifici signori del consiglio . . . esendo per esser relaxato, messer Beltramino me fa retenir a torto per essa querella, e contra ogni rasone . . ." (fol. 1103).

41. Marquis Ludovico advised Sixtus IV of Beltramino's coming in letters of 18 and 25 September 1471: AG, b. 2891, lib. 68, fols. 6r, 14v.

42. AG, b. 1101, fol. 567, Beltramino to Marquis L. Gonzaga, Siena (29 Sept.); for Cardinal Gonzaga's sake (on some unspecified matter) he was going to consult the well-known lawyer Francesco da Arezzo.

43. AG, b. 2891, lib. 68, fol. 47v.

44. Platina's letter, dated 26 August (no year shown), which begins "defere ad vos orator vester dominus Beltraminus," seems to have been written rather long in advance: AG, b. 844, fol. 229; A. Luzio, "Il Platina e i Gonzaga," *Giornale storico della letteratura italiana* 13 (1889): 439.

45. Platina [B. Sacchi], *De Principe*, ed. G. Ferraù (Messina, 1979), 120. On the text, see N. Rubinstein, "Il 'De optimo cive' del Platina," in *Bartolomeo Sacchi il Platina*, ed. A. Campana and P. Medioli Masotti (Padua, 1986), 136–44. See also the conclusion in the present study.

46. D'Arco, *Studi*, 6:73.

47. AG, b. 2412, letters of 26–31 Jan. 1471.

48. AG, b. 1141, fol. 289, Cardinal F. Gonzaga to Marquis L. Gonzaga, Bologna (17 Feb. 1473).

turage rights.[49] During most of November and December 1479 Beltramino was again in this area. A first letter from Sermide reported that he was having to deal with large-scale robberies of livestock (oxen, cows, and sheep were being seized at night and taken down river on barges), but his main commission was about boundaries.[50] He went on to Ferrara for consultations, receiving priority treatment from Ercole d'Este, whereas the Venetian ambassador had allegedly been kept waiting for six days without an audience.[51] Back on site, at Sermide and Felonica, Beltramino outlined some of his problems, among them the excessive number of Ferrarese contestants and the poor turnout and unpreparedness of the Mantuans; he declared that at Bondeno he was so desperate that he had to use his wits, by which he meant his professional skill in totally confusing the Ferrarese commissary over the way a legal deed should be interpreted.[52]

Beltramino's on-site inspections were evidently very meticulous and—so he wrote on 14 December in the course of another trip to Ferrara—involved the services of a painter to record the topographical details;[53] on yet another trip to Sermide, in May 1481, he stressed the importance of such visual records.[54] Beltramino's westward trips to the river Oglio were equally recurrent. He was at Canneto in May 1471[55] and wrote on 2 July to the marquis about "the rights concerning those waters that flow from Castel Goffredo, Mariana, and Redondesco," threatening penal action against those communes unless they "let some of the water flow beyond to their neighbors for their mills and irrigation."[56] He was at Brescia on similar business early in 1475, making an approach to the Venetian governors there. On 28 February he reported that on the first morning the governors had not been able to see him because they were conducting some interrogations under torture ("al tormento per certi malfactori"),

49. AG, b. 2894, lib. 83, fols. 21r–22v, letters of Marquis L. Gonzaga to Beltramino (14–17 Aug. 1477), sending him a sketch map of the site; AG, b. 2418, from Beltramino, 14 Sept. and 4 Oct. 1477.

50. AG, b. 2423, Beltramino to Marquis L. Gonzaga, Sermide, 7 Nov. 1479.

51. Ibid., Sermide, 17 Nov. 1479.

52. Ibid., Sermide, 22 Nov. 1479; Felonica, 7 Dec. 1479; Quatrelle, 11 Dec. 1479.

53. "ho fatto fare uno dissegno di punto in punto e di loco in loco andasevemo, menando cum nui sempre il depinctore" : AG, b. 1229, fol. 97, Beltramino to Marquis L. Gonzaga, Ferrara (14 Dec. 1479).

54. "Gionto qua a Sermido cerchai de havere quello designo de domino Zohanfrancesco [Gonzaga?], e subito me feci fare uno simile": AG, b. 2426.

55. AG, b. 2412, letters of 13–23 May 1471.

56. AG, b. 2413, fol. 391.

professional business to which Beltramino could hardly make objections, but when he was later told that it would take three days for the judges and other experts to study his submissions, he replied that he was not sent to litigate and stay for a long time in Brescia, but only to make them aware of the specific wrong that had been done.[57] Evidently his refusal to be pushed around had worked; on the next day, he reported a long discussion before the podesta,[58] and on the day after that, in another encounter with the podesta, he reiterated that the marquis only wished to emphasize his position on the matter, not to litigate.[59]

It was to contest the judgment about the waterways affecting Asola, given in 1475 by the same podesta of Brescia, Luca Navagero,[60] that in June 1477 Beltramino was sent to Venice. As a citizen of Crema with previous experience of Venetian government and judicial administration, Beltramino was well qualified for this and wrote some interesting dispatches about the difficulties he experienced. He had an interview with Doge Andrea Vendramin, which was just as useless as he had expected,[61] but he pinned more hopes on the influence of a former podesta of Crema, Francesco Giustinian, whom he knew well ("mio amicissimo").[62] It is likely that Beltramino's high contacts with Venetian patricians, particularly his acquaintance with successive governors of Crema and Brescia, was another asset making him indispensable to the Mantuan regime; for instance, Antonio Venier, Luca Navagero's successor as podesta of Brescia, wrote to Marquis Ludovico Gonzaga on 13 October 1475 that he had talked about various matters with Beltramino, whom Antonio declared—sincerely or not—he "loved like a brother."[63] Giustinian was now one of the *Savi di Terraferma,* who, Beltramino observed, carried more weight than the *Auditori.* By the latter he meant the *Auditori nuovi,* who had appellate jurisdiction within the *terraferma,* "young men," he wrote, "who easily let themselves be corrupted by the prayers of friends and relatives"; nevertheless, he had urged the *Auditori* to give the case

57. ". . . io gli respuosi che non era mandato lì per littigare e stare in tempo ma solum a fare intendere il torto expresso che ne era stato fatto": AG, b. 1599.

58. "hozi siamo stati in longa disputatione fin ad hore decenove denanti al potestate sopra la causa da Canetto . . .": ibid., 1 Mar. 1475.

59. Ibid., 2 Mar. 1475.

60. AG, b. 92.

61. AG, b. 1432, fol. 3, letter from Venice (26 June 1477).

62. Ibid., fol. 5, letter from Venice (30 June 1477)

63. ". . . el spectabile misser Beltramino Cusadro el qual amo come fratello": AG, b. 1599.

priority.[64] Things did not go the way Beltramino had hoped, and despite more lobbying, he failed to get the judgment reversed. He wrote in disgust on 11 July, "This *Signoria* that bears the name of Justice is, I see, contaminated by the pleadings of relatives and has resolved that it cannot overrule the decision of the podesta."[65] He made one final attempt to work the system by approaching the podesta's brother, Francesco Venier, but when this failed he wrote in disgust on 13 July, "it is just a waste of time to stay here and spend money."[66] With a final grouse about the problem of *homini grossi* controlling everything, "God help justice!" was his parting shot from Venice.[67]

Beltramino's reputation was such that his opinion was sought and his judgment generally respected on all manner of disputes, large and small. Ludovico degli Ippoliti, cited by Beltramino in a civil matter, wrote in July 1473 that illness prevented him from coming to Mantua, but that he would pay the costs demanded, seeing that Beltramino regarded him as the party in the wrong.[68] In September 1475, when a certain Pendaglia was accused of cutting down a hedge that belonged to Benedetto Mastino and his brothers, the judge, Paolo da Pozzo, declared that as there was some doubt in his mind, he wished first to confer with Beltramino.[69]

In 1477 it was not a hedge but a political frontier on which Beltramino was called to pronounce. Marquis Ludovico commissioned Beltramino to act on his behalf as the arbitrator in a border dispute between the republic of Lucca and the town of Pietrasanta, which was then in Genoese territory.[70] Beltramino and Baldassare Castiglione (grandfather of the famous writer), whom he had recently partnered in investigating a dispute between the Torelli and Nuvolara families,[71] reported on 10 November that they had met the Genoese emissaries at Pietrasanta, where board and lodgings were provided for them by the citizens. The Lucchesi, somewhat worried by the danger of a popular uprising, wanted

---

64. AG, b. 1432, fols. 5, 6 (4 and 5 July 1477)

65. "mi lamentai con d. Francisco Diedo, Francisco Justiniano ed Zacharia Barbaro, digando che questa Signoria portava il nome di Iustitia e che mi pareva vederla contaminare a preghere de parenti" : AG, b. 1432, fol. 8 (9 July 1477).

66. ". . . stare qua a perdere tempo e spendere": ibid., fol. 11.

67. "E ciò che scrive Zorzo mi parono bubole e tale cosse tractate da homini grossi che non se gli po fare fundamento. Ma Dio aiutare la iusticia!": ibid., fol. 12 (15 July 1477).

68. AG, b. 1795, L. degli Ippoliti to Marquis L. Gonzaga, Gazoldo, 30 July 1473.

69. AG, b. 2416, fol. 670, "Paulus de Puteo" to Marquis L. Gonzaga (25 Sept. 1475).

70. A provisional agreement between the parties, dated 21 Sept. 1477, is preserved in AG, b. 44.

71. AG, b. 2418, letter of 12 Feb. 1477.

to meet the adjudicators at Camaiore to discuss their side of the dispute; in the meantime they were taken by the Genoese to the site where a house built by Lucchesi had been destroyed. Beltramino regarded the Genoese as quibblers and the Lucchesi as more open to compromise, but he kept his own counsel.[72] He and Castiglione arrived in Lucca on 19 November, when Beltramino at once called on the new bishop, Cardinal Ammannati, a longstanding friend of the Gonzaga family. Since last writing, Beltramino reported, he and Castiglione had ridden all round the border areas with both Genoese and Lucchese contingents and examined the written evidence on both sides; he barely concealed his expectation of a favorable outcome for Lucca.[73] Baldassare Castiglione fell ill, however, and remained first at Camaiore and then at Pietrasanta, while Beltramino concluded the mission on his own[74] and went several times to Milan to explain the recommendations; he declined to adjudicate claims for damages, but he went armed with all relevant documents and painted charts of the disputed area, impressing first the dowager Duchess Bona of Savoy and then the Council,[75] though he was called back for further clarifications in January 1478, again delaying the ratification.[76]

Between his trips to Venice and Sermide in the summer of 1477 and his more distant mission to Pietrasanta, illness in Beltramino's family had briefly interrupted his work; the episode needs to be mentioned for the light it throws on his personality and his attitude toward official duty. On 30 July Beltramino wrote from Mantua that he had received on the previous evening a message that his wife was ill and on the point of death,

---

72. "Conosciamo questi gienovesi molto più cavilosi che Luchesi, ma nuy se sforzamo star stretti di parole . . .": AG, b. 1138, fol. 67, Beltramino and Baldassare Castiglione to Marquis L. Gonzaga, Pietrasanta (10 Nov. 1477).

73. Ibid., fol. 68, Beltramino to Marquis L. Gonzaga, Lucca (20 Nov. 1477).

74. Ibid., fols. 69–72, letters from Beltramino and Baldassare Castiglione (Camaiore, 23 Nov. 1477; Pietrasanta, 28 Nov. 1477; Lucca, 1 Dec. 1477).

75. "heri sera arivò lo prefato d. Beltramino tanto tarde che vix potete io habere l'adito nel castello et obtenire l'audientia . . . Questa matina sono stato inseme con lui a la presentia de la prefata Illustrissima Madona dove ha exposto la cosa notabilissimamente . . .": AG, b. 1626, fol. 102, P. Spagnoli to Marquis L. Gonzaga, Milan, 17 Dec. 1477. To the Council Beltramino "explicò el tuto mostrandoli el designo et ad tute le parti et risposte satisfacendo": ibid. See also A.R. Natale, ed., *Acta in Consilio Secreto in Castello Portae Jovis Mediolani*, (Milan, 1963–69), 1:101 (28 Dec. 1477): "In quo Consilio fuit vocatus dominus Beltraminus, orator et nuntius illustris d. Marchionis Mantuae, qui portavit iterum designum et picturam territorii, in quo est differentia confinum inter Lucenses et Petrasanctenses . . ."

76. Ibid., 129, 135, 137–38.

which was a great shock to him.[77] Although a notarial deed earlier in the
same year records that Beltramino also had a house in Mantua,[78] his
main home was still at Saviola, where he had recently received another
grant of land for his heirs to hold in perpetuity.[79] Upon hearing the news
of his wife's illness, he had hurried home to Saviola, he told the marquis
in his letter of 18 July (promising to keep his letter brief and not weari-
some), but his main worry was that he had not obtained permission to
leave Mantua. He had found both his wife and his brother Guido in very
bad health.[80] The marquis wrote from nearby Borgoforte a sympathetic
letter, assuring Beltramino that his sudden departure was of course
excused and urging him to stay away for as long as might be necessary,[81]
though he did not spare him letters about items of public business.[82]
Characteristically, however, Beltramino was back at work within four
days; he did not mention his wife's illness again, though he did write several letters about his brother, who was too sick to take any nourishment.
Presumably Beltramino thought that the marquis would be more inter-
ested to hear about Guido, who since 1472 had been vicar, or governor,
of Marcaria, a Gonzaga castle on the road toward Parma;[83] Ludovico did
in fact write that he was glad to hear of Guido's improvement.[84] Beltramino also mentioned the arrival of his brother Giovanni, the physician, who had fallen from his horse near Cremona and continued the
journey on Guido Cusadri's mule.[85] Evidently Beltramino's wife recovered and continued coping for another year with their large household—

---

77. ". . . heri sera a le tre hore mi fu scritto la donna mia essere per morire, che mi fu
grande passion ad intendere": AG, b. 2418, Beltramino to Marquis L. Gonzaga, Mantua,
30 July 1477.

78. Payment of a sum of 178 ducats was witnesssed "in domo habitationis mag. dom.
Beltramini Auditori Mantuae in contra. Monticellorum alborum": AN, Registrazioni
notarili, 1477, fol. 28r (15 Jan. 1477).

79. AG, Lib. decr. 19, fol. 140r (21 Feb. 1476). More was to follow at "Pozo de Valle,"
near Suzzara, by a grant on 28 Feb. 1482 (AG, Lib. decr. 20½, fol. 105r).

80. "e per non dare tedio a Vostra Signoria né rompergli il sonno, subito mi partì,
sperando la Vostra Signoria mi debba havere excusato se forse havesse commesso errore a
partirme senza licentia e domandogli perdono. Ho trovato la donna mia e maestro Guido
nostro in pessimi termini": AG, b. 2418 (30 July 1477).

81. AG, b. 2894, lib. 87, fol. 89v (31 July 1477).

82. AG, b. 2894, lib. 87, fols. 92r, 96v, 97r, 97v, letters from Borgoforte (1, 3, and 4
Aug. 1477).

83. There are letters from Guido Cusadri, 1472–77, in AG, b. 2414 and 2419 (Marcaria). Beltramino wrote again about Guido's illness on 5–6 Aug. (b. 2418).

84. AG, b. 2894, lib. 87, fols. 96v–97v (3–4 Aug. 1477).

85. AG, b. 2418, Beltramino to Marquis L. Gonzaga, 2–6 Aug. 1477.

in August 1478 Beltramino wrote that his house was so crowded he needed to build an extension[86]—but she succumbed again to illness and died in October 1478. Again Beltramino apologized[87] for having to go home so suddenly, and there is little grief or even decorum in the letter he sent on 16 October. He wrote to Marquis Federico that he would have returned to Mantua immediately after she died, but since there was nobody to run the house he had to stay on for a few days to make arrangements.[88] On the next day, as though nothing had happened, he wrote with his customary precision about an official matter; he explained that he did not have by him a document that Marquis Federico had asked him to produce, and that in any case he never retained official documents in his possession.[89]

During the short reign of Federico Gonzaga as marquis from 1478 to 1484, Beltramino seems to have been more than ever in the confidence of the Gonzaga family and to have remained active in public affairs. He was, for instance, a witness to the will of Barbara of Brandenburg on 3 February 1479,[90] and the following year he was invested with some land at Felonica by Cardinal Francesco Gonzaga,[91] though there was local resistance to his taking possession of it.[92] Cardinal Gonzaga also helped to find an appointment for Beltramino's eldest son, Geremia, in another cardinal's household.[93] It was to Beltramino that Marquis Federico wrote in 1481 when a loose-tongued wretch called Francesco Tondello was denounced for speaking offensively about Barbara of Brandenburg. Beltramino and the *sindico* Donino were ordered to examine Tondello, after which the marquis would let them know his wishes. But even before the

---

86. ". . . Non habiando io commoda habitatione per la mia famiglia, per essere molti a numero, e volendo fare presso questa alcuna particella di casa": AG, b. 2421, fol. 714, Saviola (23 Aug. 1478).

87. Ibid., fol. 715 (letter of 5 Oct. 1478).

88. "subito morta la donna mia, cognoscendo il bisogno . . . me serìa transferito da quella, ma siando tolto quanto governo havia in casa e non havere persona sufficiente a simel cosa ma in mane di persone estranee lassare le cose mie, m'è stato forza restare alcuni dì . . .": ibid., fol. 716.

89. "non è mio costume de retignere manuscripto alcuno spectante a la Vostra Signoria": ibid., fol. 717.

90. AG, b. 20.

91. AG, b. 2897, lib. 98, fol. 12v.

92. Ibid., fol. 13v, Marquis L. Gonzaga to the podesta of Sermide (4 Feb. 1480).

93. Cardinal F. Gonzaga wrote on 22 January 1480 to Cardinal "Agriensis" (i.e., Cardinal Gabriel Rangoni, bishop of Erlau [Eger] in Hungary) that he was glad Geremia was to be among the latter's *familiares*: AG, b. 2896, lib. 96, fol. 172r.

examination, the marquis informed the examiners that Tondello should be advised to confess and then prepare his soul to meet God.[94] Federico assured his aging mother (she died only two months later), that justice would be done.[95]

Beltramino continued to be chosen for routine assignments within his special competence—for example, he was back at Asola and Mariana in October 1481 concerning the waterways[96]—and also for more exalted commissions. In April 1480 he played a crucial part in the betrothal of Federico's son Francesco to Ercole d'Este's daughter Isabella.[97] This was no simple agreement, but as his letters from 7 to 17 April make clear,[98] Beltramino handled Ercole's wife Eleonora of Aragon with great tact and acuteness. He had assured her, he wrote to the Marquis on 8 April, that a dowry was the last thing the Gonzaga family were thinking about: they wanted a pact with Ferrara for mutual defense and, above all, an Italian wife for the heir, not a money-seeking German or other foreigner ("non todesco on oltramontanno che prima cerchavanno il dotte che la donna"). Eleonora played into his hands by protesting that of course they must have a dowry as a form of security ("perché la dotta è la segureza de la donna").[99] The dowry was settled on very satisfactory terms at twenty-five thousand ducats, half of the sum to be paid immediately, with a back debt of an additional eight thousand ducats to be written off.[100] Beltramino even interviewed the intended bride. Thus the dreaded interrogator of malefactors found himself for a change cross-questioning a female infant. Isabella acquitted herself very well, as Beltramino remarked dryly, "to me it seemed a miracle that a child of six replied so cleverly."[101] Altogether, Beltramino wrote on 17 April that it was a

---

94. AG, b. 2897, lib. 100, fol. 78r, Marquis F. Gonzaga to Beltramino, Gonzaga (13 Sept. 1481).

95. Ibid., fol. 80v, Marquis F. Gonzaga to Barbara of Brandenburg (16 Sept. 1481).

96. AG, b. 2426, letters of 4 and 12 Oct. 1481.

97. See A. Luzio, "Isabella d'Este e Francesco Gonzaga Promessi Sposi," *Archivio storico lombardo* 35 (1908): 34–69 (especially 42–45).

98. AG, b. 1229, fols. 113–20.

99. Ibid., fol. 115, Beltramino to Marquis F. Gonzaga, Ferrara (8 Apr. 1480).

100. Undated letter from Beltramino (ibid., quoted in Luzio, "Isabella d'Este e Francesco Gonzaga," 43–44).

101. ". . . Doppo fo condutta lì in camerino d. Isabella e fo fatta rasonare, et interrogata di più cosse da mi come da li altri, rispondeva con tanta intellecto e con lingua tanto expedita, che a mi parve uno miracolo che una puta di sei anni facesse cossì digne risposte": AG, b. 1229, fol. 114, quoted in Luzio, "Isabella d'Este e Francesco Gonzaga," 44.

"dolce conclusione," and he again praised Isabella's "mirabile intelletto et inzegnio."[102]

Six weeks later he returned to Ferrara, accompanied by Francesco Secco, Marquis Ludovico's son-in-law (the husband of his illegitimate daughter Caterina), for the official betrothal ceremony on 28 May,[103] and in June he was again sent to Ferrara to see Isabella.[104] It was probably Beltramino's astute conduct in this matter—as well as his proven skill concerning boundaries and his general reputation as a prosecuting magistrate—that drew the attention of Duke Ercole d'Este to his merits and desirability as a future employee. Ercole already favored Beltramino with a knighthood on the next occasion of a Gonzaga marriage—that of Federico's daughter Chiara to Gilbert de Montpensier, in June 1481.[105]

Beltramino was closely involved, too, in Chiara Gonzaga's marriage, for he was one of the party who accompanied her to France, a distinguished escort that included Sforza Bettini, the former Milanese ambassador to Louis XI, and the poet Niccolò da Correggio, with his wife Cassandra Colleoni (daughter of Bartolomeo, the *condottiere*).[106] Beltramino wrote from Magenta on 25 June 1481 describing their reception by the rulers of Milan,[107] from Vercelli on 27 June, and from Ligorno in Monferrato two days later,[108] but his most interesting letter was dated at Turin on 1 July, mentioning Chiara's happy state of mind and eagerness for entertainment. She had gone to hear organs being played in the cathedral, then she had attended a ball (presumably Beltramino was also present); unfortunately the party had had to stay at an *osteria* at their own expense, because insufficient notice had been given for the duke of Savoy to provide hospitality.[109] One more letter from Beltramino about this trip survives, dated from the castle of Avigliano ("Vianna") later on 1 July, on the way to Susa.[110] But there are others, covering the whole journey,

---

102. AG, b. 1229, fol. 120; quoted in Luzio, "Isabella d'Este e Francesco Gonzaga," 45.

103. Ibid., 45–47. Letters jointly addressed to Beltramino and Secco on 19 and 22 May contained their instructions: AG, b. 2897, lib. 99, fols. 19v–20r.

104. AG, b. 2897, lib. 100, fol. 11r.

105. Schivenoglia wrote, "Essendo lo ducha de Ferrara venuto a Mantoa per la spoxa de la fiola de messer Federigo Marchexo de Mantua, lui fece lì sotti sei chavalleri: primo messer Beltramino di Achuxadis da Crema, el qual era dottore e si era in conseio in Mantoa": BCMn, MS 1019, fol. 86v.

106. On all these persons, see *DBI, ad voces.*

107. AG, b. 2426.

108. AG, b. 731, fols. 26–27.

109. Ibid., fol. 28.

110. AG, b. 629, fol. 79 (filed as from Vienne, France).

from the outward stop at Vercelli on 27 June to the return stop there on 13 August, written by Sforza Bettini.[111] He describes the journey over the Alps, by which Chiara was quite undaunted; the entertainment received at Chambéry on 11 July; and the safe arrivals at Lyons on 17 July and at Roanne the following day, where they were met by the duke of Bourbon. It was at the royal castle of Cusset ("Cusseto") near Vichy that the nuptial meeting was to take place. According to Sforza Bettini on 21 July, Chiara had been observed arriving by her husband, standing at a window, but their encounter was arranged by jocular deception; "Madonna Cassandra" pretended to be ill in her room, so Chiara went to see her, accompanied only by Beltramino and Cassandra's husband Niccolò da Correggio. Then Gilbert de Montpensier appeared; the couple kissed and repeated their marriage vows made at Mantua, and finally, Sforza Bettini adds discreetly, the marriage was consummated.[112] The party proceeded to Aigueperse on 22 July and were presented to the bridegroom's father, but from there—a point that had brought Beltramino almost to the center of France—they turned back; on 27 July Bettini wrote from Vichy ("Vixi") that they were dividing into two parties for the journey back to Italy; he, Niccolò da Correggio, and Beltramino were going to travel ahead of the *gentildonne*.[113] Beltramino must have been back in Mantua by about 20 August.[114]

Beltramino went again on his official travels in the spring of 1482, as the prospects grew of Mantua being drawn into a major war supporting Ferrara against Venice. At the beginning of April he had consultations with Francesco Secco at the Po fortress of Ostiglia and then continued to Ferrara; there he reviewed the political situation with Duke Ercole d'Este, who accommodated him in the apartment of Niccolò da Correggio. Later the same month, after Federico da Montefeltro had been appointed commander of the allied army, Beltramino was again at Ferrara. He had been sent to invite the duke of Urbino to Mantua; Marquis Federico thought he might like to revisit the Ca' Gioiosa where Vittorino da Feltre had taught him long ago. Ercole d'Este told Beltramino that Federico was coming overland from Bologna, and Beltramino managed to meet the

---

111. AG, b. 751, fols. 26–43. Bettini gives the correct place name, Avigliano, in his letter of 30 June.

112. Ibid., fol. 40.

113. Ibid., fols. 41–42.

114. AG, b. 2897, lib. 102, fol. 80r, Marquis F. Gonzaga to the podesta of Cremona (25 Aug. 1481), refers to "Beltramino nostro consigliero ne lo suo ritorno de Franza . . ."

duke at Lugo. From there he dispatched a letter that, in his hurry or distraction, he dated 2 April instead of 2 May; however, he wrote another letter on the same day from Argenta, repeating that the invitation had been well received.[115] At Ferrara he had to contend with some Milanese emissaries who urged Duke Federico to take the most direct route toward Parma for an urgent meeting to discuss military policy, but—with some support from Ercole d'Este—Beltramino's dogged insistence prevailed.[116] Beltramino accompanied Federico da Montefeltro up the Po to Figarolo and Revere, and Federico did make a flying visit to Mantua on 5–6 May.[117] Afterward Beltramino accompanied the duke to Casalmaggiore; the talks there were held in secret, but Beltramino made a point of insisting that Marcaria would be the only good crossing point of the river Oglio for the troops promised to strengthen the Po fortresses and cut off the Venetian advance.[118]

As well as performing these special missions for the ruling dynasty and regime, Beltramino's role as a sort of judicial overlord of Mantua continued under Marquis Federico Gonzaga. Beltramino still described himself as "doctor et Auditor" in September 1478, three months after Ludovico's death, in a letter written from Reggiolo about an interrogation he was conducting in the castle there.[119] His victim was a certain Antonio di Rozi, who was thought to have heard Filipino di Durachino speaking abusively against the marquis or his late father. In a second letter, responding to the marquis's demand that he should put the accused man on the rope hoist, Beltramino asked that three or four reliable men be sent to operate it;[120] but it may be significant that this time—although this letter was not written in Beltramino's own hand—he is merely styled "fidelissimus servitor." In fact, he did not resume the title of auditor in later signatures after September 1478.

Perhaps this uncertainty about Beltramino's official title was symptomatic of the judicial confusion that must have prevailed for some time after Federico's accession, aggravated by a serious outbreak of plague

---

115. D.S. Chambers, "The Visit to Mantua of Federico da Montefeltro in 1482," *Civiltà mantovana* 28 (1993): 5–15; see ibid., 6–7 and 10–11, respectively, for the letters (AG, b. 846, fol. 606, and b. 1230).

116. See ibid., 7–8, app. 4, for Beltramino's letter of 3 May from Ferrara (AG, b. 1230).

117. Ibid., 8–9, with text for Beltramino's letter of 3 May from Ferrara (app. 4).

118. AG, b. 1627, letter of Beltramino, Casalmaggiore, 8 May.

119. AG, b. 2421, Beltramino to Marquis F. Gonzaga, Reggiolo, 8 Sept. 1478.

120. ". . . tri o quatro fidatissimi che habiano a dare essa corda per la confessione che fano molte volte li malfactori su quella": ibid.

and enforcement of quarantine regulations. The court of the vice-podesta and his judges was first transferred to Governolo, the river fortress near the junction of the Mincio with the Po. Gasparino Lanci, the *giudice del maleficio*, was at a complete loss at the end of September 1478, writing— in the manner of a judge readily subject to political pressures—that he had been waiting in vain for two weeks to know the marquis's intentions about pending trials and criminal cases;[121] a few weeks later he complained that his living and sleeping conditions—he was sharing a subterranean room with three notaries—were intolerable.[122] Writing from Governolo and Borgoforte in October and November 1478, the vice-podesta, Baldassare Gabrieli, also complained of great inconvenience and of the presumptuous demands of his notaries and foot soldiers.[123] He was still at Governolo in January 1479, complaining bitterly and asking to be extended in office for another year and to know when he would be recalled to Mantua.[124]

But the most serious source of confusion after Federico Gonzaga's accession must have been the potential loss to the podesta's jurisdiction, and hence to Mantua's fiscal administration, of large swathes of the recently united dominions of the *marchesato*. For, although Ludovico Gonzaga's last testament could not be found, Barbara of Brandenburg insisted that whereas Federico, their eldest son, should inherit as marquis, much territory west of the river Oglio should pass as appanages to the other sons: Cardinal Francesco, Gianfrancesco, Rodolfo, and Ludovico (protonotary and bishop-elect of Mantua). The uncertainty lasted until the final settlement was confirmed by Emperor Frederick III, granting to the fraternal beneficiaries "merum et mixtum imperium." The settlement in June 1479 involved much horse-trading between the brothers, but at least it enabled Marquis Federico to regain the *podestarie* of Viadana and Canneto.[125] The repercussions, in judicial terms, are wholly uninvestigated—but they must have presented problems, not only to the marquis but also to his brothers. Just to give an example, in July 1480 the then vice-podesta of Mantua, Almerico Almerici, wrote that

121. AG, b. 2420, G. Lanci to Marquis F. Gonzaga, Governolo, 30 Sept. 1478.

122. Ibid., 19 Oct. 1478.

123. Ibid.

124. "questa pesta hè stata la mia totale consumptione e desfactione": AG, b. 2423, Gabrieli to Marquis L. Gonzaga, 1 and 4 Jan. 1479.

125. For details see Mazzoldi, *Mantova*, 2:36–38. On this recurrence—to become permanent—of the separated Gonzaga territories *oltre Oglio*, see also R. Navarrini, *Il princi-*

Cardinal Francesco Gonzaga had denounced to him certain malefactors in his lands. Almerico pointed out that he could do nothing since they did not come within his jurisdiction.[126]

Despite administrative confusion, which must have been compounded by Federico's long absences on military campaigns and by the illness and death of Federico's wife, Margherita of Bavaria, in the autumn of 1479, Beltramino seems to have performed virtually the same functions as before. Even if he was no longer called auditor, he remained a senior member of the marquis's Council of Justice and also served as prior of the recently founded college of Mantuan judges and advocates.[127] In fact, during Federico's rule the position of the vice-podesta of Mantua must have become more intolerable than ever, with Beltramino, now an elder statesman, able to bypass or overrule any judgment that conflicted with his own opinion of a case. The apologetic note in a letter of Baldassare Gabrielli on 5 November 1478 concerning a poor man "who just wanted his sheep back and did not want to start a civil law action" may have been owing to some ruling by Beltramino against initiating a prosecution: "I invoke the entire palace of justice of Mantua," wrote Gabrielli, "[as witness that] I do not want to favor rogues but to persecute them—just as much as the devil hates the cross of Christ—particularly robbers; if there is any one man in the world who hates thieves, it is me."[128] Beltramino was directly entrusted with prominent cases. In July 1480 he was investigating the theft of a vase *(taza)*, the property of Duchess Eleonora of Ferrara. He had interrogated the suspect, Pedro Firentino, who claimed he was out of Mantua at the time of the duchess's visit. Beltramino had been assured by another functionary, Luca da Mariana, that Pedro had been in charge of the valuables and that many witnesses could testify to his presence. No such witnesses had appeared, but Beltramino was so convinced of Pedro's guilt that he proposed going ahead ("de procedere più oltra") without waiting longer, unless the marquis could make Luca produce them.[129] However, Beltramino was careful not to intrude in a case unless authorized; in one long-standing civil dispute he insisted that the parties must go before the "giudice ordinario," that he could not

pato e la città: Giulio Cesare Gonzaga da Bozzolo, Quaderni di Civiltà mantovana, 2 (Mantua, 1994), 21–23.

126. AG, b. 2424, fol. 122, Almerico Almerici to Marquis F. Gonzaga (9 July 1480).
127. D'Arco, *Studi,* 6:141 n. 78.
128. AG, b. 2420 (Governolo).
129. AG, b. 2424, fol. 16, Beltramino to Marquis F. Gonzaga, Mantua (7 July 1480).

interfere in judicial matters unless he had an explicit commission from the marquis to do so.[130]

Explicit evidence that Beltramino's opinion could count above all others is shown in letters in the autumn of 1480 from the vice-podesta Almerico Almerici of Pesaro. Almerici was hesitating to pass the death sentence on a certain Giovan Pietro de Cereno: a number of eminent jurists had given opinions in his defense. Beltramino, however, had resolved that all these jurists were wrong, and he was shocked by the idea that the prisoner's only punishment might be confiscation of his goods and exile. Almerici declared to the Marquis[131] that while he was glad the decision did not rest on his shoulders alone, and while he would of course be willing to defer to one so worthy and valiant as Beltramino, he felt humiliated and calumniated. Almerico had already risked disfavor for complaining to Marquis Federico that soldiers were terrorizing the city at night and even attacking his security patrols.

> Yesterday evening eight *provvisionati* gave chase to one of my knights all the way to the palace and ripped his *zornea* off his back. He would have been cut to pieces if he had not been so fast on his feet. A public example is needed to curb their temerity and audacity. I regret to say so, but unless Your Excellency does something about this continual disorderliness day and night on the part of your *provvisionati,* it will be necessary, to my dishonor and the dissatisfaction of Your Excellency, to keep my knights and retinue shut up at home.[132]

The presence in Mantua of many soldiers or armed retainers led to more and more violent incidents, and it was not always the marquis who was responsible for them. On 14 December 1480 Almerico reported another outrage, when seven soldiers in the pay of Francesco Secco had wounded two men, killing one of them. The vice-podesta had sent members of his staff with the notary of the *giudice del maleficio* to Secco's imposing palace, but to no avail.[133]

---

130. Ibid., fol. 17, Beltramino to Marquis F. Gonzaga, Mantua, (2 Aug. 1480).

131. Ibid., fols. 131, 132, 134 (letters of 27 and 30 Sept. and 18 Oct. 1480).

132. ". . . Doleme fare intendere ad Vostra Excellentia che se quella non provede al disordine continuo si fa cossì de die come di nocte per li suoi provisionati, serà necessario, cum mio dishonore perhò, et cum pocha satisfactione de Vostra Excellentia, che li mei cavalieri et famiglia stiano richiusi in casa..": ibid., fol. 121, letter of Almerico Almerici, Mantua (5 June 1480).

133. Ibid., fol. 130. On Secco, who in 1466 bought a "stancia grande vechia a mezo el

Whether or not any of these matters played a part in forming his decision, at the beginning of 1481 Marquis Federico Gonzaga decided to reinstate the office of podesta, abolishing the downgraded form that had existed since Beltramino's appointment at the end of 1466. Even Marquis Ludovico, shortly before his death, seems to have been disillusioned about the post of vice-podesta, which was acquiring some of the least desirable features of the office it replaced. He complained in a letter of 31 July 1478 that it was already bespoken until the 1490s.[134] Marquis Federico laid down the reasons for his decision in a letter to the protonotary Ascanio Sforza, who was sponsoring two candidates—considered too lightweight in any case—for the posts of vice-podesta and *giudice del maleficio*. Up to now, Federico wrote on 15 February 1481, "the vice-podestas of our city have been doctors [of law] and men of great experience, as the nature of the office requires; now that we have turned this office into podesta, it is [all the more] necessary that [the podesta] should be a doctor of law, and that his officials or judges are tried and experienced, particularly the *giudice del maleficio,* since he has power over men's lives and power [to inflict] corporal penalties. . . ."[135]

The restored podesta was to all appearances much the same as before 1467. He was required to have three assistant judges (two of whom had to be doctors of law), one constable and presumably a posse of sergeants (though these are not mentioned), four domestic servants, four squires with horses, a page, and a cook. The salary was now 277 lire per month—rather more than Beltramino had had—though Federico laid down that 200 lire should be paid by the commune of Mantua and that the extra sum should be found from the judicial fines collected.[136] The first neopodesta was Leonello Tolomei Assassini from Ferrara, whose appointment (to take effect for six months from 1 April) was announced in a letter of 17 January 1481. It contained some of the same stock

borgo de San Giacomo in Mantoa, elli el marchexo ge comenzoe uno magno palazzo," as described by Schivenoglia, see I. Lazzarini, *Gerarchie sociali e spazi urbani a Mantova dal comune alla signoria gonzaghesca* (Pisa, 1994), 162.

134. AG, b. 2895, lib. 87, fol. 32v (letter of 31 July 1478); also cited in chap 2 n. 96.

135. AG, b. 2897, lib. 101, fol. 63v.

136. AG, Lib. pat. 3, fols. 2v–3v (revised statutes of the *podestaria*). The restoration of the office is noted by D'Arco, *Studi,* 6:76–77; Mazzoldi, *Mantova,* 2:376–77; Mozzarelli, *Mantova e i Gonzaga,* 39. It is difficult to agree with Mozarelli that this reinstatement of the podesta was a sign of the "aristocratisation" of the regime; the individuals elected as vice-podesta since 1470 seem to have been little different in rank or even in identity from the podestas of 1481 onward: see the following discussion in text for the example of Giovanni Calzavachi.

phrases about salubrious government used in the first letter appointing
Beltramino as vice-podesta in December 1466.[137] Leonello Tolomei was
well aware of his office's renewed dignity, for he wrote, before his term
came to an end, to ask that he be given a banner to be painted at his own
expense and bearing the imperial eagle, as had been customary before the
institution of the vice-podesta.[138] This was an unnecessary demand since
the reward of a banner was already laid down under the new statute
(penultimate clause). Also allowed was the practice whereby a retiring
podesta could have himself commemorated on the palace walls by a
plaque bearing his name and heraldic arms. Giambattista's successor, the
Florentine Gabriele Ginori, left an exceptionally decorative ceramic
plaque (see plate 3), displaying not only his own and the Gonzaga arms
but also the arms of Florence, of the Medici family, and of several other
cities or dynasties to which he was obliged.[139]

Certainly the revival of the podesta made little difference to the marquis's supervisory role in judicial matters. He wrote, for instance, to his
son Francesco and to the podesta in August 1481 to ensure that a murderer was duly executed.[140] The podesta in 1482, Giovanni Calzavachi
(the same man who in 1470 had been vice-podesta as immediate successor to Beltramino) was writing typical letters asking Federico for clarification of the law. For instance, he asked what sentence was appropriate
for being on the streets without a light at three hours of the night and
singing *mattinate*, one of the offenders playing a lute, the other equipped
with a wind organ—he had found many different proclamations, including one issued in 1455 that prescribed three hoists of the rope.[141]

Probably the revival of the podesta also made little difference to Beltramino's role. He was sent on a mission to hear cases in Reggiolo in the
summer of 1482,[142] and after the outbreak of the anti-Venetian War of
Ferrara, he seems to have been more indispensable than ever. In the second half of 1483 he was given a special commission on the Brescian borders to interrogate suspected spies and collaborators, a task to which he

137. AG, Lib. pat. 3, fol. 3v; see the end of chap. 3.
138. AG, b. 2430, fol. 265 (6 Mar. 1482); for the text, see Bertolotti, *Prigioni e prigionieri*, 9–10. A later podesta, Giovanni Battista da Castello, wrote on 30 Oct. 1493 asking the marquis to pay "Lucha depintore" for making his standard (ibid., 10).
139. See intro. n. 44.
140. AG, b. 2897, lib. 102, fols. 67v–68r, 71r, 80v.
141. AG, b. 2430, fols. 266, 269, letters of Calzavachi (5 and 12 Aug. 1482).
142. AG, b. 2428, letters of Beltramino, Reggiolo, 28 and 31 July and 8 Sept. 1482.

applied all his usual zeal;[143] his son Matteo is also recorded in Gonzaga service at this time, as delivering an urgent message from the marquis to Francesco Secco.[144] In the course of his investigations at Asola, Beltramino kept Antonio Masono dangling for so long on the rope, at a height of fifteen *braccia,* yet failing to get a word out of him, that, he reported, "all the man's nerves suddenly seemed to relax and his body became as distorted as though he had had four jerks." Frightened that the wretch might die even if a single jerk was inflicted, Beltramino had him lowered.[145] One accused, a certain Carlo Piacano, detained in the castle of Asola and formally interrogated by Beltramino, acknowledged that he had behaved suspiciously—having been seen with enemy archers, and not having reported the encounter to his superiors—but nothing more could be extracted from him, so he was taken under guard to Mantua.[146] Beltramino boasted that he talked to the soldiers *(provvisionati)* in such an oblique way that he gained their confidence and they did not perceive what he was really getting at.[147] With much to busy himself with in the year before Marquis Federico died, including the acquisition of more property near Mantua,[148] it may be that Beltramino had little premonition of the storm gathering about his own head.

After the death of Marquis Federico Gonzaga on 14 July 1484, Beltramino faced such orchestrated hostility that he fled from Mantua, bringing to an ignominious close his quarter-century of service to the Gonzaga dynasty. The full story of this nemesis has not come to light, but many details can be fitted together. Letters from Beltramino himself provide most of the information, although of course they presented it very one-sidedly. The attack was officially sanctioned by a judicial investigation, or sindication, of his acts as councillor and judge: he had undergone

---

143. E.g., AG, b. 2431, letter of Beltramino dated at Cavriana, 6 Sept. 1483.
144. Ibid., letter from Matteo Cusadri, Asola, 13 Oct. 1483.
145. Ibid., Beltramino to Federico Gonzaga, Asola, 16 Dec. 1483.
146. Ibid., "Johannes Nagelus" and Beltramino from Asola, 18 and 19 Dec.
147. "per il voltzare ch'io feci ne lo mio parlare non se acorgessero troppo quale fosse il mio principale intento": AG, b. 2430, fol. 444, Beltramino to Marquis Federico Gonzaga, Mantua (20 Dec. 1483).
148. AN, Registrazioni notarili, 1483, fols. 25v–26r, records a purchase on 11 Apr. 1483 by "domini Beltramini de Cusatris civis Mantuae" of a nine-year lease of land "in territorio Aquedrugii" near the road to Curtatone, from the rector of the church of S. Simone and S. Giuda, Mantua, for thirty-two ducats. On 2 July 1484 Beltramino at last received formal investiture of the estate at Felonica previously bestowed on him by Cardinal Francesco Gonzaga (ibid., 1484, fol. 971).

the procedure before (after retiring as vice-podesta in January 1470),[149] but without ill consequences. On 22 September the marquis suspended the proceedings, having been informed by Amato Cusadri and other sons of Beltramino that Beltramino's lawyer Gabrielle Ceppi was ill and could not prepare their father's defense. But the Council of Justice was empowered to do as it thought fit,[150] and only a short delay was gained. In early November the marquis addressed a letter to the "sindicho" affirming his decision to go ahead, on account of the "complaints and lamentations made about him [Beltramino], for the sake of our public interest and that of particular persons."[151] Not long after this, decrees were addressed to the current podesta and two practicing lawyers, Benedetto Tosabezzi[152] and Ludovico Ghisi. The first of these decrees, dated 19 November 1484, ordered them to investigate the charges of extortion in frequent cases heard by Beltramino ("former councillor of our father"); the second, dated 27 January, confirmed the first and ordered them to proceed to pass sentence.[153]

Beltramino's pen was active in his own defense even before these decrees were issued; the prospect of prosecution had evidently been building up for some time, and he knew what charges were being brought, or concocted, against him. His poignant appeals to the young marquis emphasized the trust placed in him over so many years by Ludovico and Federico Gonzaga. Although the circumstances are not altogether clear, there can be little doubt that his fall—as a too powerful tool of the old regime—had been desired and organized by Francesco Secco d'Aragona, and by Eusebio Malatesta[154] and others of the same faction in the Gonzaga court. Secco was a senior figure; born in 1423 (so slightly older than Beltramino), he sprang from a family territorially powerful at Caravaggio—very close, in fact, to Crema. He married Marquis Ludovico's illegitimate daughter Caterina,[155] and their daughter Paola married Marsilio Torelli, count of Guastalla. A professional *con-*

---

149. See the end of chap. 3.

150. AG, b. 2901, lib. 121, fol. 62r.

151. AG, Lib. decr. 22, fol. 17v.

152. On Tosabezzi, see E. Marani, *Il Palazzo D'Arco a Mantova* (Mantua, 1980), 82, 95–96.

153. AG, Lib. decr. 22, fols. 106r–107r, 137r.

154. On Secco, see also chap. 7. Eusebio was, according to Andrea Schivenoglia, a converted Jew brought up by Paola Malatesta (Marquis Gianfrancesco's wife) and close to Federico Gonzaga since childhood: BCMn, MS 1019, fol. 83v.

155. According to Schivenoglia she was one-eyed and hunch-backed (ibid., fol. 53v).

dottiere of extraordinary physical strength and powers of endurance, Secco had been knighted by Emperor Frederick III in 1451, and for his services to King Ferrante of Naples in the late 1470s he was allowed to add the title "of Aragon" to his name.[156] It is likely that Secco had for many years been a potential rival or threat to Beltramino: he personified just that brand of Ghibelline, territorial nobility, proud of its immunities and bellicosity, to which the Cusadri, representing an urban professional elite, were opposed. Various earlier occasions have been noted when Secco's own armed retainers had created just the sort of disorder that Beltramino deplored; true, he and Secco had at times been paired to work together in Mantuan affairs—notably, over the betrothal of Francesco Gonzaga with Isabella d'Este in 1480—but it is hard to imagine their relationship was ever an easy one. At all events, Secco was specially commended by Federico Gonzaga on his deathbed,[157] and he quickly assumed a dominant role over the young Francesco, who was no doubt in some awe of Secco's military distinction.

The news that Beltramino had lost his position of trust in the Mantuan administration quickly reached Ferrara: maybe Beltramino himself had spread the word. Already a letter of Duke Ercole d'Este, dated 30 October, asked the marquis to allow Beltramino to transfer to his service; he was looking for a man of strong character to conduct a vigorous campaign ("uno homo vivo . . . di fare questa impresa gagliardamente") against criminality:[158] but this consent was to be delayed for several years.

From Beltramino's own letters it emerges that after the campaign to denigrate him had developed in Mantua, he took refuge at the monastery of San Benedetto Polirone, where he probably took advantage of the extensive new quarters built to accommodate visiting laymen and pilgrims.[159] He claimed that he did not return to Mantua to defend himself because his life was in danger, and (on the advice of the abbot) he had then gone to Crema, where he stayed for the next few years. He was

---

156. For a summary of his career, see F. Secco d'Aragona, "Francesco Secco, i Gonzaga e Paolo Erba," *Archivio storico lombardo* 83 (1956): 210–13.

157. Letter of Leonardo Aristeo to Rodolfo Gonzaga, quoted in Luzio, "Isabella d'Este e Francesco Gonzaga," 53–54.

158. "Nui havemo intentione de punire alcuni giotti et homini de mala sorte": AG, b. 1183.

159. See P. Carpeggiani, "La rinascita del '400," in *I Secoli del Polirone*, ed. P. Piva (San Benedetto Po, 1981), 195.

already there when the orders were issued for the investigation to proceed. The first of his letters in self-defense is dated at Crema on 4 November 1484. Having heard that he was to be sindicated in his absence, he appealed to the marquis for clemency and grace.[160] Other members of the Council of Justice, he complained, who had not done a hundredth part of the work he had done, were not to be sindicated. Such was his reward, he lamented, after twenty-seven years of service, including innumerable journeys throughout Italy on behalf of the Gonzaga regime. There were many, he declared, from all ranks of society in Mantua, who (although they kept quiet about it) deplored the treatment he was receiving. "The thing that makes me grieve most of all," he went on, "is that those who glory in my ill fortune are the enemies of the regime of your ancestors. I don't mention Francesco Secco," he remarked obliquely, "but you know to whom I refer: and I will prove it, when this can be done on equal terms." He then specified some of the charges against himself: having many innocent people imprisoned and tortured without legal authority, and having had such people released after taking from them enormous amounts of money or possessions. Finally, a key passage, which does not wholly exonerate himself, throws a new and sinister light on Marquis Federico.

> My lord, you know that no one could be put in prison without your father knowing about it, because all applications by prisoners for their release were seen by him. The truth is that his Lordship ordered that so-and-so should be detained, and I obeyed. Nor should they be put to [the torture of] the rope [without the marquis's knowledge]. Many times I and also d. Donino, when he was the *giudice del maleficio,* told his Lordship that to us it seemed right not to apply the rope to someone, and his Lordship said that he wanted it, and that we should give him one, two, or three hoists as appropriate; they know that such orders are given by word of mouth and cannot be proved.

Beltramino justified his conduct about the leak of an official document, apparently one of the specific charges against him, and then reverted to the more serious issue, his moral integrity as a judge.

---

160. AG, b. 1432, fol. 269v, Beltramino to Marquis F. Gonzaga, Crema (4 Nov. 1484); for the text, see app. 1.

They also say that I am guilty of great chicanery [*barataria*] and have betrayed Christ—that I have borrowed money from many whose cases were being tried by myself. This is a great corruption: I know perfectly well that the Magnifico Francesco Secco, when he lent me a hundred ducats, did not have a case pending before me, nor did Gianfrancesco Gonzaga, or Angelo Bonzani, or others who have served me with courtesy as friends do among themselves, and not in the course of litigation. They say that I have received presents from men of Mantuan territory and elsewhere and have become rich in this way. Nor is it enough for them to investigate me for receiving presents from Your Lordship's subjects, but if, say, a friend from Verona had sent me hares or pheasants. They say that I have left Mantua without Your Lordship's permission or that of the passport office [*ufficio delle bollette*]: Your Lordship knows that the abbot of San Benedetto did not want to keep me there and wrote asking Your Lordship if you wanted him to detain me or issue your license for me to go elsewhere. And because he did not wish to detain me, he wrote to you about my coming here.

Beltramino closed on a note of mordant piety: "May God who knows the hearts of men hear me. Naked came I into the world and naked shall I end beneath the earth."

Several weeks later he resumed his pleading.[161]

Up till now I have never tried to recommend myself to you or to any other lord, hoping that my innocence and the love and favor I have received in the past would be sufficient recommendation of themselves, and I think Your Lordship would have acknowledged this had there not been such continuous personal attacks and malice poured into your ears. There are certain people who want every imaginable evil to befall me and think that I should be expelled from both heaven and earth. But I shall never cease to hope for your grace, because I know you are more ready to bestow clemency and grace than any other prince I have ever known . . . I said and wrote to Your Lordship that I had a debt of six hundred to seven hundred ducats, but I had to pay out over one thousand ducats without my defense [being heard]. I have been forced to pay immediately, and some I have had to pay

---

161. Ibid., fol. 271, Beltramino to Marquis F. Gonzaga, Crema (28 Nov. 1484).

received payment previously. In order to disgrace me, they said that I wanted to enter the Benedictine Order, then that I went off to Crema and to other places, although Your Lordship wrote that you were content that the monks should take me in. On the abbot's advice I was obliged tearfully to depart; father Guglielmo, who came to San Benedetto from Pavia, said that I should go to Crema. God so willed it that father Guglielmo died, so that I would have to wait until Easter when there would be a chapter meeting and they would decide what to do about me. Please ask the abbot and the monks [about this], and concerning Pelegrino Calderino who came to murder me in the monastery . . . It is untrue that I have been anywhere except to Crema, and here I live like a hermit, not getting involved in anything.

Protesting again about his detractors, Beltramino denied some further allegations of misdeeds he had committed.

Eusebio [Malatesta] may say things to exculpate himself, but I did not teach or counsel him to rob your father of jewels, money, and silver, or to take money, cups, vases, and silver from various people . . . Had I felt assured of my personal safety on leaving San Benedetto I would have gone to Mantua and pleaded my case, but there were people who wanted to kill me or threaten me and poison me; even Evangelista [Gonzaga] said he had sent two men to murder me. So I followed the advice of those good men who advised me to come here . . . All my life has been praiseworthy and not at all damnable as others make out.

This high note[162] on which Beltramino ended his self-justification seems to confirm that, however cruel his present treatment, he had little self-awareness or conscience about misdemeanors in the past, whether the homicidal escapade in his youth at Pavia or his rigor and severity (and perhaps even some acts of self-interest) as a judge.

The third letter in the series, written two weeks later,[163] strikes an even more querulous note. Beltramino declared that, though in a Christlike spirit he had resolved to bear all his adversities, he believed that anyone who neglected his own honor was in fact committing murder. In Mantua

---

162. ". . . la vita mia è stata laudabile e non cossì damnabile como altri lo fanno": ibid., fol. 271v.

163. Ibid., fol. 270, Beltramino to Marquis F. Gonzaga, Crema (10 Dec. 1484).

it seemed that nobody had time for anything but the destruction of "that rogue Beltramino": in fact, he went on to emphasize, the marquis's forebears had no man more faithful and devoted to their affairs.[164]

Reiterating that he could not come to defend himself because he would be in danger, he dropped an innuendo about one of his investigators and commented interestingly about the demand of Leone, a well-known Jewish moneylender, that Beltramino should refund to him a sum of money that Leone had paid to Marquis Federico. Beltramino insisted that this payment had not been according to any judicial sentence he had passed but was a matter of agreement between Leone and the marquis. "So," he continued defiantly in this letter to Marquis Francesco, "you should sindicate your father, not me. I simply obeyed, in my usual way, without any dissembling."[165]

This was not the first time, as we have seen, that Beltramino had used the defense of just "obeying orders" or had shifted responsibility to Marquis Federico Gonzaga. It is another nice illustration of the way he was ready to reconcile legality with arbitrary rule; seeing himself as a lion of justice, he was, when he so chose, decidedly content to lurk beneath the throne. Beltramino even went on to recall how different it had been when he was sindicated after his three-year term as vice-podesta. He commented that Marquis Ludovico had protected him from rather similar allegations and criticism: "Your grandfather said—against those who had banded together against me, just like now—that they should not sindicate Beltramino but himself, and thus he silenced them."[166]

Although Beltramino had been fairly discreet about naming his persecutors in the correspondence so far quoted, it is clear from a letter in November 1493[167] that he believed Francesco Secco had much to do

164. "Ben che io habia deliberato tollerare ogni adversitate per rispetto di colui che indebitamente porto e sofferi tante tribulatione e pene, non posso però se non dolermi de le cosse mi lassa fare V.S.; non per rispetto tanto di robba quanto del'onore, che Dio vole l'omo ne debba far grande caso, digando caduno essere homicida che non ha cura de l'onore suo . . . pare che a Mantua non se tendi ad altro cha la destructione de quello ribaldo de d. Beltramino": ibid.

165. ". . . mai non feci parola ni atto se non tanto quanto mandava soa Signoria; unde se sindica il signore vostro patre, non io, che ho obedito segondo l'usanza mia senza alcuna simulatione": ibid.

166. ". . . et altre volte fazandosse il sindicato mio per essere stato vicepotestate trei anni de cosse simile, lo Illustrissimo Signor vostro avo diceva contra quelli che erano uniti e colligati contra mi, como è anchora adesso, che non volevanno sindicare domino Beltramino ma soa Signoria, e gl'impose scilentio": ibid.

167. AG, b. 1289, fol. 399; for the text, see app. 1; discussed in Epilogue.

with his disgrace. Secco's dominant role for seven years after 1484 and the final phase in Beltramino's long-standing relationship with Mantua's rulers will be discussed in the epilogue.

Meanwhile, for several years after November 1484 Beltramino continued to lurk in Crema, where he soon resumed his earlier role in that city's affairs. He was elected a member of the Council of One Hundred by 31 December 1484 and regularly attended its meetings throughout 1485; he was appointed a *provisor* to the podesta on 1 January, and although he resigned this office only two weeks later, he seems to have accepted it for July and August and again in January 1486.[168] His name disappears from minutes of Council meetings in 1486 but as late as April 1487 he was co-opted as an *adiuncto* of the Council.[169] He was resilient enough to write again to Marquis Francesco Gonzaga on 20 March 1486, pointing out that he had been without a job for two years and that Duke Ercole d'Este had made him a firm offer. He asked if the marquis would write to Ercole that he would be content to release Beltramino into his service. Since Ercole had made the same request in 1484, it seems that Beltramino had never been formally released from his Mantuan obligations and lived, moreover, in the shadow of Marquis Francesco Gonzaga's ill will. Such disfavor would have compromised him in his prospect of employment, particularly since the marquis was betrothed to Duke Ercole's daughter. Another year was to pass before the consent was given for Beltramino at last to take up the appointment. Beltramino understood that Ludovico Gonzaga (the bishop-elect of Mantua and the youngest of Marquis Federico's brothers) had interceded for him, and he warmly thanked the marquis, in a letter of 17 April 1487, affirming once more—and despite his downfall—that all the credit he possessed was owing to the Gonzaga family, that he was their "fatura" and "creatura."[170]

---

168. BCCr, Archivio storico II, reg. 9, fols. 150r, 157r–v, 190r, 215v.
169. Ibid., fol. 273r.
170. AG, b. 1432, fol. 406.

5

Judicial Crisis in Ferrara, Modena, and Reggio

Within weeks of Beltramino's Mantuan downfall in 1484, Ercole d'Este was asking about his availability for office; that he persisted with this request is evidence both of his determination to get the right man for the job[1] and of Beltramino's high reputation as a fighter against crime. Ercole held out for Beltramino because his appointment was part of a general hardening, in the late 1480s and early 1490s, of his policy toward crime and public order. A commissioner, with a troop of mounted archers, was briefly sent to Argenta to deal with the serious breakdown of authority there.[2] A stern new captain of justice, Gregorio Zampante da Lucca, was appointed in Ferrara. A respected, elder official in the Romagna was recalled, dismissed, and severely punished for letting two murderers escape in return for a bribe of eighty ducats.[3] Against the suspect tide of requests to waive sindication, Ercole ordered that all officials were to be sindicated, notwithstanding any testimonials *(lettere del ben servito)* written in their favor by local communes.[4] Ercole became irritated by the lobbying for pardons to which he was subjected and in which officials were involved. In February 1493, the ducal secretary wrote:

> For some weeks, Ercole has much hardened against giving pardons
> for murder, even if peace has been obtained [from the victim's family]
> and one or two years have elapsed, and he is very ill disposed toward

---

1. Cf. W.L. Gundersheimer, *Ferrara: The Style of a Renaissance Despotism* (Princeton, NJ, 1973), 215, for whom Ercole was "neither so thorough nor astute a judge of men, nor so careful and effective a supervisor," as his predecessors.

2. RdS, Ferrara, b. 13, letters of Filippo Bardelli, 4 Nov. 1490, and Bartolomeo Pioli, 8 Mar. 1491.

3. Biblioteca apostolica vaticana, MS Chigi I.I.4, Ugo Caleffini, "Cronaca ferrarese," fol. 291v.

4. ASCMo, Carte sciolte, b. 1, 28 Aug. 1491; ASRe, Comune, Provvigioni, reg. 98, fol. 237 (11 Apr. 1491).

Modenesi, as it seems to him that they do nothing else. And some reports from the podesta of Modena have arrived that much mitigate some homicides for which pardon is requested; nevertheless, his lordship has not agreed to a single one.[5]

In 1492 Ercole lamented that his clemency of past years had not been accepted in the right spirit but had emboldened some, both men and women, to become more disobedient and disrespectful. More people were making armed opposition to officials, exciting popular tumult, ringing bells to sound the alarm, and impeding justice and executions—all of which he considered to be against his princely majesty and the tranquillity of the country and of the *uomini da bene*. In consequence, he confirmed heavy penalties (announced earlier) for opposition to officials, set the penalty of death and quartering for the unauthorized ringing of alarm bells, and reiterated that noblemen were not to shelter bandits.[6] Then in 1496 came Ercole's great, Savonarola-inspired Easter proclamation against blasphemy, gambling, sodomy, prostitution, Jews, and Sunday trading.[7] So the duke took sterner action at all levels of judicial process: issuing warning proclamations, heightening penalties, ensuring heavier policing, refusing pardon, and taking exemplary action against official corruption. What could have occasioned such a comprehensive hardening of attitude?

One answer would point to Ercole's religious policies in these years. Gundersheimer observes that "Ferrara in the 1490s became a kind of

---

5. "Il nostro Ill.mo signore duca da alcune septimane in qua si e multo indurito nel far gratie de homicidii, se bene se habia la pace et sia passato un anno e dui et in questa parte e molto mal disposta verso modenesi parendoli che non faciano mai altro et sono venute alcune relatione del podesta de Modena che alezeriscono molto alcuni homicidii de li quali si e domandate gratie, nondimeno sua Signoria non ne ha voluto fare nessuna": ASE, Cancelleria, Carteggio di referendari, consiglieri, cancellieri e secretari, b. 4, Siviero Sivieri to Eleonora d'Aragona, 11 Feb. 1493.
6. ASE, Gridario, B, Registri di gride, b. 1, vol. 1, fols. 236–39; cf. the misunderstood clemency of James VI, king of Scotland: K.M. Brown, *Bloodfeud in Scotland* (Edinburgh, 1986), 215.
7. ASE, Gridario, Gride manoscritte, 1, 1 Apr. 1496; *Diario ferrarese*, 174; J. Burckhardt, *The Civilization of the Renaissance in Italy* (London, 1955), 302. For the Savonarola connection, see A. Cappelli, "Fra Girolamo Savonarola e notizie intorno il suo tempo," *AMMo* 4 (1867): 371. Cf. Carlo Malatesta's 1387 decree against blasphemy, pagan idolatry, incantation, and sodomy, specifically imposing penalties above and beyond "la pena spirituale": G. Bagli, "Bandi malatestiani," *AMRo*, 3d ser., 3 (1884–85): 79–82. Cf. also Amedeo VIII di Savoia's laws, inspired by the preacher Vincenzo Ferrer, on blasphemy, Jews, prostitution, and saints' days: Comba, "Gli Statuti di Amedeo VIII," 39.

Mecca for the religious, a city of new monastic and lay foundations, a city in which such mystics as Suor Lucia da Narni was persuaded to resettle, a city in which vanities were burned, sumptuary-laws enforced, public morals carefully watched."[8] This new discipline was also enforced on clergymen and their churches, for it was in 1490 that Ercole took up with Pope Innocent VIII the twin problems of criminous clerks and sanctuary. In January of that year, he instructed his ambassador in Rome that there was in Ferrara great popular discontent at the abuse (corruptella) of criminals taking shelter in churches, and that he feared some popular outburst, "because when citizens are attacked in their property or persons and they see their adversaries, malefactors, and thieves save themselves by this means, they can hardly be held from overstepping the mark [male ponno stare al segno]."[9] So the ambassador was to ask the pope to allow ducal officials to enter churches to arrest fugitive criminals. Apparently unaware of the controversial nature of his request, Ercole was "sure that his Beatitude [the pope] will easily grant all of this as it tends to a good and just end."

Ercole's first request to the pope met with the predictable refusal, on the grounds of infringing ecclesiastical liberties. Ercole responded that he had no intention of ruining such liberties, and that he wanted only what had already been granted to other lords and cities of Italy (was this true?) in order to repress "insolence."[10] Eventually, the pope saw the point and issued a bull curtailing both sanctuary and benefit of clergy, in the interest, which he now adopted as his own, of protecting the "honest decency" of the clerical order. Now Ercole's secular judges could proceed against those in minor orders who at the time of the alleged crime were not in habit or tonsure, and they could also remove and punish murderers who fled into churches and other "ecclesiastical places" (provided that, before punishment, an ecclesiastical judge agreed that the killing had been deliberate).[11] Though dispute still arose over the application of

---

8. Gundersheimer, Ferrara, 197.

9. ASE, Ambasciatori, Roma, b. 7, XXII, no. 5 (12 Jan. 1490).

10. ASE, Minutario, Lettere sciolte, b. 3, 6 Mar. 1490.

11. ASE, Carteggio, Principi esteri, Roma, b. 9, no. 75 (5 May 1492), briefly mentioned in Frizzi, Memorie, 4:163. Cf. Sigismondo Malatesta's creation of new sanctuary: Jones, Malatesta, 303 n. 9. This acquiescence in secular action against "unworthy" clerics seems typical of the fifteenth-century papacy: J.A.F. Thomson, Popes and Princes, 1417–1517 (London, 1980), 183–93. The real debate between papacy and secular states lay in matters of papal taxation and appointment to benefices: E. Laruelle, E.-R. Labande, and P. Ourliac, L'Eglise au temps du Grand Schisme et de la crise conciliaire (1378–1449) (n.p., 1962),

this license to particular cases, it was clearly used by the duke and his officials.[12]

There was, though, more than religious policy here. Short- and long-term problems in ensuring good order are revealed in the Ferrarese chronicles from these years. The diarist Bernardino Zambotti, who in later years held judicial office first at Reggio and then at Mantua,[13] provides some evidence for the character of criminality and justice in Ferrara in the 1470s and 1480s. His diary allows us to perceive, through his eyes, both the background pattern of violence and the deterioration toward the end of the 1480s. Three types of conflict featured in his chronicle especially stand out: first, violence in the university milieu (fights among students, broader conflicts within the university at times of rectoral election, student violence against others);[14] second, disorders arising from the rowdy band of Este servants, especially those of Ercole's brother Sigismondo (one killed a cloth merchant in a gamblers' brawl; three others, including Sigismondo's chaplain, were involved in a two-year campaign of nocturnal thieving from stalls on the main square);[15] and third, the apparently unpunished woundings and killings committed by members of the urban elites.[16] While the main sites of violence, according to Zambotti, were the university, the Este entourage, and the local aristocracy, punishment hit the poor more than the rich. Corporal punishment he records in the forms of whipping and mutilation for perjury[17] and execution (mainly by hanging) of foreigners, *contadini,* and lower-class folk

---

332–90; G. Chittolini, "Stati regionali e istituzioni ecclesiastiche nell'Italia centrosettentrionale del Quattrocento," in *La chiesa e il potere politico dal medioevo all'età contemporanea,* ed. G. Chittolini and G. Miccoli, Einaudi *Storia d'Italia, Annali* vol. 9 (Turin, 1986), 160–63. But acquiescence can also be read as a return to an older, thirteenth-century severity, in canon law and practice, by which clerics who dressed or behaved contrary to clerical duty ipso facto lost their legal privileges: R. Génestal, *Le privilegium fori en France du décret de Gratien à la fin du XIVe siècle* (Paris, 1921), 174–83, 208–24. Also in the 1480s, King Henry VII of England obtained papal approval for similar limitation of sanctuary and benefit of clergy: R.L. Storey, *The Reign of Henry VII* (London, 1968), 151.

   12. LD, C 12, fol. 34; LD, C 14, fol. 70; RdS, Ferrara, b. 1, 21 Feb. 1492. See P. Rasi, "I rapporti tra l'autorità ecclesiastica e l'autorità civile in Feltre," *Archivio veneto,* 5th ser., 13 (1933): 96–98; Chittolini, "Stati regionali e istituzioni ecclesiastiche," 161.

   13. *Diario,* 216, 254, 263, 286, 295.

   14. Ibid., 44, 49, 51, 65, 71, 72, 84, 87, 122, 200.

   15. Ibid., 73, 181, and, for the servants of Rinaldo d'Este, 180–81.

   16. Ibid., 73, 86, 191, 200; see J. Larner, "Order and Disorder in Romagna, 1450–1500," in *Violence and Civil Disorder in Italian Cities, 1200–1500,* ed. L. Martines (Berkeley, 1972), 50, 54.

   17. *Diario,* 95, 201.

for theft and murder. The murders punished fall into several types in Zambotti's diary: opportunistic killings associated with theft,[18] crimes of passion,[19] unintended killing in disputes over debt,[20] and assassination in furtherance of enmity.[21] The years 1488–89, however, did see a change and worsening in the pattern, with the killing of two officials in the *contado*,[22] two breakouts from the Ferrarese prison,[23] and the beginnings of a feud involving the banker Rigo San Vitale and his family[24]—in addition to the ordinary catalog of murderous assaults on citizens and students in the streets.[25]

A similar breakdown in public order is apparent in parts of the countryside, particularly at Argenta. The podesta there in 1490–91, Filippo Bardelli, collapsed under the pressure of the challenge to his authority. Already in June 1490 he reported his inability to take action against armed bandits returning to Argenta with ducal pardons and touring the town hunting for their enemies.[26] In July the "great disturbance and danger" warned of by an earlier podesta erupted, as two members of the Quieti family were killed on the piazza.[27] In October the podesta's constable was assaulted by armed men just outside the podesta's house: "I don't want to stay here if I don't have the force to stay securely, for tonight I have had greater fear than I have ever had," reported the podesta.[28] In the following month, in response to an order to proceed against some named criminals, he asked to be excused from prosecution of more than one of them, "hoping that your lordship loves me more alive than dead," for he maintained that in proceeding against these men, "I am certain I would lose life and belongings."[29] If he has to proceed, he continued, he would like to do so from the safety of Ferrara. The same

---

18. Ibid., 141–42, 208.

19. Ibid., 85, 166, 180.

20. Ibid., 72, 200.

21. Ibid., 207.

22. Ibid., 199, 210.

23. Ibid., 208, 210.

24. Ibid., 191, 203, 207.

25. Ibid., 200, 202, 211.

26. RdS, Ferrara, b. 13, Filippo Bardelli to Ercole d'Este, 21 June 1490.

27. Ibid., 10 July 1490.

28. "non volgio stare qui se non ho tale forza che ge possa stare securo, perche questa nocte ho habuto magior paura che mai havesse": ibid., 30 Oct. 1490.

29. "Persuadendome che la v. S. me ami come suo charo fidellissimo servitor et me habia piu achato vivo che morto . . . Supplico quella non me volgia necessitare a procedere contra de epsi perche facendollo sunto certo perderia la victa et la roba": ibid., 2 Nov. 1490.

fear, he insisted, gripped the local town council: when he had asked them
to write to the duke about recent assaults, they had refused, out of fear
for their lives and property. "If the men who live here have this fear," he
wrote, "consider what the officials must feel, given that *they* are at home,
and *we* are outsiders."[30] Such officials felt isolated, as if "in enemy territory."[31]

The problem lay not just in Bardelli's own inadequacy: even under his
more energetic successor, Bartolomeo Pioli, the same difficulties can be
glimpsed. But Pioli offered solutions, where Bardelli had sought merely to
escape. Pioli suggested changes to the selection of the constable's *fanti*, as
the "local innkeepers and peasants" were insufficient to the task;[32] advised
amendment to criminal procedure, to avoid the flight of suspects between
citation and examination;[33] and urged Ercole to have his archers show
their faces in Argenta "at least once a month," "to keep this place in
fear."[34] Though he dealt with problems in a less alarming way, the message
of Pioli's letters was the same: the need for more dedicated staff, procedures
offering fewer safeguards to suspects, and an intensification of fear.

It was presumably dissatisfaction of this sort with the existing judicial
structure and available personnel that led to the appointment in Ferrara of
a supplementary captain of justice in 1490, in the person of the former
podesta, Gregorio Zampante. The proclamation announcing his appointment made his role crystal clear: he had "the fullest authority, jurisdiction,
and power to proceed against any criminal for any crime and to punish
them as best he thinks in his *arbitrio*, without observing the rule of law or
of the statutes."[35] Princely intolerance with the ordinary judiciary and
with statutory restrictions had led finally to the overriding of both.

---

30. "e se epsi homeni hano questo dubio che son de la terra, considera v. S. quello che
debbe havere li offitialli atento che gli sono in casa e nui siamo forasteri": ibid.

31. Chittolini, "L'onore dell'officiale," 13.

32. RdS, Ferrara, b. 13, 10 Apr. 1491.

33. Ibid., 3 Mar. 1491.

34. Ibid., 20 June 1491. Ercole d'Este was sufficiently impressed with Pioli to recommend him as podesta for the city of Bologna: ASBo, Comune, Lettere del comune, reg. 5,
fol. 95v (15 Feb. 1493). Pioli also served Ercole in the Garfagnana, and during his term of
office there judicial fines amounted to seventeen hundred lire, having reached only five hundred lire under his predecessor: LD, C 10, fols. 210–11 (24 July 1487).

35. "La Excellentia del nostro Illustrissimo Signore Duca de Ferrara, desiderosa de tenir
purgata questa sua cita de Ferrara e suo destreto e contato de li mali homini e che se
delectano de mal vivere, confidandosi de la integrita, sufficientia e fede del Magnifico cava-
liero e doctore M. Gregorio di Zampanti da Luca, . . . ha constituto e electo el predicto M.

The activity of Zampante in Ferrara has left two, completely contra-dictory records: the letters that he wrote to the duke, and the Ferrarese chronicles.[36] To the duke he was a highly trusted and favored official: as even the chronicles report, Zampante was knighted by Ercole, who also stood as godfather to his son, appropriately named Ercole Benedetto.[37] To the "respectable opinion" represented by the chroniclers, however, Zampante was one of the damned, not the blessed. This dichotomy is very revealing of the nature of ducal government in Ferrara, for it con-trasts an inside view of the intentions and effects of Zampante's actions with outsiders' dislike of his methods. The dichotomy follows precisely the dividing line, made evident in chapter 1, between judicial efficiency and financial profiteering. Whether or not Zampante really made the for-tune that one chronicler alleges, his methods seemed to be those of a judge merely concerned with financial gain.

Let us first look at the official record. Zampante's expeditious way with criminals, officials, and statute law is very clear from the start. He criticized his subordinates for impeding justice.[38] He similarly dismissed objections to his application of torture, contrary to the statutes, in order to extract confessions.[39] His staff greeted the new podesta with insults, and Zampante interfered with the podesta's business.[40] When Ercole ordered that the collection of fines for arms carrying belonged to local exactors, Zampante advised him that he had been badly counseled, tricked under the cover of fine words. How can it be better, he argued, for citizens to levy these fines on other citizens, when they fear neither God nor the duke and seek only to serve one another? Would not a for-eigner, "who has no regard for anyone save for justice and for your excel-lency," do better? Zampante saw precisely what lay behind the duke's order: "they cannot manipulate me to do favors as they wish," he

---

Gregorio per suo Capitaneo de Iustitia in la prefata cita . . . cum amplissima auctorita iuris-dictione e balia de procedere contra de cadauno delinquente per cadauno delicto e punirli secundo che meglio parera alo arbitrio suo senza servare ordine de ragione o vero de statuti . . .": ASE, Archivio militare, b. 2, Capitano di giustizia, s.d.

36. The chronicles alone were used by Burckhardt, *Civilization of the Renaissance,* 33, 302.

37. Zambotti, *Diario,* 210.

38. RdS, Ferrara, b. 1, Zampante to Ercole d'Este, 11 Dec. 1489.

39. Ibid., s.d. 1489; ASE, Archivio militare, b. 2, 20 Apr. 1491.

40. RdS, Ferrara, b. 1, Antonio Gazzoli to Ercole d'Este, 13 Jan. 1491.

wrote.[41] He was certain when he had spotted lying and perjury.[42] He objected to ducal pardons and tried to invalidate or reverse them.[43] When ordered to release a man for nocturnal vandalism, he argued that he had complaints and evidence that he had held a "diabolical school of sodomy" in his house: true or not, this was the sort of allegation almost certain to win Ercole's mind.[44] Unlike other judges too, Zampante told the duke what to do: following the death of the Ferrarese nobleman Galeazzo Trotti, he reminded Ercole of the need for "a man who is good and thoroughly trustworthy" in Trotti's place on the Ferrarese city council;[45] of the outgoing captain of Modena in 1491, he thought it would be better to confirm him in office, rather than let him go to a post in Lucca, "because he has clean hands . . . though bad things have been said of him" (very bad things, in fact).[46] Of Zampante's effectiveness there can be no doubt: the notary to the criminal court complained of loss of income because of the reduction in crime (or was it merely that Zampante had efficiently channeled all lucrative business into his own hands?).[47]

However, the Ferrarese chroniclers agree with only a small part of this picture. The most detailed account is given in the *Diario ferrarese*, whose anonymous author certainly notes Zampante's fearlessness and expedition. The chronicler records that while detaining the bastard son of Ludovico Orsini, Zampante also detained the aged Ludovico, who had come to speak to the duke;[48] and that when Zampante arrested a "poor man" suspected of involvement in a recent rash of criminal vine cutting, he immediately gave the man "twelve jerks of the rope" to make him confess.[49] This, according to the chronicler was Zampante's method: to

41. "perche non me possano manezare in fare gratie a loro modo": ibid., Gregorio Zampante to Ercole d'Este, 31 Jan. 1490. See also Chittolini, "L'onore dell'officiale," 35 n. 66, who finds, among Sforza officials, that Tuscans refer more frequently to civic conscience than do those from Sforza territories.

42. RdS, Ferrara, b.1, Zampante to Ercole d'Este, s.d. 1490; ASE, Archivio militare, b. 2, 15 July 1491.

43. RdS, Ferrara, b. 1, Zampante to Ercole d'Este, s.d. 1490.

44. ASE, Archivio militare, b. 2, 16 July 1491.

45. Ibid., 12 July 1491.

46. "per le mani nette che epso ha": RdS, Modena, b. 2e, 23 May 1491. The Reggian *anziani* had earlier complained of his many and great extortions, imposed "at his pleasure, against custom and the constitution of his office": ASRe, Comune, Provvigioni, reg. 98, fol. 125 (12 Feb. 1489).

47. Cam. duc., Mandati, vol. 30, fol. 161v.

48. *Diario ferrarese,* 138.

49. Ibid., 149–50 and, for what follows, 182–84.

torture first and to ask questions afterward. But it was the motive of public and private profit that most enraged this chronicler: Zampante's first question, on receiving an accusation, was to ask how much money the accused had (poor men he remitted to the podesta); if the rich could pay a thousand ducats to the duke, he would obtain a pardon for them; his fines were always in hundreds and thousands of ducats; he always insisted on his own fees being paid first; he put away for himself and his sons over two thousand ducats a year. Whoever fell into his hands did not escape with both life and property intact. He was "the greatest, pitiless ribald," "an enemy to God and all the duke's subjects," and his death was therefore God's anger at such "cruelty and ribaldry."

Zampante's term of office was brought to an abrupt end in 1496, when he was murdered in his bed: two foreign students at the University of Ferrara and a converted Jew forced their way into his house at night, knifed and disemboweled him, and then rode triumphantly around the city and away into the countryside. Zambotti writes, "The people ran up with enormous joy to see the corpse . . . and many took bits of his guts out of vendetta, for they had been harmed by him."[50] Though the duke's son, Alfonso, endeavored to give Zampante an honorable funeral, many of the nobility, university men, and citizenry refused to attend: no clearer evidence could be made of the alienation by Zampante of the *uomini da bene*. On the night of his death, the people had shouted, "Death to such ribalds! Viva casa d'Este e chi vive bene." At once a number of songs and poems were circulated about Zampante: in one, Charon refuses to ferry him across the Styx, because Zampante had made so much work for him in the past; in another, those tortured by Zampante appeal to Satan for justice to be done; a third celebrates the manner of death of this "gran latrone."[51] In all, the themes of judicial torture and theft are prominently conjoined.[52]

The contrast between Zampante's presentation of his activities and the perception of them among the citizenry reveals the distances that had opened up between ducal judicial policy and the civic world it was intended to protect and police. There is, however, a third perspective on Zampante. Eleonora had her doubts about him: it seemed to her that he made crimes out to be worse than they were, that he pressed on with cases in his own way (resisting her desire to supervise), and that he

---

50. Zambotti, *Diario*, 262.
51. Catalano, *Ludovico Ariosto*, 99–100.
52. See Jones, *Malatesta*, 323.

moved too quickly to conviction.[53] And Ercole too found himself, in response to petition, canceling many of the monetary fines Zampante imposed for gambling, arms carrying, and assault. The arguments used by petitioners provide some indication of the considerations and interests that were disregarded by Zampante in his expeditious court but that the duke was more sensitive toward. They included youth, poverty, accidental injury, provocation, and ignorance. Departures from statute law were alleged in Zampante's citation of the accused, gathering of testimony, and award of sentence. Petitioners clearly believed that an appeal to the provisions of the statutes could prevail against Zampante's arbitrary powers, alleging that he proceeded "more from passion and hatred than anything else" and imposed fines "de facto."[54] Rationality and legitimacy resided, for these petitioners, in the statutes; anything else had to be emotional or arbitrary.[55] Ducal concession to such argument, suggesting a distaste for excess, concentrated judicial decision-making even more in the duke's arbitrary hands: increased clemency was the concomitant of increased severity.

Zampante's activity in Ferrara also throws fresh light on the debated late-fifteenth-century "crime wave" in that city. The chronicles certainly pay considerable attention to crimes and punishments in Ferrara in this period, and historians were once led by this to believe in an increase of crime, seeking explanations in the duke's frequent absences, his lack of attention to government, and the sale of office,[56] in large-scale immigration of criminous foreigners,[57] or in the social tensions of growing inequalities following impoverishment in war and increasing fiscal pressure.[58] However, Gundersheimer's analysis of the register of capital punishments performed in Ferrara seemed to disprove that there was a crime wave at all: discounting political offenses, the increase in executions was slight between the mid–fifteenth century and 1500, with no indication that foreigners were committing a higher proportion of crimes. In only three years did criminal executions exceed six in number, and these years were all before 1471.[59] However, Gundersheimer does tend to assume

---

53. CS, b. 132, 23 Dec. 1492, 27 June 1493.

54. Cam. duc., Mandati, vol. 31, fols. 25, 63v, 68, 71, 85v, 88, 98, 109v, 110v, 134v.

55. Statutes were a "product and symbol" of urban autonomy: G. Chittolini, "Statuti e autonomie urbane: Introduzione," in Chittolini and Willoweit, *Statuti città territori*, 8, 23–24.

56. Frizzi, *Memorie*, 4:160–61.

57. Gundersheimer, "Crime and Punishment," 109.

58. Gundersheimer, *Ferrara*, 217–18.

59. Gundersheimer, "Crime and Punishment," 110–13.

that the number of executions is a measure of broader levels of crime, and the weakness in his analysis lies in the particular nature of his source (a register of capital punishments). Conversely, Zampante's main *modus puniendi,* as we have seen, was the pecuniary penalty. It was for torture and heavy fines, not hangings, that he earned his disrepute.

Zampante's actions do not necessarily imply a crime wave, even though some contemporaries claimed that crimes were multiplying. In response to this perceived problem, "new remedies to correct delinquents" were created. There would seem to be only three possible explanations for Zampante's appointment and actions: that they reflect a genuine increase in urban crime, that they reflect an intensified concern about crime, or that they were ducal instruments for extracting more revenue from crime. These are not mutually exclusive: it has been argued that in this period there was a rise in crime, a rise in unpunished crime, and a rise in revenue from the prosecution of crime.[60] On the assumption that economic distress fosters criminality, there was cause enough for a rise in crime and violence in late-fifteenth-century Ferrara (food shortages, heavy taxation, extortionate interest rates). At the same time, extensive smuggling, illegal trading, and counterfeiting combined to reduce tax revenues, encouraging the government to focus policing and prosecutorial energies on the more remunerative (that is, nonviolent) offenses. The duke, however, became convinced that fiscal losses were caused by fraud among his own officials, and he was therefore led to generalize the sale of office as a means of ensuring more efficient collection of revenues.

At roughly the same time that Zampante was installed as captain of justice in Ferrara, similar problems in Modena and Reggio led to a similar solution in the appointment of a special commissioner. But though the general problem was similar—a lack of judicial grip on the state of public order—the precise features were very different. In Modena, no trial records survive from this period. In Reggio, those for most of the last two decades of the century are missing, and the latest to survive cover the years 1481–82.[61] These contain a number of features that might have justified ducal concern. First, there was a substantial number of "not proven" verdicts, which arose because of the failure of witnesses to confirm the indictment.[62] Second, there was a preponderance of prosecu-

---

60. R.G. Brown, "The Politics of Magnificence in Ferrara, 1450–1505" (Ph.D. diss., University of Edinburgh, 1982), 163–200.

61. ASRe, Curie della città, Libri delle denuncie.

62. Such verdicts were handed down in fourteen out of twenty-eight trials in the first semester of 1481.

tions of insult, bloodless assault, and threatening behavior, presumably because fines for these lesser offenses went to the commune.[63] This is not to say that more serious crime was not prosecuted or punished—three killings and an infanticide were prosecuted in 1481—but it does suggest that witness intimidation and concerns for local (rather than ducal) revenue determined the broad pattern of criminal prosecution.

Other evidence for the nature of the difficulties and disorders in Modena and Reggio during the 1480s is much more plentiful. In the years 1486–88 we hear of repeated failure to effect arrests,[64] of invasion of a nunnery by ladders and wall breach,[65] of raiding by the men of Sassuolo on the lands of the bishop of Luni,[66] of the urgent repairs needed to the fabric of the civic law court to stave off collapse,[67] of fraud in the office levying straw from the *contado* while the city pleaded poverty to the duke,[68] and of peasant clamor against extortion in the rural small-claims court.[69] In Reggio, errors and frauds in the salt office in the years 1484–88 caused large losses to the revenue,[70] while toward the end of 1488 the commune tried to put its own house in order by taking action against notarial abuses in the rural and criminal courts.[71] In the same years there were complaints about the conduct of the podesta of Frignano, about the activities of bandits in the Reggian hills, about the strong-arm tactics and exorbitant expense demands used in pacifying peasant brawls, and about the "stupendous" extent of extortion by "exactors" in the *contado*.

So far, this is perhaps little more than the ordinary stuff of subject-community misgovernment and complaint, but that the disorder was of a more substantial kind is suggested by letters from the vicar of the podesta of Reggio in June 1485: he and the appeals judge had been assaulted at their bench; those who had committed crimes were going unpunished and standing about on the piazza, such that officials could not do their work; one criminal had become a servant of the captain of the *cittadella*

---

63. These offenses were prosecuted in seventeen out of twenty-eight trials in the first semester of 1481, in twelve out of seventeen in the second semester of 1482.

64. LD, C 10, fol. 28 (2 Apr. 1486).

65. Ibid., fol. 82 (and fol. 164 for burglary of a nunnery).

66. Ibid., fol. 73 (11 Aug. 1486).

67. ASCMo, Vacchetta 1487–88, fol. 68 (28 Apr.); 1489, fol. 38 (4 May).

68. ASCMo, Vacchetta 1487–88, fols. 37v, 62v (3 Sept. and 18 Mar.).

69. Ibid., fol. 68 (28 Apr.).

70. ASE, Carteggio di ufficiali camerali, b. 1, Ercole to the *fattori generali,* 1489.

71. ASRe, Comune, Provvigioni, reg. 98, fols. 108, 110.

and was threatening the judicial notaries whenever they tried to register denunciations of his crimes; the *massaro*, seizing the keys to the city jail, had released a prostitute, falsely claiming that jurisdiction over prostitution belonged to him. The vicar wrote: "It seems to me that your officials here take little account of your lordship . . . but act *proprio motu* . . . I cannot but cry out to the sky when I see ruffians and such prostitutes being favored by those who should extirpate them . . . I have decided that I do not want any more involvement in criminal matters and I wish . . . to return to my dear *patria* and to take up some other office than this one . . . where little account is taken of me and of the office of podesta . . . because your officials want to do things in their way only."[72] Two years later, the podesta warned the duchess that crimes were multiplying daily, that it was impossible to proceed in many criminal trials because the summoners refused to cite suspects, "fearing their power" as they were threatening to kill them. No one else would take on this task. The result, the podesta believed, was that "this city seems to me to live 'in liberta e a popolo' and not in any fear of obedience."[73]

There was also in these years an explosion of feuds ("enmities"). In April 1487 Ercole wrote to the podesta of Frignano to record his concern at recent disturbances that had arisen there because of three enmities. Though the podesta had prosecuted and condemned those involved, Ercole wanted them settled by a good peace, and he dispatched a delegate envoy to this end.[74] At the same time, Ercole had to involve himself personally and directly in the pacification of the men of Sassuolo following several murders committed there. A first attempt was aborted: the difficulty lay in the number of "principals" involved and now scattered, but Ercole knew where they were and how to exert pressure on them. However, the truce remained precarious, too ready to collapse at the slightest provocation (such as an attempt to collect public debts in Sassuolo).[75]

---

72. "Mi pare che quisti vostri officiali facino pocho conto di v. S. . . . ma proprio motu se governano. E certo non posso se non cridare fine al cielo quando vedo ruffiani e simile meretrice essere favoriti da quilli che doverebbeno quilli extirpare . . . Et circa maleffitia . . . me delibero piu non impaciare e desidero . . . redurme ad la dolce patria exercitarme in altro exercitio cha questo de biraria dove come olditi puocho conto se fa di mi et de l'offitio del podesta e questo e perche quisti vostri officiali non voleno fare se non a suo modo": RdS, Reggio, b. 112, Antonio Leuti to Eleonora, 18 June 1485.
73. ASE, Carteggio di referendari, b. 166, 24 June 1487.
74. LD, C 10, fols. 139 (8 Apr. 1487), 142–43 (10 Apr.).
75. LD, C 10, fols. 139v, 146, 147, 148, 194–96, 214, 223, 245–46, 314–15.

The same year saw violent clashes in the city involving the major families and civic churches. As these became the immediate cause of Beltramino's appointment, they deserve extended treatment here. In unraveling the complex fabric of these conflicts, one place to start is with the monastery of San Pietro. This Benedictine community had, under the reforming zeal of the Congregazione di S. Giustina, led an invigorated campaign to reclaim lands and rights at San Cesario, a small place in the Modenese plain devastated in the mid–fourteenth century and occupied by the Boschetti family.[76] The result was a series of disputes and negotiated settlements in which the Boschetti were forced to make large cash payments and property transfers to the monastery.[77] As the monastery continued in the late fifteenth century to buy up land at San Cesario, for which it then claimed ecclesiastical exemption, the Boschetti complained of being forced out of their ancestral lordship, and eventually (in the 1490s and 1500s) they reacted with violence, chasing out the monastery's chaplain, imprisoning its workers, imposing "unjust" corvées, and assaulting its servants.[78] Perhaps the Boschetti were hopeful of riding a general resentment against the monks: in April 1487 the governors of the city had contrasted the poverty of the city priests with the monks' wealth—San Pietro had, they alleged, over fifteen hundred ducats of annual income, a sum that dozens of poor families in the city could put to better use.[79]

In this context of Boschetti concessions to the monastery, dispute arose over the benefice of San Michele, Zena. This had been held by a canon of the cathedral, Gaspare Petrezani, who in 1481 invested his brothers with patronal rights over the benefice. However, Albertino Boschetti had a previous title, granted him by the pope, which he in turn had transferred to San Pietro.[80] This situation caused lengthy litigation between the monastery and the cathedral chapter in the mid-1480s, and the monks' savoir faire in Rome eventually won out over ducal support

76. G. Tiraboschi, *Memorie storiche modenesi* (Modena, 1793–94), 3:182–84; ASMo, Soppressioni napoleoniche, 2653. For the general history, see G. Soli, *Chiese di Modena* (Modena, 1974), 3:103–9; P. Golinelli, "Il monastero, la città, il territorio," and G. Spinelli, "Mille anni di vita monastica," in *S. Pietro di Modena, mille anni di storia e di arte* (Milan, 1984), 24–25, 37.

77. Ibid.

78. ASE, Particolari, b. 213, letters of Albertino Boschetti, 31 Oct. 1490, 16 Apr. 1504, and 3 Apr. 1505.

79. RdS, Modena, b. 1a, Reggimento to Eleonora d'Aragona, 21 Apr. 1487.

80. ASE, Particolari, b. 213, Diamante Boschetti to Ercole d'Este, 31 May 1490; ASE, Minutario, Lettere sciolte, b. 3, Ercole to the bishop of Reggio in Rome, 10 Aug. 1487.

of the canons.[81] During this litigation, in June 1487, Gaspare Petrezani, "subverting the Modenese clergy," as one report had it, led them, banner in hand, to take violent possession of the benefice.[82] To this, the wife of Albertino Boschetti replied by maintaining bandits to rob and raid around San Cesario, to damage the canons' hold on the benefice and its properties.[83]

The character of this dispute, in which the monastic reform movement collided with the interests of cathedral canons and lay landowners, was a familiar one in fifteenth-century Italy, but in this case Gaspare Petrezani had already been at the center of another cause célèbre earlier in the decade: imprisoned for several years in Rome on obscure criminal charges, he was eventually released after much lobbying from the duke and his ambassador in Rome.[84] The aftermath of his trial created much bitterness: he was a "diabolical man," "excommunicated and defamed throughout Italy," according to Diamante Boschetti;[85] he was also the cause of a much resented papal interdict imposed on the cathedral of Modena;[86] and the pope's anger against him was pungent and lasting—he was a "son of perdition," an abuser of papal clemency and of ducal protection, who deserved to be expelled from Modena and stoned.[87] Even the duke of Ferrara, once his supporter, refused him audience later on.[88]

Gaspare Petrezani provides the link with other feuds in the city, for in 1502 he was killed in the cathedral by men acting for the dal Forno family.[89] Between the dal Forno and the Petrezani families there was, across the late fifteenth and early sixteenth centuries, a series of reciprocal killings, only briefly halted by a laboriously constructed peace in 1491–92.[90] Among the Petrezani, Rangone, Gaspare, and Giberto were

---

81. Ibid., 10 Aug. 1487, 16 Dec. 1487; ASE, Ambasciatori, Roma, b. 7, Ercole d'Este to bishop of Reggio, 16 Mar. and 29 Apr. 1488.

82. ASE, Particolari, b. 213, Diamante Boschetti to Ercole d'Este, 6 June 1487.

83. Ibid.; LD, C 10, fols. 165, 189 (15 May and 14 June 1487).

84. ASE, Ambasciatori, Roma, b. 6, XII, nos. 3 and 66; b. 6, XVII, nos. 11, 15, and 46; b. 7, XVIII, nos. 3, 4, 11, 14–17, and 23.

85. ASE, Particolari, b. 213, Diamante Boschetti, 6 June 1487.

86. ASCMo, Vacchetta 1490, fols. 32v (8 June), 56v (7 Oct.); Carte sciolte, b. 1, 25 Oct. 1491.

87. ASE, Carteggio, Principi esteri, Roma, b. 9, no. 64 (12 July 1491).

88. ASE, Particolari, b. 1087, Gaspare Petrezani to Eleonora d'Aragona, 18 Aug. 1492.

89. Ibid., Alberto Petrezani to the duke of Ferrara, 19 July s.a.; Zambotti, *Diario*, 343.

90. RdS, Modena, b. 1a, Reggimento to Ercole d'Este, 24 Nov. 1490; ASE, Minutario, Lettere sciolte, b. 3, 1 Dec. 1491 and 30 Dec. 1492. The act of pacification (14 Sept. 1492), largely the work of Eleonora and concluded in her rooms in the Ferrarese castle, is in ASE, Particolari, b. 558, letters of Gabriele del Forno.

killed by or for the dal Forno;[91] Gianfrancesco dal Forno was killed by Alberto, the nephew of Rangone Petrezani in 1489,[92] and others were killed by various hands: Mesino in 1476, Giorgio in 1497, Giovanni in 1500.[93] What had pitted these two families against each other was in origin, yet again, dispute over a benefice, specifically the dispute between Andrea Petrezani and Tommaso dal Forno over a cathedral canonry.[94]

Into this feud was entwined the most powerful of Modenese families, the Rangoni. Their association with the Petrezani is evident in the very name of Rangone Petrezani. Two of their number were involved in the killing of Gaspare dal Forno in 1471.[95] They were allied with the dal Forno's opponents in the Molza family.[96] Their hostility to the Boschetti family was long-standing;[97] and in 1475 they had occupied some lands at San Cesario that belonged to the monastery of San Pietro.[98] It is thus the Rangoni who provide continuity between two apparently unconnected conflicts: between the Petrezani and the dal Forno; and between Gaspare Petrezani and the cathedral chapter, on the one hand, and the monks of San Pietro and the Boschetti, on the other. Both conflicts came to a head in the month of June 1487.

The organized priestly expedition to seize property belonging to the benefice at Zena inflamed the duke's anger: he gave his governors in Modena full power to punish whoever was the principal author and his supporters, stating, "you cannot do any disorder in this case that we would not praise as great order, provided that it has a good outcome."[99]

---

91. ASE, Particolari, b. 1087, letter of Tommaso, Lanfranco, and Alberto Petrezani to Lucrezia Borgia, s.d.; Tommasino de'Bianchi, in *Cronaca Tommasino de' Bianchi,* 1:81–82.

92. ASE, Minutario, Lettere sciolte, b. 3, 5 Dec. 1489. Alberto dal Forno was later hanged: Cam. duc., Amministrazione finanziaria dei paesi, Modena, Massaria, b. 44, reg. 1497, fol. 3; Jacopino de' Bianchi, in *Cronaca Tommasino de' Bianchi,* 1:169; Zambotti, *Diario,* 273.

93. Jacopino de' Bianchi, in *Cronaca Tommasino de' Bianchi,* 1:20, 165, 190. Though Giorgio (alias Ercole) was in fact killed by the sons of Gianfrancesco: ASE, Particolari, b. 557, letters of Ercole dal Forno; Cam. duc., Notai camerali ferraresi, reg. 52, fol. 126.

94. ASE, Particolari, b. 558, letters of Gabriele dal Forno, 14 Sept. 1492; ASE, Minutario, Lettere sciolte, b. 4, 9 July 1494.

95. RdS, Reggio, b. 1, letters of Sigismondo d'Este, 2 Oct. 1471.

96. Jacopino de' Bianchi, in *Cronaca Tommasino de' Bianchi,* 1:55, 69 (through marriage).

97. A hundred years earlier, Niccolò II d'Este had ordered these two families not to allow division to arise between them, to obey his officials, and not to leave Modena without his license: LD, A 1, insert fols. 138–39 (s.d.).

98. LD, C 4, fol. 27 (8 Feb. 1476).

99. LD, C 10, fols. 165 (15 May 1487), 189 (14 June 1487).

But the worst was yet to come. On 23 June 1487 an armed fight on the piazza spread into the cathedral, where three men were wounded near the altar of San Gemignano, the city's patron saint. The governors, while attributing this disturbance to the unbridled, unregulated carrying of arms ("as there is no one who will arrest, accuse, or denounce"), also pointed the finger at a deeper root: "We understand that this happened . . . because of a legal action that Tommaso Daineri, Ludovico Molza, and Giangiacomo della Porta have with Sigismondo dal Forno."[100] According to Violante Rangone's letter to the duke, it was the witnesses who had testified against him whom Sigismondo and his accomplices surrounded on the piazza, pursued into the cathedral, and assaulted: "because of the great *parentado* on both sides, Modena is all in arms and great evil will befall unless your Excellency takes things in hand, because the governors take no action."[101]

The wounding in the cathedral—with the added offense to the city's patron saint (a "violation," according to Violante Rangoni)—was the last straw. Eleonora relayed the news to the governors of Modena: she had spoken to Ercole, who had decided to send in a commissioner "to restrain the acts of insolence," who "will set out very, very soon," "with such a commission that we are persuaded will rein in such disorders that arise there every day."[102] The governors of Modena objected, raising the issue of their own honor, but Eleonora replied that there was great cause for the appointment, as there was no punishment of any crimes in the city.[103]

There were, however, many other aspects to disorders in Modena and Reggio in the 1480s. The commission issued to Beltramino Cusadri in 1488 (see chap. 6) specified "recent wars" as the cause of the breakdown in law and order in Este territories. It is certainly true that Ercole began his efforts to hire Beltramino very soon after peace was concluded in his disastrous war with Venice (August 1484). Furthermore, one of the last letters from Reggio of Ercole's wartime governor there reported the activities of a whole company of ne'er-do-wells, many of them from good families, who had occupied a brothel on the main square, were living on

---

100. RdS, Modena, b. 1a, Reggimento to Eleonora d'Aragona, 24 June 1487. Daineri, Molza, and della Porta were married to daughters of Francesco dal Forno: RdS, Modena, b. 2c, Niccolò Cocapani to Eleonora d'Aragona, 29 June 1487.
101. ASE, Particolari, b. 1169, 23 June 1487.
102. LD, C 10, fol. 200 (26 June 1487).
103. Ibid., fol. 205 (5 July 1487).

the earnings of prostitutes, and were making themselves lords of the piazza by their frequent and indiscriminate use of violence.[104] Although Modena and Reggio had not been directly threatened in the fighting, the war had impinged severely on their social and political life. They may have been spared much of the violence and robbery of garrison troops against local populations that marked Ferrarese experience of the war,[105] but the increased demand for money and, perhaps more importantly, for foodstuffs created a crisis that led to food shortages and substantial emigration.[106] As the war approached and began, Ercole's demands on Modena rapidly multiplied: he demanded munitions, troops, carpenters, church bells (to be made into cannon), straw, money, and foodstuffs.[107] This had a grievous effect on the supply and price of food in Modena,[108] causing rioting for food over several days in November 1482, with an aftermath of armed disorders and crowd movements.[109] Order collapsed, requiring the dispatch of a commissioner with 120 *fanti* to disperse armed gangs and to carry out some exemplary hangings.[110]

In such conditions, levying taxes became more difficult. Already at the start of the war there was tax refusal in Modena, with officials reporting fearfully of the situation.[111] By the end of the war, the captain of Reggio

104. Venturi, "Relazioni," 295.

105. RdS, Ferrara, b. 19, Lodovico Garardini to Ercole d'Este, 20 July 1483; ibid., Francesco Maria Montachiesi to Ercole d'Este, 29 July 1483; ibid., Massari, 1 Dec. 1483; ibid., b. 45a, Bartolomeo Canali to Ercole, 5 Dec. 1483. But see RdS, Reggio, b. 1, Paolo Antonio Trotti to Ercole d'Este, 18 Dec. 1482: "quisti citadini qui si gravano molto de quisti soldati e fanti, dicendo che li fano magiore guerra de li nemici."

106. For "carestia" in Reggio, see RdS, Reggio, b. 2, Lippo Boccamaiori to Ercole d'Este, 14 June 1483; for other problems, see T. Dean, "After the War of Ferrara: Relations between Venice and Ercole d'Este, 1484–1505," in *War, Culture, and Society in Renaissance Venice*, ed. D.S. Chambers, C.H. Clough, and M.E. Mallett (London, 1993), 73–74.

107. Jacopino de' Bianchi, in *Cronaca Tommasino de' Bianchi*, 1:55–61, 66–67, 76, 80.

108. Ibid., 62, 64, 77, 82; G.L. Basini, *L'uomo e il pane: Risorse, consumi e carenze alimentari della populazione modenese nel Cinque e Seicento* (Milan, 1970), 63–65, 89, 155. Cf. the difficult extraction of foodstuffs from Reggio: Venturi, "Relazioni," 264, 268.

109. Jacopino de' Bianchi, in *Cronaca Tommasino de' Bianchi*, 1:67–71, 76, 77–78, 91; L. Chiappini, "Eleonora d'Aragona, prima duchessa di Ferrara," *Atti e memorie della Deputazione ferrarese di storia patria*, n.s., 16 (1956): 53. See also O. Rombaldi, "La comunità reggiana nello stato estense nel secolo XV," *Annuario del Liceo-Ginnasio statale "L. Ariosto" di Reggio-Emilia*, 1965–67, 112.

110. Ibid., 92. Cam. duc., Amministrazione finanziaria dei paesi, Modena, Massaria, b. 40, reg. for Feb. 1483–May 1484, records payments for eight hangings and two whippings (fols. 73, 118, 131, 135v, 139v, 146v, 156v, 159v, 169v); cf. the regs. for 1481 (one hanging: fol. 71) and 1482 (one hanging: fol. 72).

111. CS, b. 131, 9 July 1482.

was complaining of the behavior of the *massaro* in keeping *giotti* to extract payments and in devouring the poor, who were so exhausted by extortion that already one-third had left the city.[112] Evidence of fiscal difficulties in later years in Modena are abundant: revenue from indirect taxes was in decline at the end of the 1480s;[113] there were grain shortages in these years too, causing fear of popular unrest;[114] the commune declared that it could not continue work on the city walls because it was "weak and exhausted";[115] and even the horse provided by the commune to Alfonso d'Este for a Michaelmas festival was judged to be "sad and slight," entirely unsuitable for the purpose.[116] These local difficulties were reflected at the center: at the end of 1487 one of the presidents of the ducal revenue office *(fattori generali)* wrote with some concern to Ercole that, for the coming year, "I do not see a way of paying off debts and providing for your lordship's living, as the debts due and the expenses are beyond measure more than the income."[117]

The war seems to have brought a general slackening of the reins of political control as well as a brutalization of tax collection. In February 1484, Eleonora wrote to Ercole despairingly of three evident, daily problems: the military danger on all sides, the lack of money, and "the disobedience and lack of reverence of everyone."[118] Mainly she had in mind disturbances among troops, widespread defections, and surrenders, but her words have a general application: "everything stands in danger here, because from no one can obedience be had, no one wants to do their duty, everyone complains and all turn to robbing your poor subjects because they do not have food to live on, for not having any money, so they have to force others and use all sorts of violence."[119] Such conditions would naturally exacerbate the collection of taxes and repression of violence after the war: there was, for example, loud peasant protest at

---

112. RdS, Reggio, b. 2, Lippo Boccamaiori to Ercole d'Este, 31 July 1484.

113. RdS, Modena, b. 2e, letter of Giovanni Girolamo Marchesi, 27 Mar. 1490. Between 1486 and 1487 indirect revenue fell 6 percent, and though it largely recovered in 1488–89, it fell again in 1490, by 4 percent: Cam. duc., Mandati, vol. 31, fol. 158.

114. ASCMo, Vacchetta 1487–88, fols. 84r–v, 87; 1489, fols. 23v, 24, 28v, 30v–31.

115. ASCMo, Vacchetta 1487–88, fol. 62v.

116. "tristis et levis": ibid., fols. 101, 102.

117. ASE, Carteggio di ufficiali camerali, A.M. Guarneri to Ercole d'Este, 30 Nov. 1487. See Gundersheimer, *Ferrara*, 202–3.

118. CS, b. 131, 11 Feb. 1484, quoted in Chiappini, "Eleonora d'Aragona," 56–57.

119. CS, b. 131, 25 Jan. 1484.

land purchases by citizens that left the rural tax burden to be shared among fewer peasant landholders.[120]

It was precisely the combination of fiscal severity and judicial laxity that was depicted as *malgoverno* in a letter of complaint from Reggio. The letter starts with a vivid picture of groups of "exactors" constantly touring the *contado* to take tribute from villages in exchange for merely leaving them in peace; of a salt office that refused to take account of deaths, so forcing "the living to pay for the dead"; and of the migration that these pressures caused (to Carpi, Mirandola, Pisa, Siena). The author then proceeds to indict judicial officers of inadequacy: in the hills and *contado*, "whoever wants to carries arms, provided he has money," while poor *contadini* are arrested for arms carrying at the urban market on Saturdays; *giotti* go around unchallenged at night, robbing churches and shops, knocking down the doors of poor women; no one upholds the law, "because there is no constable or *fanti* willing to do their duty, nor does the podesta know how to, as he does not keep any staff" (see chap. 1); at present, anyone with money is not safe in his or her own house, and the *contado* needs a foreign constable with twenty *fanti*, a captain worth his price.[121] The "law-abiding subjects . . . were more aware of too little government than of too much: save always in the sphere of taxation."[122]

None of this was totally new, of course: complaint at the erosion of the rural tax base had been heard in Modena before[123] and was a commonplace phenomenon. Evidence of fiscal crisis would also be easy to mount for other periods; for example, in 1471 the *massaro* was berated by the duke for failing to supply cash, a crowd burned the public account books, long letters were penned to the duke by officials regarding clerical exemption and financial mismanagement, and the commune wrote of its "impossibility with very burdensome expenses and debts greater than ever."[124] Nonetheless, there is some evidence of greater fiscal pressure being applied in the years after the War of Ferrara. In 1490 it was noted that the almost daily appearance of public-debt collectors in Ferrarese territory and their excessive and extraordinary demands were forcing

---

120. LD, C 10, fols. 205–6 (6 July 1487), 227–28 (31 Aug. 1487); ASCMo, Vacchetta 1487–88, fol. 42v (16 Oct.); ibid., 1489, fol. 39 (13 May).

121. RdS, Reggio, b. 166, s.d.

122. Bueno de Mesquita, "The Place of Despotism," 325.

123. RdS, Modena, b. 1a, Borso d'Este to Reggimento, 29 Dec. 1470, and Reggimento to Borso d'Este, 1 and 3 Feb. 1471.

124. RdS, Modena, b. 1a, *savi* to Ercole d'Este, 15 Oct. 1471, and Reggimento to Ercole d'Este, 29 Nov. 1471; ibid., b. 2e, letters of Francesco da Mosto, 1 Mar., 16 June, and 29 Aug. 1471. See also Torri, "'Allegrezze'," 216–20.

emigration and the purchase of (controversial) immunities from the Venetian consul.[125] Some of the most eloquent complaints about "exactors" come from these years (see chap. 1). The *anziani* of Reggio claimed that Ercole had broken the custom that its tax demand be one-third less than that of Modena.[126] A new tax demanded in Modena in 1490 created an enormous popular uproar, with a murderous manifesto being pinned to the door of an inn,[127] and the governors were forced by public opinion to convene a general council *(consiglio generale)*—something so foreign and uncongenial to them that they did not know how it was to be composed or how to conduct themselves before it.[128] A loan of two thousand ducats requested by the duke in 1489, for his daughter's dowry, had encountered difficulties in collection,[129] but Ercole refused to accept the commune's pleas of impossibility,[130] and when requesting another dowry subsidy of three thousand ducats in 1490, he warned the commune that it should not even try to have the amount reduced. Faced with substantial noncollection, the central revenue office was forced to attach the city's tax farms to pay what was due.[131] But these direct taxes depressed economic activity in Modena, and the yield of gabelles on commerce and contracts fell from levels in 1488, the former by 8 percent, the latter by 55 percent.[132]

Clear evidence of increased fiscal pressure also comes from the territories governed by the Modenese and Reggian nobility, the *gentiluomini*. Inhabitants in Fogliani territory in 1487 complained against the levying of new imposts and the appropriation of the emoluments of the podesta's office.[133] The Montecuccoli were found to be imposing export duties

125. RdS, Ferrara, b. 41, Tommaso Catanelli to Ercole d'Este, 8 Oct. 1490. For the issue of these immunities, see T. Dean, "Venetian Economic Hegemony: The Case of Ferrara, 1200–1500," *Studi veneziani,* n.s., 12 (1986): 90–93.

126. RdS, Reggio, b. 2, Massaro to Ercole d'Este, s.d.

127. "DEFENDIVE CANALIA DA / QUESTO TIRAM / CHIAMA LIBERTA / AMAZA DIPESI GROSI / AMAZA LOFITIALI / LAMBASADORE COMISARIO": RdS, Modena, b. 1a, Reggimento to Ercole d'Este, 25 Apr. 1490. "Quella scripta cussi abhominevole," as Ercole described it: ASCMo, Carte sciolte, b. 1, 4 May 1490.

128. RdS, Modena, b. 1a, 25 Apr. 1490.

129. ASCMo, Vacchetta 1490, fol. 5ff.

130. ASCMo, Carte sciolte, b. 1, 8–9 Aug. 1490.

131. ASCMo, Vacchetta 1490, fols. 23v–24, 27v–28, 28v, 29v, 30v, 31v, etc.; Vacchetta 1491, fols. 6v, 25v, 35, 36; Carte sciolte, b. 1, 20 July 1491. Cf. the gentler pressure in similar circumstance of Giangaleazzo Visconti: F.E. Comani, "I denari per la dote di Valentina Visconti," *Archivio storico lombardo,* 3d ser., 15 (1901).

132. Cam. duc., Mandati, vol. 31, fol. 158.

133. LD, C 10, fols. 229–30 (15 Sept. 1487), 244–45 (14 Oct. 1487).

contrary to custom;[134] while the men of Olina, Ranocchio, Camatta, and Riva, in justifying their request to be removed from Montecuccoli lordship, complained of having to pay for castle guard that was not mounted, of seizure of their local mills to force them to use the seigneurial mill at inflated prices, and of the Montecuccoli in-laws who served them as podestas but did not care to administer justice.[135] In Manfredi territory, it was revealed in 1491, a huge increase had taken place in the past twenty-five years in the burdens placed on the inhabitants. Under Taddeo Manfredi's predecessors, the Reggian governors reported, the inhabitants had paid nothing for their land (no entry fine?), and the local *estimo* was used only to raise the sum needed for the podesta's salary. But after his father's death, Taddeo began diversifying imposts, such that the governors reported they "are now more or less at Messer Taddeo's will and pleasure." The governors said that Taddeo began imposing the *estimo* much more frequently, appropriating all the fines collected from transgressions on the common pastures, and forcing communities to provide and transport wood and straw, to hoe his vineyards, to build and dig at his command, and to pay his legal costs.[136] And this report came ten years after Ercole's previous settlement of dispute over dues and services on Manfredi lands.[137] In the same year of that settlement, 1481, "the men governed by the Rangoni" had complained to the duke of extortion. The Rangoni, it was alleged, had usurped common woodland, divided it among themselves ("and don't let us put a foot in it"), but still insisted on the villagers supplying them with wood (due out of goodwill, not obligation, the Rangoni asserted). Similarly, the Rangoni had appropriated common pasture, such that inhabitants now had to pay to graze their animals. Faced with peasant resistance, the Rangoni were threatening to spill some blood and, as the complainants put it, "to dig the wood out of our eyes."[138] The Rangoni responded haughtily: these men were ingrates of "il nostro bom e amorevole governo"; the *honoranze* at stake were ancient custom and of such small value that the men should be ashamed. "We have more consideration for our honor than for profit," they eva-

---

134. Ibid., fols. 263–64 (23 Nov. 1487).

135. G. Campori, "Cesare Montecuccoli," in idem, *Memorie patrie* (Modena, 1881), 105–7.

136. RdS, b. 112, Domenico Boldrini to Ercole d'Este, 23 July 1491.

137. RdS, Reggiano, Albinea. Cf. Jones ("Communes and Despots," 92) "though commonly said to have shown favour to the peasantry, [the despots] in fact did little to moderate rural burdens."

138. ASE, Particolari, b. 1176, 16 Nov. 1481.

sively replied.[139] Peasant "audacity" against civic officials could thus have its roots in the aggravation of aristocratic burdens and demands. In a process found in several parts of Italy, and indeed of Europe, agrarian conflict intensified, especially over common lands, from the late fifteenth century onward.[140] In these circumstances, it was the state that was called on both to pacify disputes and to punish violent outbursts.

The disorders at Modena and Reggio had a further dimension, distinguishing them from those in Ferrara: the presence of *gentiluomini,* privileged, castle-owning aristocrats, deeply rooted in the economy and society of these subject cities and their political histories. This is not the place to attempt a history of these families—the Rangoni and Boiardi, the Roberti and Fogliani, the Boschetti, Contrari, and Montecuccolo, to name only a few—but some lines of general development are relevant here. Their rural properties, as we have seen, constituted seigneuries, combining castles and jurisdiction, dues and services from the inhabitants, milling monopolies and tax exemptions. Their relation to the prince was defined by feudal investitures and by their appearance at court and in princely armies. With the creation of the imperial duchies of Modena and Reggio for the Estensi, a transformation does seem to have taken place, in outward forms at least, in the relation of these provincial aristocracies to the prince. No more is heard of them as *raccomandati,* that is, as allies or adherents with a certain independence:[141] now they are governors, exercising delegated authority over the duke's subjects. Not too much should be made perhaps of this surface change: it had partly been anticipated in the first half of the fifteenth century, while even toward 1500 some aristocrats (e.g., Albertino Boschetti) still sought service careers independent of the Este court.[142] Nevertheless, a contrast exists that suggests a possible weakening of these seigneurs' political independence and of their control of the rural population between the early and late fifteenth century: in 1429, an Este envoy sent to negotiate the surrender of the castle of San Martino in Rio from the Roberti family was confronted by a popular assembly asserting its will to keep the

139. Ibid., b. 1169, Vincislao and Gerardo Rangoni to Ercole d'Este, 28 Sept. 1482.

140. See Muir, *Mad Blood Stirring,* xxv, 102–3, 122, 143, 150; C. Rotelli, *Una campagna medievale: Storia agraria del Piemonte fra il 1250 e il 1450* (Turin, 1973), 103–6; P. Blickle, "Peasant Revolts in the German Empire in the Late Middle Ages," *Social History* 4 (1979): 234.

141. Dean, *Land and Power,* 166–78.

142. *DBI* 13 (1971): 170–74.

Roberti as its lords;[143] conversely, in 1481, the Rangoni subjects declared that the "Cha da Este" was the only one they adored, and it governed their bodies and souls.[144] Two episodes do not, of course, make a crisis, and we should recognize that displays and statements of adherence to either the Este or the local seigneurial family were a tactic used by both the peasantry and the aristocrats, depending on the circumstances. Uguccione Contrari could plaster his castle walls with Este emblems and devices,[145] just as Vincislao Rangoni could in 1472 report that the inhabitants of Castelvetro had celebrated Ercole's marriage to Eleonora d'Aragona with the full festive panoply of bonfires, bell ringing, and book burning.[146] Conversely, as we shall see, peasants could rally to the name of their governing family in resistance to civic "exactors." The trend, however, does seem to have run toward greater expression of peasant allegiance to the ducal overload.

The role of aristocrats, alongside civic officials, in the maintenance (or disturbance) of law and order requires our attention. Three features are immediately apparent: their own jurisdictional rights and powers, and the relation of these to ducal law and jurisdiction; their own behavior, especially their violent family disputes; and their (alleged) use and protection of bandits. Aristocratic preference for "easy and remote surveillance"[147] led them to object to the audience given by ducal officials to complaints regarding their justice. Ercole had firmly to instruct the Calcagnini, seigneurs of Cavriago, to allow complaints to be heard by the *reggimento* of Reggio.[148] However, the *reggimento* continued to experience difficulties in supervising such gentlemen, as it was "difficult to prove anything, because the local inhabitants will not speak against their governors."[149]

It would certainly be easy (though misleading) to depict the "gentlemen" as turbulent and overbearing, petty tyrants, representatives of a territorial nobility still proud and independent, not (or not well) integrated into the princely state, confounding princely law and order. These "gentlemen" were of the sort who, when asked to post bond for good

143. RdS, Modenese, Campogalliano, Pietro Marocelli to Niccolò d'Este, 2 Sept. 1429.
144. ASE, Particolari, b. 1176, 16 Nov. 1481.
145. L. Franchini, *Simboli, emblemi, impresi nel castello di Vignola* (Vignola, 1977); Dean, *Land and Power,* 161.
146. ASE, Particolari, b. 1169, 13 Nov. 1472.
147. Jones, *Malatesta,* 332.
148. LD, C 10, fols. 238, 241 (4 and 11 Oct. 1487).
149. RdS, Reggio, b. 1, *reggimento* to Ercole d'Este, 12 Mar. 1498.

behavior, felt shame at being treated like mere civic notables;[150] or who felt slighted, reduced to the level of "mechanics," when asked to pay indirect taxes (while not caring that their peasants be required to pay).[151] Evidence enough of their harsh landlordism has already been presented, and other evidence confirms their potential for generating disorder. At times of poor harvest, they sold grain to foreigners, leaving the local city to provide for their own hungry subjects.[152] They disrupted markets and trade.[153] Above all, rural aristocrats sheltered and maintained bandits. In 1479 Eleonora, picking up reports from Modena of this, wrote to Ercole, "it seems to me the weirdest thing in the world," to allow those banned from places he ruled to find shelter in the territories of his gentlemen, vassals, and feudatories.[154] The case of the Montecuccoli will here be allowed to stand for them all. In the 1470s and again in the 1490s, Bologna complained repeatedly to Ercole of brigands sheltering in and operating from the territory of Cesare Montecuccoli and, with the aid of Cesare's son, raiding across the border for women and horses, inciting "capital enmities" in Bolognese territory, and counterfeiting coin.[155] Ercole himself berated Cesare for failing to detain two criminals and for instead keeping them in his home to eat and drink "domesticamente," "as if they were the best men in the world."[156]

However, other interpretations of the social and political role of the gentlemen are indicated in the evidence. The first stresses their role as protectors of country folk against the city.[157] Giacomo Boiardo's sympathies for poor rural communities in the Ferrarese have already been cited (see chap. 1). As officials the aristocrats listened to peasant complaints of oppression; as landlords they complained of increased civic charges on "their" men.[158] Seigneurial officials constituted a barrier against the excesses of civic exactors, as the latter had to collect debts through local podestas, "so that the poor men are not consumed in expenses";[159] simi-

---

150. ASE, Particolari, b. 1157, Helena Rangoni to Eleonora d'Aragona, 12 Apr. 1488.

151. ASE, Particolari, b. 213, Diamante and Alberto Boschetti to Ippolito d'Este, 1 Apr. 1499.

152. RdS, Modena, b. 1a, June 1497.

153. Dean, *Land and Power,* 152.

154. CS, b. 131, 28 Mar. 1479.

155. ASBo, Comune, Lettere del comune, reg. 1, fol. 38; reg. 5, fols. 11r–v, 46, 50, 51, 57, 69, 71, 131.

156. LD, C 11, fol. 183 (21 May 1496).

157. G. Chittolini, "Feudatari e comunità rurali nell'Italia centro-settentrionale (secoli XV–XVII)," *Studi storici Luigi Simeoni* 36 (1986): 15–16.

158. ASE, Particolari, b. 1155, Antonio Rangoni to Ercole d'Este, 13 June 1497.

159. ASE, Minutario, Lettere sciolte, b. 4, 10 Jan. 1497.

larly, criminal summonses of Rangoni subjects had to be made in a special form.[160] And gentlemen professed—however insincerely—a desire to help their subjects: later we shall find Cesare Montecuccoli assuring his men that he would, through personal interview with the duke, save them from the predatory attentions of the civic exactors (see chap. 6). When challenged with maintaining bandits or with causing flooding by their river works, the Rangoni replied that they had acted only to help people or to protect their own communities from flooding.[161] And others in the city accepted this altruistic image: when Lanfranco Rangoni died, the chronicler Jacopino de' Bianchi wrote that there was much grief in Modena, "because he had always been good for the 'republic.'"[162]

Another interpretation might stress aristocratic weakness, not strength. A revealing comment on public order in the Reggian hills was occasioned by the city governors' efforts to prosecute an armed assembly and fight at Sarzano, which was governed by the Fogliani family. The gentlemen-governors, they concluded, command "little reverence and less obedience" at Sarzano: because judicial fines do not go to them, they do not proceeed sincerely or properly. Moving to a more general level, the Reggio governors continued that many perpetrators of crimes go unpunished in the lands of the nobility, "either for money or for fear," and that many people involved in armed assemblies and murders are never punished, owing to the timidity of the gentlemen and the poverty of the malefactors.[163] We might therefore be led to conclude that banditry in aristocratic territories was such a persistent problem not because aristocrats recruited criminal bravos to enforce and extend their dominion but because they lacked the will, the capacity, or the resources to round criminals up and drive them away.

A further source of weakness was the deep, often violent division within noble families. Divisions of property between coheirs or joint owners were frequent: that among Vincislao, Violante, and Gerardo Rangone, for example, was said to involve passionate shouting and unresolvable discord.[164] Taddeo Manfredi, for all that he was said to be

---

160. LD, C 10, fol. 210 (24 July 1487).

161. ASE, Particolari, b. 1159, 2 May 1488 ("sempre me son sforzato de servire ogni persona"); ibid., b. 1166, 1 Apr. 1493 ("noi non siamo homini de volere fare dare danno ad nostri vicini"); ibid., b. 1169, 1 Sept. 1491.

162. *Cronaca Tommasino de' Bianchi,* 1:94.

163. RdS, Reggio, b. 1, *reggimento* to Ercole d'Este, 20 Mar. 1496.

164. CS, b. 131, 9 Mar. 1479. See also RdS, Reggiano, Albinca, 1451 and 1472; ASE, Particolari, b. 1159, 28 July 1495; ibid., b. 1169, 26 June 1472, 18 Jan. 1471, 3 Nov. 1472; ibid., b. 1176, 26 Mar. 1471.

crushing his peasants with imposts, could not control his own disorderly sons and had to ask for them to be rounded up by the captain of the Modenese piazza.[165] Taddeo was also in dispute with his cousin, Giovanni Manfredi, who himself, as we shall see, ran into difficulties as a result of the criminal activities of his wife (see chap. 6). Carlo Boschetti complained of the violent and threatening behavior of Ludovico Boschetti, who kept bandits and thieves in the house to threaten and assault whom they pleased, who prevented the local podesta from doing justice and punishing wrongdoers, and who refused to pay tax on land that he bought.[166] The Rangoni family were divided between Guelfs and Ghibellines.[167] Cristoforo Rangoni was so disgusted with his own brother Giovanni's behavior that he tried, so as to prevent him succeeding to any of his property, to break a *fedecommesso* set up by their father. When the brothers had divided their joint property in the 1480s, Cristoforo became frustrated at Giovanni's delays and obstruction and sought ducal remedy: "it seems to me too much that I cannot separate myself from ne'er-do-wells, and that I have to stay in a house with my enemies and with those who every day lay into my servants or give me rudery."[168] Dispute among the da Sesso clan over who should have the government and jurisdiction of Casteldaldo led to the killing of one of them in 1494.[169] Discord between Giberto Pio and his cousin was said to arise from "riotous people," favored and defended by both sides, and from their crimes passing unpunished.[170]

Aristocratic divisions thus exacerbated disorder in three areas: they interfered with and incapacitated the exercise of justice; they produced violence and killings; they attracted and mobilized groups of bandits. If the gentlemen could not control their own households and kinsmen, if they had need of ducal intervention even within their own families, how likely was it that they could ensure justice and order in their territories?

---

165. ASE, Minutario, Lettere sciolte, b. 3, 14 Dec. 1487.

166. ASE, Particolari, b. 213, 5 Aug. 1490.

167. Jacopino de' Bianchi, in *Cronaca Tommasino de' Bianchi*, 1:69–70, 81–82.

168. ASE, Particolari, b. 1157, 1 July 1484; Jacopino de' Bianchi, in *Cronaca Tommasino de' Bianchi*, 1:167–68.

169. RdS, Reggio, b. 1, *cancelliere* to Ercole d'Este, 28 June, 3 July, 9 July, and 25 Aug. 1494; N. Campanini, "Lettere edite ed inedite di Matteo Maria Boiardo," in *Studi su Matteo Maria Boiardo* (Bologna, 1894), 432–35, 438, nos. 107–8, 110, 112, 116; Venturi, "Relazioni," 318–20.

170. ASE, Minutario, Lettere sciolte, b. 4, 23 May 1497. See also A.L. Trombetti Budriesi, "Sui rapporti tra i Pio e gli Estensi: Lo scambio Carpi-Sassuolo," in *Società, politica e cultura a Carpi ai tempi di Alberto III Pio*, vol. 2 (Padua, 1981).

We do have some indication of the quality and conduct of justice by two families: the Fogliani and the Rangoni.[171] The Fogliani seem to have favored the concentration of judicial power in local hands. In 1442 Guido Savina obtained from Leonello d'Este license to appoint a notary, especially for judicial matters, because of the alleged inconvenience of calling notaries from the city. In 1487 Ercole took up local complaint that the podesta of Sarzano had been in office "for an age" and was a native of the area.[172] Vincislao Rangoni was reproved by the duke in 1476 for the frequency of crimes at Castelvetro and Levizzano—including robberies, Easter woundings, and seven recent murders.[173] According to Cristoforo, his brother Giovanni had been worthless as ducal podesta of Sestola.[174] Yet considerable leeway was ordered by Ercole in the Modenese treatment of Rangoni jurisdictions. In 1476 he restrained the governors of Modena from taking cases from Rangoni territories at the request of one of the parties;[175] in 1482 the governors were instructed to arrest those criminals nominated by the Rangoni for punishment by that family's officials (though the duke did order them not to allow this prerogative to be used within the city, "so that it should not seem that they have any superiority");[176] and in 1488 Ercole ordered the podesta of Modena to release a Rangoni official charged with assaulting a *mezzadro*.[177]

Such caution was doubtless required given the extent of Rangoni power and influence in Modena.[178] The Rangoni had brought the city into Este rule in 1288, and according to Guicciardini, they had the city at their disposal in 1510 when it submitted to Pope Julius II.[179] Across the centuries the signs of their unbreakable primacy are clear. Unlike almost all other Modenese families in this period, they suffered no punitive

171. See Muir, *Mad Blood Stirring*, 99–100, 181; Bueno de Mesquita, "The Place of Despotism," 325.

172. LD, B 5, fols. 182, 265; LD, C 10, fols. 229–30. Only in the sixteenth century, it is claimed, did the state control more strictly the feudatories' exercise of jurisdiction: Chittolini, "Feudatari e communità," 22–23.

173. LD, C 4, fol. 75 (4 May 1476).

174. ASE, Particolari, b. 1157, Cristoforo Rangoni to Eleonora d'Aragona, 1 July 1484.

175. LD, C 4, fols. 71, 112.

176. RdS, Modena, b. 1a, Ercole d'Este to *reggimento*, 5 Oct. 1489.

177. LD, C 10, fols. 311, 327.

178. On the Rangoni in general, see L. Rangoni Machiavelli, *I Rangoni* (Rome, 1908); P. Litta, *Famiglie celebri italiane* (Milan, 1819–74; Naples, 1902–23).

179. F. Guicciardini, *Storia d'Italia*, IX, vi.

confiscations or expropriations by the Este overlords.[180] The family stood head and shoulders above not only its co-citizens but also its Ferrarese counterparts, boasting a thirteenth-century *beato,* fifteen-century condottieri, and a bishop in Hungary. They enjoyed a variety of tax exemptions, for themselves and their families, for their mills, and for their tenants,[181] in addition, of course, to practicing avoidance of other taxes.[182] They enjoyed leading honors and offices at Ferrara and Modena and elsewhere in Este service: Gerardo had served as Este captain of Parma in 1419;[183] from 1495 Francesco Maria was Ercole's captain of Reggio, before being seconded, again for Ercole, as captain of the Castelletto of Genoa;[184] earlier Francesco Maria had been one of Ercole's companions in his aborted pilgrimage to Santiago;[185] Cristoforo was Ercole's "beloved secret councillor" and one of his envoys to the new pope in 1485.[186] In the city itself, the Rangoni could always be relied on: the *reggimento* called Niccolò Rangoni "father";[187] the family did not fail to provide an escort for some foreign ambassadors when the city was otherwise "empty of suitable persons";[188] and when a son was born to the then podesta, Cristoforo was one of the commune's representatives at the baptism.[189] For these varied services, they received varied rewards: grants of land[190] and revenues,[191] tax exemptions, and even delegated authority to distribute salt (and collect the salt levy).[192] Their wealth and influence in Modena were extensive. They owned a huge granary, which sometimes attracted thieves,[193] but from which, at times of shortage, the Rangoni grain was sold "at an honest price."[194] They maintained both a right

---

180. See Dean, *Land and Power,* 155–59.

181. LD, A 4, fol. 231 (1 Jan. 1416); LD, B II, fol. 300 (11 Mar. 1395); ASCMo, Vacchetta 1490, fol. 27v; ASE, Particolari, b. 1164, 13 Feb. 1504.

182. LD, A 1, fol. 23 (15 Oct. 1363); ASE, Minutario, Lettere sciolte, b. 3, 22 Nov. 1487.

183. LD, A 4, fol. 310.

184. LD, C 11, fols. 111, 151; Jacopino de' Bianchi, in *Cronaca Tommasino de' Bianchi,* 1:141.

185. Zambotti, *Diario,* 183.

186. LD, C 4, fol. 60; Zambotti, *Diario,* 165.

187. RdS, Modena, b. 1a, *reggimento,* 9 Sept. 1429.

188. RdS, Modena, b. 2e, letter of Francesco da Mosto, 8 June 1471.

189. ASCMo, Vacchetta 1491, fol. 22 (16 Apr. 1491).

190. Dean, *Land and Power,* 61, 86–87.

191. LD, B IV, fol. 191v (2 Mar. 1430).

192. ASE, Particolari, b. 1160, 31 Oct. 1500.

193. RdS, Modena, b. 2c, 25 Sept. 1471.

194. ASCMo, Carte sciolte, b. 1, 28 Oct. 1496.

to elect the *massaro* of the cathedral fabric (though disputed with the cathedral canons)[195] and a claim (disputed with the canons again) to participate in the election of the weights officer in the city gabelle office.[196] And they played a supervisory role, as "sindics," of a local hospital.[197]

Contemporary chroniclers were well aware of the political, military, and social importance of the Rangoni. The family acted decisively to quell disturbances in the city during the War of Ferrara.[198] They raised troops and fought under Ercole's banner, both in defense of his state and under his command during the Pazzi War, while also being hired independently as condottieri by Florence.[199] They accompanied Ercole's son, Ferrante, to the French court in 1493.[200] They were linked by marriage to the wealthiest of Modenese citizens and by godparenthood to the Estensi.[201] At their palace on Canalgrande visiting dignitaries might be lodged.[202] Their building projects in the city (a palace, a chapel), their marriages and deaths, and their internal divisions and disputes were thought worthy of extended recording.[203] Above all, their hold on popular and respectable opinion seems clear from the case of Cristoforo Rangoni, who calmed a food riot by going into the crowd and using "sweet words,"[204] and from the chronicler's words on Lanfranco (quoted earlier) and on Niccolò ("he was a decent man, he was very attached to masses, sermons, and indulgences and was seen every day on the streets").[205]

Against this complex background, it was events in the city streets that finally ensured the dispatch of the long-threatened commissioner. Perhaps in response to the action of the captain of Modena in their dispute with San Pietro, the cathedral clergy began refusing to say mass in his

---

195. ASE, Ambasciatori, Roma, b. 8, G.B. Ferrari to Ercole d'Este, 17 June 1502. For this office held by their Petrezani allies, see O. Baracchi, "Volte a crociera e affreschi del Duomo: Nuovi documenti del '400 e '500," *AMMo,* 11th ser., 15 (1993): 131, 133. For this office held by Francesco della Molza, see ASMo, Archivio notarile, Modena, Libri memoriali, 332, fol. 117v.

196. ASE, Particolari, b. 1176, 29 Oct. 1488.

197. ASCMo, Vacchetta 1491, fol. 46 (26 Sept.).

198. Jacopino de' Bianchi, in *Cronaca Tommasino de' Bianchi,* 1:68, 69–70, 71, 81–82.

199. Ibid., 40, 155.

200. Ibid., 107.

201. Ibid., 55, 69, 107.

202. Ibid., 156.

203. Ibid., 54, 142, 167–68, 185, 190.

204. Ibid., 68.

205. Ibid., 190.

presence, declining to doff their caps to him, laughing behind his back, and running at him with weapons in hand.[206] In January 1488 the Modenese *anziani* requested "most urgently" that Ercole take measures against the many crimes and woundings in the city, "so that the lower classes are not trodden down by the greater and more powerful."[207] The governors of Modena reported in May that the statutes against the receipt and harboring of bandits were altogether ignored there.[208] In December came the final trigger for the dispatch of the commissioner: a letter from the podesta that plumbed new depths in helplessness.

> It pains me to my soul . . . that I must every day take my pen in hand and trouble your lordship's head with the scandals and disorders that happen every day in this city of yours, and that I cannot do my office or my duty . . . It is a pity to see this poor city of yours: ruffians and rowdies go armed about the piazza, armed gatherings and celebrations go on at night, every day someone is wounded . . . I work with my pen, I inquire and condemn, but this does not make them stop. I do not use force as I cannot . . . My knight and my poor staff are as timid and enclosed as cats . . . It shames me to tell the truth to your lordship, like an ass . . . that is reduced to such shame and misery . . . Pardon me if I seem presumptuous in writing: the love and sincere faith that I have toward your lordship and your state meant that I could not keep quiet.[209]

Into such an arena stepped one of the most experienced, one of the most feared and fearless of criminal investigators of the time: Beltramino Cusadri da Crema.

---

206. ASCMo, Vacchetta 1487–88, fol. 65v (11 Apr.). The cathedral was interdicted shortly afterward: ibid., fols. 69v, 72v.

207. "ut inferiores non conculcentur a maioribus et potentioribus": ibid., fol. 51 (10 Jan. 1488).

208. RdS, Modena, b. 2c, Giacomo Compagni to Eleonora d'Aragona (s.d. May 1488).

209. RdS, Reggio, b. 112, Antonio Oldoini to Ercole d'Este, 11 Dec. 1488.

6

Beltramino in Modena and Reggio

It was usual for late-medieval judicial officials to make a solemn entry into the cities where they were to hold office. At Modena and Reggio, the incoming podesta was received by the other officials of the *reggimento,* by a crowd of nobles and citizens, and by *domicelli* and armed *fanti* bearing banners and shields. He was then escorted, preceded by trumpeters, to the piazza and the cathedral. There, at the altar, before the communal *anziani* and in the presence of the *popolo,* the letters of his appointment would be read out, there would be an oration, and the outgoing podesta would hand on to his successor the scepter of office. The new podesta would then present his other staff and swear, in the hands of the chief of the *anziani,* to serve well in office and to administer justice according to the civic statutes.[1] As suggested in some contemporary poems and novellas,[2] the pomposities of these events could certainly attract sarcastic remarks and contemptuous challenges—reminders not to take the symbolism too seriously. Nevertheless, the underlying political significance of such entries is clear. Although the podesta was appointed by the duke, each stage of his installation (except for the reading of the ducal letters) emphasized the podesta's contract with the civic authorities—with its past and present officials, its communal leaders, its citizens, its patron saint, its statutes. The new podesta was received not so much as a delegate of the duke but as a lineal successor to his outgoing predecessor, entering a position not of dominance but of obligation. The ceremonies were outward signs of hoped-for collaboration between official and community.[3]

---

1. ASRe, Comune, Provvigioni, reg. 98, fols. 131v, 185; ibid., reg. 100, fols. 24v–25, 89–90; ASCMo, Vacchetta 1490, fol. 26; etc. See also E. Santini, "La *protestatio de iustitia* nella Firenze medicea del secolo XV," *Rinascimento* 11 (1959).

2. A. Cappelli and S. Ferrari, eds., *Rime edite ed inedite di Antonio Cammelli detto il Pistoia* (Livorno, 1884), 125; F. Sacchetti, *Il trecentonovelle,* ed. A. Borlenghi (Milan, 1957), no. 42; Poggio Bracciolini, *Facezie,* ed. M. Ciccuto (Milan, 1983), no. 9.

3. Chittolini, "L'onore dell'officiale," 14; Connell, "Il commissario," 607–8.

For Beltramino there was no such ceremony. He arrived; he started work. Because that work involved the disregarding of local statute law and the reassertion of ducal authority over cities leaning too much toward liberty, such ceremony would have been impossible. Beltramino's commission (dated 16 January 1489) specified both his task and his powers: Ercole d'Este, aware that his towns and territories had, because of recent wars, deviated from "right living" and had turned themselves over to wickedness and crime, and in order to return them to good habits and old order, sends his councillor Beltramino Cusadri to investigate all crimes unpunished in the past or committed in the future, with full power, both in the places immediately subject to the duke and in those mediated to others (the gentlemen-governors), to proceed, sentence, and punish as he thinks fit. In pursuing his inquiries, Beltramino was to have at his disposal two squads of mounted archers—a truly awful instrument of power—under the captaincies of Guizzardo Riminaldi and Alessandro da Fiorano.

This is the commission that Ercole had been threatening since 1487. As we have seen, it was not until 1488 that Beltramino was released by the Gonzaga. From July of that year, he was on the Este payroll. The further delay in sending him to Modena is explained by the problems elsewhere needing his attention. One Ferrarese chronicler recorded that it was crimes across the whole state—from Finale and Modena to Consandolo and Argenta—that forced Ercole to hire "uno commissario teribilissimo."[4] Indeed, so urgent was Ercole's need for Beltramino's expertise that within two days of his arrival in Ferrara he was sent off to Finale to deal with some murderous "excesses" there.[5] In August he was investigating the killing of the podesta of Massafiscaglia (see chap. 1) and a murder at Lugo.[6] Having evidently proved his worth, in September he was enrolled as a ducal *salariato* at the considerable rate of forty lire per month and was paid the arrears for July and August.[7] By December he was put in charge of the trial in Ferrara of two Modenese malefactors.[8] Soon in 1489, he had trans-

---

4. Biblioteca apostolica vaticana, MS Chigi I.I.4, Ugo Caleffini, "Cronaca ferrarese," fol. 263v.

5. AG, b. 1289, 2 July 1488.

6. ASE, Minutario, Lettere sciolte, b. 3, 2 Aug. 1488; Cam. duc., Mandati, vol. 31, fol. 6v.

7. Cam duc., Memoriale del soldo, reg. 10, fol. 59.

8. ASE, Minutario, Lettere sciolte, b. 3, 1 Dec. 1488.

ferred to Modena, leaving his large family in a rented house in Ferrara, with his son Amato enrolled in the university (where he took his degree, in civil law, in 1490).[9]

That a new era in law enforcement had dawned with Beltramino's arrival quickly became clear in the Finale murder case. In his sentence Beltramino followed the letter of the local law that ordered confiscation of part of a father's property for killings committed by a son. Thus two fathers of the powerful Vecchi family found themselves penalized for their sons' crime. They protested to the duke, "this statute has never been observed in similar cases in Finale." They asked that Ercole should not "enforce against them what has up to now not been enforced against others." Ercole, however, was adamant: the statute had been made for the best of reasons, namely, to prevent homicide, and if it had not been needed in the past, it certainly was now, "because homicides have become so frequent, and the malice and cruelty of men has so increased, that it is reasonable and lawful to exacerbate laws and statutes as well."[10] The significance of Ercole's resolution acquires added force when we read a former podesta's report on the domineering attitudes of the Vecchi family.

> There are many of them, of a large family *[parentado]*, rich, powerful, and leaders of faction. As one of them says, they could in a day bring together a thousand men ready to do their bidding, and not only do they seek to supplant others, taking what is theirs by force, but also they give out beatings, which they would not do if they were lords *a baccheta* of this place. And the poor, oppressed by the fear and terror they have of them, dare not open their mouths, and get on as best they can . . . They persuade themselves that they have the lordship of this place by prescription, and they want to keep everyone under themselves.[11]

Investigating crimes committed by this family was not just a judicial matter but a political one. It had to be demonstrated that Ercole, not the Vec-

---

9. RdS, Modena, b. 2d, s.d.; O. Venturini, "Dei gradi accademici conferiti dallo studio ferrarese nel primo secolo di sua istituzione," *Atti e memorie della Deputazione ferrarese di storia patria* 4 (1892): 96.

10. RdS, Finale, b. 1, Ercole d'Este to podesta, 15 Oct. 1488.

11. Ibid., Bartolomeo Trotti to Eleonora d'Aragona, 19 Oct. 1479. On Trotti, see chap. 1.

chi family, was lord of Finale, and this could only be done by a commissioner with special powers.

The appointment of such plenipotentiary commissioners, overlapping or supplanting the existing judiciary, and with the power to set aside statutory procedures and penalties in the interests of security and tranquillity, was no new expedient in the history of the Italian *signorie*.[12] The difference here lies in the facts that Beltramino became a permanent presence (unlike the transient Florentine commissioners, quickly recalled following local lobbying)[13] and that he left correspondence exceptional both in its quantity and its quality. It is therefore strange that these hundreds of letters have been almost completely overlooked by local historians and by those literary biographers who have touched on the cities of Modena and Reggio at the end of the fifteenth century, when the poet Matteo Maria Boiardo was captain of Reggio, and when Ludovico Ariosto's father was captain of Modena. The local historian Vicini omitted all reference to Beltramino in his study of the podestas of Modena.[14] Venturi, in publishing the correspondence of the "Este governors" in Reggio, included none of Beltramino's, while conducting in his introduction a vigorous defense of Matteo Maria Boiardo from the criticisms leveled against him by the sixteenth-century chronicler Panciroli.[15] Only one Boiardo biographer, it seems, has delved into the Beltramino correspondence, but he unquestioningly took Matteo Maria's side: we can but smile, he wrote, at Beltramino's blatantly overwrought attempt to blacken Matteo Maria's reputation.[16] Such exculpation of Boiardo has been the norm, as if it could not be accepted that an exceptional poet could be an unexceptional official.

12. A. Gianandrea, "Della signoria di Francesco Sforza nella Marca," *Archivio storico lombardo* 8 (1881): 332–36; A.R. Natale, ed., "I Diari di Cicco Simonetta," *Archivio storico lombardo,* 8th ser., 2 (1950): 159–60, and 6 (1956): 61–62.

13. E. Fasano Guarini, "Gli statuti delle città soggette a Firenze tra '400 e '500: Riforme locali e interventi centrali," in Chittolini and Willoweit, *Statuti città territori,* 102–4.

14. E.P. Vicini, "I podestà di Modena: Serie cronologica dal 1336 al 1796," *AMMo,* 5th ser., 10 (1917): 288–95.

15. Venturi, "Relazioni," 231–33; G. Panciroli, *Storia della città di Reggio* (Reggio, 1848), 2:73–74.

16. G. Reichenbach, *Matteo Maria Boiardo* (Bologna, 1929), 178–79, 205–15. F. Forti, "Boiardo Matteo Maria," *DBI* 11 (1969): 214–15, repeats the quotations used by Reichenbach. See also E.G. Gardner, *Dukes and Poets in Ferrara* (London, 1904), 274: Gardner maintains that Boiardo was "much harassed . . . by the perpetual intrigues of the ducal commissary, Messer Beltramino . . . , who tried to undermine his authority and insisted upon regarding him as a personal enemy."

Panciroli's comments arose in order to explain Beltramino's appointment as commissioner: Boiardo had been too benign and placid; he was more suited to writing verses than to punishing criminals; brigands, holding his authority in contempt, had been emboldened to pillage and extortion. Panciroli's criticisms were not groundless. Boiardo's own letters speak of his mildness, incompetence, and reluctance: he asserted that he was unable to punish a group of murderers, even with the aid of twenty or thirty *fanti;* he preferred to pacify disputes; he released without fine some boys arrested for wearing masks during Carnival.[17] His ineffectiveness was also implied by praise in Reggio for his successor (see later in this chapter). Panciroli, however, does leave the impression that Beltramino was dispatched to deal with only one bandit, and that, with that man's capture and execution, his task was done: this too, has had the effect of minimizing Beltramino's perceived impact on Reggio in the 1490s. As will become apparent, his role was much more far reaching.

Beltramino seems to have spent most of the first months of his commission in Reggio rather than Modena: nineteen of his twenty-one letters from Reggio in 1489 fall in the weeks from March to late May (though he did make occasional trips to Modena in this period). He then turned his full attention to Modena in the summer months (writing ten letters from there from late May to late September), before being dispatched by Ercole on unspecified business to Pesaro,[18] from where he returned to Modena by mid-December. What type of cases did Beltramino deal with in his first year?

Among his first investigations at Reggio was the fatal wounding of a nobleman's son, of the da Bebio family, by the *fanti* of the constable of the piazza (Borso Magnanino) as they tried to break up an illicit nocturnal assembly. This killing caused Beltramino to act in haste, as "tumult" was feared in Reggio. Beltramino's views on this excess of repressive force was clear: "I do not understand what necessity forced them to kill him, as they could easily have arrested him."[19] He nevertheless took on the task of protecting Borso Magnanino and his staff: "when I got here he was shut up in his house," he wrote, "not daring to come out . . . fearing the power of the da Bebio . . . I sent the archers, made him come out

17. Campanini, "Lettere di Matteo Maria Boiardo," 415–16; Venturi, "Relazioni," 310.
18. Cam. duc., Mandati, vol. 28, fol 204v.
19. RdS, Reggio, b. 1, 27 Mar. 1489.

and go around the city . . . as if no one thought themselves offended by him."[20] A few days later, Beltramino was supervising a more properly restrained use of force in the capture from a church tower of a "pernicious ribald," one Squadrone, guilty of murder, burglary, rape, and assault: though the man defended himself by throwing stones from the tower, and though "there was fighting as at a castle," Beltramino surrounded the area with his archers and forced his surrender.[21] In late March, he also sent the archers to the hills, as a result of which he reported that "all the bandits have retreated over the Apennines [*alpe*],"[22] but he also reported that his desire actually to capture and punish bandits was being frustrated by other officials and by local assistance.[23]

Protection of a different sort arose in Beltramino's attempted prosecution of three brothers for seizing a prisoner from the custody of the podesta's staff: the brothers claimed to be clerics who could not be touched by a secular judge; the commissioner's intolerant attitude to such claims was manifested in some forthright expressions.[24] In May Beltramino was prosecuting Francesco da Dallo and Giacomo Canichia for highway robbery and rape: having examined them under torture (the *corda* as usual, as Beltramino admitted that "in other tortures I have little confidence"),[25] he sent a list of their confessions to Ercole, concluding, "these are enough . . . It did not seem necessary to dig out everything, so as not to dirty too much paper."[26] Beltramino also tried to investigate a case of rape and sodomy that he heard of at Montecchio,[27] successfully caught a "giotto vagabundo" who had robbed a Frenchman traveling to Rome,[28] and secured confessions from one Matteo da Minozzo to many robberies and assaults.[29]

---

20. AG, b. 1289, 23 Mar. 1489.

21. RdS, Reggio, b. 1, 17 Mar. 1489; Panciroli, *Storia della città di Reggio*, 2:73–74; A. Balletti, *Storia di Reggio nell'Emilia* (Reggio, 1925), 257–58; Reichenbach, *Boiardo*, 209.

22. RdS, Reggio, b. 1, 24 Mar. 1489.

23. Ibid., 24 Mar. and 17 Apr.

24. "E perche li preti qua per esser preti sogliene fare spesso simili excessi": ibid., 17 Apr.; "costoro sono laici come mi, ne credo che vadano pur in chiesia ad oldire messa . . . a questo modo ogniuno se potria fare chierico senza chierica, poi fare ogni male e allegare de non esser suppositi al judice laico . . . che non e da comportare": ibid., 28 Apr.

25. Ibid., 22 Apr.

26. "bastandomi queste . . . non me parso andare in cavo dil tutto per non imbratare tante carte": ibid., 5 May.

27. Ibid.

28. Ibid., 22 Apr.

29. Ibid., 23 May.

At the end of April he was particularly perturbed by a *mattinata* (charivari). When Messer Alessandro Anguissola took a widow as his wife, there was contention between two companies of men and youths over who should perform the *mattinata,* and Beltramino promptly banned it, informed that weapons were being laid by. He was subsequently persuaded that *mattinate* were an old custom ("usanza vechia") and allowed it to go ahead, as long as both companies agreed to unite and eschew violence. But he was not convinced that this was an old custom worth preserving: "it seems to me a very dangerous thing, of a kind easy to generate scandals and to put schism and division in this town," he wrote, and he asked Ercole to "take it away."[30]

The most atrocious crime that Beltramino had to deal with in these months at Reggio was one that began to emerge in mid-April. He heard that a notorious counterfeiter, Gaspare dell'Amante, had returned to the area to recover his forging equipment, which he had buried under a house near Scandiano. Beltramino sent his archers to arrest Gaspare, but the counterfeiter hid ("according to what I was told," wrote Beltramino) and escaped.[31] Was Beltramino aware that the Venetian Council of Ten believed, "not out of rumor, but out of clear certainty and truth," that Gaspare had been forging ducats near Scandiano "with the protection and favor" of Matteo Maria Boiardo?[32] Whether or not he knew, he seems to have pushed the inquiries into a slightly less scandalous channel: a few days later, he was working hand in hand with the podesta of Reggio, gathering information on large-scale counterfeiting of coins at the castle of Albinea, with the consent of the count, Giovanni Manfredi, and his wife, Gabriella. He reported his findings as follows:

> And one Giovanni Giacomo, a painter, who is at Rubiera, was one of the protagonists in this forgery, because he had been asked by Count Giovanni to paint in the castle, when the count married his

---

30. Ibid., 28 Apr.

31. Ibid., 17 Apr.

32. G. Ferrari, "Documenti particolari alle notizie della vita di Matteo Maria Boiardo," in *Studi su Matteo Maria Boiardo* (Bologna, 1894), 470–71; Reichenbach, *Boiardo,* 212–13. In the early 1470s Venice had pressed Ercole hard to prosecute and punish alleged counterfeiting of ducats by former courtiers of Borso d'Este, claiming that "ex civitate Ferrarie et tota illius Ill. domini ducis ditione, ut omnibus haud ignotum est, confluunt omnes fere monete false et viciate sub forma stampe nostre que in hanc civitatem nostram. . . feruntur et expenduntur": Archivio di Stato, Venice, Consiglio dei Dieci, Misto, reg. 18, fols. 82–88v.

daughter to Cristoforo Cantello; and as he was an attractive youth, the count's wife coupled with him and he made her pregnant. And this painter brought a Franciscan friar . . . to make these coins in the castle tower at the instigation of the woman and with the count's consent, for four months, and he also brought two Ferraresi, one of whom was called Niccolò . . . , but at length the count became aware of his wife's adultery, and the painter had to flee . . . and Niccolò continued the making of these coins with the count and his wife for more than six months, and they were disbursed by two of his servants in Venetian territory, and Gaspare dell'Amante helped them.[33]

Given the identity of those involved, Beltramino would not act without ducal approval, and he saw the need to proceed secretly, not writing down information received, "so as not to reveal the matter,"[34] and "lightly feeling" his way without revealing too much.[35] With Podesta Oldoini leaving office and with no one else who could be trusted present, there was no further progress in following weeks. However, by July Beltramino had discovered the whereabouts of Gaspare, who was now offering "to bring prisoner into my hands an infinite number of people, including *grandi*, who have forged coins with him," in return for assurances of immunity from prosecution.[36] In September Beltramino had a meeting with Gaspare and received a list of names: "they are all men of the hills," he reported, "and I firmly believe that they arranged with those gentlemen to share the coins between them."[37]

Beltramino was then dispatched to Pesaro. During his lengthy absence, the case developed in the hands of the new podesta, the Ferrarese Giacomino Compagni. A thief confessed under questioning that he had seen counterfeit coins being made in Massenzatica by a Franciscan friar (Fra Bernardino) and others, at the instance of the local priest, Don Filippo. Armed with a list of a dozen names of those allegedly involved in the making and spending of false coin, Compagni set out to question them. Most of them fled, and he was able to hold only three in prison. However, these did include the friar, a man of some sixty years, who confessed

---

33. RdS, Reggio, b. 1, 22 Apr. 1489. It was likewise Cesare Montecuccolo's wife who was suspected of involvement in counterfeiting in the 1480s: G. Campori, *Memorie patrie* (Modena, 1881), 105–6.

34. RdS, Reggio, b. 1, 22 Apr. 1489.

35. "non mi discopro troppo ma vado attastando de intendere": ibid., 5 May.

36. RdS, Modena, b. 2d, 8 July 1489.

37. Ibid., 22 Sept; Reichenbach, *Boiardo*, 214–15.

to repeated involvement in forging in many parts of northern Italy, from making false ducats in Monferrato in the 1460s, to supplying the stamps for the Albinea forgers while he served as chaplain to Gabriella, at her instigation and that of her nephew, Niccolò Piccinino. Compagni prosecuted some of these cases but reported, "I have not begun any process at all against Count Giovanni Manfredi, his wife Gabriella, Niccolò Piccinino, or Messer Branca di Messer Taddeo [Manfredi], because it did not seem to me that I could without a special order from your lordship, as they are gentlemen and not subject to this court, and as they have separate jurisdiction in those places where these coins were made." Nor did he institute proceedings against four gentlemen-clerics, five priests, and a friar, "because they are ecclesiastical persons altogether removed and separate from my jurisdiction."[38] Again, the incapacity of the podesta's court made clear the need for a commissioner.

Though it is clear that Beltramino limited his inquiries to "atrocious" crimes, he also received mandates to hear and determine civil disputes. He handled a case between Taddeo Manfredi and Matteo Maria Boiardi, a case concerning nondelivery of some dotal lands by the Canossa family, a dispute between the ducal *massaro* and chancellor in Reggio, and a conflict over nonpayment of debts by the commune of Cavriago.[39]

In the middle of May, Beltramino reported that the citizens of Modena "are urging me not to spend all my time here in Reggio,"[40] and by the end of the month he had reappeared in Modena, where over the summer months, he inquired into a slightly more varied group of crimes: a murder,[41] a case of adultery and abduction of a wife,[42] a violation of a pacification,[43] and a serious armed gathering in which 150 men attacked the houses of the Schidoni and Schianchi families at Sassuolo, "out of the old enmity between them on account of mutual killings."[44] Also away from the city itself, in June he took the confession of a man of San Felice who had killed two of his wife's lovers and had attempted to poison her too.[45] In

---

38. RdS, Reggio, b. 112, 31 Jan. 1490; see also ibid., 23 and 31 Dec. 1489 and 2, 11, 13, 19, 20, and 23 Jan. 1490.
39. RdS, Reggio, b. 1, 24 Apr., 28 Apr., and 23 May 1489. For the Manfredi-Boiardi dispute, see Campanini, "Lettere di Matteo Maria Boiardo," 390.
40. RdS, Reggio, b. 1, 11 May 1489.
41. RdS, Modena, b. 2d, 5 Aug.
42. Ibid., 28 May.
43. Ibid., 5 Aug.
44. Ibid., 19 and 20 Sept.
45. AG, b. 1289, 18 June 1489.

July Beltramino's suspicions were aroused at the conduct of the podesta of the Frignano (that he was in the habit of taking "a stack of ducats" from suspects and then letting them go). Later that month, Beltramino made an excursion into the Frignano: in his own account, this was a whirlwind of executive action, ensuring the levying of fines, making peace between enemies that had seemed "almost impossible," having weapons laid down, torturing suspects, and giving sentence in several cases of breaking private pacification.[46] When he returned to Modena in December, he had to deal with a case of violent resistance to the captain of the piazza (Matteo Calabrese) and an assault in San Cesario by Ludovico Boschetti on the citizen notable Francesco Carandini.[47]

The letters from Beltramino to the duke in 1489 reveal certain features that were to become characteristic in subsequent years. Two broad categories are apparent: first, Beltramino's own rectitude and promptness; second, the suspect, corrupt motives of other officials and of the "gentlemen." Beltramino declared his own incorruptibility in rebuffing a charge, carried to Ercole, that he had extorted forty ducats during an inquiry: "if this were true," he wrote, "I would not want to live any longer, having had so much time and experience in this profession that money cannot corrupt me."[48] And to threats he responded coolly: when he heard that a counterfeiter he had convicted in Mantua had come to Ferrara and was "going about armed from top to toe . . . , boasting that he will not leave without taking revenge on Amato," Beltramino simply asked the duke to ensure that nothing happened.[49] His inquiries could be lightning-swift, as shown in the case of the French traveler robbed on the road: although the traveler could speak no Italian, and though no one had seen the crime, Beltramino quickly understood the Frenchman's complaint, dispatched his archers to scour the inns, and found and arrested the culprit, who tried to dispose of his loot by throwing it into the moat while he was being escorted into the castle.[50]

As a general rule, Beltramino favored harsh punishment: against bandits he wanted to proceed according to the letter of the law and without

---

46. RdS, Modena, b. 2d, 5 July and 5 Aug. 1489.

47. Ibid., 17 Dec.

48. RdS, Reggio, b. 1, 17 Apr.

49. Ibid., 24 Apr. Amato's servant was killed in 1493: Biblioteca apostolica vaticana, MS Chigi I.I.4, Ugo Caleffini, "Cronaca ferrarese," fol. 311.

50. RdS, Reggio, b. 1, 22 Apr.

pardoning any of them (whereas the captain of Reggio wanted to pardon those bandits who captured other bandits);[51] he recommended that all those he prosecuted for sheltering bandits be convicted, "so that the report of this conviction goes round and everyone knows they were not pardoned";[52] against the ducal archers who let a suspect escape, he fulminated, "if they were at my disposal, I would have given them due punishment."[53] He went in person to Sassuolo to investigate the armed assembly there and reported, "had I not feared doing something that would displease your lordship, I would have seized the men of that faction, and there, where they had congregated, would have had them cut to pieces, because it is necessary, if one wants to extirpate such evil habits, to use similar medicine."[54] Such bold talk, distinctly Machiavellian in tone, probably exceeded Beltramino's real intentions, but his sternness is not in doubt: he tortured suspects,[55] yet he also knew how to extract confessions "more through the industry of words than with the rope";[56] he raised the tempo of public executions.[57] He even fined those who used charms to keep them from confessing under torture.[58] Later, Beltramino spoke of himself as a schoolmaster disciplining unruly children: "Those who commit these outrages seek any way they can to escape from my school, because in all the others they can find some relief, except in mine."[59]

Beltramino's methods of obtaining information and pursuing cases

---

51. Ibid., 24 Mar.
52. Ibid., 27 Apr.
53. Ibid., 16 Apr.
54. RdS, Modena, b. 2d, 19 Sept.
55. Ibid., 5 Aug.; Reggio, b. 1, 22 Apr.
56. AG, b. 1289, 18 June.
57. Cam. duc., Amministrazione finanziaria dei paesi, Modena, Massaria, b. 41, reg. 1487, fols. 102, 104; b. 43, reg. 1492, fols. 101, 105; b. 43, reg. 1496, fols. 181, 186; b. 44, reg. 1497, fol. 216; b. 44, reg. 1498, fols. 92, 96, 102, 203; b. 44, reg. 1499, fol. 208.
58. He learned that the father of Jacomo Canichia had supplied his son and Francesco da Dallo with "boletini da mangiare quando se conducevano ala corda, et una fugacina impastata di latte di matre e fiola che lattassenno, acio che non potessenno confessare," and he consequently fined the father ten ducats: RdS, Reggio, b. 1, 30 Apr. 1489. For a similar case at Mantua, see app. 1, Letter to Marquis Ludovico Gonzaga, 20 Oct. 1468. See also J. Sprenger and H. Institoris, *Malleus maleficarum* (Speyer, 1485), III.xv, as quoted in *Witchcraft in Europe 1100–1700: A Documentary History,* ed. A.C. Kors and E. Peters (Philadelphia, 1972), 172.
59. RdS, Reggio, b. 1, 29 Jan. 1491. This brand of thinking was later satirized by Dickens in "The Finishing Schoolmaster," *Household Words* 60 (1851).

was impressively dogged and varied. Obviously he received instructions from Ercole to investigate crimes that had come to ducal attention, and he also received denunciations and accusations direct from lesser officials and injured individuals.[60] However, he was not merely reactive. He used his powers to search for crimes and corruption: he summoned judicial notaries and inspected their registers;[61] he extracted information from suspects about accomplices and other delinquents;[62] he tracked down informants and used spies to locate suspects;[63] he searched the houses of suspects to uncover evidence of further criminal activity;[64] and, forewarned of their intentions, he lay in wait to catch criminals in the act.[65] He also used his powers to the full to expedite cases, activating extradition treaties to get hold of suspects;[66] sending the archers to capture known bandits, *giotti,* and *ribaldi;*[67] instructing other ducal officials to arrest and deliver suspects;[68] trying to get "gentlemen" to do the same;[69] persuading witnesses to testify;[70] and excavating evidence overlooked by the podesta.[71] In other words, the existing judicial "machinery" was thoroughly set in motion, a new chain of coordination and command was set in place, and sources of information were sought out and exploited. Beltramino seemed intent on turning a commission to investigate unpunished crime into a judicial generalship.

Such a presence stirred up the alarm of both the local and the central establishments, which were fearful of a loss of control over judicial fines. At Reggio, within weeks of Beltramino's appointment, the communal *anziani* noted that the commissioner was interfering "in so many things that nothing seems to be left to be decided by the podesta," and that he was "burdening those who carry arms with the great expenses of his

60. RdS, Reggio, b. 1, 8 Mar. and 16 Sept. 1490; RdS, Modena, b. 2d, 11 Jan. and 28 May 1490.

61. RdS, Modena, b. 2d, 2 May 1490; RdS, Reggio, b. 1, 16 Mar. 1489 and 16 Sept. 1490.

62. RdS, Reggio, b. 1, 17 Mar. and 16 Apr. 1489 and 13 Oct. 1490.

63. RdS, Reggio, b. 1, 30 Apr. 1489, 28 Sept. 1490 and 29 Jan. 1491; RdS, Modena, b. 2d, 14 June 1490.

64. RdS, Reggio, b. 1, 21 Feb. 1491.

65. RdS, Modena, b. 2d, 14 June 1490.

66. RdS, Reggio, b. 1, 24 and 27 Mar. 1489.

67. RdS, Reggio, b. 1, 27 Mar., 9 Apr., 5 May, and 11 May 1489, 8 Mar. 1490, 29 Jan. 1491, etc.

68. RdS, Reggio, b. 1, 18 May 1489; RdS, Modena, b. 2d, 4 Jan. and 29 Mar. 1490.

69. RdS, Modena, b. 2d, 23 Apr. 1490.

70. RdS, Reggio, b. 1, 5 May 1489.

71. RdS, Modena, b. 2d, 11 Jan. 1490.

archers." The real source of Reggian anxiety here was the threat to its income from lesser crimes and from rural *danni dati*.[72] They resolved to depute a committee to speak to Beltramino and tell him "that he should not do those things about which there could be complaint."[73] The *anziani*, Beltramino replied, had misunderstood his purposes: faced with so many complaints from those who claimed to have been denied justice, he had sent for the judicial notaries to inspect their registers, to see if "by fault of the podesta or of the notaries, or rather by some bribe or favor, anyone has been acquitted who should have been punished," especially in the more serious crimes, for which fines go to the ducal camera; but the citizens thought he wanted to interfere with the fines for lesser offenses that go to the commune and to transfer all the podesta's current cases to himself. "After a long discussion with them, they seemed to go away happy," he thought.[74]

The commune had reacted so swiftly to protect "its" judicial fines because it was in the habit of remitting dozens of them every year, compounding with the convicts for smaller sums or for no sum at all.[75] These remissions or pardons—so-called *gratia*—were approved in batches at intervals during the year, by the *anziani*, and related to the whole range of criminal activity (from blasphemy, working on holy days, and disobedience, to theft, assault, and even homicide),[76] as well as to criminal damage in the *contado (danni dati)*. Such *gratia* were in essence a fiscal resource: despite the occasional profession of charitable motive, their purpose was to raise money quickly for pressing needs—as stated specifically in 1496, for example[77]—or more generally to ensure that the *contadini* had the wherewithal to support other fiscal burdens.[78] *Gratia* also retained a certain power of patronage within the local community, as also occasionally revealed.[79] The possible transfer of both trials and

---

72. Cf. Ferrara, where the duke had taken such income away from the commune in 1474: Biblioteca apostolica vaticana, MS Chigi I.I.4, Ugo Caleffini, "Cronaca ferrarese," fol. 37.

73. ASRe, Provvigioni, reg. 98, fol. 125v (12 Feb. 1489); Reichenbach, *Boiardo,* 210.

74. RdS, Reggio, b. 1, 16 Mar. 1489.

75. Cf. Dean, "Criminal Justice in Mid-Fifteenth-Century Bologna," 28–29; A. Ryder, "The Incidence of Crime in Sicily in the Mid-Fifteenth Century: The Evidence from Composition Records," in Dean and Lowe, *Crime, Society, and the Law.*

76. ASRe, Provvigioni, reg. 98, fols. 85, 110v, 112, 126v, 145, 159v; reg. 100, fols. 51, 119, 196v; reg. 102, fols. 18, 38v.

77. To pay for the annual horse race: ibid., reg. 100, fol. 274.

78. Ibid., reg. 100, fol. 64v.

79. Ibid., reg. 98, fol. 145; reg. 100, fol. 96v.

fines to an outside commissioner threatened all these local interests: the display of charity, financial liquidity, the rural tax base, and noble and official patronage. The commune of Reggio, too aware already of its own weakness, could not permit such a transfer (even though none was intended), and in later years (as we shall see) it turned to any argument to keep Beltramino at bay.

Similarly, at Modena the captain, Niccolò Ariosti, responded to the commissioner's presence by jealously trying to protect his own status as the duke's superior official in the city. Beltramino reacted nonchalantly: "I have never shown, to him nor to the podesta nor to any other official, any desire for superiority, because I never took pleasure in such smoke, nor do I look for it now when I have less need than in the past. I take pains to honor everyone, even those of lower standing than myself, and it has always seemed to me that humanity is a better thing than ambition."[80] Beltramino was tireless in portraying himself in a flattering light: here he professes indifference to the ambitious posturings of those over-concerned with rank and status; he had a job to do, and such issues were irrelevant to it. Nevertheless, we should note that when there was a dispute over precedence in the Corpus Christi procession in Reggio in 1493, which Beltramino was required to settle, he ensured that the place of greatest honor—behind the bishop and the host, in front of the podesta, *anziani*, and gentlemen—was taken by himself.[81]

An alarm at Beltramino's activities was also quickly sounded in the central revenue office. In the summer of 1489 the *fattore generale*, Filippo Cistarelli, happened to visit Reggio on business and was present when the captain of the piazza levied a fine of twenty-five lire that Beltramino had imposed. Offering to cancel this fine from the lists of those outstanding, Cistarelli was told that it was not written down, that the Reggian *massaro* had an instruction from Beltramino not to write down any of his fines. "At which I took no little amazement," Cistarelli wrote, ". . . because in large numbers of fines some could easily be lost." At Modena, Cistarelli found the same thing: no account was kept of Beltramino's fines.[82] As a jealous defender of the camera's rights and powers over its subordinate officials, Cistarelli urged Ercole to correct this dubious practice; but there is no evidence that the duke did so. Rather,

---

80. RdS, Modena, b. 2d, 25 Dec. 1489.
81. ASRe, Comune, Provvigioni, reg. 100, fols. 91v–92.
82. ASE, Cancelleria, Carteggio di ufficiali camerali, b. 1, Filippo Cistarelli to Ercole d'Este, 3 Aug. 1489.

receipts at Modena from judicial fines continued to fall, from 1,639 lire in 1488 to 1,059 in 1489 and to 479 for the period from May 1490 to June 1491.[83] Were these "losses" finding their way into Beltramino's hands?

That Beltramino's actions were not themselves entirely above suspicion also becomes clear from his continuing correspondence with the Gonzaga about matters in Modena and Reggio.[84] It was the marquis of Mantua who urged him to take Borso Magnanino into his protection,[85] just as the marquis also pressed him to ensure that the San Felice poisoner escape the death penalty and that Galvano Castaldo and Giacomo Canichia be released from custody. Hopeful, as we shall see, to return to Mantua, Beltramino obviously wished to present a compliant face to the Gonzaga. He wrote to the marquis: "I wish for nothing but to do what I can to show you that I recognize the rewards received from you and your predecessors . . . If I can do anything more, let me know and I will always do anything to satisfy you";[86] "God knows I have no other desire but to show that I am your faithful, absent servant . . . [and] that I hold you as my lord as if I were at Mantua."[87] This attitude creates a dilemma for the historian: which master was Beltramino serving?[88] And how did his performance of personal favors to the Gonzaga affect his administration of justice to Este subjects?

In the case of Borso Magnanino, his reports to Ercole are full of investigative successes (detentions, extraditions, questionings), while his letter to Marquis Francesco Gonzaga brims with faithful favors (aiding and protecting Borso and his staff, taking his belongings into safekeeping, releasing those *fanti* "in whom there was little suspicion").[89] In the case of Galvano Castaldo, Beltramino satisfied the Gonzaga desire for his release, while telling Ercole that there was insufficient evidence to justify his further detention.[90] In the case of Giacomo Canichia, Beltramino not

---

83. Cam. duc., Amministrazione finanziaria dei paesi, Modena, Massaria, b. 42, "Libro autentico" for 1490, fol. 245.

84. Cf. the "double correspondence" of Renaissance ambassadors: M. Mallett, "Ambassadors and Their Audiences in Renaissance Italy," *Renaissance Studies* 8 (1994): 241–42.

85. AG, b. 1289, 23 Mar.

86. Ibid., 18 June.

87. Ibid., 23 Mar.

88. See D.M. Bueno de Mesquita, "Niccolò da Correggio at Milan," *Italian Studies* 20 (1965): 45.

89. AG, b. 1289, 23 Mar.

90. Ibid., 23 Mar. and 9 Apr.; RdS, Reggio, b. 1, 24 Mar.

only suspended the trial to allow Francesco Gonzaga to write to Ferrara to obtain his release but said that he had seconded Gonzaga's efforts with his own letter to the same effect (though there is no trace of such a letter),[91] while to Ercole he complained of interference in the trial from the bishop of Modena (who claimed Giacomo as a cleric) and from Milan (in protection of Giacomo's accomplice, Francesco da Dallo).[92] Finally, in the case of the San Felice poisoner, Beltramino himself admitted being "totally confused": having the ducal go-ahead to proceed to execution, Beltramino had then received a Gonzaga letter "commanding" him to ensure that the condemned man's life was spared. Here, Beltramino's response was to delay execution until Ercole went to Mantua, so that Francesco Gonzaga could there persuade him to clemency. In none of these cases is the evidence clear of the subordination of judicial action to personal interest, but the open potential for such distortion certainly is present, given Beltramino's authority to disregard statute law. More striking perhaps is the masterly way that Beltramino shapes his reports to suit his relationship with their recipients: to the Gonzaga he is all dutifulness and solicitude; to Ercole he is the no-nonsense, expeditious man of action.

While Beltramino was honing his own image as the stern man of justice, he readily inculpated others of failures of duty. When the archers shot and killed a man for attempting to escape as they escorted him to the city, Beltramino was quick to blame their neglect ("though he deserved to die, he should not have died without legal process, and I believe they killed him to cover up their negligence").[93] He alleged that the podesta of Castelnovo drew a murder trial out for months and then acquitted for money;[94] that the podesta of Sestola was selling arms licenses;[95] that the podesta of Carpineti had used his power to seize bandits "not to punish them but to let them go for money" and that he was guilty of "negotiating with those who should be punished, releasing thieves for money";[96] and that the podesta of Montecchio had let go a rapist and sodomite ("some say the podesta had money from him").[97] Beltramino presented himself as the lone champion of justice against this ubiquitous corrup-

---

91. AG, b. 1289, 11 Apr.
92. RdS, Reggio, b. 1, 22 Apr. and 5 May.
93. Ibid., 16 Apr.
94. Ibid., 17 Mar.
95. RdS, Modena, b. 2d, 16 Aug.
96. RdS, Reggio, b. 1, 27 Mar.
97. Ibid., 5 May.

tion. His work was inevitably frustrated by other officials: "my misfortune," he wrote, "has been to find everywhere officials who seek to undo what I do for the good of this place."[98] In addition, there were few he could trust: at Reggio, apart from the podesta (Antonio Oldoini) and the *massaro,* who had been prompt with information about local people and past events, there was no one who would speak honestly to him. "If I need to dig out the truth, everyone fears to tell me."[99]

Facing such widespread noncooperation, Beltramino felt justified in suspecting others' motives. When the Reggian citizens held a "parlamento," "fearing that I wanted to interfere in the money fines that belong to this commune," Beltramino thought their assembly was not spontaneous but "pushed by others for some private interest, or for that of friends and relatives who perhaps in the past have avoided punishment."[100] When taking the confessions of those who had harbored bandits, Beltramino reported that "some said [they did it] because they were relatives, some because friends, some because of fear," but "I, for my part, knew that they did it to make themselves lords *[capitani]* of those places."[101]

All these elements—negligence, noncooperation, fear, and private interest—come together in Beltramino's general depiction of the corruption in city and countryside that was held at bay only by his own fearsome presence. Witnesses feared to testify: "so much have these *giotti* intimidated men and women with their threats, that it seems that they still have them at their backs, fearing that when I leave, they will return and cut them to pieces."[102] "It is with the greatest difficulty in the world that I have been able to find witnesses to prove these things, because they were reluctant, saying that your lordship would grant a pardon and then they would be cut to pieces."[103] The captain at Reggio (Matteo Maria Boiardo) obstructed his examination of suspects held in the castle. "This," Beltramino believed, "happens out of envy, as he sees me being visited every day by . . . innumerable *uomini da bene,* and as he sees so

---

98. "Pare che per mia disgratia habia trovato per tutto officiali che cercano de desfare cioche io facio al bene de questo paese": RdS, Modena, b. 2d, 16 Aug.

99. "non ho dove mi possa voltare a persona che mi tenga dritto di simel cossa che se debbo cavare una veritate ogniuno teme de dirla e bisogna con grande sagacitate extirparla": RdS, Reggio, b. 1, 30 Apr.

100. Ibid., 16 Mar.

101. Ibid., 27 Apr.

102. Ibid., 30 Apr.

103. Ibid., 5 May.

many *cattivi* fleeing and others being punished whom perhaps he would not want punished."[104] Beltramino also claimed that there were so many bandits in the hills, despite the presence of officials and gentlemen who should keep them away or capture them, because they were harbored by those who aimed to become "principali" and "to be feared and obeyed out of fear."[105]

Despite these difficulties, Beltramino was confident of his corrective presence. By late March, he wrote, "things are going from good to better";[106] at Modena, shortly after his return in the summer, he had arms deposed throughout the city;[107] and by 16 August he could report that "things are in good order, and since I came here few serious excesses have happened."[108] The only flies in this ointment were the gentlemen: "since these two cities . . . are very well settled, and since the lands of the gentlemen, of the Reggiano and the Modenese, do not obey likewise, things will go ill," Beltramino predicted, "so it is necessary to make good provision."[109] This provision, effected toward the end of the year, comprised a reinforcement of the archers and a proclamation reasserting Beltramino's powers over gentlemen as well as citizens.[110]

In fact, things were going badly wrong with the Rangoni. As early as April 1489, Beltramino already had three grievances against this over-mighty family. The first was that Francesco Maria had refused to give him a list of his servants as requested. The second was that Beltramino had heard that Francesco "has in one of his rooms several *giotti,* who eat, drink, and sleep there, and they think they are safe and embolden all the others to return in my absence in the hope of this refuge" (note how Beltramino here uses the argument of disorder in his absence in an attempt to control the aristocratic household). Finally, Beltramino reported that Guizardo Riminaldi, captain of his archers, in pursuing some *giotti* who had fled into the house of Francesco Maria, was refused entry there, Francesco's servants offering to fight him, and Francesco's wife saying that the family had a privilege by which no one could be taken in their house. Beltramino was outraged at such presumption: "we will have to come to grips with him [Francesco]"; "that family must be more obedi-

104. Ibid., 17 Mar.
105. Ibid., 27 Apr.
106. Ibid., 27 Mar.
107. RdS, Modena, b. 2d, 5 Aug.
108. Ibid., 16 Aug.
109. Ibid., 20 Sept.
110. Ibid., 14 Dec.

ent."[111] In this he was supported by Eleonora, who thought that Guizardo should not have let himself be fobbed off by Francesco Maria's wife. In September Beltramino sent Guizardo and the archers to the Rangoni castle at Levizzano in pursuit of the band of men who had made an attack on the Schianchi and Schidoni of Sassuolo: the archers were not simply refused entry but attacked from the castle with stones, while the alarm bell was rung and scores of men and women ran up from the surrounding area.[112]

This incident prompted the strengthening, by proclamation and extra *fanti*, of Beltramino's power and authority. Immediately Beltramino reported that the Rangoni had resolved to conduct a united campaign, together with all the other gentlemen, to have the proclamation revoked. They claimed they would spend whatever it cost and would write to Ercole, the marquis of Mantua, the duke of Milan, and Giovanni Bentivoglio.[113] Beltramino professed indifference to these threats, robustly asking Ercole that, "if these gentlemen come to you, . . . you give them such a warning that they do not allow anyone to carry arms who is not their servant or who does not live at their expense, because I would be happier for the arms carried by their followers under their protection to be laid down . . . And I would also like your lordship to show them that you know of the threats they make to me and that such presumption displeases you."[114] Ten days later, he could report more calmly that the Rangoni had not in fact gone to Ferrara, because the other gentlemen had not agreed with their wishes, especially Count Niccolò Rangoni, who had sent a message of support to the commissioner, thankful that Ercole had opened his eyes to the lamentable state of the city, nostalgically recalling the days of his youth when it was possible to go out at night without meeting people carrying weapons or making a nuisance, and asserting that "your lordship could not do too much here, because the place is too corrupted."[115]

There was still the danger, however, of Francesco Maria alone persuading Ercole that Beltramino should not prosecute "his men": if this immunity were allowed, Beltramino solemnly forewarned, "everything done up to now would be shattered and everyone would be emboldened

111. RdS, Reggio, b. 1, 9 Apr. and 1 May.
112. RdS, Modena, b. 2d, 20 Sept.
113. Ibid., 14 Dec.
114. Ibid.
115. Ibid., 25 Dec.

to have little respect for what I do. I advise you that this proclamation has been the curing of this state *[la medicina de questo stato]* and that the whole town and all the other gentlemen are as content as it is possible to say, because everyone knows their own ills and whence they originate and are greatly pleased to see them remedied."[116] Here then is another familiar figure: the judge as physician, diagnosing the ills of society and prescribing medicines (sometimes harsh) to cure them.[117] The medicine, however, did not bring a rapid cure, and in 1490 we find the commissioner talking more of the need for patience, "for the great corruption that over past years has become so rooted that it cannot easily be removed, but it is necessary little by little to accustom people to *ben vivere.*"[118]

The year 1490 was to prove Beltramino's earlier forewarnings. He was present at Reggio at the beginning and end of the year (in January and from September to November), spending a few days in January and, as before, the summer months (May to August) in Modena. From Reggio he reported on nearly twenty cases, from Modena over forty—a distribution that seems to reflect the intensity of disorder in the two cities in the 1480s. In both cities his caseload continued to include some civil business, as he was used by the duke and by private parties more as a general supreme judge than as a specifically criminal investigator. These civil cases ranged from a small dispute over clothing pawned to a Jew[119] to the disputed accounts of the Modenese gabelle farmers,[120] from a widow seeking return of her dowry[121] to conflicts over benefices.[122] The more serious civil cases were again Modenese. So were the more serious criminal cases: Reggio troubled Beltramino with only notarial forgery,[123] perjury,[124] horse stealing,[125] armed assembly,[126] and counterfeiting (includ-

---

116. Ibid., 28 Dec. 1490 (= 1489).

117. See O. Capitani, "L'incompiuto 'tractatus de iustitia' di fra Remigio de' Girolami," *Bollettino dell'Istituto storico italiano per il medio evo* 72 (1960): 125–28.

118. RdS, Reggio, b. 1, 21 Jan. 1490.

119. Ibid., 19 Jan.

120. Ibid., 6 Oct; see also later in this chapter.

121. RdS, Reggio, b. 1, 27 Jan.

122. Ibid., 24 Sept.; RdS, Modena, b. 2d, 31 Dec.

123. RdS, Reggio, b. 1, 16 Jan. and 8 Mar.

124. "Io faro il dovere . . . a correctione de questa cita che in questa falsita de testimonii e instrumenti e tanto corrotta che questi homini da bene non ponno stare securi de le faculta e rasone sue": ibid., 27 Jan.

125. Ibid., 8 Mar.

126. Ibid., 29 Jan.

ing the eventual arrest of Gaspare dell'Amante),[127] as well as with various assaults and thefts[128] and, more importantly, a rape[129] and a murder.[130] Even within this rather limited list, Beltramino found corrupt matter to expose to the duke. Presented with some earlier ducal letters ordering credence to be given to Jews' allegations of injuries inflicted on them by Christians, Beltramino found this "absurd" and "beyond common law," as it allowed "that when a Jew wants to attack a Christian, he can do so safely and then say that the Christian started it, which I do not believe was your lordship's intention."[131] In September he found the podesta proceeding in a leisurely and unsatisfactory way in a murder case (it was alleged that friends of one of the murderers had paid him money), and so he intervened to prosecute more swiftly and comprehensively.[132] He wrote to Eleonora to enlist her support with Ercole, "that he might let this sort of fault be uncovered for once, so that other officials abstain from this practice."[133]

Much more serious matters came to Beltramino's attention in Modena: murders and attempted murder, attacks on officials, highway robbery, assaults and thefts, abduction, incest and rape, forgery, fraud, and counterfeiting. In addition, it was in this year that judicial action in the Petrezani–dal Forno feud was transferred to the commissioner. As soon as he returned to the city in January, he was vigorously resisting requests to allow Carnival masking (arguing that masking was "dangerous because of the great enmities there are among the citizens and people"),[134] he was attempting a pacification among the Schidoni of Sassuolo and their enemies at Dinazzano,[135] and he was coolly fending off the insults of Niccolò Ariosti and the threats of Gerardo Rangoni, whose servants he wanted to prosecute for an assault on Matteo Calabrese's *fanti*.[136] This latter assault had happened the previous month as Matteo had tried to seize some meat that had entered the city without tax being

---

127. Ibid., 28 Sept. and 1, 3, 13, and 17 Oct.
128. Ibid., 19 Jan., 21 Jan., 29 Jan., 17 Sept., and 24 Sept.
129. Ibid., 8 Mar.
130. Ibid., 16 and 17 Sept.
131. Ibid., 21 Jan.
132. Ibid., 16 and 17 Sept.
133. Ibid., 17 Sept.
134. RdS, Modena, b. 2d, 4 Jan.
135. Ibid., 5 Jan.
136. Beltramino wrote that the captain of Modena "non cessa in consiglio e in altri lochi . . . de dire che sono uno ribaldo, ladro, poltrone": ibid., 12 Jan.

paid. Two of his *fanti* were wounded. The *reggimento* (according to Beltramino) did nothing for weeks afterward, until it heard of the commissioner's imminent return; then it hurriedly examined a few witnesses
(including the wounded *fanti*), who, however, deposed that they did not
see who had hit Matteo's men. Beltramino wrote to Ercole, "And so your
lordship can see how things go here: that such a disorder as this, committed in the presence of the people against the officials and against your
revenues, should be covered up in this way, and it will appear neither
likely nor credible to you that, in the middle of the day, in a crowd of
people, there is not someone who saw who wounded these men."[137]
Within days the *fanti* were telling Beltramino the truth and excusing their
earlier statements, which were made, they said, at Count Gerardo's
request and in fear of assault by his men. "This city is so contaminated
with favors," noted Beltramino, "that the truth can hardly be discovered."[138]

At this point Beltramino's relations with the Rangoni turned decisively
toward open confrontation.

> I had resolved not to write to your lordship the improper and
> threatening words used yesterday by Count Gerardo in the captain's
> house in the presence of the podesta and many people, but as the count
> is coming to Ferrara, I believe that he is coming for this in the fear that
> I had written to you. When the count was in the captain's room, they
> sent for the podesta, and when he arrived the count asked him to write
> to your lordship that it was not true that he had threatened the wit-
> nesses with being cut to pieces if they testified against him and his men
> . . . Then the count began to fulminate and say that I would not always
> be commissioner at Modena,[139] but that if I ever had to go to Mantua
> or Crema, he would make me regret it, and that if I were a gentleman
> he would make me go as far as France, reviling me with many words,
> and no less did the captain, saying I was a poltroon, constantly incit-
> ing the count to go to Ferrara and to write such that it would be bet-
> ter if I had let the matter stand . . . than to shame him and others, say-

---

137. Ibid., 17 Dec. 1489.

138. "questa cita e tanto contaminata de compiacerse l'uno l'altro che apena se po
trovare verita alchuna": ibid., 30 Dec. 1490 (= 1489); see also ibid., 29 Dec. 1489.

139. Cf. "tu non serai sempre antiano" and "quando tue sarai fuora dell'officio, io ti ne
paghero": S. Bongi, "Ingiurie, improperi, contumelie ecc. Saggio di lingua parlata del Tre-
cento cavata dai libri criminali di Lucca," *Il propugnatore*, n.s., 3, no. 1 (1890): 103, 105;
Istorie di Giovanni Cambi, ed. I. di San Luigi (Florence, 1785), 2:254.

ing to those present, "Look at this ribald, who is not ashamed to go against these gentlemen, who would not be worthy to wash their feet," recalling that I had fled from Mantua and other things that would be long to write down . . . I of all these words take little account, and less of the threats; indeed I intend to show that I have not understood them. It really sorrows me that those who should help me . . . do the opposite . . . The truth is that this task you have set me to is of a kind that cannot please, doing justice, which no one wants to hear of in their own house . . . You should know that the citizens and people and all the place raise their hands to the sky at my arrival . . . and only these three, that is the captain, Count Gerardo, and Francesco Maria do not welcome me, for wanting to have things their way.[140]

Again we may note the assured literary control of this letter: Beltramino's initial declaration of reluctance, overcome only by his adversary's fearful decision to talk directly to the duke; his portrayal of himself as the people's champion against a tight oligarchy, as the friend of justice in a city that resisted reform; his inculpating of other officials for not performing their duty. Against Beltramino's self-depiction in terms of official duty, the Rangoni are portrayed as angrily transforming the issue into one of honor (Beltramino is no gentleman) and shame (theirs, caused by one who had none), as turning to the illicit methods of insult and threat, of using their wide aristocratic contacts to prevent a prosecution of their servants and to endanger Beltramino's life outside Ercole's state. Beltramino, in constructing his version of events, thus plays on a public-private polarity: as a public official he embodies both the authority of the duke and the expectations of the general populace against the aristocratic weapons of honor, shame, and the clientele; and so too he refuses to do battle with aristocrats on their terms, publicly refusing to acknowledge the meaning of their words ("I intend to show that I have not understood them").

However, Beltramino's best literary efforts were no match for Rangoni influence: when he moved on to Reggio in the middle of the month, he received Ercole's instruction not to proceed against Gerardo's servants. Beltramino made a half-graceful bow to an obviously political decision, noting that because the duke always acted according to considerations of which Beltramino was ignorant, he remained content. But he

---

140. RdS, Modena, b. 2d, 10 Jan 1490.

firmly added: "Do not believe that I would not willingly ingratiate myself with these gentlemen as others do, if justice did not weigh heavier on the other side . . . I also see that the complaisancy of your lordship's officials to these gentlemen, which makes them lords of the citizens against their will, ruins this city, because it is then necessary for everyone reluctantly to do things their way. And it also happens that they make themselves poodles *[cagnetti]* and followers to do what they command . . . I shall do according to my habit of persecuting the *cattivi*, whoever they are, gentlemen or their followers, regardless, and with justice, then I shall leave it to your lordship to dispose as you think fit for your state."[141]

The assault on the forces of law continued, and only a few weeks later, Matteo Calabrese himself was killed. Beltramino recommended swift and exemplary punishments against the killers (seizing their properties, destroying their houses) and tried, without success, to extract them from their hideaways at Mirandola and Carpi (where the gentlemen-governors seemed unable to hand them over).[142] The failure to bring these men to trial represented another victory for noble power.

Beltramino was more successful in handling crimes not apparently connected to aristocratic interest. He had much success, for example, in taking bandits,[143] arranging for the arrest of known "thieves and ribalds,"[144] apprehending and hanging a highway robber who had attacked a friar,[145] torturing suspects,[146] and handing down sentences, even if sometimes in the absence of the accused.[147] However, the record for 1490 is perhaps marked more by failure than success. The case of the two bandits brought in on 12 June is exemplary. One was hanged within days;[148] but process against the other was suspended at Ercole's order,[149] and Beltramino soon recorded why: "he has many supporters, lords and gentlemen, who have obtained a list of all the thefts he has confessed. And I fear that they have, by fear or by private concord or by promise of compensation . . . , corrupted those who were robbed to say that they were not robbed, for, having interrogated them, they say that they were

---

141. RdS, Reggio, b. 1, 16 Jan.
142. RdS, Modena, b. 2d, 17 and 23 Apr.
143. Ibid., 12 June 1490.
144. Ibid., 4 Jan. and 4 Aug.
145. Ibid., 23 June, 24 June, 6 July, and 13 July.
146. Ibid., 11 Jan, 29 Mar., 23 June, 9 Sept., etc.
147. Ibid., 23 Apr., 12 May, 27 July, and 9 Sept.
148. Ibid., 19 June.
149. Ibid., 23 June.

not robbed."[150] Though there remained enough verified charges on the sheet to hang the bandit, Ercole spared his life.[151]

At almost every turn, Beltramino found his way blocked, his action stifled by the power of the gentlemen. Instead of executing a convict, a gentlewoman-governess (Marietta Calcagnini) was "seeking to make an accord with him, as all the castellans do, which is something that ruins this country, because no one is ever punished, but they fix things for money."[152] When Beltramino took in the Rangoni miller to discover the truth regarding a rape perpetrated in his mill, he had to release him after two days, none the wiser; "I believe that the count [Antonio Rangoni] had trained this miller in what to say, so that the malefactors should not be found," he reported, "for it is said that they were Rangoni servants."[153] Pursuing a priest-assassin in June, Beltramino's archers dared not follow him into Antonio Rangoni's house, and by the time Beltramino arrived on the scene, no trace of the priest could be found ("search the house if you like," said Antonio: Beltramino did but found nothing).[154] In a benefice dispute, Taddeo Manfredi and his podesta at Borzano forcibly seized crops that Alessandro da Fiorano had consigned to the rightful incumbent: "if it is tolerated that gentlemen come with armed men into your lordship's territory and not allow legal right to prevail but do things de facto," Beltramino warned, "things will take such a form that neither law nor good order *[bono costume]* will be found here."[155]

Similar forebodings litter Beltramino's reports on the worst excess of the year, a long joust with Count Cesare da Montecuccolo, lord of a number of castles in the Apennines.[156] This confrontation arose from the case of one Gaspare da Castagneto, who had been forced to seek ducal protection against the many attacks on him by Cesare and his men. In April, Cesare's son, Giovanni Ludovico, with a band of eighty armed men, went at night to Gaspare's house, with tools to break in and gunpowder to destroy it. Ercole instructed Beltramino to proceed. Beltramino's summoner was assaulted; his citations were ignored at Cesare's

150. Ibid., 13 July.
151. Ibid., 13 July and 25 Aug.
152. Ibid., 3 May.
153. Ibid., 21 May.
154. Ibid., 14 June
155. Ibid., 17 June.
156. On Cesare, see G. Campori, "Cesare Montecuccoli," in idem, *Memorie patrie*.

order. The archers, sent to bring in some witnesses, were met by an armed crowd and the ringing of the alarm bell and were forced to withdraw. "All these men say they have an express command from Count Cesare not to come and testify," Beltramino reported, explaining that Cesare "has told them that he does not want them to obey me, that he has nothing to do with me, that they should go to work and leave the matter to him as he will provide."[157] All of this, Beltramino advised, deserves great punishment: "the ink is not dry on the proclamation about this sort of thing," he wrote, adding that as this was the first case since that decree, "what is done here will give law to the whole country." Beltramino recommended sending in a good number of soldiers and razing a few houses.[158] Repeatedly he asked to be allowed to do justice in this case, arguing that the path of law and patience is the only way to correct the country.[159] Cesare had his own plan. Beltramino heard that he had gone straight to Ferrara, having told his men not to worry because he would defend them, and praising what they had done; but at Ferrara he was refused audience by the duke and was told to ensure that his men obey the commissioner.[160] However, he returned to Reggio telling a different story, that Ercole had been too unwell to see him, and that he did not think he could make his men attend, "because of the little obedience he has over his subjects."[161] Ordered to deliver ten of his men within five days, Cesare doubted they would come, but he had at least earned time for them to make off: "From what I understand," reported Beltramino, "in the time Cesare has been here, they have emptied their houses and fled."[162]

Given all Beltramino's strictures in this case, it is surprising to find him suddenly reporting that he had negotiated an accord between Cesare and Gaspare, something that, in pressing for exemplary punishment, he had earlier declared Gaspare specifically did not want (Gaspare wanted justice, not an accord, because despite several accords in the past, Cesare had still tried to kill him). What had happened? Beltramino was partly bowing to events: the men had fled and would not be delivered for questioning; Cesare had at least been given a reprimand. But Beltramino's

157. RdS, Modena, b. 2d, 14 May and 1 June 1490.
158. Ibid., 14 May.
159. Ibid., 14 and 15 May.
160. Ibid., 1 June.
161. Ibid., 1 and 7 June.
162. Ibid., 7 and 11 June.

correspondence with the Gonzaga tells a different story. In early May the marquis wrote in support of Cesare, "pressing more than you have ever done for anyone else, that I might take him into my protection . . . as if he was of your own blood."[163] Given this display of "great affection," Beltramino felt obliged "to do everything possible for the said Count Cesare, so that he know that your lordship has servants everywhere, through whom you can assist those who are loved by you." Beltramino does admit that he could not alter the prosecution and that he would continue to inform Ercole truthfully of the affair, but he agrees to exhort the duke to clemency, recalling to the marquis that "by this route I always obtained what I wanted from . . . your grandfather and father, that when they had the truth of things from me, they then let me do and decide things as I thought best." So, at the beginning of July, Beltramino related to the marquis the fact of the accord and the ducal annulment of the trial, noting that Cesare was "very pleased" to have received such a service from the Gonzaga through him, and that Beltramino puts himself yet again at Gonzaga disposal ("everyday you will find me more ready to show my servitude and loyalty").[164] As in the past, when severity against the delinquent ran counter to service to his first master, Beltramino's vigor melted into subservience. Or at least he made it seem so: was the truth of the matter that he so played with the appearance of things as to turn Cesare's stonewalling into a stepping-stone on his own path back to Mantua?

The appointment of a successor to the murdered Matteo Calabrese brought back into Beltramino's company Borso Magnanino, the man with "clean hands," praised for his good work by Gregorio Zampante, and damned for his extortions by the Reggian *anziani* in 1489 (see chap. 5). Although in 1489 Beltramino had assured the marquis of Mantua that he had always loved Borso, "as he was raised in the same school as I was nourished and raised in,"[165] he now rapidly came into conflict with him over rights to levy fines for arms offenses. Guizardo had happened to arrest a man for arms carrying, and Borso complained that Guizardo was "ruining my office." Beltramino reports, "I marvel at how he can complain, as he has only been here a day . . . and we have been here so long with Matteo Calabrese, who did not make as many complaints as this one makes in a day; rather, he had an understanding with Guizardo . . .

163. AG, b. 1289, 19 May.
164. Ibid., 3 July.
165. Ibid., 23 Mar. 1489.

and what he did not dare to do himself, he was happy for Guizardo to do."[166] Beltramino suspected the worst: that Borso was being prompted to complain by those who were corrupting the city with their armed followers (the Rangoni?), "so that they can do worse than ever, because here it is only Guizardo who is feared, as they have all the others doing things their way."[167] The duke instructed his commissioner not to interfere in Borso's office or in searching for illicit weapons. Beltramino resentfully obeyed in what he regarded as pernicious policy, "such that, from that moment on, I have not concerned myself with who carries and who does not carry arms . . . and I have left Borso and the *capitano del divieto* to perform their offices in their own way. And the result is that now every man carries arms in this town, and it is a stupendous thing to see every day so many arms carried that it seems there is a war, whereas before . . . , by the inquiries that I made, so many arms were not to be seen, and even those who had a license did not dare to carry them."[168]

It was perhaps this new laxity that led to a recrudescence and extension of the Petrezani–dal Forno feud. In January Beltramino was pressing the dal Forno to let the law take its course against the killers of their father, Gianfrancesco, while he was privately admitting to the duke that evidence was almost nonexistent against the Petrezani and that he hoped that, if the killer, Giacomo Petrezani, could be extradited from Cremona, "it would extinguish this fire."[169] But Giacomo entered the defense that the killing of Gianfrancesco was legitimate and unpunishable, because he was a bandit.[170] By May, the dal Forno were reaching the limits of their patience with the law and complained that Beltramino was dragging the case out, denying them justice. Beltramino explained that he could in reality do no more against the murderer, because he was a cleric; Beltramino hoped that time would diminish the pain and make the parties more ready to forget their injuries.[171] Gaspare Petrezani was also dissatisfied with the commissioner's handling of the case.[172] The same complaints—that Gianfrancesco dal Forno could be killed because he was a bandit, and that Giacomo Petrezani could not be prosecuted because he was a cleric—surfaced in the embittering sindication of Podesta Oldoini in May (see the following discussion).

---

166. RdS, Modena, b. 2d, 29 Apr 1490.
167. Ibid.
168. Ibid., 29 June.
169. Ibid., 4 and 6 Jan.
170. Ibid., 22 Apr.
171. Ibid., 6 May.
172. Ibid., 25 May.

By August the feud had returned to the path of violence, as Don Andrea Petrezani and Giacomo Rangoni, in furtherance of the original benefice dispute with Tommaso dal Forno, insulted and attacked Antonio Zavarise in the street.[173] "Your lordship has granted license to the Petrezani to carry arms for their defense, and now they want to use them to attack others," wrote Beltramino; no good could come of these licenses, he insisted, in support of his oft-repeated view that it was not enough just to ban weapons, but that existing licenses had to be revoked as well.[174] With his attempt to prosecute Don Andrea for this assault "inhibited" by the episcopal court ("everyday I have some quarrel with these clerics"),[175] Beltramino seems to have given up. By November, the case was back with the *reggimento*. Seeking to implement Ercole's order that both sides lay down their weapons, they met with refusal: Alberto dal Forno replied that he did "not believe that your excellency could want to take away his weapons, having granted him them for his defense."[176] And because the dal Forno would not comply, Girolamo Fontana and his brothers also wanted an arms license, on account of their enmity with the Petrezani. So licenses multiplied. With the city governors so powerless, Eleonora was obliged to intervene personally, with the assistance of the distinguished lawyer Gianluca da Pontremoli, to negotiate a pacification of the feud.[177] It was only several years later that Beltramino had anything more to do with this case, in his execution of Alberto dal Forno in 1497.[178]

As one feud was laid to rest, another began to take shape. In December 1490 Ercole learned that Giovanni Cortesi and his cousins were threatening Giacomo da Fogliano and Gregorio Calora, seeking to provoke them to some disorder. Because of the great *parentadi* on both sides,[179] this could generate some "gran scandolo," Ercole thought, and

173. Ibid., 4 Aug.

174. Ibid., 12 June, 4 and 14 Aug. 1490, 14 Mar. 1491. Eleonora at least was listening: her Ferrarese arms decree of 1492 innovated in annulling all licenses: Cam. duc., Mandati, vol. 31, fol. 66v.

175. RdS, Modena, b. 2d, 27 Aug.

176. RdS, Modena, b. 1a, *reggimento* to Ercole d'Este, 24 Nov. 1490.

177. ASE, Particolari, b. 558, Gabriele dal Forno, 14 Sept. 1492.

178. Beltramino's *cavaliere* "Joanne Buratino" was paid for performing this execution: Cam. duc., Amministrazione finanziaria dei paesi, Modena, Massaria, b. 44, reg. 1497, fol. 216. Some of the property of Alberto and his brothers was confiscated and sold to Rinaldo d'Este: ASFe, Archivio notarile, Ferrara, Bartolomeo Goggi, *pacco* 6, 26 Mar. 1498.

179. Alberto Cortesi had married Sigismonda Molza, which would link him to the Rangoni: *DBI* 29 (1983): 715.

he ordered the *reggimento* to give the Cortesi a sound warning.[180] This enmity was not unrelated to the Petrezani–dal Forno dispute, as Giacomo da Fogliano had gathered and pressed charges against the outgoing podesta on behalf of the Petrezani (as we shall see), and as he had been responsible for the arrest of Gianfrancesco da Balugola for the murder of Matteo Calabrese.[181] But the root seems to have lain elsewhere, in Giovanni Cortesi's behavior as a newlywed in his father-in-law's house: having married Giacomo da Fogliano's niece, he frequently visited her at home, making her pregnant, but also consorting with and impregnating his new sister-in-law. "The thing is so open and known about throughout the city that nothing else is talked about except this abominable incest," reported Beltramino, keen to investigate, but held back only by the difficulty of proof.[182]

The curtain was also lifted in 1490 on the malicious milieu of officialdom in Modena, when the departing podesta, Antonio Oldoini, wrote to Ercole contrasting the honorable farewell given him by the commune with the "secret plots, betrayals, and malignity of the *massaro* and of Giacomo da Fogliano, who I believe to be an evil man, without scruple and angry." The origin of this animus against Oldoini lay in dispute over Giacomo da Fogliano's position as farmer of the city's gabelles.

> They waited until the last moment within the deadline for laying complaints, then they incited some rowdies and their satellites to complain of some of my sentences . . . Giacomo da Fogliano gathers all these complaints to himself and is constantly in court and pays the expenses of each complainant . . . I thank God that in this examination . . . I am coming out better than I thought: he has not found anyone who has been able to say that I made any extortion or robbery or fraud, and he has searched hard. What he has charged me with are all trifles, fancies, and gossip *[frasche, zachare et novelete]*. But he is troubling me and delaying the sentence of acquittal . . . such that he is keeping me here at expense with my staff and with great harm and shame. The anger that moves him is because I did not implement the commissioner's sentence in his favor against the commune . . . and, the reason moving me, I wrote to your excellency, who commended it . . .

---

180. RdS, Modena, b. 1a, Ercole d'Este to the *reggimento*, 5 Dec. 1490.

181. RdS, Modena, b. 1a, *reggimento* to Ercole d'Este, 18 May 1491, reporting on Gianfranceso's assault on Giacomo in Mirandola.

182. RdS, Modena, b. 2d, 10 Aug. 1490.

The *massaro,* who is totally with this Giacomo—they are companions in Christ who go around the city arm-in-arm—is waging such a war against me that if I had killed his father he would not do any more. There are here your lordship's *capitoli,* and there are also the statutes that set down the office of *massaro,* but he breaks the rules fearlessly: he plots against me . . . he appears in person before the sindicators, sends orders to the notaries in the criminal court . . . , he preaches that your lordship is my enemy and hates me . . .[183]

Anger at being denied revenue by the podesta's decision seems to have lain at the origin of this dispute between the commune and its tax officials; the podesta had sided with the former, unleashing against himself a fiercely maintained, vindictive campaign of denigration,[184] which gathered up into itself all manner of resentments, even at judicial handling of the Petrezani feud.

The following year, 1491, is the last for which large numbers of Beltramino's letters survive. By September of that year the former epistolary torrent had turned into a trickle. The year brought an inversion of the commissioner's previous pattern of residence: he was at Reggio from early January to mid-March, then in Modena until early June, when he went to the Mantovano on some Gonzaga business. He then spent July and August in Reggio, but his last letter of the year to Ercole comes from Finale. There is also an inversion of his concern with corruption: it is now public and private mores in Reggio that occasion his literary flights, as we shall see. At Modena, Beltramino dealt with an attempted joint action, with the Bolognese government, against border bandits (it failed: the Bolognese of course were to blame);[185] two murders in the spring, one over some stolen oxen, the other by Niccolò Cortesi, who left the body displayed on the piazza;[186] more counterfeiting;[187] more violence for possession of rural benefices;[188] an unspecified "enormity" in the hills at Bismantova, perpetrated by the men of Mocogno;[189] an "excess" at Sas-

---

183. RdS, Modena, b. 2c, Antonio Oldoini to Ercole d'Este, 11 May 1490.

184. This legal action between the commune and its former gabelle farmers was a long-drawn-out episode: ASCMo, Vacchetta 1490, fols. 10, 10v, 13v, 15v, 37, 41, 49v, 60v; Vacchetta 1491, fols. 10, 11v, 12, 12v, 34v, etc.

185. RdS, Modena, b. 2d, 13 Mar; RdS, Reggio, b. 1, 19 Mar.

186. RdS, Modena, b. 2d, 14 Mar. and 17 Apr.

187. Ibid., 8 Apr.

188. Ibid., 21 Apr., 23 Apr., and 11 May.

189. Ibid., 8 Apr.

suolo, related to the persistent feud there;[190] and an enmity between two families at Nonantola.[191] It is noticeable that Beltramino's action seems to have been directed more to the *contado* now. Had life been made too uncomfortable for him in the city? He did, nevertheless, report on a fresh episode of Rangoni-Petrezani violence, on the Cortesi killing, and on the arrest of a citizen for nocturnal arms carrying.

These last three incidents are suggestive of Beltramino's weakening power and authority in the city. Returning to Modena on 8 May after a brief absence, he found that the Rangoni brothers, Counts Sigismondo and Guido, were "going around all day and all night, armed, with the Petrezani, in a group of twenty-five or thirty"; he noted that "they give their encouragement to the Petrezani to come to blows with the dal Forno, and one night recently they wounded Borso Magnanino's secretary and two of his *fanti* . . . and in this way the Rangoni are turning this city upside-down."[192] Beltramino, previously so confident in his own abilities to control and correct such behavior, was now reduced to advising that Ercole keep the Rangoni out of Modena for a year or two: "make them stay in Ferrara, or wherever," he recommended, "so that this city can bring itself back to health."

In the same days of May, the archers (now apparently working in harness with Borso Magnanino) arrested a citizen found abroad at night who refused to give his name; but the communal council pressed for his release, and he escaped custody the next day (not without the collusion, Beltramino implies, of the captain and the podesta).[193] Only with the Cortesi killing did Beltramino have some success, but even that inquiry revealed how confident the Modenese establishment was of returning to its leisurely, corrupt ways under the commissioner's very nose. Again Beltramino had been out of the city, when one Giacometto da Verona was killed on the piazza. The podesta investigated but extracted little information from the witnesses—according to Beltramino, "because of the deals and suborning that are practiced today in this town, by which the thing was kept in silence." He thought it was shameful that "a murder is done on the piazza, and then it is said that nothing can be found out and that the law cannot take its course." Resolved not to let the matter rest, Beltramino began some inquiries of his own and discovered enough evi-

190. Ibid., 14 and 20 May.
191. Ibid., 8, 9, and 18 Apr.
192. Ibid., 8 May.
193. Ibid., 8, 9, and 10 May.

dence to detain two men on suspicion of being accomplices. "And already it is rumored that the relatives of the murderer (believed to be Niccolò di Alberto Cortesi) are coming to your lordship with three hundred ducats to stop the prosecution," Beltramino reported.[194] However, Beltramino's correspondence with Mantua again reveals that he was not himself alien to the world of "deals" that he so reviles in his letters to Ercole: lamenting that his former Gonzaga masters rarely wrote to him now or made requests of him, he all the more readily acceded to their letter in support of Antonio dal Bambaso, one of the two suspected accomplices. He had released him immediately, he said, solely to please the Gonzaga (or was it that he had insufficient evidence to proceed?).[195]

Other letters from this year help to explain Beltramino's seeming weakness. In January there were thefts from his rooms after the doors were mysteriously left open for some days: Beltramino thought the captain, Matteo Maria Boiardo, was responsible for this act of attempted destabilization.[196] At the same time, he found cause to complain of Alessandro da Fiorano, captain of the ducal archers, for lingering in Ferrara to see the festivities that were to accompany the arrival of Alfonso d'Este's wife. Beltramino said that he needed him at his post, "so that these archers are not left without their chief, and because, with him here, things can be done that without him cannot."[197] "I seem to be without a hand, lacking the chief of these archers," he wrote.[198] Beltramino found himself at odds with Alessandro again in May: having criticized some of the archers for "going around here and there telling their business, such that many of my affairs have failed," and for robbing in houses that they entered, he thought it would be better to dismiss those who had never held a bow in their hands before, as the rest would be more effective without them. However, Alessandro insisted that he be the one to do any cashiering, and he proceeded to dismiss the very men Beltramino wanted to keep, including one Andrea da Cremona, "an experienced, valiant, and industrious soldier," whom Beltramino found invaluable for tortures and executions and for informing on his colleagues.[199] Though Beltramino got his way with the reinstatement of Andrea, he was less than

---

194. Ibid., 17 Apr. On Niccolò Cortesi, sometime Este ambassador in Venice (1476–82 and 1484–87), see *DBI* 29 (1983): 714–15.

195. AG, b. 1289, 23 Apr. 1491.

196. RdS, Modena, b. 2d, 5 Jan.

197. RdS, Reggio, b. 1, 9 Jan.

198. Ibid., 12 Jan.

199. RdS, Modena, b. 2d, 14 May.

satisfied with those who remained: "they are all servants of citizens, who were put forward for this job to your lordship," he reported, "and they don't know what to say or do, such that every day they let some prisoner flee. I tire myself out working to arrange things so as to have such ribalds in my hands, and these archers, because they do not know what they are about, ruin everything."[200] Indeed their record looks poor in 1491: one bandit escaped from their custody in January and another in August;[201] and though one bandit chief was taken at Carpineti, another was forewarned and fled ("it is two months that I have been after them with spies to locate them, which I have never been able to do except on this occasion").[202]

Against the eleven cases reported from Modena in 1491, Beltramino reports on fifteen from Reggio. These included a fraudulent or forced pacification;[203] a man taken for barn burning who also confessed to horse stealing, incest, and counterfeiting;[204] another wedding-night disturbance, with woundings;[205] notarial forgery;[206] murders at Mirandola, San Felice, and Finale;[207] and threats to a gabelle official, followed by a fatal attack, by the same man, on the *massaro*'s son.[208] In addition, three brothers from near Toano, imputed of homicide and incest, were found with counterfeit coins in their house and were later investigated for procuring the abortion of an incestuously conceived fetus;[209] the men of Sarzano made an armed attack on the *capitano del divieto* for attempting to levy some fines;[210] and a Jew was detained for keeping a young Christian mistress.[211] Several bandits were captured, including one who had (allegedly) impregnated his niece and strangled his wife.[212]

Two of these cases deserve our attention. In the first, Beltramino was challenged by the duke to justify his prosecution in a murder case, as it apparently duplicated a trial conducted by the podesta of San Felice. Bel-

200. RdS, Reggio, b. 1, 13 Aug.
201. Ibid., 24 Jan. and 13 Aug.
202. Ibid., 29 Jan.
203. Ibid., 15 Jan.
204. Ibid., 24 Jan.
205. Ibid., 26 Jan.
206. Ibid., 29 Jan. and 12 Feb.
207. Ibid., 22 July, 31 July, and 23 Aug.
208. Ibid., 26 Feb. and 28 June.
209. Ibid., 21 Feb., 25 June, and 28 June.
210. Ibid., 11 Feb.
211. Ibid., 18 Aug.
212. Ibid., 24 Jan., 29 Jan., and 13 Aug.

tramino explained, "these podestas have a custom that if three or four men commit a murder, they prosecute and convict only one of them, and all the rest they let pass unpunished and in silence, for a bribe, and they confiscate the property only of the one they have convicted."[213] Something similar seems to have been going on in a trial in 1490.[214]

In the second case, a violent tumult at Sarzano outraged Beltramino's sense of the respect due to ducal and official authority. The men of Sarzano had been in dispute with Count Antonio da Bebio over some pasture; the sentence had gone in favor of the count, with fines on the men, who resisted the levying. The manner of the resistance shocked Beltramino: the captain's men had their retreat cut off, shouts were uttered of "Carne, carne," "a la morte, a la morte," and, as Beltrame da Fogliano loosed the first shots, "Foglie, foglie," the family battle cry, to which the captain's men vainly tried the countervailing power of the Este emblem-shout, "Diamante, diamante." This "exorbitant" challenge to ducal officials, the insolence of bell ringing and shouting, and the lack of respect for "the name of the Diamond" led Beltramino into high-geared action. The local podesta was detained so as to learn the names of those involved. Beltrame da Fogliano was told to present himself in Reggio on pain of one thousand ducats and disgrace. The men of Sarzano were summoned to enter their defense against a fine of fifteen hundred ducats for transgressing the ducal decree on disturbances.[215] But nothing happened. In June the men, again led by Beltrame da Fogliano, seized some of Count Antonio's cattle and sheep and cut some wood from his trees; they then, in like fashion as before, resisted Alessandro da Fiorano when he came to recover the seizures at Beltramino's order. They continued in this violence because they had not been punished the last time, wrote Beltramino, who complained, "your lordship knows that I wanted to punish them, if you would have let me do so." He now urged going to the head and root of all this trouble: Beltrame da Fogliano, "perché punito lui, seriano puniti tutti."[216]

Beltramino had begun the year in more effective action, enforcing a new arms decree that, at last, included an obligatory review, but not yet a comprehensive revocation, of all licenses—though as Beltramino interpreted the decree, review meant revocation.

---

213. Ibid., 22 July.
214. Ibid., 16 and 17 Sept. 1490.
215. Ibid., 11 and 14 Feb.
216. Ibid., 28 June.

> Some have come to present their licenses, and I asked them why they carried these weapons, and they replied, because they had the license, and I, knowing that they did not carry them out of necessity nor for any good reason, told them that I wanted them to lay down their weapons.[217]

Within three days he proudly informed the duke, "this town is already half-healed." Five days later, he could say that the task was now complete: "I have had the archers go out at night, but they have found no one going abroad without a light, which is a good thing and a sign of great obedience."[218] The only problem now was the constable of the piazza, who predictably was bewailing the loss of his earnings and pressing that inquiries for arms be left to him and his men. Beltramino's response was brusque: "I replied that he had no cause to complain, because if he did his inquiries properly, it would not be necessary for the archers to interfere."[219] The commissioner did recognize that the constable's interest lay in arms being carried, "for the profit he takes from licenses he gives to this one and that one," but he argued that "it would be an improper thing to issue a decree and not to implement it."[220]

The constable did not go away satisfied. He enlisted the *capitano del divieto* and began issuing threats ("that if he found the archers, he would see who was the better fighter"),[221] going around the city with a crowd of armed men to find and fight the archers. When the *capitano del divieto* came to excuse himself to Beltramino, the latter replied politely, asking him to do his office "virilely," as a *uomo da bene;* but he reported to the duke that he could hardly contain his anger ("And if I were not awaiting your lordship's opinion [on this], I would have laid hands on him and demanded to know what these assemblies and *secte* were that he was holding throughout the town").[222] Next to join this fray was the captain of Reggio, Matteo Maria Boiardo, who wrote to Ercole that Beltramino had arrested one of his *famigli* for arms carrying. Beltramino parried the captain's charge: he was not "of so little sight as to interfere in his *famiglia*" for arms carrying; the captain, "to steal a march," had

217. Ibid., 9 Jan.
218. Ibid., 14 Jan.
219. Ibid.
220. Ibid.
221. Ibid., 15 Jan.
222. Ibid., 17 Jan.

reported untruthfully, for the man arrested was not on his staff but was a Modenese bookbinder who had nothing to do with the captain, except that the captain had illegally given him a license to carry arms.[223] The real abuse here, Beltramino insisted, was that the captain allowed men to carry arms under his protection who were not members of his *famiglia*.

Beltramino's relations with Matteo Maria Boiardo had never been cordial; now they became venomous. This animosity had arisen from the moment of Beltramino's first arrival in Reggio, when Matteo Maria showed "to everyone he speaks to that he does not much like my being here," envious, Beltramino thought, at the concourse of people bringing their complaints to him.[224] "He seems to have no desire to punish, nor does he like others to punish, and he spreads threatening rumors that if he were well he would not let me do such things."[225] Two years later, Matteo Maria had moved from threats to subterfuge: "He has constantly sought to draw me into battle, and I have always eluded him," remarked the commissioner, but now Beltramino suspected that the captain had arranged some leave from Reggio so that his *famiglia* could have a quarrel with the archers, in such a way that it would seem that the archers were to blame, as the captain was absent.[226] Despite Beltramino's foresight, the archers fell straight into the trap, for on the very next day one of them responded to a farting insult by one of the captain's men by drawing his sword, and this triggered a general skirmish on the piazza among the two companies.[227]

Between the end of February and mid-March, Beltramino was away from Reggio. In that time, he reported on 17 March, one person had been killed and four wounded, and everyone had taken up arms again. It was the captain's laxity, in allowing law and good habits to be overturned in his absence, that was the occasion for Beltramino's most eloquent depiction (now tinged with despair) of corruption.

If a judge decides to do justice, he is threatened by those who have weapons in their hands, and he fears to carry through his good intention. If someone is owed money, he is threatened that if he ask for it his head will be knocked off, and he does not dare ask for what is his.

223. Ibid., 24 Jan.
224. RdS, Reggio, b. 1, 17 Mar. 1489.
225. Ibid.; Reichenbach, *Boiardo*, 210–11.
226. RdS, Reggio, b. 1, 24 Jan. 1491.
227. Ibid., 25 Jan.

If a witness has to be summoned in some legal action, whether civil or criminal, immediately he is intimidated by the other party, with weapons and threats to take his life if he testifies against them, and so it happens that they [witnesses] do not want to tell the truth and justice cannot be done. If my father is murdered, at once they [the murderers] ask me for peace, and if I do not give it, they threaten to kill me too, so that it is necessary to give them peace, and when they have it, your lordship immediately pardons them . . . And all this proceeds from this arms carrying.[228]

After 1491, Beltramino's letters become few, one or two a year until the last in June 1499. The reason is not clear: more letters were certainly written than survive, for the duke replied to them. Those letters we do have continue to display the same vigor, even though Beltramino must now have been approaching seventy. For example, in 1492, he complained to Eleonora that he had been instructed not to proceed against the podesta of Modena (Gianniccolò da Correggio) for corruption in office (for acquitting and releasing for money those who deserved death), and that Ercole had not allowed him to punish the podesta of Carpineti for his gallows-deserving faults, because he was a *parente* of Gianniccolò.[229] In February 1494, on returning to Modena, he found the male youths, orchestrated and led by Giacomo da Fogliano, all inflamed against Alessandro da Fiorano and his archers, insulting them with the name *sbirri*, threatening them on the piazza, and shouting "as if Christ had just been betrayed."[230] Following the Martinelli family's display of arms at a *fiera* at Sorbara, contrary to an official order, Beltramino began to proceed against them, remarking that "many have asked me to proceed slowly, with a blind eye, which is not my habit." Rather, Beltramino was animated to his task by two considerations: first, if this offense were not punished, he feared that "all the peasants would dare to go against every official"; second, he saw a need to stop the Martinelli, who, he wrote, "though they are men of substance and rich, are so petulant and proud, and do not fear God and the saints, and behave so that their peers submit to them, like the quail to the hawk."[231]

Significantly, all these reports come from Modena; from Reggio only

228. Ibid., 17 Mar.
229. RdS, Modena, b. 2d, 22 June 1492.
230. Ibid., 14 Feb. 1494.
231. RdS, Modena, b. 2d, 18 July 1497.

four letters survive, all in 1493, one reporting a cold and fever Beltramino suffered in the early days of January, another telling of the mockery Matteo Maria Boiardo did him in moving his belongings out of the castle so as to accommodate Ercole and Ludovico Sforza on a visit to the city, and, in connection with that visit, a third on the theft of a horse that was to be used to fetch some wine from Parma.[232] The image these letters leave is of a sick man, humiliated by his rival, and reduced to petty matters of fetching and carrying.

However, a strange inversion happens in the records in 1493. For the first years of Beltramino's commission, there is a gap in the series of ducal letter registers, but we have scores of Beltramino's letters to the duke and duchess; for the later years, we have few letters from Beltramino, but many more addressed to him, both registered and loose.[233] A good number of letters to other officials too relate to Beltramino's business. These latter are mainly aimed at clearing the commissioner's path of obstructions and interference. The podesta of Reggio was told not to meddle in any prosecution begun by Beltramino;[234] Marietta Calcagnini (governess of Cavriago) was told not to attempt to review any of Beltramino's sentences, just as Ercole himself did not;[235] the podesta of Rubiera was told to allow Beltramino to proceed regarding the murders committed between two families there;[236] the *capitano della piazza* and the *capitano del divieto* of Modena and Reggio were told to obey Beltramino in all his requests, as they would the duke's own person;[237] and so on. The dispatch of ducal letters was also required to compel civic and village podestas to surrender their registers to Beltramino for inspection.[238]

Ducal letters continue to show Beltramino's indefatigable responses to disorders of all kinds. They show him sending the archers to Varano following an attack on the podesta there by the local inhabitants,[239] wanting to fine heavily the notary at Toano who erased some words from the local statutes,[240] wanting to punish the sodomy of a prominent Floren-

---

232. RdS, Reggio, b. 1, 4 Jan. and 10, 16, and 17 May.
233. LD, C 11; ASE, Minutario, Lettere sciolte.
234. LD, C 11, fol. 12 (9 Feb. 1493).
235. Ibid., fol. 14 (19 Feb. 1493).
236. Ibid., fol. 39 (5 Aug. 1493).
237. Ibid., fol. 111 (27 Jan. 1495).
238. ASE, Minutario, Lettere sciolte, b. 4, 22 May 1494; RdS, Modena, b. 2d, 2 May 1490.
239. LD, C 11, fol. 3 (19 Jan. 1493).
240. Ibid., fol. 49 (3 Oct. 1493).

tine,[241] seizing ribalds in the *contado*,[242] and investigating murders and woundings.[243] The duke continues to commit cases to Beltramino's "valiant" attention, including illegal assembly by a nobleman,[244] an act of insolence by two men against the wife and children of the captain of Rubiera,[245] local resistance to a gentleman-cleric taking possession of a benefice in the hills,[246] assault with a sword in the episcopal court,[247] and blasphemy by one of the Rangoni on being summoned by the captain of Modena.[248] Even the Rangoni sought Beltramino's assistance, against a "ribald" of Levizzano who insulted Gerardo's wife, and against men who wounded Gerardo's servant.[249] The Modenese *anziani* too, faced with a rash of robberies in the city, about which no official took any action ("now we are slaves in our own houses"), asked for Beltramino to be instructed to investigate.[250] Of Beltramino's evergreen efficacy we are further assured by Ercole, who in 1498 told the Bolognese government that Beltramino had "a stronger, swifter arm than other officials."[251]

The archers, however, continued to be a source of disorder and dissatisfaction. In 1493 Ercole told Beltramino to take action regarding periods of unauthorized absence from Alessandro's *squadra*, saying of the archers, "we keep them over there so that they are always in readiness, and not to go off on pleasure trips."[252] Four years later, there was a bloody fight on the piazza between the archers and the *fanti* of the captain of the piazza, in which one of the latter was killed and four were wounded.[253] Nevertheless, the potency of the archers and of their leader was still acknowledged: Ercole refused to let them be used to collect other officials' fines, even though he recognized that this would be the easiest way,[254] and it was Alessandro da Fiorano who was entrusted with the important task of extricating Suor Lucia da Narni from the jealous hands

---

241. Gabriele Ginori (on whom see introduction, app. 2, and plate 3): ASE, Minutario, Lettere sciolte, b. 4, 22 Aug. 1495.
242. Ibid., 9 Aug. 1496.
243. Ibid., b. 3, 6 Aug. 1493; b. 4, 29 Nov. 1496 and 2 Mar. 1498.
244. LD, C 11, fol. 32 (19 July 1493).
245. Ibid., fol. 59 (7 July 1494).
246. Ibid., fol. 125 (30 Apr. 1495).
247. LD, C 12, fol. 5 (17 June 1495).
248. ASE, Minutario, Lettere sciolte, b. 4, 19 July 1497.
249. ASE, Particolari, b. 1160, 7 and 17 Oct. 1498.
250. RdS, Modena, b. 1a, *savi* to Ercole d'Este, 10 Jan. 1497.
251. ASE, Minutario, Lettere sciolte, b. 4, 11 July 1498.
252. LD, C 11, fol. 4 (21 Jan. 1493).
253. RdS, Modena, b. 1a, *savi* to Ercole d'Este, 10 Jan. 1497.
254. ASE, Minutario, Lettere sciolte, b. 3, 8 Oct. 1492.

of the citizens of Viterbo and bringing her to Ercole's new nunnery in Ferrara.[255]

It was also in the years after 1492 that complaint about the commissioner was carried to Ferrara. In 1493 there was barely concealed rivalry between Beltramino and the podesta of Reggio (Giovanni Maria Guidoni of Modena). Late one February evening, the podesta heard a clamor on the piazza and found Beltramino about to hang a peasant just outside the podesta's door. Guidoni, in remonstrating that this was neither the time, the place, nor the method to do this, recognized the (doubtless intended) slur on his conduct in office and reported the incident to the duke.[256] A few weeks later, Guidoni proposed a motion to the communal council that they write to the duke to stop Beltramino from interfering in his judicial proceedings and to report (unspecified) extortions of which Beltramino had (allegedly) been guilty.[257]

The subsequent discussion of these issues with Ercole reveals that the extortions complained of were only the legitimate expenses of the commissioner's archers, knight, and notary, but Ercole did give a little ground, promising that they would in future be approved before exaction. On the other issue, he also clarified his intentions: Beltramino should not impede the podesta's proceedings where the podesta began prosecution first, but, the duke explained, "if Beltramino starts to proceed against any malefactor before the podesta, it does not seem to me that it can be said that the podesta is impeded"; if the podesta were vigilant and diligent, maintained Ercole, this latter situation would not arise.[258] By June, the *anziani* were trying a different tack. Beltramino, they said, wanted to put his hands in every little crime, and they claimed that whenever the podesta tried to proceed, Beltramino said that he had already started prosecution. They maintained that this severely damaged the commune's revenues from fines (see the discussion of Reggio earlier in this chapter). Beltramino should be attending more to crimes in the duchy (i.e., the territory), they argued, and only to "atrocious" crimes in the city: otherwise, the *anziani* thought, it was like setting an eagle to catch flies.[259]

---

255. A. Prosperi, "Brocadelli, Lucia," *DBI* 14 (1972): 382; ASE, Minutario, b. 4, 31 Jan., 6 Feb., and 17 Apr. 1498, etc.
256. ASRe, Comune, Provvigioni, reg. 100, fol. 74v (1 Mar. 1493).
257. Ibid., fol. 77 (17 Mar.).
258. Ibid., fols. 81, 87v (29 Mar. and 20 May).
259. Ibid., fol. 92v (11 June).

While Matteo Maria Boiardo was the captain of Reggio, however, cause enough for Beltramino's presence could be found in continuing abuses: in April 1494 the communal *sindico generale* complained publicly that the podesta was not proceeding and sentencing in criminal trials according to local law, to which the podesta replied that he did not have a legible copy of the statutes;[260] in August of the same year, one of the *anziani* spoke in council of the large congregation of pimps in the city, "such that we cannot move around the piazza," and of the consequent corruption of morals among the city's young, citing as proof the already numerous nocturnal burglaries from urban shops;[261] and in January 1495 there was a communal enactment to prevent the continued concealment of crimes by the notaries of the criminal court.[262]

Nevertheless, underhanded attacks on Beltramino may be seen in the requests made to the duke to sindicate "all the officials who are not usually sindicated" and not to confirm officials in office beyond one year.[263] And after the appointment of Francesco Maria Rangoni as captain in January 1495, the *anziani* now had what they thought was a trump card: "that there is no need of the commissioner, as the captain well and diligently and virilely does the office of both captain and commissioner," better than any captain in the past, "and also because now meeting such expenses is impossible for this commune."[264] The argument of financial impossibility was then developed into an inability to provide Beltramino and the archers with accommodation and stabling, and for the moment Ercole seems to have promised (though not in writing) that Beltramino would not visit the city, given the captain's good conduct ("he keeps criminals in fear, proceeds without expense, and prosecutes no one unjustly," according to the *anziani*).[265]

However, Francesco Maria was soon removed by Ercole to act as his captain of the Castelletto of Genoa, a Sforza castle entrusted to Ercole to ensure observance of a treaty with the king of France. When Francesco Maria was no longer in post, Ercole expressed his incomprehension at the uncooperative attitude of the *anziani*: as the archers are there for the universal benefit of the community, to extirpate *tristi* and *giottoni,* and so that the *uomini da bene* may live peacefully, the commune should pro-

---

260. Ibid., fol. 140v.
261. Ibid., fol. 155.
262. Ibid., fol. 190r–v.
263. Ibid., fol. 192v (23 Jan. 1495).
264. Ibid., fol. 200 (30 Mar. 1495).
265. Ibid., fols. 204v–205 (30 Apr. 1495).

vide sufficient accommodation for them.[266] Without Francesco Maria, the commune lacked a shield against Beltramino: when ordered in January 1496 to prepare accommodation for him, they complied without murmur.[267] Given the vagueness of complaints of Beltramino's "extortions" and "injustices," it is obvious that it was merely the expense of the commissioner that was objected to. In addition, men such as Francesco Maria Rangoni or Matteo Maria Boiardo, with bases of local power to which individuals and institutions could relate, were seen as preferable to stern foreigners with full powers and ducal favor. But even Francesco Maria admitted the need for the commissioner: in excusing his own arbitrary sentences in some criminal cases, he argued that the "statutes impose very light penalties in these crimes, such that no one refrains from crime out of fear of the penalty," and that as a result there had been "very good cause" for the duke to send in a commissioner.[268] And despite the praise lavished on him by local opinion, Francesco Maria was certainly not altogether successful: he threatened to resign unless Ercole put order among his men-at-arms stationed in the city, and he complained about unpaid arrears of his salary (something that Beltramino never did).[269]

Just as Beltramino's arrival as commissioner was marked by no ceremony, so too his departure was made without those gifts and signs of gratitude that cities usually made to their outgoing podestas (citizenship, banners and shields with the communal crest, depiction of the podesta's coat of arms in his official residence, etc.).[270] Beltramino simply disappears from the record. The last letter to him is dated 13 September 1499;[271] "sick in body," he made his will on 18 November;[272] and by November of the following year he is mentioned as deceased.[273]

266. LD, C 11, fol. 175 (6 Apr. 1496); Minutario, Lettere sciolte, b. 4, 11 Sept. 1496.

267. LD, C 11, fols. 158 (21 Jan. 1496), 175 (6 Apr. 1496); ASRe, Comune, Provvigioni, reg. 100, fol. 253v (though they did seek to be excused the burden of providing accommodation for the archers); Venturi, "Relazioni," 348–49.

268. ASRe, Comune, Provvigioni, reg. 100, fol. 231 (1 Nov. 1495). One such example had arisen in 1493, when a case of abduction and rape deserved more serious penalty than the statutory one hundred lire, and Ercole had appointed a penalty of six hundred ducats: ASE, Minutario, Lettere sciolte, b. 3, 13 Dec. 1493; Campanini, "Lettere di Matteo Maria Boiardo," 409–12, nos. 71–73. See also E. Fasano Guarini, "The Prince, the Judges, and the Law: Cosimo I and Sexual Violence, 1558," in Dean and Lowe, *Crime, Society, and the Law.*

269. Venturi, "Relazioni," 379–80, 384.

270. See Chittolini, "L'onore dell'officiale," 14.

271. RdS, Modena, b. 2d.

272. AN, Registrazioni straordinari, 19, fols. 471–v (discussed further in the epilogue).

273. RdS, Modena, b. 2f, 17 Nov. 1500.

However, Beltramino's powers as commissioner did not die with him. They were assumed first by one Bernardino Montelini d'Arezzo and later by Beltramino's own son, Amato.[274] In Amato we find Beltramino's self-righteousness mixed with a less persuasive, more offensive manner. Like his father, he had apparently had to leave office in Mantua under charges of extortion; like his father, he did judicial favors to those whom the Gonzaga recommended, in the hope of being allowed to return.[275] In 1496 he seems to have played a piece of trickery in order to advance himself up the long waiting list for judicial office in Ferrara.[276] As gabelles inspector in Modena, he outraged the *anziani* by calling all citizens fraudful as regards ducal revenues and by making what were seen as illegitimate and exorbitant exactions.[277] Libelous papers were pinned to Modenese churches purporting to announce his excommunication.[278] Amato held the post of commissioner, for the new duke, Alfonso d'Este, from January 1506 until the summer of 1507. In that time Duke Alfonso urged Amato on to forceful action against malefactors, entrusted important cases to his "usual dexterity and prudence," and praised his investigations. When, in September 1506, the Modenese *anziani* suggested to Alfonso that the post of commissioner appeared to them "superfluous and unhelpful," Alfonso insisted that "to us it appears . . . extremely necessary . . . for the peace and safety of the 'persone da bene.' "[279] However, a stream of complaint from precisely such persons forced Alfonso to replace Amato. In January 1507, following Niccolò Pio's complaint of harassment of his servants by the archers, Alfonso had to remind the commissioner "to have some respect" for Niccolò, "given his privileges and the rank of his family."[280] In February, Alfonso took up local complaints that the prisons were being overcrowded by excessive arrests made "for the purpose of fleecing them" and that those arrested for arms carrying were being imprisoned in the castle, rather than the city jail.[281] Alfonso did not find Amato's explanations altogether satisfactory and ordered that, though Beltramino had established a custom of imprisoning in the castle, in future the communal jail should be used, and that the fees

274. RdS, Modena, b. 2d.
275. Catalano, *Ludovico Ariosto*, 1:213.
276. LD, C 13, fols. 181 (17 Nov. 1498), 183 (10 Dec.).
277. ASCMo, Carte sciolte, b. 1, 5 Sept. 1498 and s.d. 1498.
278. ASE, Particolari, b. 453, Cusadri, s.d.
279. LD, C 14, fols. 309–10.
280. Ibid., fol. 46.
281. Ibid., fols. 332, 335, 339.

of the commissioner and his archers were not to exceed the tariff laid down in the statutes. Then, in July and August, Alfonso made repeated interventions to halt Amato's activities in response to aristocratic or elite complaint,[282] while the Modenese notaries scurried for protection against punishment for the "constant forgeries and frauds" that Amato had discovered in their drawing-up of contracts.[283]

Finally, Amato was dealt a knockout blow by an eloquent piece of Modenese pleading to Alfonso. This lamented the fact that Alfonso's resolution to sindicate all his father's officials had not lasted so long as to catch Amato, who was being preserved from sindication by avarice and favor. To describe all his extortions, injustices, and ribaldries would fill a book, claimed the complaint's anonymous author, who urged the duke not to let so many perish for the sake of one person, to seize Amato's papers and trial records and measure him against the measure he has used against others.[284] Terminate his powers, the author demanded, otherwise no one will dare to say anything against this man, who is used to having the world tremble at his pillaging and injustices. The author of the complaint then appeals to the famed justice of the house of Este, to the glory it can acquire with God in removing such a plague, to the perpetual renown it would earn, more even than Cambyses, who removed a vicious judge.[285] "Che sono i regni?," the author concludes, "remossa la iustitia, una cosa infame e non durabil molto."[286] Quoting St. Augustine to the duke seems to have had the desired effect, for Amato was thrown into prison in Ferrara for months, while complaints against him were investigated. In this time, he penned several humble letters of penitence to Cardinal Ippolito d'Este, who seems eventually to have worked in his favor to clear him of the charges.[287] But Amato's reputation for giving "false sentences at little cost" survived, to be recalled as evident fact by Ludovico Ariosto (Satire 6.115–16), who, however, seems to have had a profitable hand in Amato's removal.[288] Amato thus lasted eighteen months in a post his father had held for over ten years. Like Beltramino,

282. Ibid., fols. 46–47, 49, 50–51, 52, 247.

283. Ibid., fols. 193, 343, 350, 354, 361.

284. Luke 6:38.

285. Herodotus, The Histories, V. 25.

286. ASE, Particolari, b. 453, letter to Ippolito d'Este, s.d.

287. Ibid., 1 and 14 Nov. 1507, 22 Apr. 1508, 14 July 1508; Catalano, Ludovico Ariosto, 1:214.

288. See the strange contract between Ludovico Ariosto and Bernardino Medogno, of Oct. 1507, in Catalano, Ludovico Ariosto, 2:81–82. In this, Bernardino, fearful of Amato's

he stirred up local animosity against his presence; unlike Beltramino, he also gathered a reputation for extortion and corruption. This is further evidence perhaps that Beltramino was an unusually "clean-handed" official.

To base a historical assessment solely on official letters is a hazardous exercise. A cautionary example from English history would be the early biographies of King Charles I's "great administrator" and "devoted servant" Thomas Wentworth, earl of Strafford, whose own "flattering elucidation of his policy as it appeared in his eloquent letters" supported an interpretation of him as "the brain and hand of . . . authoritarian government which was at least in intention benevolent," as a man with "an ideal of government that was far nobler than the means by which he tried to realize it." Beltramino had something of Strafford about him: the latter has been described as a man of "enormous energy," with a "guiding faith in the necessity of order and authority," who "constantly represented himself as modest, forbearing and straightforward." The simplicity and strength of this portrait was later undone by research into Strafford's financial interests and his "remarkable talent for accumulating wealth," and by greater awareness of the general "ineptitude, corruption and confusion" of seventeenth-century administration.[289]

A key issue to be addressed, therefore, is that of profit. Was Beltramino's exceptional eloquence, suspicious and expeditious forcefulness, and exposure of corruption only a cover for enormous profiteering on a par with that alleged against Zampante? It has to be admitted that the records here are not as helpful as they might be. We could start with Beltramino's salary, of forty lire a month, which was paid, if intermittently, though the source was maddeningly variable: in 1490–91 he was paid from the central revenue office;[290] but in 1496 he was paid through the Modenese office.[291] Beyond that, the financial registers are irritat-

---

prosecution of him for breaking a private pacification, undertook to pay Ludovico ten ducats; in return, Ludovico, as a *familiare* of Cardinal Ippolito d'Este, promised to ensure that Amato would not hear Bernardino's case and would cease to be commissioner in Modena. Did Ludovico Ariosto write the anonymous letter of complaint against Amato?

289. C.V. Wedgwood, *Thomas Wentworth First Earl of Strafford 1593–1641: A Revaluation* (London, 1961), 11–14.

290. From Feb. 1490 to Feb. 1491 he was paid a total of 453 lire, close enough to his notional annual salary of 480 lire: Cam duc., Memoriale del soldo, reg. 11, fols. 24, 29, 31, 40, 40v, 43, 49v, 55, 75v, 79v, 84, 85, 90, 107v, 117, 119.

291. From Mar. 1496 to Feb. 1497 he was paid a total of 280 lire: Cam. duc., Amministrazione finanziaria dei paesi, Modena, Massaria, b. 43, reg. 1496, fol. 101.

ingly silent about payments to or from Beltramino. At Modena, the registers of the *massaria* only once give him the double-page spread used to record the debits and credits of every other official, from the captain to the minor tax collectors. Instead, he appears (but rarely) only in composite entries of expenses paid directly on ducal account. He does not appear among the "salariati ala buleta hordinaria," nor does he appear in lists of "spexe extraordinarie." In other words, he escaped the ordinary mechanisms of financial control. It is therefore difficult to assess how much he earned even from legitimate ducal sources.

Even more difficult, then, is any assessment of other profits. He was allowed his fees and expenses, but how far these were inflated is impossible to know. We should note, however, that complaints of exorbitance in Beltramino's expenses are infrequent (usually it is the archers' expenses that attract criticism). Indeed, Beltramino is to be found just as often having difficulty collecting his expenses as he is responding to complaints of their impropriety or excess.[292] In 1490 he claimed that his usual rate was two ducats a day, hardly an enormous sum.[293] In a case in 1491, Alessandro charged nineteen ducats for himself and his archers for two days and two nights, whereas Beltramino charged only ten ducats for himself and three for his secretary.[294] Of less legitimate profits, we know that Beltramino professed (at least) to have rejected several bribes,[295] though he did not write to the duke about a small gift that the commune of Reggio made him in 1489.[296] We should note, though, the nature of complaints made against him: complainants argued not that he amassed a fortune through enormous fines and bribes, like Zampante, but that he interfered with the business of the podesta, that he prevented the captain of the piazza from earning a living, that he did not respect local custom and practice, and so forth. Only later, and against Amato, was it suggested that the commission was tantamount to a license to rob.[297] Beltramino

292. RdS, Reggio, b. 1, 31 July 1491; ibid., Modena, b. 2d, 25 June 1490, 25 Aug. 1490, and 15 Apr. 1491.

293. RdS, Modena, b. 2d, 1 Sept. 1490. This was precisely the rate set by Ercole in 1480 for councillors sent out of Ferrara on commissions: ASFe, Libro delle provvigioni, fol. 65–v. At Florence, it was two florins per day: Connell, "Il commissario," 605.

294. RdS, Reggio, b. 1, 31 July 1491.

295. RdS, Reggio, b. 1, 21 Jan. 1490 and 31 July 1491.

296. ASRe, Comune, Provvigioni, reg. 98, fol. 130 (26 Apr.), mandate to the treasurer regarding five lire, six soldi, and six denari spent "in certis rebus presentatis et dono datis . . . domino Beltramino Cusatro."

297. ASE, Particolari, b. 453, letter to Ippolito d'Este, s.d.

did not display an extortioner's remorse in his will, nor does his personal wealth seem to have been very great (see epilogue).

Any assessment of Beltramino's decade in office in Modena and Reggio must start with the evidence for the disordered state of these cities in the years following the War of Ferrara. That evidence, from the commune itself, from foreign officials such as the podesta, and from prominent members of local elites, speaks clearly enough of financial mismanagement, economic decline, and overmighty families who engaged in, promoted, and protected violent feuding. These problems were worse at Modena than at Reggio. Such distempers gave at least one podesta the impression that the cities had almost returned to the chaos of communal rule and had abandoned obedience to ducal order and authority. Though the Este liked to think of themselves as "liberators,"[298] this sort of freedom was going too far. Though it was not specified in his commission, part of Beltramino's function must therefore have been political: certainly he soon saw the problem in political terms. The problem thus became one of the sort beloved by Machiavelli: how to govern a corrupt people, how to reform their standards of behavior. Machiavelli's prognosis was not, however, encouraging.

> No individual can possibly live long enough for a state which has long had bad customs to acquire good ones . . . For corruption of this kind is due to the inequality one finds in a city, and to restore equality it is necessary to take steps which are by no means normal, and this few people either know how to do or are ready to do.[299]

---

298. "Wishing to maintain his peoples in that liberty and freedom that naturally should be loved and desired by each person," Ercole in 1474 forbad the citizens and *contadini* of Reggio from swearing fealty and vassalage to any nobleman, castellan, or prelate: RdS, Reggio, b. 166, 1474; see also Dean, *Land and Power,* 118. In response to a complaint of the suppression of free speech in the local council of Castelnovo (Garfagnana), Ercole expressed his surprise, "because it seems to us very right and proper that everyone should have freedom to say what he thinks regarding the needs of that community in debate pro and contra": LD, C 10, fol. 285 (21 Jan. 1488). Communities submitting to Este rule were welcomed into "liberty": Dean, *Land and Power,* 160. See Gundersheimer, *Ferrara,* 278–84, on "despotic myths"; that scholar suggests that such an abstract value as liberty had no place in the ideological supports of despotism, because it was suppressed under their rule.

299. *I discorsi* 1.17; cf. G. Cozzi, *Repubblica di Venezia e stati italiani: Politica e giustizia dal secolo XVI al secolo XVIII* (Turin, 1982), 28 (on viceroy Juan de Vega).

Indeed, politically Beltramino's mission was a failure: in 1500 Ercole had to issue a proclamation against the invoking of "names and surnames of lords other than ourselves"[300] (a sign of incipient revolt), and his successor, Duke Alfonso, lost both Modena and Reggio to the forces of Pope Julius II, largely through the defection of the Rangoni.

The strong evidence of disorder in the 1480s also largely counters the possible objection that the real villain in this piece was Beltramino himself. He did not invent the problems he was dispatched to solve. But his manner of dealing with them does pose a difficulty: Was he hero or hypocrite? Was he the man who brought to life Ercole's planned "reformation" of social life,[301] or was he merely one more level of enforcement and influence, a ruthless instrument for extracting money for his own and the duke's profit? Was he, like commissioners in late-medieval England, "a public nuisance," who contributed to disorder by encouraging accusations and litigiousness, and who was regarded not as a potential carrier of justice but as an enemy intruder?[302] Beltramino's very suspiciousness of all others make us suspicious of him. Corruption, errors, and abuses he "discovered" as relief to his own rectitude; but he himself, an indicted murderer and dealer in favors to the Gonzaga, perhaps conceals as much as he discloses. His own insistent self-portrayal as a "bribeless officer" conflicts both with his desire to *appear* to satisfy Gonzaga requests and with his refusal to be accountable in the normal way.

Judicially, his decade in Modena and Reggio was uphill work from the start. He faced local opposition, from citizen communities and aristocratic individuals. He was surrounded by corrupt officials. As a result of exposing cover-ups, provoking aristocratic hatred, probing noble enclaves, and inducing witnesses to testify, he became isolated. There were few he could trust; even the ducal archers became an unreliable tool, open to local influence. He could not always depend on the duke endorsing his action, and he could find his work wasted and his authority undermined by the duke's grant of pardons or refusal to support him in overriding local privileges. And whatever short-term benefits he

---

300. RdS, Modena, b. 1a, Ercole d'Este to *reggimento,* 7 Feb. 1500.

301. "la reformatione del ben vivere de quella nostra citade": RdS, Modena, b. 2d, Ercole d'Este to Beltramino Cusadri, 12 Jan. 1497.

302. M. Clanchy, "Law, Government, and Society in Medieval England," *History* 59 (1974): 77–78; C. Carpenter, "Law, Justice, and Landowners in Late Medieval England," *Law and History Review* 1 (1983): 228.

brought, they were completely nullified by later events. After Modena's surrender to the pope in 1510, the same disorders resurfaced: weapons were openly carried on the streets, bandits went about the piazza armed as if going to battle, there were daily killings and woundings, there were armed confrontations between the Tassoni and the Fogliani families and factions (the former supported by the Rangoni), and no one felt safe in their own home.[303] Advisors to the new papal government alleged that the city under the dukes of Ferrara had been badly administered and that the *capitano della piazza* and his *fanti* were useless: they advised doubling the number of *fanti* and installing a more substantial governing circle (a lieutenant and six counselors).[304] Beltramino himself failed to make an impression on local chroniclers, who refer to him vaguely as "the commissioner" or "a man called . . ."; and for a mid-sixteenth-century chronicler, the death of Gregorio Zampante in Ferrara was the only memorable part of Ercole's new judicial order.

Part of Beltramino's difficulties came from the uncertainty of his relationship to existing officialdom: was he in charge of this, working alongside it, or clearing up those cases it failed to deal with? The duke had not articulated this at the outset. Beltramino tended to turn his commission into a supreme judgeship; the civic captains and communes tended to see him as supplementary, not superimposed. The Reggian *anziani* thought he should concentrate on crimes in the territory. They and their Modenese counterparts tried to resist his interference in "little things" in the city, especially as they had governors enough (captains, podestas) already. The captain of Reggio, in suggesting that Beltramino's cases be dealt with by himself during Beltramino's absences, argued that "if in all the incidents that arise we have to wait for Messer Beltramino to provide, sometimes things would drag on for a very long time," and that when Beltramino leaves the city, "and some small thing happens here, we don't know what to do, if he later is going to put his hands into what has been started."[305]

It is also possible to see the appointment of energetic judges, such as

303. L. Beliardi, *Cronaca della città di Modena (1512–1518)*, ed. A. Biondi and M. Oppi (Modena, 1981), 31, 33, 43, 44, 62, 63, 64 (though note that the formula "not safe in our own homes" was a common piece of exaggeration: see E. Basaglia, "Il controllo della criminalità nella Repubblica di Venezia. Il secolo XVI: Un momento di passaggio," in *Venezia e la Terraferma attraverso le relazioni dei rettori* [Milan, 1981], 70).

304. "Modus et ratio qua Mutinensis civitas dudum malis afflicta recte ac ordine administrari possit": RdS, Modena, b. 2f.

305. Campanini, "Lettere di Matteo Maria Boiardo," 405–6, no. 64 (26 Jan. 1493).

Beltramino and Zampante, as part of broader economic and monetary policies, unrelated to previous social disorder. The Ferrarese chronicles for the 1490s give attention especially to four features of urban life: thefts and burglaries; ducal decrees banning the use of clipped, false, or foreign coin; heavy direct taxation; and food shortages and poverty.[306] It is not difficult to see how these features could be related: monetary shortage at times of poor harvest increased poverty and thieving. In 1493 Caleffini noted that "there was almost no silver coin to be found in Ferrara, nor ducats," such that the law courts had to close, "as there was no money to live on, let alone litigate with."[307] This situation had, in the government's eyes, come about through an influx of bad coin, and it banned all foreign coin (save Venetian), whether good or false. Compounding the monetary difficulties was the ducal policy in favor of monetary uniformity throughout Este territory: the only legal tender throughout the state was to be a small range of Ferrarese and Venetian coins. Ercole declared that he was acting for the common good and reducing the cost to individuals—whether as tradesmen, taxpayers, or rent payers—of changing bad or foreign coin into good. This was not mere rhetoric: artisans did raise complaints against clipped coin,[308] though the ducal camera was also concerned at its own losses. Unfortunately for this virtuous policy, there was very little Ferrarese or Venetian coin in the further parts of the state (such as Modena and Reggio), as local institutions were not slow to point out.[309] The ducal policy, if implemented, could only have had a deeply disruptive effect on local economies. Ercole ceded ground; but his firm intention remained to reduce drastically the number of bad and foreign coins in circulation, and decrees to this effect continued to be issued.

At the same time, tax demands seem to have been raised—or perhaps people short of coin were more sensitive to the state's demands and made more eloquent complaint. Meanwhile, periods of poor weather caused loss of crops and livestock and thus higher food prices, and the predations of exactors, distraining on peasant belongings, were felt more

---

306. E.g., Biblioteca apostolica vaticana, MS Chigi I.I.4, Ugo Caleffini, "Cronaca ferrarese,"fols. 270, 271v, 272, 273v, 275, 275v, 278, 281, 281v, 282, 286v, 287, 290, 294, 296, 297, 297v, 300v, 306v.

307. Ibid., fol. 305v.

308. Jacopino de' Bianchi, in *Cronaca Tommasino de' Bianchi*, 1:111 (1494).

309. In 1496, following a fresh coinage decree, the Modenese *anziani* considered measures "ad inveniendum monetas ferrarienses . . . pro subveniendis pauperibus . . . ut . . . possint providere sibi et suis necessitatibus": ASCMo, Vacchetta 1496–97, fols. 9v, 22. See also, Rombaldi, "La comunità reggiana," 112–15.

harshly, as peasants too lacked the coin to pay their debts, taxes, and fines (hence the complaint that exactors were distraining even for their expenses). In these circumstances, counterfeiters served a function, supplying much-needed and good-seeming Venetian ducats to those pressed for payment. Counterfeiting was yet another "service" that aristocrats (or more precisely, aristocrats' wives) provided to "help" their subjects and neighbors. The pursuit of counterfeiters (prompted by Venice),[310] which was a significant part of Beltramino's work, was thus as much a part of economic and monetary policy as of judicial. It was also the punitive side of a socioeconomic policy that included the promotion of trade and industry (through tax reductions and concessions) and the creation of new charitable institutions aimed specifically at relieving poverty.[311]

Other aspects of Beltramino's judicial activity can likewise be placed in the context of contemporary social trends. His pursuit of abductors could be said to reflect a general trend to reinforce paternal authority within families, in order to reduce the incidence of clandestine marriage. His attempt to revoke Jewish judicial privilege reflected the more intense anti-Semitism of the times, when preachers promoted the establishment of *Monti di pietà* in both Modena and Reggio. His vigorous pursuit of pear thieves at Mantua mirrors the extension of penalties for similar thefts in Ferrara, as one consequence of renewed population growth (market gardening) was protected from another (poverty).

Beltramino's commission needs also to be placed in the context of the sale of office in the late fifteenth century. Ercole d'Este has earned a great notoriety as a seller of office, partly thanks to Burckhardt.[312] Historians usually condemn sale of office as an expedient introduced by rulers needful of revenue and careless of the consequences. Such expediency is usually presented as having inevitably and uniformly reprehensible results (official corruption and oppression, a strengthening of noble clientage, and so on). In Ferrara, the full extent and precise consequences of sale of office have yet to be investigated. Often reported is one chronicler's claim that in 1485 Ercole d'Este opened up all offices to the highest bidders. Yet this seems to have been intended as a *remedy* to corruption and fraud, a means of ensuring more efficient collection of revenue and of

---

310. Ferrari, "Documenti"; see also Grubb, *Firstborn of Venice,* 116, for more direct Venetian intervention in counterfeiting cases in the 1490s.

311. Biblioteca apostolica vaticana, MS Chigi I.I.4, Ugo Caleffini, "Cronaca ferrarese," fol. 285; Gundersheimer, *Ferrara,* 189–91.

312. Burckhardt, *Civilization of the Renaissance,* 31.

squeezing out fiscal losses through financial pressure.[313] It also seems to have been a temporary policy, for in 1498 Ercole proudly proclaimed to his subjects that, despite the many offers of money he had received, he was making all appointments free that year—a "holy measure," he insisted, that would be of universal benefit, especially to poor gentlemen and citizens who could not afford to buy offices,[314] and that would ensure that his subjects were treated well by officials.[315] We should note that such second thoughts regarding the value of sale of office accorded with princely opposition to a private market in office (through subcontracting: see chap. 1) that long predated the duke's first sales.

It is also necessary to place Beltramino's experience in the context of modern study of patronage, corruption, and "bastard feudalism." Beltramino creates a vivid picture of systematic noble domination of urban society. The aristocratic palace was recognized as an off-limits area, a refuge for bandits. Officials were corrupted by bribery or "custom." The culture of favors and deals permeated the judiciary and their staff. Armed intimidation deflected judges, witnesses, and creditors from their legitimate intentions. Aristocratic honor was used as a weapon to protect the clientele from justice. The license permitted to noble households to bear arms was a prime source of disorder. Aristocratic identities—given graphic voice in their emblem-shouts—created disruptive rival loyalties. The aristocrats' frequent defense, when they were challenged, was to assert that they intended only to help friends, tenants, and neighbors, but this revealed the gulf between their world and that of the duke's officials, as it was against officialdom and against official policy that aristocrats helped "their" men.

Such a picture would be all too familiar to historians of late-medieval England, a land in which the "normal machinery of law enforcement was paralysed or perverted by local forces" and in which the law could provide no remedy against harassment by those who were "grete kynred and alyed," while the king used his prerogative of pardon with "characteristic abandon";[316] a land in which legislation aimed to suppress "the casual recruitment of idle and potentially lawless hangers-on to the

---

313. On sale of office "come forma di disciplinamento e controllo di ceti di officiali," see Chittolini, "Il 'privato,' il 'pubblico,' lo Stato," 575.

314. ASCMo, Carte sciolte, b. 1, 4 Jan. 1498.

315. ASE, Minutario, Lettere sciolte, b. 4, 9 Jan. 1498.

316. R.A. Griffiths, *The Reign of King Henry VI: The Exercise of Royal Authority, 1422–1461* (London, 1981), 593, 595.

fringes of households,"[317] in which "an upper class household could har-
bour felonious followers,"[318] in which "everyone who was not a gentleman did not expect justice from the law,"[319] and in which even kings
found it "hard to throw off the habit of regarding the law as something
capable of being bent or bought."[320] If this was "bastard feudalism," it
was alive and well in northern Italy as well as in England.

The direction taken by recent research would, however, take out of
such practices any stigma of illegitimacy. The positive functions of corruption and of informal networks of favor are now more commonly
stressed. For Waquet, corruption "may contribute to the stability of a
given social and political organization."[321] For Blockmans, the growth of
state power fostered a corresponding growth of brokerage and patronage, as local communities tried to protect themselves from central interference.[322] For Chittolini, corruption was a natural part of the early-
modern state's "permeability" to private interests and forces, and it was
"an instrument in the very creation of a social group that drew its social
legitimacy from the exercise of public functions," while within closed
aristocratic elites, it was an aspect of cohesion and consolidation.[323] In
this regard, it is the contradictions of Beltramino's actions that are most
significant. Even he sought favors, to have or to give. These, however,
form only a small part of the story: more significant, surely, is the fact
that his appointment reflected a widespread feeling, both in Modena and
at the center of the ducal state, that there was something rotten that was
destabilizing the state and that needed cleansing. Beltramino's commission was an attempt by Ercole d'Este to make his state less "permeable":
Beltramino's successes and failures showed how far this could be
achieved.

---

317. K.B. McFarlane, *The Nobility of Later Medieval England* (Oxford, 1973), 106.
318. J.G. Bellamy, *Bastard Feudalism and the Law* (London, 1989), 99–100.
319. C. Richmond, "An English Mafia?" *Nottingham Medieval Studies* 36 (1992): 241.
320. Carpenter, "Law, Justice, and Landowners," 212, 234.
321. J.-C. Waquet, *Corruption: Ethics and Power in Florence, 1600–1770,* trans. L.
McCall (Oxford, 1991), 20.
322. W. Blockmans, "Patronage, Brokerage, and Corruption in Symptoms of Incipient
State Formation in the Burgundian-Habsburg Netherlands," in *Klientelsysteme im Europa
der Frühen Neuzeit,* ed. A. Maczak (Munich, 1988), 123–25.
323. Chittolini, "Il 'privato,' il 'pubblico,' lo Stato," 569, 575–76.

After Beltramino: Crime and Punishment in Mantua, 1484–99

What had been happening in Mantua since 1484? How did investigations, prosecutions, and penalties in criminal matters proceed after Beltramino left the scene? For most of the first seven years of Marquis Francesco Gonzaga's rule—the period from 1484 to 1491 dominated by Francesco Secco—the source material is sparse, but it seems probable that Secco himself, armed with a grant of almost boundless arbitrary jurisdiction, including the power to pass sentences of death without appeal,[1] was much more of an "uomo tyrannico" than Beltramino had ever been. Some idea of his interference in political matters can be gained from the surviving registers kept by the chancery secretaries, where letters to a variety of addressees are headed in his name ("nomine magnifici d. Fr. Sicci").[2] These letters include discussions of criminal cases, and it may be—to give him the benefit of the doubt—that as a military man Secco was genuinely outraged by reports of violent and disorderly behavior among the civilian population. In September 1488, having heard of an attack on a woman in the public street and of her abduction, he wrote indignantly to the marquis, "people say that this city is a thicket full of rogues."[3] However, in this case the assailant turned out to be one Ambrosio Galuppo, probably not a civilian at all but a soldier; Secco reported, "I sent for Galuppo and had him imprisoned in the castle, and will do the same for anyone else who commits similar crimes." In other words, Secco acted like a military governor rather than a civilian official,

---

1. A. Fino, *Scielta degli huomini di pregio usciti da Crema* (Brescia, 1576), 21.

2. There are many examples in AG, b. 2903, lib. 131, fols. 55v–60r, 80r–93r (June–Oct. 1488). Incoming letters do not provide much supportive evidence, because there is only one *busta* from the "Mantova e Paesi" series covering the five years 1484–88 (AG, b. 2434).

3. ". . . se dice questa terra essere uno boscho per la licentia che li cativi se pigliano in committere li inconvenienti": AG, b. 2903, lib. 131, fols. 80v–81v, letter to Marquis F. Gonzaga (11 Sept. 1488).

who would normally refer such a case to the proper legal authority. Yet he was quite capable of using the means of that authority to enforce order as and when he pleased, and in February 1489 he informed the marquis, who was absent from Mantua: "since your departure there have been various robberies. I ordered out the knights of the podesta. I did not find anyone except some members of your company. I hope with dexterity to collect some names together."[4] This sounds like a rather contemptuous way of outflanking the podesta, as does Secco's nomination of a substitute judge of appeals following the sudden death of the incumbent later in the same year.[5]

The podesta in 1490, Giacomo Baiardi of Parma, must have resented such acts. He was already humiliated because his salary was not paid regularly, and he complained in July 1490 that he was badgered by creditors, being obliged to maintain fourteen persons and four horses and having no private income to draw on.[6] Another example of disrespect for the podesta's authority is revealed in Giacomo's report to the marquis that "a man of ill-fame called Quatrochino had been detained in prison by Francesco Secco without a charge being brought against him"; meanwhile, a certain Comino had told Giacomo that Quatrochino had stolen a silver chalice, so the podesta rather cravenly asked the marquis what he should do.[7] But even if his own job might be usurped, Giacomo seems to have shared Secco's opinion that Mantua was in the throes of a crime wave. His own officers were at risk; soon after Giacomo had taken up his appointment in December 1489, his knight, Biaxio, went to purchase a dagger from Michele, the marquis's armorer, who then stabbed him in the chest beneath the portico of Sant'Andrea—a scandalous assault that set all Mantua talking.[8] On 14 June 1490 he reported to the marquis that his knight had twice been wounded in the course of duty and that another member of his *famiglia* had been assaulted by three armed men outside the Borgo di Porto; rather vaingloriously, he pledged himself to purge Mantuan territory of such criminals.[9]

As these episodes suggest, part of the problem lay in the large number of military retainers quartered in Mantua and in the degree of exemption they seem to have enjoyed from normal restraints—a problem, it has

4. AG, b. 2438, fol. 263, Secco to Marquis F. Gonzaga (12 Feb. 1489).

5. Ibid., fol 288, Secco to Marquis F. Gonzaga (26 Aug. 1489).

6. Ibid., fol. 571.

7. Ibid., fol. 569, Giacomo Baiardi to Marquis F. Gonzaga (15 July 1490).

8. Ibid., fol. 36, Giacomo Baiardi to Marquis F. Gonzaga (16 Dec. 1489).

9. ". . . purgare la provincia de homini cativi": ibid., fol. 567.

been noted, that was already growing serious under Marquis Federico. Some control of the situation had been attempted by proclamations condemning those who fraudulently claimed to be the servants of *provvisionati* and those who applied their energies to terrifying "war games" *(bataioli)* in the streets of Mantua,[10] but exemption from the prescribed three jerks of the rope hoist, now the standard punishment for carrying weapons about, was still allowed for soldiers and courtiers.[11] On 6 January 1490 Secco wrote that there had been various "scandals" in the marquis's absence, and that on one occasion a number of people had been seriously wounded, but that he did not wish to interfere with the *provvisionati*.[12] The marquis replied (he was not far away, only at Marmirolo) that he was shocked to hear of such misdeeds, and he ordered the delinquents not to be spared in several cases.[13] Nevertheless, a protective attitude toward military persons continued. In the case of a *stradiotto* called Zorzo who had wounded a poor Mantuan street porter, Secco simply had the assailant confined to barracks.[14] And the podesta himself examined and then let go one Rizolo, an archer who had threatened to kill a man called Cecchetto in an argument over a woman. The ground for such leniency was that the woman who was the cause of the trouble was Cecchetto's mistress, not his wife; had she been Cecchetto's wife, beheading might have been Rizolo's punishment.[15]

Some of the dangers of having numerous unemployed men-at-arms hanging around the town seem to have been perceived by Marquis Francesco. After the fall of Francesco Secco, the marquis was dismayed when many members of Secco's private army sought to enter the marquis's own service;[16] he insisted that his contract with Venice (he had been appointed governor-general of the Venetian army in 1489) only permitted him to have a private company of twenty-five archers; already he had twice that number, as well as a hundred *stradiotti;* he could not take on any more.[17] Nevertheless, the semiprivileged status of the military men continued.

---

10. AG, b. 2038–9, Gride, fasc. 8, fols. 1r–v (21 Nov. 1488, 4 Jan. 1489).

11. Ibid., fol. 3r (4 May 1490).

12. AG, b. 2438, fol. 610, F. Secco to Marquis F. Gonzaga (6 Jan. 1490).

13. AG, b. 2903, lib. 135, fol. 12.

14. ". . . Io ho facto restare in Castello in bon loco, cum animo perhò de rellaxarlo": AG, b. 2438, fol. 263, F. Secco to Marquis Francesco, Mantua (12 Feb. 1489).

15. AG, b. 2438, fols. 37, 38 (letters of 18 and 24 Dec. 1489).

16. AG, b. 2903, lib. 135, fol. 68v.

17. AG, b. 2904, lib. 139, fol. 45v, letter to Giorgio Brognolo (2 Sept. 1491).

There even seems to have been some use made of superfluous soldiers for police work. A *stradiotto* with the daunting name Hercule Turco, described in March 1491 as "caporalis stratiorum," served at the same time as *stradiotto* and *capitano del divieto*,[18] and in the summer of the same year he was appointed "guard of the piazza," a special officer in charge of a company of fifteen *provvisionati*.[19] As one might have expected, Turco's men seem to have turned a rather blind eye toward unruly fellow soldiers; "the citizens were amazed" when a stabbing incident in the piazza was allowed to pass without any arrests being made.[20] Turco subsequently claimed greater success, having divided his company into two patrols, though the only achievement he had to report was the arrest of two Jews caught in the street at night without lanterns.[21] In fact, the incoming podesta next winter reported very badly to Isabella d'Este about Turco's foot soldiers *(fanti)*; they showed no respect toward either the marquis, himself, or his staff and had caused, rather than prevented, discord.[22]

Militaristic and extralegal, Francesco Secco's style of government did not have much in common with that of his onetime colleague and eventual victim, Beltramino Cusadri. While the process of downgrading and complementing the ancient authority of the podesta was hardly a novelty in the late 1480s and early 1490s, it was taking different and rather cruder forms than it had done under Marquis Ludovico Gonzaga. Secco, this overbearing survivor of an older generation, acted nevertheless with the full trust and consent of Marquis Francesco, who later declared that he had felt physically ill, as though bereaved, upon the discovery of Secco's deceptions and his flight from Mantua.[23] Nevertheless, the marquis may have become more alert to the situation after the coming to Mantua of his wife Isabella d'Este early in 1490. Isabella—who would have remembered both Secco and Beltramino from childhood, when they both came to Ferrara for her betrothal—seems to have recognized the serious threat behind Secco's domination. Already in March 1490 she wrote to her husband that she had opened many letters and that in her

---

18. AG, Lib. decr. 24, fol. 27v.

19. AG, b. 2440, Hercule Turco to Marquis F. Gonzaga, Mantua, 8 Aug. 1491.

20. "Io non faria cosa alcuna contra li soldati de Vostra Signoria se Quella non nul comanda": ibid.

21. Ibid., letter of 18 Sept. 1491.

22. AG, b. 2441, Antonio Oldoini to Isabella d'Este, 30 Jan. 1492.

23. AG, b. 2905, lib. 142, fols. 19r–20r, Marquis F. Gonzaga to his sister Chiara Gonzaga (3 Dec. 1491).

judgment many of them required decisions to be made by him (i.e., not by Secco); one month later she declared that there were many supplications from condemned persons that again she thought he, the marquis, ought to decide.[24] Isabella felt concern over criminal matters. She might occasionally urge a degree of leniency—for example, she proposed in the case of two men, whose crime may only have been trapping pheasants, that instead of the two being put to death, the elder should have a hand cut off and the younger should get three jerks on the rope[25]—but she approved of ruthless detection and law enforcement; her feelings were outraged, for instance, over the case of a mangled dead baby found in March 1491.[26] In view of her strongly held views and force of personality, it is hardly surprising that Beltramino—an employee of her father— extolled her and appealed to her for support in his own affairs.

Francesco Secco maintained, of course, that he was the victim of intrigue by his enemies, and from his refuge in Pisa he declared that his priority had always been only to love and serve the marquis.[27] "Did I wait all my life to offend the marquis, as he has been told?" Secco protested to Ercole d'Este on 31 October 1492. He attributed the latest round of persecution to *giotti* who alleged he had plotted to kill the marquis, whereas, even after all the wrong done to him, he would not dream of hurting one hair of his head. "No father loves a son more than I do him," he claimed.[28] For all this, Secco's downfall had rid the Gonzaga regime of an additional source of arbitrary jurisdiction, and it is significant that in their flight both he and his wife first sought the refuge of castles controlled by their daughter Paola, countess of Guastalla, widow of Marsilio Torelli:[29] not even Mantua was wholly free of the potential danger from backwoods nobility.

---

24. AG, b. 2904, lib. 136, fol. 13r; b. 2903, lib. 133, fol. 73r.

25. AG, b. 2451, Giacomo da Capua to Marquis F. Gonzaga (8 Mar. 1498), referring to "quelli da li fasani."

26. AG, b. 2904, lib. 136, fol. 82v; lib. 137, fol. 12r (22 and 26 Mar. 1491).

27. "La Excellentia vostra scia le cose succedute ali die passati fra lo Illmo. S. marchese mio e me, dopoi vedendo io ogni die le cose andare pegiorando contra me per suggestione de mei inimici . . . io mi sum ridacto qui a Pisa . . . et in dicti et in facti mi forzaro fin che mi durarà questa vita essere fidelissimo servitore di Sua Signoria": ASMo, Archivio per materie, Capitani di ventura, b. 2, Secco to Ercole d'Este, Pisa (18 July 1491). On 6 August he wrote to Ludovico Sforza that apparently the marquis had read out to a large assembly of citizens "certi processi facti contra me," and again he wrote to Ercole d'Este on 30 September about his honor and innocence, promising to send a copy of his defense: ibid.

28. Ibid.

29. Mazzoldi, *Mantova*, 2:86, 124 n. 124.

However, Secco's disappearance may not have made so much differ-ence to the long-term pattern of decline in the office of podesta. Humili-ations similar to those suffered by Giacomo Baiardi, mentioned earlier, were also inflicted on his successors after Secco's fall. The nonpayment of salaries was so recurrent by the spring of 1492 that the podesta's assis-tant judges threatened to resign;[30] this at least provoked an urgent letter from the marquis telling his secretary, Antimaco, to take up the matter with the *massaro* or the *magister intratarum,* whose duty it was to pay these salaries.[31] They in turn remonstrated that it was not their fault if no one had been paid; Cristoforo Gori pointed out that the judges were sup-posed to be paid out of the judicial fines they themselves imposed, but that these funds had already been raided to pay for the marquis's build-ing works.[32] The same trouble continued down the scale. Hercule Turco protested in August 1492 that the *massaro* was supposed to pay him twelve ducats and the cost of maintaining his police guards: nothing had been received.[33] (Hercule Turco may, however, have done better from his cut of judicial fines; no respecter of persons, he was, for instance, even bringing a charge against the countess of Guastalla—daughter of his fallen patron—for the unlicensed transport of corn through Mantuan ter-ritory).[34] Three years later the podesta Cesare Valentini declared that he and his staff had been paid no salaries for the last six months. Cesare complained that no podesta before him—certainly none over the last fifty years—had been treated so badly.[35] It may seem surprising, in view of such humiliations, that there was still any demand at all for the job of podesta of Mantua.

In the meantime, violent attacks on officers of the podesta and disre-spect for his jurisdiction continued. In the winter of 1492, Giambattista da Castello was appalled by the *disordeni* in the city. Of one evening he reported, "Tonight my knight was assaulted by about ten armed men—it was as though war was raging at the gates of Mantua, and wrongdoers were emboldened to go from bad to worse."[36] Much the same was

---

30. AG, b. 2904, lib. 141, fol. 47v, letters to the *massaro* and podesta of Mantua (13 May 1492).

31. Ibid., fol. 55r (letter of 25 May 1492).

32. AG, b. 2441, letter of 7 July 1492.

33. Ibid., letter of 3 Aug. 1492.

34. AG, b. 1390, Paola, countess of Guastalla, to Marquis F. Gonzaga, 5 Aug. 1492.

35. AG, b. 2447, fols. 99, 100 (17 Sept. 1495).

36. "come se la la guerra fusse a le porte de Mantua . . . li cativi pigliarano animo de pegiorare": AG, b. 2441, 7 Dec. 1492.

reported by Pandolfo Malatesta, the podesta of Viadana, which he declared to be infested by thieves and other malefactors; he complained that the prospect of sindication inhibited him, but that he needed a free hand to use torture, which was the right way to clean up the place.[37] Antimaco, reporting on the exemplary execution (beheading and quartering) of a violent criminal in September 1496, declared that it was everywhere said—even as far away as Germany—that Mantua was a murderous place.[38] Armed retainers of the marquis were involved in all manner of crimes of violence. In April 1497 the podesta reported a case in which two archers, Niccolò and Antonio del Maio, had been incriminated in hiring a barge to rob wood from the stables; but because they were knights and members of the marquis's household, the podesta was reluctant to take any action.[39] Even within the walls of the Palazzo della Ragione it could happen that a *provvisionato* committed an assault with impunity, as was reported in March 1497 by the podesta; Giovanni Merlo was unsure whether or not the contempt of court was outweighed by the marquis's protection.[40] On 5 June 1499 Francesco Tonso, then podesta, complained that his men had been assaulted on three occasions and that executions could not be carried out.[41] Impeding a public executioner was punishable, according to a proclamation of 28 February 1492, by a fine of twenty-five ducats or by ten jerks on

---

37. "questa sarà la via de purgare el paese de ribaldi": AG, b. 2422, letter from P. Malatesta, Viadana, 28 Nov. 1492, published in Pavesi, *Relazioni sui delitti,* 1–3 (the only pre-1500 case cited in this book).

38. ". . . essendosi pur havuto da Verona quello tristo che fece li dì passati quelli insulti, sino assasinamenti, qui fuora de la porta de San Zorzo, sabato passato che fu a li XVII del presente, fu inco[l]pato per el maestro de la iusticia suso uno tribunale constructo presso il loco de la berlina, poi squartati e li quarti posti suso due forche pur fuora de la porta predicta. L'opera è stato tanto necessario et al proposito quanto dir si potesse, per la vociferatione che erano da ogni canto, dico fin in la Elemagna, che intorno Mantua se assasinavano le gente. El statuto de questa terra non disponeva che il fosse se non impichato, ma considerato il bisogno, il podestà cum la corte sua, volse arbitrarli la pena predicta": AG, b. 2449, fol. 320r, Antimaco to Marquis F. Gonzaga (21 Sept. 1496).

39. ". . . per essere di la famiglia di V. Ill.ma S. e per non volerli pigliare li cavalieri . . .": ibid., fol. 484, Giovanni Peregrino Merlo to Marquis F. Gonzaga (8 Apr. 1497).

40. "questa matina per Stefano da Mozanica provisionato di Vostra Excellentia fu facto assalto contra uno mestrale nela sala ove se administra ragione, zetandoselo sotto pedi e dandoli di multe percosse, delicto avenga non grave in se, pur per il loco di male exemplo ad astanti a cui lo intende. Unde tenendo questo loco et essendo di la famiglia di Vostra Illustrissima Signoria, mi è parse debito mio darne noticia . . .": ibid., fol. 483, Giovanni Peregrino Merlo to Marquis F. Gonzaga (15 Mar. 1497).

41. AG, b. 2453, fol. 418.

the rope,[42] and it could even be punished by hanging, as on the occasion of the political executions in November 1491, which will be discussed later. For impeding the podesta or his officials the punishment decreed was less severe—merely three jerks on the rope or a fine of twenty-five ducats.[43]

It may be that some older citizens felt rather nostalgic for the more efficient days of Beltramino and Marquis Ludovico Gonzaga. But taking a longer perspective view, the trend in the 1490s looks familiar. From the surviving correspondence between successive podestas and the marquis, it seems clear that in judicial matters deference and reference to the marquis's authority continued and grew, whether this authority was expressed by himself personally or by his increasingly empowered Council of Justice. For there is no doubt that the marquis preferred his authority to be buttressed by the expert and experienced, and it is notable that in the 1490s retiring podestas were sometimes invited to stay on or to return to serve as members of the Council; thus Ermolao Bardolini and Antonio Oldoini were both co-opted in November 1492. Oldoini, expressing his thanks for the customary banner presented to him on retirement as podesta, added that the new honor conferred on him was the culmination of his career and a perpetual glory for his family and heirs.[44] Giambattista da Castello was similarly honored, so he informed Isabella d'Este, early in May 1493.[45] The pattern of Beltramino's career, his appointment as auditor and councillor after his long-term as vice-podesta, comes to mind here as a precedent.

Some specific examples will underline the point. Giacomo Baiardi, who has already been quoted as a particularly browbeaten podesta, admitted to bafflement in December 1489 when a prisoner whom he was interrogating for the alleged theft of a cap fell asleep on the rope hoist. Awakened and threatened with other tortures, either fire or the *stanghetta*, Zoan Tomaso of Venice decided to make a full confession. "But what should I do now?" the podesta asked his master.[46] Similarly, in July 1490, with regard to a case of false testimony confirmed by confession, which earned the statutory penalty of being paraded through the streets and having both tongue and right hand removed, Giacomo asked

42. AG, b. 2038–39, Gride, fasc. 8, fol. 6r.
43. Ibid., fasc. 9, fol. 1r (15 Dec. 1495).
44. AG, b. 2441, letter of 10 Nov. 1492.
45. AG, b. 2443, fol. 157.
46. AG, b. 2438, fol. 35 (letter of 11 Dec. 1489).

for the marquis's approval before he proceeded to pass sentence.[47] In other words, the marquis's personal will determined judicial sentences and sometimes even anticipated or replaced formal hearings. For instance, Giacomo Baiardi replied obediently to instructions that a man who had wounded one of the marquis's serving-boys would be punished with three hoists on the rope in public.[48]

The podestas who followed Giacomo Baiardi took much the same line. Ermolao Bardolini asked the marquis on 16 November 1490 how he ought to deal with a thief "condemned by my predecessors to be hanged";[49] two horses and a number of lambs and hens had been stolen, so the law was fairly clear. Antonio Oldoini sometimes displayed a trace of compassion, though he was generally more stalwart than some of his predecessors in making and standing by his own judgments. On 6 February 1492 he expressed reluctance to obey instructions to interrogate on the rope hoist a poor man who had been denounced by someone with no hard evidence; Oldoini reported that the man was "not really a robber at all, and claims the cows in question were his own."[50] In contrast, a week later he was urging the marquis to let justice take its course in the case of Ludovico da Tonino, who had been condemned to be hanged (not beheaded) at the place where he had shoved a woman into the Po.[51] Oldoini was certainly far from squeamish, as is shown in the case of Antonio di Bartoletto in December 1491. This Antonio was condemned for false testimony to the statutory parade of infamy, followed by amputation of a hand. He had tried to commit suicide by banging his head against a wall and had lost much blood, but the podesta dryly remarked, "he will have to be carried to the place of execution and seems a bit out of his mind. Will the 20th be all right?"[52]

More to the point, Antonio Oldoini was not afraid to express himself forcibly, or at any rate irritably, when the marquis failed to back him. On 26 October 1492 he was infuriated that a capital sentence had not been carried out: flagellants had spent the night with the condemned man and the first bell had sounded at break of day, but the marquis's mandate failed to arrive so the execution had to be postponed.[53] If last-minute

47. Ibid., fol. 570 (letter of 16 July 1490).
48. Ibid., fol. 575 (letter of 6 Sept. 1490).
49. Ibid., fols. 779–80 (letters of 16 and 19 Nov. 1490).
50. AG, b. 2441.
51. Ibid.
52. AG, b. 2440, 19 Dec. 1491.
53. AG, b. 2441.

omissions could anger the podesta, so could last-minute interventions, as happened with Giambattista da Castello, who wrote on 10 July 1493: "I had intended this morning to sentence the robber Tomaxo Sghargiotto of Crema to be hanged. But afterward your order to suspend the sentence arrived." He asked what he was meant to do next.[54] Oldoini was even more exasperated in the case of Ludovico dalle Margonaze in April 1492. "You wrote to tell me not to molest him further," he protested to the marquis, "but if you had heard his case you would have kept him in prison for four months. Truly he is a wretch and a rogue." This Ludovico twice confessed to bearing false testimony but—fearful of having to wear a miter of infamy and lose a hand—had denied his confessions and appealed. It was quite clear to the podesta that the marquis favored Ludovico because he was a skilled employee in the Gonzaga stables. Indeed, Antonio Oldoini mentions in the same letter that Antimaco had several times told him that, as the marquis had need of Ludovico, a way should be found to release him. "I should gladly be corrupted into letting out all the other prisoners rather than him. My business is to enforce the law," he declared.[55]

It is hard to imagine such bending of justice being attempted by the marquis's grandfather, though if Beltramino's allegations in October 1484 were fair, his father Marquis Federico had not been above reproach.[56] Clemency could, therefore, be just as arbitrary as punishment, and it is remarkable how often sexual offenders benefited from it. In February 1496, for instance, a wife-murderer was released, and five days later a wife-sodomizer was let go.[57] Another case in which the offender against the law got off more lightly than the victim occurred in March 1500, when the podesta Francesco Tonso reported that on the marquis's instruction he had released from prison one Bartolomaio Baron *sodomitta*, but that the twelve-year-old boy he had violated remained in jail and the podesta did not know what to do with him.[58]

The marquis's intervention was not always capricious and unmindful of judicial practice. For instance, in a case of *laesa maiestas* in 1494 he insisted that the accused must be allowed to appeal ("even the devil has a right to justice") against the podesta's sentence of decapitation; accord-

---

54. AG, b. 2443, fol. 155.
55. AG, b. 2441, 25 Apr. 1492.
56. See end of chap. 4.
57. AG, Lib. decr. 29, fols. 68r, 69v (13 and 18 Feb. 1496).
58. AG, b. 2455, fol. 3r.

ing to the podesta, Gabriele Ginori, no lawyer or notary had offered, or dared to offer, his services.[59] But the frequent irregularities, and the prevalence of the marquis's will in prosecutions and punishments, remain very striking.

In Mantua as elsewhere, the period after the War of Ferrara—coinciding with the period after Beltramino's fall—may have been characterized by an increase in crime and by a variety of expedients used to oppose it. Terror was the main instrument, and although there are no statistical controls, evidence from correspondence suggests that more corporal and capital sentences were carried out than formerly, despite the fact that the catchment area for prosecutions had diminished, owing to the dividing-up of the *marchesato* in 1478–79. Sometimes the marquis insisted on severity, sometimes the law officers, but there is no doubt that Marquis Francesco Gonzaga could be remorseless in brutality as well as in partiality.

There was, for instance, the case of Angelo the baptized Jew, who was accused of various ill deeds in the summer of 1491. The marquis was in no two minds about it. On 27 August he ordered the podesta (Bardolini) that although Angelo had undergone the statutory three jerks on the rope and had confessed nothing, it could not be allowed that he had purged his guilt: the torture must be repeated.[60] On 30 August the podesta wrote that, as Angelo had not only stolen goods but consorted with a Christian prostitute, he presumed that the marquis wanted him to be hanged.[61] This was indeed Francesco's wish, and he gave the order to go ahead on 10 September.[62] Five days later the marquis wrote again, expressing his surprise on hearing that nothing had been done.[63] It transpired that the

59. AG, b. 2446, fol. 19, G. Ginori to Marquis F. Gonzaga (5 Jan. 1494). For Ginori's heraldic plaque, see plate 3, introduction, and chap. 4. Malacarne has cited various cases heard by Ginori and emphasizes his cold zeal ("lo zelo funesto"), though in the light of the present study Ginori hardly sounds exceptional ("La stemma del podestà": 48), nor does Marquis Francesco betray much greater humanity (ibid.: 43). Ginori's insistence on hanging the culprits who had painted graffiti on the walls and stuck horns over the door of Ermolao Bardolini is hardly surprising since Bardolini was formerly podesta and now a member of the Council of Justice. Ginori's letter of 13 Sept. 1494 (AG, b. 2446, fol. 29, cited by Malacarne: 50–51) speaks for itself: "non si debba usare nessuna clementia, non che uno tanto homo, ma al più vile officiale di Vostra Signoria, et quando si facia una degna punitione si darà exemplo alli altri a tenere la mano a loro. Habbiamo trovato una crida registrata che mette pena la forcha a chi farà lettere, scrite o brani deffamatorii . . ."
60. AG, b. 2904, lib. 139, fol. 36r.
61. AG, b. 2440.
62. ". . . volgiamo lo condemnati, et lì procediati": AG, b. 2904, lib. 139, fol. 56r.
63. Ibid., fol. 60v.

archpriest of Mantua cathedral had intervened on behalf of Angelo, on the ground that his baptism had purged the guilt of his previous crimes. This cut no ice with the marquis. "Hang him at once on the gallows at the Te," he ordered on 20 September 1491, issuing a special proclamation that no one should be allowed to cut down the corpse, which must remain there as an example.[64] Even so, Ermolao Bardolini hesitated; "I see what you have written," he wrote on 27 September, "ordering me to have him hanged on Monday morning . . . but I find there are two opinions in the matter."[65] Antimaco wrote on 28 September to reiterate the canon-law standpoint of Benedetto Mastino.[66]

The most gruesome and extended account of public execution in Mantua records that November day in 1491 when Paolo Erba and two others were beheaded; Paolo was the pawn or scapegoat of Francesco Secco and after the latter's downfall was denounced for inventing the whole conspiracy in 1487. The writer of the description, Antimaco, professed that it pained him to write about such horrors, but he seems to have aimed at providing his readers (the marquis or Isabella) with a degree of sadistic titillation. Thus on 16 November, after reporting a hand amputation (he named the executioner as Niccolò Ruca), he noted that the platform was being constructed for the imminent beheading and quartering. In another letter two days later, he forecast that vast crowds would attend the event—in other words, this triumph of justice—and that there would have to be extra guards at the gates. "The whole city is jubilant," he declared. On the nineteenth his long letter gave dramatic details of the event: "there was a dead silence such as I never witnessed at any sermon"; after the beheading of Bartoletto, Paolo Erba ran in desperate eagerness to the block; then their bodies were hacked into quarters, which had to be distributed to different display points. All this took so long that it was already an hour before sunset when the third victim, Zohanfrancesco Barbaro, who had had to watch the fate of the others, was brought down to be blinded and branded and to have his ears cut off. "I am telling you this as my duty," Antimaco wrote, "I would like to tell pleasanter things." On 23 November he rewrote his account for the benefit of Isabella d'Este.[67]

---

64. Ibid., fol. 63r.
65. AG, b. 2440.
66. Ibid.
67. AG, b. 2440. Secco d'Aragona, "Francesco Secco, i Gonzaga e Paolo Erba," 244, prints the letter of 23 Nov.

This was of course a special occasion weighted with political significance in Mantua. But ordinary beheadings, hangings, and mutilations, preferably performed on Saturday (market-day) mornings, may have become a more routine spectacle by the 1490s than formerly. An urgency just to get through the list can sometimes be detected in podestas' letters. Thus on 16 January 1493 Giambattista da Castello went over the outstanding cases for which sentencing had been delayed by the recent holiday period: two were to be hanged, Gallottino and Giacomo Cantino (though the latter was expected to appeal), and the robber Domenico de' Sartori was to be blinded and to have an ear cut off; the podesta supposed the marquis would wish the executioner—by name Matello—to do the blinding.[68] The *sindico,* Donato de' Preti, wrote, also on 16 January, that the order had been given to the podesta (note that it is by order from above) for the blinding to take place on the following Saturday, but that the ear was to be spared thanks to an act of Christmas clemency by the marquis; the hanging of Gallotino was to be on Friday.[69] Two weeks later he noted that the marquis, setting aside all clemency, now wanted Matello to behead Domenico and to operate on the ears of Giampaolo da Piacenza, whose theft did not qualify him for death.[70] Sometimes executions were deliberately hurried to forestall special pleading; on 21 January 1499 Francesco Tonso, insisting that a famous robber deserved the gallows, asked the marquis to turn down his appeal immediately, so that he could be dispatched on the following Thursday, "before he has time to get some outside power to intercede for him."[71] In some cases, statutory death penalties might be made additionally horrific, by special order or even by error. In September 1496 Baldassare Soardi wrote to Isabella d'Este that according to the podesta assassins had to be hanged (normally they were beheaded), and that a certain Francesco da Gonzaga was judged worthy to be quartered as well, with the quarters to be displayed in the place where he had committed his crime. Once Isabella's mandate arrived the podesta would have the execution carried out during the Saturday market, to be sure of its lesson reaching the largest public possible.[72] This seems to have been the same case about

68. AG, b. 2443, fol. 163.
69. Ibid., fol. 93. See also Bertolotti, *Prigioni e prigionieri,* 19–20.
70. AG, b. 2443, fol. 165.
71. AG, b. 2453, fol. 423.
72. Soardi's letter of 15 Sept. 1496 (AG, b. 2449, fol. 116) is printed in R. Signorini, "Baldassare Soardi, Dedicatoria della 'Vita' di Vittorino da Feltre del Platina," in *Bartolomeo Sacchi il Platina,* ed. A. Campana and P. Medioli Masotti (Padua, 1986), 203.

which Antimaco wrote in a letter already quoted, where he emphasized the ill reputation Mantua was getting even in Germany. The victim reserved for exemplary execution had confessed to an infinite number of robberies and also to having set fire to the Certosa when he was a doorkeeper there, seventeen years previously. He was deemed a bad lot from the day he was born: his brother had also been hanged. To give him his deserts, the *maistro de iusticia* (executioner) would be operating on a specially built platform next to the pillory, and the quarters would be exposed on two gallows erected for the purpose.[73]

It may also have been the case that penalties of monetary fines and property confiscation were being applied and exacted more ruthlessly in the 1490s than before; this might be expected under a regime chronically short of cash. Giacomino Terzo was accused in February 1493 of talking disrespectfully about the marquis, a crime that was subject (under the statutes) to punishment wholly at the latter's discretion; a fine of one thousand ducats was proposed, but for cash on the spot the marquis was prepared to accept four hundred ducats, a sum that Giacomino said he was equally unable to raise.[74] There can be little doubt that the podesta in 1497, Brancha Manfredi, had few qualms about expediting the marquis's order for the whipping and branding of two youths who had confessed to robbing a lame man of his cloak, seeing that they could not buy themselves off; in fact, they could not even pay the jailer his customary fee for their keep in prison.[75]

The collection of judicial fines was the business of the *sindico,* and holders of this office worked in close cooperation with the podesta and his assistants. Giacomo da Capua, one notable incumbent, was predictably keen on making Jews a special target for exactions. In June 1497 he had secret talks with two leading Jews called Bonaventura and Moses, who had heard that the marquis, advised by several fanatical priests, was planning to expel the Jews from Mantua; they were prepared to discuss terms that would be to the marquis's advantage.[76] Despite a judgment

73. AG, b. 2449, fol. 320r, Antimaco to Marquis F. Gonzaga (21 Sept. 1496).

74. AG, b. 2443, fols. 195–97, Donato de'Preti *(sindico)* to Marquis F. Gonzaga (8 and 26 Feb. 1493).

75. "Feci fustigare e bolare quelli dui garzoni confessorno havere robato quella capa del zoppo . . . il guardiano de la prigione non li vuol lassare che prima vuole essere pagato de la mercede soa, e loro non si trovano havere dinari alchuni": AG, b. 2449, fol. 491, B. Manfredi to Marquis F. Gonzaga (17 Dec. 1497).

76. ". . . dicono che volentieri parlariano cum la Signoria Vostra et gli fariano tal provisione osia presento che la se ne contentaria": AG, b. 2449, fol. 415, Giacomo da Capua to Marquis F. Gonzaga (16 June 1497).

given against the same Moses some months later—maybe for less damages than had been expected—Giacomo wrote on 9 September 1497, "All the Jews are throwing their weight about—it is quite incredible."[77] Giacomo seems to have combined with his duties a keen interest in intensified cruelty, particularly if the condemned person had failed to buy himself off. Thus on 16 March 1497, writing on behalf of the podesta's *giudice del maleficio,* he requested the marquis's mandate to punish on the next day Antonio Chiapino for bearing false witness (i.e., to parade him on an ass wearing a miter of infamy, before having him publicly whipped and then placed in the pillory and branded) and to execute as a public example—presumably by hanging—Antonio del Castello from Treviso, who had confessed to helping a thief who stole a confectionery dish *(confetere)* belonging to the marquis's sister, Elisabetta Gonzaga, duchess of Urbino.[78] On 27 June the same year he proposed that Giacomo Capelletto should be severely punished for swearing (presumably because he could not pay the fairly modest statutory fine of ten lire, a failure worse—from Giacomo da Capua's point of view—than the original crime): he should be whipped with a miter of infamy on his head and tied to the pillory with his tongue in the *giova.*[79]

Giacomo da Capua was probably also responsible for the raising of the level of judicial fines. For the habitual, ineradicable offense of going about at night carrying offensive weapons, the penalties became notably more severe. According to a proclamation of May 1496, offenders were to receive three punitive jerks on the rope, as well as a fine of twenty-five ducats; if more than two offenders were caught together, the penalties could be increased *ad arbitrium.* But the real breakthrough came in August 1498, when the penalty was raised to five jerks on the rope and a fine of fifty ducats—with no exemptions. Neither bona fide servants of soldiers nor soldiers themselves could claim privilege any longer.[80] A few weeks before this, the punishments for stone throwing and gang fighting in the streets *(bataiole)* were raised for adults to three jerks on the rope hoist and a fine of fifty ducats; offenders under fourteen were punished with fifty lashes and the same fine, to be paid by their fathers.[81]

---

77. "loro tuti hebrei sonno per ciò venuti in tanta superbia che è una cosa incredibili": ibid., fol. 427.

78. Ibid., fol. 417.

79. Ibid., fol. 423.

80. AG, b. 2038–39, Gride, fasc. 9, fol. 10v.

81. Ibid.

While Giacomo da Capua took up a new office, as captain of the guard, his successor as *sindico*, Andrea Ghisio, addressed himself to penalties for arms carrying in a letter that confirms that monetary considerations were of increasing importance in the Mantuan administration. He maintained that the contumacious should be punished by the fine ("more pecuniarie") simply for their contumacy, otherwise they would be better off than they were before the new proclamation.[82] Ghisio was a ruthless cost-cutter; he even cautioned the *massaro* of Mantua that the traditional banner should not be offered to a retiring podesta unless the marquis specifically ordered it.[83] He was also the equal of Giacomo da Capua in urging cruel retribution; he told the marquis in the case of Giacomo da Bozzolo, which had been referred to the Mantuan podesta's court, that his appeal should be disregarded because it was just a trick to prolong the case until after the serving podesta retired; Ghisio argued that the offender, guilty of many robberies and a murder, was an evil type who should be shown no mercy.[84] Similarly, in a case referred by the podesta of Canneto, who had sentenced the accused, Benedetto Arrivabene, to beheading and confiscation of possessions for murdering a kinsman, Ghisio insisted that the appeal brought by his father should be disregarded despite the insufficient evidence and reasonable degree of doubt. It seems very likely that it was the prospect of the confiscation that Ghisio had in mind; the Arrivabeni were a clan of substance with extensive property in the region of Canneto.[85] Ghisio's letters also seem to confirm that the breakup of the old *marchesato* among Marquis Ludovico Gonzaga's sons presented, among other problems, a loss of revenue from judicial sources, so that the fiscal motive tended to determine prosecutions. Thus Ghisio wrote to the marquis early in 1500 that it would be preferable to charge one Andrea Corradi for smuggling—since his possessions could be penally confiscated by the marquis—rather than for the more serious offense for which he could be hanged, because if he were hanged, his goods would be forfeited to the late Gianfrancesco

---

82. AG, b. 2451, A. Ghisio to Marquis F. Gonzaga, 30 Aug. 1498. Giacomo da Capua signed himself as "marchionalis capitaneus custodie" in a letter of 16 Sept. 1498 (AG, b. 2451, fol. 278). See also intro. n. 51.

83. AG, b. 2453, fol. 312, Federico Malatesta *(massaro)* to Marquis F. Gonzaga (4 May 1499).

84. "ho informatione dicto Jacomo essere homo de mala sorte et pessima vitta": AG, b. 2449, fol. 576, A. Ghisio to Marquis F. Gonzaga (13 Oct. 1497).

85. AG, b. 2453, fol. 316.

Gonzaga's sons, lords of Bozzolo (probably on account of the place where the crime was committed).[86]

All this evidence from the end of the fifteenth century is necessarily selective and miscellaneous; in the absence of official records, it cannot be otherwise. It is unknown why another *consulta* of the good and the great of Mantua took place in 1497, reminiscent of Gianfrancesco Gonzaga's opinion taking in 1430; maybe matters relating to criminal jurisdiction were raised in the course of it, but no records of any such depositions have come to light.[87] Whether the more severe penalties of the late 1490s were enforced and at last led to a reduction of violence in Mantua or whether the fiscal aspect of Mantuan justice became paramount are questions that cannot be pursued here any further. For what it is worth, the evidence seems to point to a conclusion partly vindicating Beltramino. Even if his conduct and standards of justice were not quite so clean-handed as he claimed, no better alternatives were devised to many of the expedients and practices he had used or exemplified. Some of them seem even to have been reintroduced, perhaps owing to Isabella d'Este's initiative. But it looks as though the arbitrary element grew and the respect for legality further deteriorated in the post-Beltramino era. As a magistrate who had pledged himself to fighting criminality, even if he sometimes let law be sacrificed to political or personal expediency and had a very subjective and retributive idea of justice, Beltramino had been about as clean-handed a magistrate as one could hope to find under a princely regime.

---

86. AG, b. 2455, A. Ghisio to Marquis F. Gonzaga, 23 Mar. 1500.

87. Spagnoli refers to the marquis's imminent return the following Saturday from Gonzaga to Mantua "ove fa convocare per quello dì cinquanta de li principali et megliori citadini a li quali vole parlare, et ho visto alcune litere scripte per questo a quelli citadini che sono fora quale toccano ch'el prefato signore li vole rasonare de certe cose concernente il bene publico et la salute dil stato": AG, b. 2449, fol. 438, Tolomeo Spagnoli to Isabella d'Este, Mantua (18 July 1497). For the precedent in 1430, see the beginning of chap. 2.

Epilogue: Mantua and the
End of Beltramino

Despite Beltramino's ignominious flight from Mantua in 1484, his return to Crema, and his employment by Duke Ercole d'Este from 1488 onward, he never lost touch with Mantua and its Gonzaga government. Indeed, his hope of rehabilitation and eventual return to his adoptive homeland seems to have become almost obsessional; the Mantua connection overshadowed the last years of his life. It has been seen that sometimes he even set aside his judgments as a magistrate at Modena and Reggio in response to Gonzaga pressure, and that the long delay before he took up his appointment with Ercole d'Este had probably been owing to Francesco Gonzaga's reluctance to give his consent. Maybe that delay had been aggravated in 1487 by the alleged plot against Francesco Secco and the marquis, which implicated the latter's uncles Gianfrancesco, Rodolfo, and Ludovico Gonzaga.[1] At least one and perhaps all three were sympathetic toward Beltramino, a martyred figure of their father's and brother's times.

Once launched in Este service, Beltramino had lost no time in writing to his old employer. He told the marquis that only two days after his arrival in Ferrara he had been sent to Finale on a murder investigation.[2] He acknowledged that his disgrace had made it impossible for him to return to Mantua ("where he had thought to stay for ever and leave his bones"), but he reported that, nevertheless, he was already caught up in a sensitive matter of political goodwill, since the accused murderer claimed to have been promised a pardon by the grace of Isabella d'Este. Beltramino was afraid it would be said that he was getting his own revenge on Francesco Gonzaga if he overruled the wish of the latter's bride, as Isabella's father, Ercole d'Este, had at first intended him to do.

---

1. See end of chap. 4, and chap. 7 n. 67.
2. AG, b. 1289, fol. 218, Beltramino to Marquis F. Gonzaga, Finale (2 July 1488).

Fortunately Ercole had changed his mind and ordered the murderer to be released; Beltramino protested that it upset him to think that anyone could think he might do something to displease "she whom I love as my God," revealing yet again his readiness to let the law be flexible if princes intervened.

Beltramino's new position under Ercole d'Este must have helped him gradually to regain some official respectability in Mantua, despite Secco's domination. It is possible, too, that Isabella d'Este contributed to his limited rehabilitation after she finally arrived in Mantua in February 1490. In any case—and although her husband continued to allow successive favorites to dominate him—Secco's influence did not last much longer.[3] It is worth noting that Beltramino was opportunistic enough to hope for a comeback even while Secco was still in power, expressing readiness to bury his hard feelings beneath a sanctimonious veneer of forgiveness. Thus he wrote in a letter to the duke in April 1490 that he was sending his son Matteo about a letter he had received from Secco, in which Secco asked Beltramino to intercede for the brothers of a member of Secco's retinue, who were evidently in trouble at Ferrara. Beltramino declared that he would like Secco to appreciate his good nature and readiness to let bygones be bygones.[4] This was very different in tone from what he would write after Secco's fall from power.

In the course of his duties, Beltramino continued quite often to write to Marquis Francesco Gonzaga, particularly when he had been asked to protect or intercede for individuals. He used such occasions to reaffirm his old loyalty, declaring, for instance, in March 1489 that his heart was still in Mantua;[5] some months later, when promising to intercede in another murder case (notwithstanding evidence that the accused had hired assassins to kill two of his wife's lovers and had also planned to

---

3. Mazzoldi, *Mantova*, 2:84. Marquis Francesco's susceptibility to favorites is noted by Luzio, *L'Archivio Gonzaga*, 2:67.

4. "Mando mio figliolo a v.S. per una littera me scrive messer Francesco Secco ch'io interceda presso quella per certi fratelli de uno suo homo d'arme, ad ciò che quella, intendendo la excusatione loro, gli possa fare et usare quella benignità gli parerà potere fare, et io anche lo haveria a caro, ad ciò che il prefato messer Francesco cognoscesse la mia bona natura de havermi domenticato le cose passate": RdS, Modena, b. 2d.

5. "Dio sa ch'io non ho altro desiderio cha dimonstrargli che son quello fidele servitore absente che son stato presente a li mei Ill.mi signori avo e patre di Quella, et a la V.S. et in ogni caso mi sforzaro sempre che la cognosca ch'io il tengo per mio signore come se fusse a Mantua, dove continuo sta il core mio": AG, b. 1289, fol. 248, Beltramino to Marquis F. Gonzaga, Reggio (23 Mar. 1489).

poison her),[6] he even expressed the hope that after returning to Reggio he would be able to come over to Mantua and visit the marquis. A year later he again referred to his nostalgia and then turned to a matter in which he considered himself wronged. "And although I am not now at Mantua," he wrote, "I am your servant, and when God wills it, I will return to my home with the same faithful service. In the case against Evangelista Gonzaga [son of Carlo, Marquis Ludovico's disgraced brother] concerning lands at Suzzara, Luzzara, and Gonzaga, I gave judgment against him and as reward was invested with lands at Felonica." Beltramino complained that the inhabitants of Felonica had seized some of this land, claiming that Beltramino had enclosed more than was his by right. It may be inferred that Beltramino had regained quite a large degree of confidence to be able to raise his private affairs at all in such a letter. He asked furthermore that a job in the chancery might be found for his son Matteo ("your father was very fond of him"), and he also commended another of his sons, Federico, "now aged fourteen, who says he no longer wishes to go to school, but is keen to take up the profession of arms." On a note of morbid hopefulness, Beltramino repeated his yearning to return to Mantua by adding, "I have decided to die in my own home."[7]

But it was only after the flight of Francesco Secco in September 1491, the condemnation in absentia of him and his brother Stefano, castellan of Mantua, and the confiscation of Francesco's estates at San Martino Gusnago and elsewhere[8] that Beltramino could write freely about the power that had lain behind his own persecution and exile. "Your Lordship knows," he wrote from Modena on 24 November 1493, "how great was my persecution by Messer Francesco Secco, so that I was forced in tears to leave your Excellency, the fatherland, my sons, and my property without any defender, and how he aroused the laborers [fachini] of Sermide and the whole city against me, to demand what justice did not warrant, before judges whom he had selected in his own manner." Beltramino itemized some of the possessions he had had to sell, and his letter reveals

---

6. Ibid., fol. 251, Beltramino to Marquis Francesco Gonzaga, Modena (18 June 1489).

7. ". . . el gie Matheo apto ad ogni impresa et uso in canzelaria, et era amato del Signore Suo patre . . . anche Federico de anni 14 che dice non volere più andare a la scola, ma volere usare le arme a le quale è molto apto. Io lo offerro a Quella e La prego se digni retirarli a la patria fin che anch'io megli possa rit[i]rare, perché delibero morire in casa mia": ibid., fol. 262, Beltramino to Marquis F. Gonzaga, Modena (3 July 1490).

8. Secco d'Aragona, "Francesco Secco, i Gonzaga e Paolo Erba," 216; Mazzoldi, *Mantova*, 2:85–90.

that the bitterness that had haunted him over the last nine years was undiminished. He noted that he had had to sell some property at Castel-lucchio and all his moveables, and that another property, which he had rented from the Ospedale Grande in Mantua, had been confiscated, so that Beltramino lost without compensation houses on which he had spent money in improvements.[9] Beltramino's tirade aroused more irritation than sympathy. On 1 December the marquis acknowledged receipt of his long and passionate letter ("lhonga et pasionata litera"); he resented Bel-tramino's insinuation that he had been denied justice.[10]

Did Beltramino come back to Mantua and, as he had hoped, leave his bones there? He made a short trip early in 1494 and intended to make another in April 1495 in connection with his lawsuits, but there is no other evidence about visits there, until his wish was fulfilled and he returned to Mantuan territory in a coffin.

Beltramino's combination of nostalgia and embitterment toward Mantua, was much aggravated by the aforementioned difficulties con-cerning property and his acute litigiousness. The marquis's councillors were already dealing with one of his civil disputes in November 1493,[11] and in his intemperate letter of 24 November, denouncing Secco and bewailing his losses, Beltramino had drawn attention in detail to another matter still outstanding. Some years before, Secco had supported a claim of fictitious debt brought against Beltramino by one Cristoforo dal Bosco. Beltramino had been threatened that unless a settlement was reached with Amato Cusadri on his father's behalf, Secco would confiscate more of Beltramino's property; in this way Beltramino had lost to Cristoforo his land at Borgoforte. Beltramino reveals at this point of his letter that he had made frequent appeals not only to the marquis but also to Isabella d'Este, who well understood how wronged he had been by Francesco Secco but was not old enough to be able to do much.[12] Meanwhile Cristoforo had subleased the land to one "Zoan Zacomo de Reloyo" (Giovan Giacomo dell'Orologio?), so that again Beltramino lost his outlay in improvements, including the provision of a hay loft and other items. After Cristoforo's death Beltramino claimed Ermolao Bar-dolini (podesta in 1490–91 and subsequently councillor) revealed that

---

9. AG, b. 1289, fol. 399; for the text, see app. 1.
10. AG, b. 2961, lib. 2, fol. 57v.
11. A difference between him and Zohanne di Manfredi, mentioned in the councillors' letter to the marquis: AG, b. 2443, fol. 254 (23 Nov. 1493).
12. AG, b. 1289, fol. 399; for the text, see app. 1.

Cristoforo had admitted he invented the debt claim because he needed money. Evidently Beltramino or his sons had tried to take back the property; Zoan Zacomo complained that he was being despoiled, and the Council of Justice found in his favor, which astonished Beltramino.[13] He believed that Ermolao, for one, had a grudge against him, and he asked the marquis to refer the case to an outside lawyer who would not be intimidated by the Council ("a Mantoa se haverìa respecto al Consiglio"); there were, he declared, excellent lawyers at Verona, Brescia, or Cremona. Beltramino had a particularly high opinion of the Cremonese Antonio Oldoini, most recently podesta of Mantua ("doctore singulare") and formerly a judicial colleague of Beltramino's at Modena.

Undeterred by the marquis's reproaches, Beltramino raged in a letter of 28 January 1494—dated at Mantua, thus proving that he did return there temporarily—that his antagonist Zoan Zacomo was a blockhead ("quella testa dura") who would make no just or honest concession.[14] In a letter to Isabella d'Este, dated at Modena on 30 May 1494, he pointed out with his perennial asperity that three judges had given contradictory judgments and that he was now entrusting his son Matteo to sort the matter out in Mantua.[15] He added that he wanted the Marquis to assign the case to "qualche valent'homo," one who, unlike these others, would be disinterested ("che non abia respecto alcuno ad iudicare"). Just before Easter of the following year, he expressed the wish, which may or may not have been fulfilled, to combine a penitential visit to San Benedetto Polirone with bringing his long-drawn-out legal disputes once and for all to a conclusion.[16] Despite Beltramino's tenacity, he lost this case. His preferred "doctor singulare," Antonio Oldoini, had found in his favor, but then his adversary had appealed. Beltramino had insisted that the marquis, who was away on military business, should refer the matter to Isabella d'Este; she in turn forwarded it for a ruling to the Rota, the papal court of appeal in Rome. But the Rota had confirmed the original judg-

13. ". . . mi maraviglio che dicto Consciglio habia così referito perché è contra la raxon, e cosa non digna de' suoi pari": ibid.

14. AG, b. 2446, fol. 359.

15. ". . . ho inteso che quelli tre judici che mi dette Vostra Excellentia ne la causa mia contro Zamiacomo de Roloio hano dato tre sentetie, l'una diversa da l'altra, cosa che non è usanza de boni judici, perché niuna di per se è valida. . .": AG, b. 1289, fol. 433.

16. "voglio andare questa septimana sancta a San Benedecto in Mantuana et poy a Mantua a fare li tri giorni de la pasqua et mettere qualche ordine che quelle mie cause tanto tempo principiate una volta se finiscano": RdS, Modena, b. 2d, Beltramino to Duke Ercole d'Este, Modena, 12 Apr. 1495.

ment against Beltramino. Likewise, the Council's subcommittee of appeal, consisting of Stefano Guidotti (archpriest of the cathedral) and Ermolao Bardolini, concluded—in a letter that records all stages in the matter—that Beltramino did not have a leg to stand on and must resign his claim to this property, which was based on a wrongful appropriation from Giacomo del Reloio.[17] Their conclusion followed some months after the Council had been ordered[18]—on 11 April 1496—not to proceed any further in Beltramino's case.

This unsuccessful lawsuit must have added salt to the old wounds. Nevertheless, Beltramino stayed on relatively good terms with Marquis Francesco Gonzaga and Isabella d'Este; in January 1495 he was given a formal discharge[19] from a debt or tax liability of over two hundred lire claimed by the Mantuan authorities since 1484, and he continued to be asked to do occasional services for them in Modena and Reggio.[20] Meanwhile his sons did what they could to ingratiate themselves in the Mantuan court,[21] and Beltramino went on living and working at Modena and Reggio in the later 1490s. Even so, he could never quite manage to put Mantua out of his mind; he wrote poignantly on 31 August 1498 (the pretext was his help in arranging for fifty of the marquis's archers to be lodged in Modena) that now that he was old, he wanted to retire there.[22] One of the more practical difficulties preventing this was that his house in Mantua was occupied and he needed the marquis's authority to evict the sitting tenant or tenants. Amato Cusadri, in a letter to the marquis dated 14 September 1498, mentioned that it was a month since he had sent his brother to Mantua concerning "the letting of that blessed house" ("quelli afficti di quella benedetta casa"), reminding him that Beltramino had wanted repossession in order to end his days there, now that he had

---

17. AG, b. 2449, fol. 103 (29 Aug. 1496).

18. AG, Lib. decr. 29, fol. 91v.

19. AG, Lib. decr. 28, fol. 174v.

20. E.g., AG, b. 2906, lib. 150, fol. 68v; lib. 154, fol. 75v, letters of *raccomandazione* (11 Feb. 1495 and 19 Apr. 1496).

21. Amato wrote to the marquis on 14 June 1495: ". . . sono molti mesi e anni che io ho dedicato la persona e faculta a Vostra Excellentia"; on 23 June 1495 he asked for another favor: AG, b. 2447, fols. 413–14. On Matteo and the others see the subsequent discussion in text. There are also signed letters from a "Francesco Cusatri" who purveyed gloves, cherries, and other items to Isabella d'Este (AG, b. 2447, fols. 411–12, letters of 7 and 9 May 1495), but his relationship to Beltramino is unsure; maybe he was a nephew, the son of Guido or Giovanni Cusadri.

22. ". . . per essere io ormai vechio e cerchare riposo, il quale riposo voria fare a Mantua quando V. Ex.a se dignasse farmi vodare la casa mia . . . per bisogno de la mia vechieza": AG, b. 1289, fol. 599.

become so old and immobile.[23] The brother in question must have been Rodolfo, who wrote two weeks later that he was not even able to collect the rents.[24]

Beltramino's will, drawn up by the notary Bernardino Mazzoni in the ducal castle at Modena on 18 November 1499, provides a few final details.[25] Four of his sons—Amato, Matteo, Federico, and Rodolfo—were named as heirs; there is no mention of Geremia, but because he was in holy orders and well provided for, such an omission would have been normal. No one in particular is named as executor, though Matteo was entrusted to manage the properties at Felonica and Marcaria for twenty years after his father's death.

Beltramino's sons are not of great importance in the present context, and a short digression about them will suffice here. After the death of his wife in 1479,[26] there is virtually no evidence about Beltramino's domestic arrangements; his two youngest sons would have still been children then, and Mantua appears to have remained the home of all (excepting, of course, Geremia, who was in Rome) until their father's departure. Beltramino's letter of 24 November 1493 suggests that he had had to leave his sons behind in Mantua when he took refuge at San Benedetto Polirone in 1484; maybe they followed him to Crema, staying there until he finally entered the duke of Ferrara's service. Matteo, it will be recalled, had been used by Marquis Federico as a courier in 1483 during the War of Ferrara, and in January 1490 Beltramino strongly recommended him to Ercole d'Este, who had offered to take him into his service as a secretary or courier (*canzelero* or *cavalcante*). According to his father, Matteo was "handsome, a top-class, talented writer, learned and well trained under the late Marquis Federico"; Beltramino predicted the duke would quickly appreciate that Matteo needed to be occupied and not left in idleness.[27] It seems that Ercole had been unresponsive, because in July 1490, as was mentioned earlier, Beltramino had recommended Matteo to Mar-

---

23. ". . . di farli vodare la casa sua nela quale ha desiderio finire sua vita, per non potere più exercitarsi, resistente la senectu sua": ibid., fol. 601.

24. AG, b. 2451, letter of Rodolfo Cusadri, 29 Sept. 1498.

25. Professor Rodolfo Signorini kindly provided a photocopy of the will, a registered copy of which (authenticated by the notary's brother Ludovico Mazzoni) he found in AN, Registrazioni straordinari, 19, fols. 471r–v.

26. See chap. 4.

27. "per essere lui aptissimo al'uno e l'altro exercitia, per essere apparisente, optimo scrittore di bon inzegnio, docto e ben exercitato con lo Ill. quondam Federico marchese . . . son certo quando havera gustato Matteo, gli parera comprendere ch'el non fusse da essere in otio ma da essere oprato": RdS, Modena, b. 2d, 6 Jan. 1490.

quis Francesco Gonzaga for a job and had recommended the fourteen-year-old Federico for a military career. Amato, who gained a degree in civil law from the University of Ferrara in November 1490,[28] settled there and in professional life became a disreputable caricature of his father (as seen in chap. 6), but he kept in touch with Mantua: for instance, he informed—and sometimes misinformed—Antimaco about the preliminaries of Charles VIII's invasion in 1494.[29] There is also some evidence about the later careers of Matteo and Federico.[30] There was a provision in Beltramino's will that Amato and Matteo should provide Rodolfo, the youngest, with funds to continue his studies until he had reached the age of twenty-five, and Beltramino's books were to go to Rodolfo. (The one exception, and the only book individually noted in the will, was a copy of Platina's *Historia Urbis Mantuae*—a chronicle ending in 1461, shortly after Beltramino himself had entered on the Mantuan scene—which he had acquired from the library of Cardinal Francesco Gonzaga (d. 1483). Beltramino specified, somewhat late in the day, that this book should be returned to the commissary or executors of the cardinal's estate.)[31] However, the provision for Rodolfo's education may have been in vain. For one of Beltramino's sons, working for the marquis as a secretary, was reported to have died of plague in 1503; this cannot very well have been Matteo or Amato in view of the information about them at later dates, so Rodolfo is the most likely candidate, particularly since the word "figliolo" is used to describe the afflicted and may imply a relatively tender age.[32]

Two women were also beneficiaries of Beltramino's will. A legacy of twenty-five Cremonese lire was to be paid to the convent of Santa Monica in Crema, where Beltramino's daughter Candida (of whom no other record has come to light) was a nun; this convent had been founded in Beltramino's own time at Crema, in 1451, with five Milanese nuns and

---

28. Venturini, "Dei gradi accademici," 96.

29. AG, b. 1233, letters of 6 Mar., 8 and 10 Aug., and 12 Nov. 1494; see also chap. 6.

30. See R. Ricciardi "Cusadri, Geremia," *DBI* 31 (1985): 494–95, where it is stated that Matteo was alive still in 1528, and that Federico died not long before 1525, leaving seven children still to be educated; Amato needed to be lent money by Baldassare Castiglione to visit the baths for a cure in 1515.

31. On the cardinal's books and the problems of his executors, see Chambers, *A Renaissance Cardinal*, esp. 65, 108, and 96–131 passim.

32. "dil Signor marchese se dice qui el ge morto de peste uno figliolo fu de m[esse]r Baltramino che hera suo canselero . . .": ASE, Ambasciatori, Mantova, b. 1, Stefano Pigna to Duke Ercole d'Este, Mantua, 17 Dec. 1503.

an abbess installed in 1455.[33] A previous allowance of three hundred ducats was confirmed for Ludovica, wife of Amato, to buy herself clothes, rings, jewelry, linen, silver, furs, and so on (maybe she had been attentive to her father-in-law in his decrepitude).

On the whole, it sounds like Beltramino was disposing of a rather austere and frugal patrimony. A hundred ducats was set aside to cover outstanding debts; no other sums or possessions are itemized apart from those mentioned already, and there are no other legacies, not even for pious purposes, though such an omission is consistent with the trend noted elsewhere about laymens' wills in the century and a half after the 1363 plague.[34] Beltramino specified—possibly the most interesting provision in the will—that he should be buried at San Benedetto Polirone, and perhaps, to give him the benefit of the doubt, he had already made charitable donations during his lifetime to this and other religious foundations. Whether or not they had any material cause for gratitude, the only witnesses of the will were eight regular clergy: the abbot, the prior, and two monks of the abbey of San Pietro at Modena, as well as four Dominican friars.

Beltramino's burial wishes and the exclusive presence of clergy as witnesses to his will calls for a final comment about the possible state of his mind. His refuge in the dark days of 1484 at San Benedetto Polirone, that great monastery near to his former home at Saviola on the south bank of the Po, has already been mentioned; so have his pious exclamations ("Naked came I into the world . . ." etc.) in his letters from Crema in November and December 1484, including the ambiguous remark that suggests that he had even thought of retiring to a monastic cell. That his daughter Candida was a nun may or may not point to her father's reverence for the contemplative life, but the recurrent strain of Job-like lamentations about his lot is notable in Beltramino's later letters, and it may be that he turned increasingly to religion as the years passed. This is borne out by his penitential wish to spend the three days of Easter at San Benedetto Polirone in 1495,[35] and by the remark by a fellow official at the speed with which Beltramino traveled from Reggio to Modena in 1496 to benefit from a new indulgence available there.[36]

---

33. Terno, *Historia*, 206, 217.

34. See S. Cohn, *The Cult of Remembrance and the Black Death: Six Renaissance Cities in Central Italy* (Baltimore, 1992), 79, 99, and passim.

35. See chap. 6.

36. Venturi, "Relazioni," 353–54.

According to the Crema chronicle of Pietro da Terno, who is generally so accurate in his biographical outline that there is no good reason to doubt him on this point, Beltramino died at the age of seventy-six, which could well indicate the winter of 1499–1500; in any case it is known that he was dead before November 1500.[37] A popularizing author who drew on the chronicle adds the quite plausible information that Beltramino died in Reggio,[38] and Pietro himself confirms that Beltramino was indeed buried in the church of "San Benedetto, Mantua" (*sic* for San Benedetto Polirone), even including the epitaph on the tomb, which no longer exists. Maybe it was removed or destroyed at the time of the reconstruction of the church in the 1540s by Giulio Romano, though it is odd that Pietro da Terno does not mention this if it is what happened; in any case one of Beltramino's descendants may have given the chronicler a copy of the inscription, whether or not it was still in place in the 1550s. This epitaph preserves Beltramino's image as a rigorous upholder of law and justice, not the servant, much less the corruptible servant, of any master.

DONA, PRECES, AMOR, ODIUM, TERROR, IRA, MINEVE
FLECTERE IUDICIUM NON POTUERE TUUM.

[Not gifts or prayers, not love or hate, not fear, anger, or threats could deflect your judgment.][39]

---

37. On Pietro da Terno, see the beginning of chap. 3. The letter of 17 Nov. 1500 that refers to Beltramino as deceased (RdS, Modena, b. 2f) is cited in chap. 6.

38. Fino, *Scielta*, 21.

39. Such vocabulary was conventional: see, for example, *Le dicerie volgari di ser Matteo de' Libri da Bologna*, ed. L. Chiappelli (Pistoia, 1900), 41–42; "Orfini laudensis poema de regimine et sapientia potestatis," ed. A. Ceruti, *Miscellanea di storia italiana*, 7 (1869): 65–66; and discussion in conclusion.

Conclusion

What was it that contemporaries found "terrible" or "tyrannical" about Beltramino? Something, at least, of his self-estimation, as revealed in letters to his employers, must also have been evident to the public at large: his ability to spot suspects, perhaps; or his image as a tenacious and inflexible interrogator, who could extract confessions "by the industry of words" alone or, when words failed, would use torture to the limits of safety. The commune of Reggio described him as an eagle, which conveyed a sense both of the nobility and legitimacy of his purposes and of the speed and strength of his seizure of prey. Speed was certainly something that seemed to characterize his judicial action, whether in the immediate and massive hike in penalties at Mantua or in his own accounts of some of his judicial successes. Ercole d'Este must have had these qualities in mind when he praised Beltramino as his most effective judge even as late as 1498, when we know that Beltramino was old and tired.

There was more than just investigative efficiency to Beltramino's "tyranny," however. He also attacked entrenched local and aristocratic means of social domination. In doing so, he incurred the enmity of strongly placed noblemen: at Mantua it was the power at court of Francesco Secco that led to his downfall; at Modena the Rangoni were victorious in their many jousts with Beltramino. Such aristocrats had much to defend. Systems of composition for crime were widespread: gentlemen-governors allowed their podestas to receive payments from criminals to avoid prosecution or punishment; the commune of Reggio routinely remitted large numbers of fines for all sorts of offenses. Beltramino, like other stern captains of justice, believed instead in punishment and could see these local systems for dealing with crime only as corruption ("no one is ever punished, but they fix things for money"; "this city is so contaminated with favors that the truth can hardly be discovered": see chap. 6). The inability of podestas to work outside such self-protective local networks was entirely normal, as we have seen: peasants refused to make denunciations or arrests and informed suspects of planned police raids, and the placement of loquacious or unskilled protégés among the ducal squad of archers reduced their effectiveness. Unlike most judicial officers, however, Beltramino joined his own incisiveness to his employers' irascible urgency to reduce levels of violent crime and to have those they regarded as guilty arrested, interrogated, and punished.

Beltramino also answered his employers' needs in another sense: he offered more for less to rulers seeking to cut the costs of justice and to increase its revenue. Exceptionally for an official of the period, he never complained about nonpayment of his salary, and he seems to have kept his fees at precisely the legal levels. Frugality marks his terms of office under both the Gonzaga and the Este. In addition to financial savings, Beltramino allowed the prince to move decisively against specific features of the judicial system that blunted princely power. The appointment of Beltramino as vice-podesta and then *auditore* in Mantua and later as commissioner in Modena and Reggio was part of a process of reducing both the professional independence of the podesta as contractor (his freedom to hire his own staff, set their salaries, etc.) and the rewards (monetary, heraldic) that went with it. The appointment of semipermanent judicial officers cut away the network of patronage that booked up major offices for years in advance and filled important posts with other rulers' favorites. Beltramino, though he himself felt a need to apply the laws precisely, was also the instrument by which rulers impatient with judicial norms and restraints could overcome statute law: "I am not the podesta, nor am I bound by statute law," he declared at one point.[1] In particular, princes distrusted defense lawyers and their tactics (they "pull the law about, this way and that, as they please": see chap. 3): hence their continuing effort to keep them out of the courtroom and their long-standing refusal to allow criminal appeals.[2] Beltramino's dismissal of defense lawyers' arguments, to the shame of the then podesta (see chap. 4), precisely illustrates his role as a princely weapon against a thick skein of legal learning and lawyerly solidarity.

Just as Beltramino was handpicked by the prince for specific purposes, he too was a manipulator. His letters are deceptive, allowing rulers to

---

1. RdS, Reggio, b. 1, 27 Jan. 1490.
2. Cf. Venetian intolerance of lawyers' "exceptions": Varanini, "Gli statuti delle città della Terraferma," 259.

think that their wishes and commands were being satisfied, that they were making decisions. But as is clear in Beltramino's continuing correspondence with Francesco Gonzaga after 1489, he constructed different versions of his activity depending on the expectations of his correspondent (see chap. 6). Above all, he was skilled, through long experience, in presenting himself as the lone champion of princely justice, as the cool, unemotional voice of rectitude, as the incorruptible servant. In this he conformed exactly to the pattern of proper and virtuous behavior recommended to judges by the long tradition of "podesta literature." In the thirteenth century, for example, Giovanni da Viterbo had instructed that the judge should not be a lover of vainglory or pomp; he should be neither greedy for money nor prodigal; he should avoid drunkenness, pride, anger, sadness, avarice, and lust; and he should beware of flattery, immoderate laughter, and excessive familiarity with citizens. Instead, he should be magnanimous, eloquent, modest, "of subtle intelligence," a lover of justice and truth.[3] Thus Beltramino avoided suspicion of greed by not pestering the duke for his salary and by collecting only his legitimate expenses. He reported to the duke bribes that he was offered. He deliberately distanced himself from the major family of Modena and from the local citizenry. Sobriety and frugality were the hallmarks of his tenure of office. He wisely forfended any suggestion of vainglory. His letters reveal considerable literary accomplishment. His humorous asides were written with a straight face; he did not expose to the marquis any sadness over the death of his wife.

It is within this long-established framework of ideals regarding the conduct of judges that we should approach the clash between different ways of understanding the state, as seen by Chabod.[4] Chabod saw the conflict between two ideologies—one old, one new—as characteristic of the early-modern period: noble governors viewed the state in personal terms, in terms of their chivalric and feudal loyalties to the sovereign, and saw their tenure of office as reward for military or other service; administrators, from bourgeois stock, viewed the state in impersonal terms and saw office as something detached from the self, independent of personal favor, with legally constituted responsibilities and remuneration. Though

3. "Iohannis Viterbiensis liber de regimine civitatum," ed. G. Salvemini, in *Bibliotheca iuridica medii aevi*, ed. A. Gaudenzi (Bologna, 1888–1901), 3:220–21, 235–45.

4. F. Chabod, "Lo Stato di Milano e l'impero di Carlo V," in idem, *Lo Stato e la vita religiosa a Milano nell'epoca di Carlo V* (Turin, 1971), 169–82.

Chabod's categories have recently been criticized,[5] they clearly retain some validity, at least at the level of appearances: Beltramino, though he had been knighted, displayed in office all the features of the bourgeois bureaucrat as sketched by Chabod.

This was the official persona that he pitted against aristocrats at the Mantuan court or in office in Modena and Reggio. However, whereas in Mantua Beltramino's official stance brought him success (until Secco turned the new marquis against him), in Modena his persona was more easily overcome by aristocratic "honor" and power. The times of course were different: the political and economic problems of the 1490s were of a different order to those of the 1460s–70s and may have prevented Ercole from pursuing to its conclusion his social "reformation." The cities were different: Mantua, with its resident princely court and compact territory, was a different arena to Modena, with its local "gentlemen" and distance from Ferrara. The personalities were different too: Ercole's wife, Eleonora d'Aragona, seems to have put iron into her husband's judicial fist in the 1480s, but after her death in 1493, Beltramino's role was diminished. Together, these factors prevented Beltramino from repeating at Modena/Reggio his success at Mantua.

At Modena too, the contradictions in Beltramino's position are all too evident. While criticizing the operation of favor when it impeded his investigations, he was quite willing to use it to win positions for his own sons. While reviling the "world of deals" by which lesser podestas let the guilty go unpunished, he claimed at least to offer similar benefits to those recommended by the Gonzaga. While he clashed with the Rangoni in Modena, his own son was in the service of Cardinal Gabriele Rangoni in Rome. The conduct, if not the mentalities, of bourgeois and noble officeholders were not as distinct as Chabod wished to draw them.

These contradictions are also evident when we consider Beltramino as bureaucrat.[6] In one sense his experience can be read as that of a new type of career bureaucrat in a struggle against the old aristocracy. In both the Este and Gonzaga princedoms, he was selected for his "objective suitability" for the task, not out of personal favor; he was promoted by the

---

5. C. Mozzarelli, "Patricians and Governors in Spanish Milan of the Sixteenth Century: The Case of Ferrante Gonzaga," in *Patronages et clientélismes 1550–1750 (France, Angleterre, Espagne, Italie)*, ed. C. Giry-Deloison and R. Mettam (Lille, n.d.).

6. What follows draws heavily on, while also diverging from, M. Knapton, "Dalla signoria allo stato regionale e all'equilibrio della pace di Lodi," in *Storia della società italiana* (Milan, 1988), 8:108–9, 111, 117–21.

prince and dispatched from the center; he had relevant previous experience and remained in post for a long term; his were new offices, with wide geographical competence, not part of the institutional legacy of the communal or early signorial period; he was motivated by a concept of government that was opposed to aristocratic privilege. Centrality and impersonality seem to mark his activities. Conversely, he was but one individual serving a wide area, his authority overlapped tensely with that of existing officials, he was loaded with other business outside his original commission, his rewards still came (partly) from fees and commissions, and his itineracy meant that there was still a geographical gap between the subjects and the state power that he represented. Above all, Beltramino's presence revealed the real sources and contours of power in the localities: he stung aristocrats into exercising that "protective function traditional to the feudal nobility." At Modena, both the Rangoni and Cesare Montecuccoli, in appealing direct to Ferrara and to the wider aristocratic world against Beltramino, showed that the prince's bureaucrat had broken the collaborative alliance between princely and aristocratic power on which political equilibrium in the provinces depended. And it was they, not the bureaucrat, who emerged victorious, just as at Mantua Beltramino had been overcome by Secco.

Beltramino thus reveals, both in his tales of official corruption, and in his own personal attitudes, the limitations of the Renaissance "bureaucracy." Officials could not usually separate themselves from their identities and interests as members of families and factions. It was because Beltramino could not be absorbed into local systems of patronage and "corruption" that he was treated so hostilely by local institutions and privileged groups: bureaucracy thus became tyranny. In both Mantua and Reggio there was more local affection for those gentle judges who were courtly noblemen and part-time poets, such as Matteo Maria Boiardo and Gianfrancesco Soardi. The enraging and alienation of "respectable" local opinion scarred Beltramino's experience, just as it led to the killing of his counterpart Zampante in Ferrara.

Unlike Zampante, however, Beltramino seems ultimately to have been caught up in the use of judicial power for the social domination of city over countryside and of the wealthy over the poor. As in Florence, apparent improvements in the efficiency of judicial machinery only accentuated its "class character."[7] Though Beltramino professed his keenness to pun-

---

7. Cohn, "Criminality and the State," 224.

ish wayward aristocrats (the Rangoni, Cesare Montecuccoli, Beltrame da Fogliano, Taddeo Manfredi), this was never allowed by the duke. Indeed, errant nobles such as Francesco Maria Rangoni or Branca Manfredi (and, of course, Matteo Maria Boiardo) turned up in judicial or political office alongside him. The innocence, or at least impunity, of the rich continued to be presumed, while criminal justice visited its bloody mutilations and ghastly hangings on the "delinquent poor." The Rangoni preserved their own servants from Beltramino's prosecution and punishment but later sought out Beltramino's "strong arm" against attacks on their household. Indeed, the intensification of terror that Beltramino's commission represented had a clear class significance: as a later aristocrat wrote, "no other category is lower than the small people, full of evil, full of mental confusion; and if they are not kept in terror of the death sentence, it is impossible to rule them."[8]

Despite all these failings, Beltramino's experience shows that most of the "modernizing" features of judicial policy, seen by historians in the major states of sixteenth-century Italy, were present already in minor states of the fifteenth century. This is not to claim any precocity for Mantua or Ferrara but merely to reveal early-modernist myopia. Early-modern historians have drawn attention to a new "insistence and intensity" of action by princes to remedy judicial failings. They find evidence of princes streamlining procedures and stopping the spinning out of cases by appeals, increasing penalties (especially greater use of corporal punishment), punishing all crime without consideration of social status, controlling judges by halting the sale of office and eliminating venality, and rationalizing statute law (resolving contradictions, supplying gaps).[9] The sixteenth century and the *ancien regime* brought a judicial system based not on respect for local laws and customs, nor on municipal control of the law courts, but on terror and absolutist disregard for statute law, with vastly increased numbers of public precautions demonstrating the ruler's will, force, and power.[10] In Ferrara and Mantua most of these features

---

8. G. Tocci, "Perceiving the City: Reflections on Early Modern Age," *Critical Quarterly* 36, no. 4 (1994): 37.

9. Cozzi, *Repubblica di Venezia e stati italiani,* 4–5; A. Mazzacane, "Diritto e giuristi nella formazione dello Stato moderno in Italia," in *Origini dello Stato: Processi di formazione statale in Italia fra medioevo ed età moderna,* ed. G. Chittolini, A. Molho, and P. Schiera (Bologna, 1994), 337; M. Bellabarba, "Norme e ordini processuali: Osservazioni sul principato di Trento tra XV e XVI secolo," in ibid., 349.

10. Muchembled, *Le temps des supplices,* 70–75, 82, 85, 110–12; M. Foucault, *Discipline and Punish: The Birth of the Prison* (Harmondsworth, 1979), 47f.

were present under Beltramino, if not before. The Este had long resisted criminal appeals and, with judges such as Beltramino and Zampante, dispensed with statutory procedures. The rope hoist was increasingly used not as an instrument of torture alone but also as one of punishment. Though Ercole did sell some judicial office, he also took firm action against official corruption. The legislative record in Ferrara or Modena shows a constant endeavor to update the law and to take account of new developments in criminality. The only deficiency here is the princely reluctance to prosecute or punish noble wrongdoing; but Ercole d'Este would not be the last ruler in Italian history to take no action on the politically sensitive reports of a "clean-handed" investigator.

Appendices

Appendix 1

Selected Letters of Beltramino

(Punctuation and accents added)

I. To Marquis Ludovico Gonzaga, 6 February 1467

Illustrissime princeps ac Ex[cellentissime] d[omine] d[omine] mi. La v[ostra] Illu[strissima] S[ignoria] per benignità soa, sperando in qualunque cossa la mi operasse recever da mi ogni bon frutto, s'è dignata deputarmi a questo primo offitio de vicepodestà, aciò che chaduno altro habia seguire non possa da mi pigliar exempio di cossa non dovuta. Unde per questo ho concepto esser necessario di sforzarmi che ogni mio atto habia in caduna parte perfectione. E cossì fin qua con ogni diligentia ho fatto. Al presente, vogliando chel mio zudexe del malefitio fra il tempo per li statuti limitato apresentasse al massaro l'instrumento del suo doctorato, ritrovo che l'è stato doctorato a Parma dove non è studio generale, como par voler il statuto nominando gli lochi dove vole sia doctorato on licentiato chaduno iudice di malefitio che habia vegnir a Mantoa, e non si connumera Parma. Onde per questo glio ditto che non intendo de retenirlo et maxime che a principio quando mandai per lui gli fo ditto ch'el non acceptasse di vegnire s'el non era doctorato in alcuno di lochi comprexi nelo statuto. Lui mi dice ch'el spera haver dispensa da V. S. e ch'el farà scrivere a quella e pregarla etc. Illu. S. mio, ben ch'io per questo non intenda partirme da quanto parerà a quella, ho deliberato dal canto mio non esser contento che dispensa alcuna se faza ne in questo ne in altro, aciò che a V. S. per quelli hanno a seguire non sia rotto el capo di far dispensa alcuna como a dire che a mi fosse fatto el simile, per che caricho mi serìa quando fosse ditto e non riuscirìa a V. S. li penseri l'a fatto de mi. E fra quatro giorni ne farò vegnir un'altro sufficientissimo e bono che haverà tuti i requisiti dalo statuto, per che non delibero d'esser dispensato ma che le cosse passanno per gli ordeni soi. E cha la v. Illu. S.

271

cognosca non haver fatto de mi falso concepto ala qual mi ricomando.
Mantue, die 6 februarii 1467.
(AG, b. 2405, fol. 506)

II. To Marquis Ludovico Gonzaga, 25 August 1467

Illustrissime princeps ac Ex. d. d. mi. etc. Procedando ala investigation
del furto fatto di pirri de Guidon da Bagno, feci relation ala Illu. V. S.
como trovava che i famigli de Zohan da Caravazo, homo d'arme de d.
Francisco Secco, eranno stati quelli che gliavianno robati. La prefata V.
S. me commisse che vedesse d'aver questi famigli, e cossì scrisse al vicario
da Revero che li mandasse qua a Mantoa, e tandem ne mando uno, l'altro pare che fugisse per non esser preso. Unde examinato questo
mandato, confessa esser vero che lui e l'altro famiglio con uno calzolaro
da Revero andonno a tempo di notte nel brolo de Guidon e robonno i
piri. E per che la valuta d'essi piri non ascenderìa ala summa punibile per
il statuto, ma di raxon comuna se dupplarìa la valuta d'essi, non so se la
Illu. V. S. per altro rispetto voglia che se proceda altramente, exas-
perando per qualche caxone l'excesso perpetrato. La qual cossa quando
fosse supplico la prefatta v. s. si digni far quella comission gli pare aciò
possa procedere più oltra. Mi ricomando a V. S. Mantue, die 25 augusti
1467.
(AG, b. 2405, fol. 509)

III. To Marquis Ludovico Gonzaga, 20 October 1468

Illustrissime princeps ac Ex.me d.d. mi singularissime etc. Questa matina
ho ricevuto lettera da V. S. ch'io vedesse d'aver nele mane uno Ponchione
alias famiglio de Girardo Feroldo. Unde subito l'ave a man salva et ho lo
fatto mettere ne la torre a requisition de V. S. Ceterum avixo quella che
ben ch'io non gli abbia scritto fin qua sopra quelli da Gazolo che uccel-
lanno, nichilominus non ho cessato de instar ala investigation del vero,
perché non m'è parso quello processo fatto a Gazolo esser sufficiente a
ciò, et anche lo sospetto per che lo notaro è quello che l'a scritto e ha
examinato li testimonii, neli qual trovo contradictione asai, e lo notaro
proprio è incolpato. Sì ch'el non è verisimile ch'el non habia operato ogni
inzegnio in far che la verità non si trovi. Ho mandato per alcuni de quelli
testimoni e spero di trovar il vero e quanto troverò insieme cum il consiglio se punirà e farassi intendere a V. S. Questi giorni ho havuto Mathio

Formiga ala corda, dal qual non ho possuto cavar cossa alcuna perch'el non teme la corda et anche se dormenza sula corda, credo per qualche incanto on diavolarìa che l'abia mangiato, e queste eran le longe ch'el pigliava in recusarmi sospetto et appellavassi per haver tempo di provederse de questi incanti. Ho deliberato dargli la stangetta e farò quanto mi sera possibile per cavar el vero. E la raxon comporterà. Al fatto de Zohanantonio stancharo e di quanto scrive il vicario da Borgoforte per le uve manzate e despicate ho fatto debita provisione. Mi ricomando ala Illu. V. S. Ex Mantua die 20 octobris 1468.
(AG, b. 2410, fol. 39)

IV. To Marquis Ludovico Gonzaga, 21 November 1471

Illustrissime Princeps ac ex.me d. d. mi sing.me etc Questa matina per supplire a quello no poti fare heri sera, intrai in rocha e fecime apresentare questo Todeschino carzerato e domandandogli ch'el me narrasse la casone perché l'era conducto qua. Cominzò a dire il modo come lo sera partito da d. Theophilo il quale monstrava de volere habandonare la corte, habiando tolta donna, e voleva condurlo al salario d'uno ducato, e al tempo del Duca Borso ne havia dui e mezo; e ricordandossi che alias a Parma habiando domandato lo Ill.mo Duca de Milano chi el era, et intendando che l'era stafezero de d. Theophilo, gli havia proferto che, se mai accadeva che gli potesse fare cossa grata, che l'andasse da Sua Signoria . . . [Beltramino alleges that Todeschino had traveled—somewhat circuitously—via Codigoro, Chioggia, Monselice, etc. and took the river Adige above Legnago to Isola della Scala] . . . venne a Mantua et andò a "La Campana" e, stato lì alquanto e apresentato a li bolleti, venne uno chiamato Jacomo da le Calze suo compare, che sta con d. Nicolò, il quale intexo da lui la casone del suo partire gli disse ch'el andasse con seco in corte, e cossì introrno in camera de d. Nicolò, e d. Nicolò gli parlò, digandogli che d. Theophilo suo compare l'avia ben trattato di compare. E partito de lì, andò a l'ostaria, et intendando che a l'altra hostaria, crede sia "da l'Aquila", alcuni todeschi gli eronno, andò là, e, stagando a vederli cenare, fo preso da la famiglia del podestà [= vice-podestà]; e digandogli io che la via sua de andare a Milano non era per Mantua, rispose che, s'el non fusse per havere quelle littere de recomandatione, non gli serìa venuto. Disse ancora che d. Theophilo gli avia dicto ch'el non sperasse d'aver recapito in recetto a Milano, perché l'avia scritte per modo non serìa acceptato. E digandogli io "Perché gli andavene tu adonchà?" rispoxe, "confidandomi ne gli offerte del prefato Ill. Duca, con intentione che quando non fosse acceptato, de andare a caxa mia." Vedando non potern[e] cavare altro, in presentia sempre del vicario e del castelano, gli feci la debita admonitione, monstrando che la V.I.S. non gli aveva voluto fare mettere le mane adosso, siando quella iustissima, fin tanto che la non haveva intexo il marzo de questa cossa, non specificando però mai qual fosse questa cossa, e che per questo eranno passati tanti giorni che mai V.I.S. non gli avia mandato alcuno e molte altre cosse, e ch'el se dovesse preparare poi ch'el non voleva per amore dire il vero, gli le farìa dire per forza.

Costui stette sempre constantissimo nel parlare. Questa sera con asai parole inductive e persuasive dil vicario, castelano et io, lo conducessemo a la corda, e qua cum parole mò dolce mò brusche lo feci tirare alto e lì stette per uno bon pezo con grande smaniare e dolersi; et interogandolo sempre, diceva non havere fallito, e cossì fo lassato transcorrere. Ma per non haversi ben acordati quelli tegnivanno la corda di lassarlo correre in zoxo non pigliò grande tratto; poi, ellevato un'altra fiata fin a la cirella che ho fatto mettere sotto al batiponte, è stato cossì alquanto, confortandolo ch'el dicesse il vero, e non digando altro che non haver fallito, fo lassato transcorrere e pigliò bon tratto. E colui che tegniva ferma la corda la lassò scapare de mane per modo ch'el cascò fin a terra; non però se feci troppo male, ma steti uno poco stramortito. E fatagli butare l'aqua nelo volto se rehave, et un altra fiata il feci ellevare con quelle medeme parole, e non respondando altramente ch'avia fatto prima, io feci transcorrere un'altro tratto e, sforzandomi cavarne qualche cossa, gli stetti intorno uno bon pezo. E non possandone cavare altro, ni vedando altro segnio, deliberai farlo desligare e ritornarlo al loco suo, e dil tuto darne avixo a V.I.S. per intendere da quella se senza altri indicii la vole che domane di sera il se ritorni a la corda, como a lui ho minazato di fare. E quanto comanderà V.I.S. cossì exequirò, a la qual mi ricomando. Ex Capriana, die 21 novembris 1471.
(AG, b. 2412, fol. 307)

V. To Marquis Ludovico Gonzaga, 22 August 1475

Illustrissime princeps ac ex.me d. d. sing.me etc. Subito gionto qua, andai in palazo e vitti quanto era fatto nela causa de Pedrono Sinerero, e trovo che l'è provato per cinque testimonii che l'è quello de chi parla la condemnatione e quanto a questo non bisogna altre prove, ma seguendo li

statuti bisognerìa dargli termine congruo a fare le sue diffexe, e cossì circa la innocentia sua como ad opponere a li testimonii s'el volesse opponere, che serìanno forse sette on otto dì. Preterea se porìa poi appellare la guardia se gli fa bona ch'el non fuga. La V.S. po deliberare quelo gli pare meglio. Siamo poi stati insieme, il maestro de l'entrate et io, e per essere già tardo n'è parso meglio aspettare damatina per la facenda, perché son venuto et interim non farne mentione alcuna et anche il maestro de l'entrate era occupato con d. Anselmo Folenghi e Galeazzo da Capriana circa quella sua facenda. Mi ricomando a V.I.S. Mantue, 22 augusti 1475.
(AG, b. 2416, fol. 716)

VI. To Marquis Francesco Gonzaga, 4 November 1484

Illustrissime princeps ac Ex.me d. d. mi singularissime. Scrisse a questi giorni a V. S., sperando che oramai la se dignasse per sua clementia che l'usa verso caduno, non volere comportare che tanta persecutione mi fusse fatta, ma che se dignasse metergli fine, attendando la natura de quella la quale l'era tanto prompta a fare gratia ad ogniuno che glila domandava. Ma per quello ho novamente inteso, trovo che pur adesso pare se comincia a sindicarmi, come se a li giorni passati non fosse ben trutinato il fatto mio, che non ho già commesso tradimento ne lo stato né persona né l'avere di la casa di Gonzaga. E ben che fin qua mai non fusse sindicato alcuno dil suo consiglio che fosse casso on se partisse, e mi ricordo de d. Andrea da Gatto che fu casso, d. Francesco Sangiugno, d. Antonio da Pesaro, d. Luca Vernazo, d. Raymundo e d. Amadeo, che nesuno di loro fu sindicato, et io solo sia quello che sia pegio tractato cha gli altri che non hanno fatto de le cento parte l'una di stenti che ho fatto io per la casa di Gonzaga, me ne posso dolere. Ma più che v.S. et tutta la terra sa che, per le menaze grande a mi facte e lo grande pericolo de la persona, non posso sicuramente vegnire ala diffexa, che quando gli fusse possuto essere sicuro mi serìa diffexo, come ho fatto agli altri quatro mei sindicati e non serìa sindicato absente senza alcuna mia diffexa né tanto serìa stato constretto a pagare como è stato pagato. Ma vedando che ancora me remaneva qualche cossa de le mie fatiche de anni vintisette e che gli emuli mei non havevanno per quella via possuto in tutto disfarmi, sonno saltati a farmi sindicare absente, a ciò che per contumacia sia condemnato, che non è altro cha in tutto tormi quella poca mercede ch'è parso a le bone memorie de li Ex.mi Signori vro. avo e patre di remunerarmi de tanti viagi e mei sudori e pericoli scorsi in tante andate per tutta Italia a Signori, Signorie e comunitate, che mai non fu mandato in loco che non gli portasse la conclusione che desideravanno soe Signorie e con honore, né mai gli feci vergogna. V.S. comporta che sia trattato a questo modo. Spero una fiata se dolerà che tale servitore sotto quella sia cossì malmenatto, quando la cognoscerà bene che cossa sia trovare uno bon servitore, e non dubiti quella che de questa cossa se ne parla oramai in caduno loco et a presso ogni Signore, a chi forse non pare cossì ben fatto como a quelli che mi fa fare questo. Quando mi serà tolto quello poco mi resta, non serà però ogniuno contento né per questo serà richo. Et dentro Mantua, ben che se tacia, son molti e molti a chi ne dole, e di magiori, mezani et infimi, che intendeno chi son quelli che son casone di questo e la casone, che non è legittima, ma solum per vendicarse contra mi senza mia colpa. Se la V. S. vole che habia butato via tanto mio servito e tante fatiche, sia in Dei nomine. Ciò che piace a quella piace a mi. Una cossa mi dole che li inimici mei, che sonno stati inimici di lo stato di vostri progenitori, sianno quelli che si glorianno dil mio male, como se hanno gloriato dil male di loro Signorie, ne in questi metto il M.co d. Francesco Secco che sempre è stato fidele al stato, ma ben se intende de chi parlo, e quando li termini fossenno pari, glielo provarìa se le parole di lo Illu. S. vostro patre sopra questo eranno vere. Io son sindicato che ho fatto mettere in presone e messo a la tortura molti persone senza commissione, e se le ho dovuto lassare di presone gli ò tolto dinari, robbe che non è nummero, e che dovevanno essere di V. S. etc. Illu.mo S. mio, quella sa e comprende che in presone non serìa possuto mettere alcuno che il Signore suo patre non l'avesse saputo, per che tutti gli supplicavano essere relaxati. Ma questo è per che soa S. cometteva che'l tale fosse distenuto et io obediva, né altramente constava dela commissione ne se potrìa monstrare tale comissione né di metterli a la corda, come anche d. Donino, ch'era fatto ancora lui giudice de maleficio, né informato che molte volte dicevamo a soa S. che a nui pareva non dare corda ad alcuno, e soa S. diceva che la voleva che gli dessemo uno, doi on tre tratti, como a quella pareva, e perché costoro sanno che tale comissione a boca fate non se potrìanno monstrare, mi sindicanno di questo. Se a V. S. pare iusto starò tacito e contento. Diconno ancora ch'io ho dato zuramento al notaro che haveva lo instrumento dil Tridapalo, ch'el non lo monstrasse, ma lo tegnisse occulto. Signore mio, io mi trovai priore quella settemana, e venne al consiglio il fattore con il Cornachia e domandò d. Benedetto Mastino e mi in camerino de l'audientia, digando ch'el non era usanza dare fora li instrumenti dil S. senza licentia de soa S. e che volessemo mandare per il notaro de quello instrumento e che gli comandassemo ch'el non lo desse ad alcuno senza licentia dil Signore, e cossì fu mandato per esso e fogli comandato como è dito, e, dato il sacramento, poi ne fu parlato al Signore il quale rispose ch'el nol voleva dare l'arme sue al suo adversario. Pare che io solo habia tradito Cristo. Mandi V. S. per il factore e Cornachia e vederà se merito essere sindicato per questo.

Diconno ancora che ho commesso una grande barataria e tradito Cristo, che ho tolto dinari in prestito da molti che havevanno cause denanti a mi. Questa è una grande barataria. Io so bene ch'el M.co d. Francesco Secco, quando me imprestò cento ducati, non haveva litte denanti a mi, né lo feci per che committesse barataria, né anche d. Zohanefrancesco da Gonzaga haveva licte alora, né Angello Bonzani, né altri che me hanno servito per cortesia e non per licte, como fanno gli amici insieme. Dicono ancora che ho ricevuto doni e da gli omini di Mantuana e d'altrove, per modo che son fatto richo. Questo non gli bastarà sindicarmi quando havesse tolti doni dali subditi di V. S., ma voleno sindicarmi se uno mio amico da Verona on da Cremona mi havesse mandato a donare uno livrero on fasani on livore. Diconno che son partito dil Mantuano senza licentia di V. S. ne di l'officiale da le bolette. V. S. sa che scrissi a quella como l'abbate non mi voleva tegnire a S. Benedetto, pregando V. S. gli scrivesse mi volesse retegnire on darmi licentia d'andare altrove. Quella scrisse a l'abbate, ben che l'avesse poca executione, che mi tegnisse et acceptasse, et quando non mi volse tegnire scrisse a V. S. de lo vegnire mio qua. Sì che facia V. S. vedere la lettera e vederà se debbo per questo essere sindicato. Per tutte queste cosse V. S. po vedere quante richeze ho fatte per tanto tempo e quanto ho tolto ad alcuno. S'el pare a quella di mettere fine a queste cosse fatte in mia absentia in loco dove sicuro non posso essere, supplico di gratia la si digna farlo. Sin autem Dio mi aiutarà che sa il core de gli omini. Io naque nudo e nudo anderò sotto terra, che Dio voglia essermi in aiuto che non abandona chi ha bon core. Et a V. Illu. S. mi ricomando. Ex Crema, 4ᵃ novembris 1484. (AG, b. 1432, fol. 269)

VII. To Duke Ercole d'Este, 22 April 1489

Illustrissime princeps ac Excellentissime D.D. mi singularissime etc. Per intendere meglio e più secretamente la cossa de le monete false sonno fabricate ad Albinea, non m'è parso de andare per quella via ch'io scrisse a

V. S. de havere quello regazo, perché subito la cossa serìa scoperta, ma m'è parso di confidarmi di questo podestà per cognoscerlo non manco desideroso di satisfare ale voglie di quella cha io stesso, e per havere in odio le cosse malfatte, e per haverlo provato in molte cosse qua che m'è stato aiuto asai, et era quello con chi haveva pratica de havere il regazo per la via dela matre d'esso regazo che sta ad Albinea. Unde ho operato con lui ch'el'a mandato per essa matre e da lei se ha havuto la veritate de la cossa, senza altramente mettere in scritura il ditto suo per non discoprire la cossa. L'è vero che in la rocha de Albinea sonno stampate monete false di consentimento dil conte Zohanne e di la donna sua, in grande quantitate, et uno Zohanne Jacomo pictore che sta a Rubera è stato di principali a tale fabricatione, perché costui fu richesto dal conte Zohanne a depingere la in rocha, quando il ditto conte maritò una sua fiola a Parma in Christoforo Cantello, e siando giovenne apparisente, la donna dil conte se meschiò con costui, e la ingravidò, e questo depintore condusse uno frate di S. Francesco, che staseva a Castelnovo di parmesana, a fabricare nelo torione di le rocha queste monete, instigante dicta donna, e consentiendo ditto conte, per mese quatro, e condusse anche dui ferraresi, di che quella femina non sa il nome, salvo che uno che se chiama Nicolò, homo grande e magro che va con dolore, dogliandosse nel'andare. L'altro è homo pizolo, negro, di brutta statura, veste nigro, e Nicolò veste colore meschio. Tandem il conte se acorse de lo adulterio di la donna, e bisognò ch'el depintore se ne fugisse, e credo sia a Rubera. E questa donna, dubiosa di morte, mandò a Perusa, per uno Nicolò Picenino suo parente, che la reconciliò con il conte. E questo Nicolò seguì a la fabricatione de dicte monete con il conte e la donna per più de sei mesi, e per dui soi famigli le smaltiva in terre de venetiani, et anche Gaspare delamante aiutava costoro. Questo se ha havuto secretamente da questa femina, e non ho voluto passare più oltra ad investigare di quello depintore ni di quello frate di S. Francisco ni altro motto fare fin che non habia di ciò dato aviso a v.S., per intendere da quella quanto habia a fare, che ben me bastarìa l'animo di trovare questa cossa quando a quella parerà.

Da Milano mi son mandate lettere che mi ricomanda Francesco de Dalo, et anche intendo vene scritto a V. S., et aciò la possa intendere le extorsione, sforzi e rapine, e lo sforzare de pute rapite e de maridate e robate femine sula strata, et altri excessi de dicto Francisco e di Jacomo Canichia suo compagno, per potere rispondere a chi scrive, gli mando una copia qua inclusa de ciò sonno incolpati. Vero è che non ho possuto fin qui compire lo examine de tutte queste cosse, per essere costoro rotti de sotto, et hogli facto fare li cinti per potergli dare la corda, per che in altri tormenti ho poca confidentia. [E] damatina se procederà ala tortura, e non li lasserò fin al compimento dil tutto.

Heri uno franzese che va a Roma capitato ad uno hospitale e non sapendo parlare italiano, uno giotto vagabundo, dice essere da Udene, lo tolse a menarlo a megliore hospitale, e lo condusse già notte in una stretta via e, non vedendo alcuno, caciò mane al petto di questo franzese e stratiògli la borsa dal petto con dinari e portola via, non cognosciuto ne veduto da alcuno. La matina il franzese venne a dolerse, ma non sapeva altramente darme ad intendere il fatto suo, ma per discretione pur lo intese, e deliberai trovare costui e mandai Guizardo a quelli hospitali ad intendere se con questo franzese fosse visto alcuno, et tandem se trovò chi l'aveva visto condure fora del primo hospitale e tolti li signi e le vestimenti. Cerchò tutte l'ostarie, tandem lo trovò, e menandolo in citadella, quando fu sula pontesella, gittò quella borsa con li dinari in la fossa, e li feci pescare et eranno da vinti in trenta soldi ultra ch'el ne haveva pagato l'osto. Lo examinato et ha confessato lo delicto, ch'è grave, et anche ha confessato alcuni altri furti picoli fatti altroe, e qua credo glie ne habia de magiori da confessare, perch'el mi pare di capello. Gli procederò e presto il spazarò.

S'el paresse a v.S. di scrivere a d. Jacomo Trotto che vedesse di havere copia de uno processo fatto a Milano contra uno Bernardino Tosco di Albinea, preso a Milano per monete false, il quale secondo ho intexo ha palezato il conte Zohanne e ciò ch'è fatto, quella vederà meglio la cossa che io non gli posso ancora scrivere, per che questa femina da chi se ha havuto quello che ho scritto, benchè la stasesse in casa dil conte, non posseva però cossì intendere ogni cossa. Io dal canto mio non gli mancharò, et exequirò ad unguem quanto la mi comandarà, senza rispetto alcuno, ala quale mi ricomando. Ex Regio 22 aprilis hora 4a 1489
(RdS, Reggio, b. 1)

VIII. To Marquis Francesco Gonzaga, 24 November 1493

Illustrissime princeps et Ex.me d. d. mi observandissime etc. Io continuo cum mei figlioli como fidieli di V. Ex.tia stammo vigilanti et attenti sempre accadendo di potere fare cosa che estimemo dovere piacere a quella, e così in tute le cose accadute doppo siamo in queste parte quella ha possuto comprehendere e cognoscere così essere vero, e per questo ne pare dovere havere confidentia e speranza di potere a nostri bisogni obtegnir da epsa qualche gratia che non sia exorbitante dal dovere. La S.V. scià quanta persecucione mi fece messer Francesco Seco, che forza mi fu abandonare cum lacrime la V. Ex.tia, la patria, mei figlioli e le facultade senza defensore alcuno; e como il fece saltare li fachini da Sermido e tuta la città contra de mi a domandare quello che la raxone non comportava denanti a li iudici tolti a suo modo per desfarmi, che bene gli vene facto che bisognò vendesse la possessione che havea a Castelucchio e tuto il mio mobile, e fecime tuore una possessione indebitamente ch'io teneva ad afficto da l'hospitale grande, facendomi perdere le caxe e megliora- menti gli havea facti suso contra ogni debito, dil che remasi desfacto. E più, fece che Christophoro dal Boscho mi domandò denanti a dicti suoi iudici una summa de dinari de che io non era debitore, favorezandolo poi a tuta bria, et essendo minaciato messer Amato, alhora zoveneto, che s'el non remaneva d'acordo cum dicto Christophoro remagnerìa in tuto des- facto da messer Francesco, e che acordandosi gli serìa reservato il resto. Et anche Christophoro gli promise che ciò che per lo acordio gli prom- etesse gli serìa restituito, e ciò ch'el faceva era solum a conservacione che altri non ge lo tolesseno, e cum queste vie messer Francesco mi fece poi tuore quell'altra possessione ch'io havea a Borgoforte, essendo me absente, senza aiuto, e così Christophoro intrò in possessione, de la quale tante volte ne ho facto doglianza a V.S., como a quella che scia et intexe como mi tractava messer Francesco, benché quella fusse in etade de non potergli provedere. Doppo dicto Christophoro se messe cum questo pre- sumptuoso e temerario Zo. Jacomo dal Reloyo, e fecese investire durante il novennio de la mia locacione dal priete che teneva il beneficio, non riservandomi gli megliormenti di caxe, foenili et altri che sono di valuta quanto sia la possessione per magiore iniustitia farmi. E morto che fu Christophoro, V.S. che sapeva che indebitamente era stato spoliato et anche havea bona informacione per relacione del Magnifico messer Ermolao del suo Consciglio como più volte epso Christophoro havea confessato che re vera non era creditore di quelli dinari, ma che la pover- tade l'havea facto fare, como per li testimonii examinati per il Consciglio appareva chiaramente. Quella se dignò, per suo decrieto, restituirmi a la mia pristina possessione. Doppo, la importunità de dicto Zo. Jacomo fue tanta allegando essere spoliato da mi, che quella comisse al Consiglio che intendesse ciò che volea dire dicto Zo. Jacomo, e sopra ciò pare sia facto uno grande processo, e che il Consciglio habia referito V. Ex.tia in favore de dicto Zo. Jacomo. Ex.mo S. mio, credo e mi persuado in simile rela-

cione haverni qualche experientia et intelligentia. Mi maraviglio che dicto Consciglio habia così referito perché è contra la raxon, e cosa non digna de' suoi pari. Poi cesso de admirarmi, perché scio como a cadauno è noto che poche logie gli vano per la testa, e de tale exercitio haverne pocha noticia non est mirum se così spesso faleno e cadeno in errore, e tanto più che messer Ermolao, sdegnato contra mi per non havergli lassato la caxa mia, minaciò de impagarmi, e ben l'ha facto. Et a ciò che questo loro errore e mala voluntà non mi nocia, priego, supplico e dimando di gratia a V. Ex.tia se digni remettere questa rellacione a quale collegio gli pare, on ad uno doctore che sia docto fuora di Mantoa, perché a Mantoa se haverìa respecto al Consiglio. E gli è Verona, Bressa, Cremona dove gli sono de valenti legisti et ègli messer Antonio Oldoini, già podestà di Mantoa, doctore singulare, a chi se po comettere on a chi meglio pare a quella. Et in questo gli domando gratia, se digni soccorermi aciò che in tuto non sia disfacto per queste reliquie de messer Francesco, che gli son remaste, e a quella mi racomando quanto posso. Ex Mutina, die XXIIII Novembris 1493.
(AG, b. 1289, fol. 399; not autograph?)

Appendix 2

Lists of the Podestas of Ferrara, Mantua, Modena, and Reggio

Even though the list for Reggio is incomplete, these lists do reveal both the exchange of judicial personnel between the Gonzaga and Este states and the circulation of personnel among the cities studied in this book. The traffic in both cases seems to have been heavier from the larger state to the smaller: nine men from Ferrara, Modena, or Reggio served as podesta or vice-podesta in Mantua, whereas three Mantuans served in Modena or Reggio. Eight men served in one of the Este cities before serving in Mantua (Cristoforo Almerici, Giacomo Baiardi, Gabriele Ginori, Branca Manfredi, Francesco da Mercatello, Antonio Montecatini, Antonio Oldoini, and Mastino Soardi), while only Francesco Vi(co)mercati did the reverse. In both cases too, traffic intensified significantly after 1480—after, that is, the negotiation of marriage between Francesco Gonzaga and Isabella d'Este, as presumably Ercole d'Este's recommendations, both of his own subjects and of outsiders who had served him in office, quickened or were given more credit in Mantua. Why, finally, the Gonzaga should have taken as podesta six members of the Almerici family of Pesaro is not clear.

Ferrara

1451   Niccolò Conti da Padua (from 1 Jan.: LD, A 6, fol. 9)
1452–53   Giovanni Odorno da Genova (from 1 May to 30 Apr.: ibid.)
1453–55   Giacomo Brocardi da Imola (from 1 May to 1 May: ibid., fol. 9v)
1455–56   Giovanni Megalotti da Città di Castello (from 1 May to Nov. 1456: ibid.)
1456–57   Francesco Corbino da Siena (from Nov. to Nov.: ibid.)
1457–58   Giovanni Giordani da Pesaro (from Nov.: ibid., fol. 11)

1459   Cristoforo Almerici da Pesaro (from Nov.: ibid., fol. 11)

1461–62   Benedetto Graziani da Borgo San Sepolcro (from Nov. to Nov.: ibid.; RdS, Ferrara, b. 1, 4 Sept. 1462)

1467   Luchino da Savona, "eques et doctor" (Rds, Ferrara, b. 1, 12 May)

1469   Scipione Roberti, "comes et miles" (ibid., 13 June)

1470   Luchino da Savona (ibid., 30 Apr., 30 July)

1472   Marc'Antonio Scalamonti da Ancona, "eques" (ibid., 23 June, 18 Sept.)

1474–75   Giovanni "Schamado siculo" (Zambotti, *Diario*, 4)

1476   Antonio Gazzoli da Reggio, "legum doctor" (entered office 1 Jan.: Zambotti, *Diario*, 3)

1478   Ludovico Martinozzi da Siena (Zambotti, *Diario*, 49, 78)

1478   Cristoforo Bianchi da Parma, "jurisconsulto e cavalero" (entered office 1 May: Zambotti, *Diario*, 48)

1480   Niccolò Bonzagni da Reggio, "jurisconsulto" (entered office 2 May: Zambotti, *Diario*, 75)

1482   Cristoforo Bianchi (RdS, Ferrara, b. 1, 24 July)

1484–85   Antonio Oldoini da Cremona, "jureconsulto e cavalero" (entered office 3 May 1484: Zambotti, *Diario*, 153; RdS, Ferrara, b. 1, 12 Mar. 1485)

1485   Niccolò Coccapani (ibid., 13 June)

1487   Giacomo Baiardi da Parma, "legum doctor" (entered office Jan.: Zambotti, *Diario*, 177)

1488   Gabriele Ginori da Firenze, "cavalero" (entered office 1 Jan.: Zambotti, *Diario*, 191; RdS, Ferrara, b. 1, 23 Aug.)

1489   Gregorio Zampante da Lucca, "jureconsulto e cavalero" (entered office 10 Jan.: Zambotti, *Diario*, 203; RdS, Ferrara, b. 1, 11 Jan., 11 Dec.)

1490   Idem (ibid., 22 Sept.)

1491   Antonio Gazzoli da Reggio (ibid., 13 Jan., 6 Oct.)

1502   Giovanni Valeri, "eques et doctor" (ibid., 10 Mar., 6 Oct.)

Mantua

(D'Arco, *Studi intorno al municipio di Mantova*, 6:64–81, supplemented, clarified, and corrected by reference to AG)

1432   vice-podesta: Maggio Maggi da Verona (AG, b. 3452: 14 Mar.)

1434–36	Giovanni de' Medici da Verona
1437	Bartolomeo da Campagna da Verona, "de la Campanea" (AG, b. 3452, fol. 285: Aug. 1436)
1437–38	Giovanni de' Medici da Verona
1438–39	Piergiorgio Almerici da Pesaro (from July)
1439–40	Sceva Corti da Pavia (AG, b. 3452, fol. 316)
1441	Giovanni Almerici da Pesaro
1442	Ambrogio Magistri da Milano
1442–43	Lonardo Picenardi da Cremona
1445	Giorgio Spinola da Genova (AG, Lib. pat. 2, fol. 2: Jan.)
1445–46	Francesco Beccaria da Pavia (ibid., fol. 3v: 1 July, 4 Feb.; AG, b. 3452, fol. 434: 31 July)
1446–47	Gaspare Bandelli da Tortona (AG, Lib. pat., 2 fol. 4: renewed 1 Apr.; AG, b. 3452, fol. 475v: May 1447)
1447	Giovanni Francesco Butigelli (da Pavia?) (AG, Lib. pat. 2, fols. 4, 39)
1448	Giacomo Tolomei da Siena (AG, Lib. pat., 2, fols. 4v, 6: withdrew 1 Feb.) Guido Almerici da Pesaro (ibid., fol. 6v: 1 Mar.)
1449	Ludovico Coccapani da Carpi (ibid., fol. 7: 1 May, 1 Oct.; AG, b. 3452, fol. 536: 16 May)
1450–51	Giovanni Almerici da Pesaro (AG, Lib. pat., 2, fol. 7v: 1 May)
1451	vice-podestà: Francesco Carenzoni da Cremona (ibid., fol. 8: Mar.)
1451–52	Mastino Soardi (da Bergamo?) (ibid., fol. 8v: 6 Apr. 1451)
1453	Folco Ariosti da Ferrara (ibid., fol. 9; AG, b. 2390: 28 July)
1454	Ugolino Crivelli da Milano (AG, Lib. pat., 2, fol. 6; AG, b. 3453: Aug.)
1455	Manno Donati da Firenze (AG, Lib. pat., 2, fol. 9: appointed May 1454 to start Feb. 1455, but postponed) vice-podesta: Andrea Cattanei da Novara (ibid., fol. 9v: Feb. to Apr.; AG, b. 3453: June, Sept.)
1456	Manno Donati da Firenze (AG, Lib. pat., 2, fols. 10v, 11: from Aug.)
1457	Giannozzo Strozzi da Firenze (ibid., fol. 11: 1 Jan.)
1458	Bernardo Maggi da Brescia (ibid., fols. 10, 11v)
1459	Guzono Guzoni da Modena (ibid., fol. 10v: 1 July)

1460	Giacomo Cesarini da Roma (ibid., fol. 11v: 1 Mar.; AG, b. 2395)
1461–62	Rainero Almerici da Pesaro (AG, Lib. pat., 2, fol. 12v: 1 Mar.)
1462	Giovanni Sbarra da Lucca (ibid., fol. 12v: 1 Mar.)
1463	Ludovico Coccapani da Carpi (ibid., fol. 12v: 1 Mar.)
1463–64	Cristoforo Almerici da Pesaro (ibid., fol. 13: 1 May, 1 Oct.; AG, b. 2390)
1464	Bartolomeo Ianfiliaci (= Gianfigliazzi da Firenze?) (AG, Lib. pat., 2, fol. 13v: 1 May)
1465	Chierechino Chieregati da Vicenza (ibid., fol. 14: 1 May)
1466	Gianfrancesco Soardi da Bergamo (ibid., fol. 12: 1 May)

Vice-Podesta

1467–69	Beltramino Cusadri da Crema (ibid., fols. 14v, 15, 15v, 16: 1 Jan. and 1 July 1467, 1 Jan. and 1 July 1468, 1 Jan. and 1 July 1469)
1470	Giovanni Calzavecchi da Parma (ibid., fols. 16v, 17) (Battista Bendedei da Ferrara withdrew)
1471	Antonio Montecatino da Ferrara (ibid., fol. 17r–v: 1 Jan., 1 July)
1472	Lazzaro Scarampi da Asti (ibid., fols. 17v–18: 1 Jan., 1 July)
1473	Ermaclide Soardi da Bergamo (ibid., fol. 18r–v: 1 Jan.)
1474	Donino Puelli da Parma (ibid., fol. 18v: 1 July)
1475	Federico Beni da Gubbio (ibid., fol. 19: 1 Jan.–1 July)
1476	Francesco Vicomercato da Crema (ibid., fols. 19v–20: 1 Apr., 1 Oct.)
1477	Francesco Mercatello da Urbino (ibid., fol. 20r–v: 1 Apr.)
1478	Baldasare Gabrielli da Parma (ibid., fol. 21; AG, Lib. pat., 3, fol. 1: 1 Apr., 1 Oct.)
1479	Niccolò Sfondrati da Cremona (AG, Lib. pat., 3, fols. 1v–2: 1 Apr., 1 Oct.)
1480	Almerico Almerici da Pesaro (ibid., fol. 2: 13 Jan., 1 Oct.)

Podesta

| 1481 | Leonello Tolomei degli Assassini da Ferrara (AG, Lib. pat., 3, fols. 3v–4: 1 Apr.) |

1482–83   Giovanni Calzavacchi da Parma (AG, Lib. pat., 3, fol. 4: 1 Apr., 1 Oct.)

1483–84   Giambattista da Castello da Bologna (ibid., fol. 6v: 1 Nov.)

1484   Ambrogio Maraviglia da Milano (AG, Lib. pat., 3, fols. 4–6: 1 Apr., 1 Oct.)

1485–86   Alfonso Galeotti da Ferrara (ibid., fols. 7, 7v: 1 Nov. 1485)

1486   Giambattista da Castello da Bologna (ibid., fol. 8: May 1486)

1486–87   Pellegrino Prisciani da Ferrara (ibid., fol. 8: 1 Nov.; AG, b. 3441, 16 Sept. 1486)

1487–88   Francesco Vicomercato da Crema (AG, b. 2434: Nov. to Sept.)

1489–90   Francesco Munaro da Correggio (AG, Lib. pat., 3, fol. 8: 1 Nov.)

1490   Giacomo Baiardi da Parma (ibid., fol. 8v: 1 May; AG, b. 2438)

1490–91   Ermolao Bardolini da Venezia (AG, Lib. pat., 3, fol. 8v: 1 Nov; AG, b. 2438 and b. 2400: Nov. to Apr.)

1491–92   Antonio Oldoini da Cremona (AG, Lib. pat., 3, fol. 9: 1 May; AG, b. 2440)

1492–93   Giovanni Battista di Castello da Bologna (AG, Lib. pat., 3, fol. 9: 1 Nov; AG, b. 2441 and b. 2443)

1493–94   Gabriele Ginori da Firenze (AG Lib. pat., 3, fol. 9: 1 Nov., 1 May; AG. b. 2446)

1494–95   Cesare Valentini da Modena (AG, Lib. pat., 3, fol. 9v: 1 Nov., 1 May)

1495–96   Giovanni Maria Guidoni da Modena (ibid., fol. 9: 1 Nov., 1 May)

1496–97   Giovanni Pelegrino Merlo da Correggio (ibid., fol. 10–10v: 1 Nov., 1 May; AG, b. 2449)

1497–98   Branca Manfredi da Reggio (AG, Lib. pat., 3, fol. 11: 1 Nov., 1 May; AG, b. 2551 and b. 2453)

1498–99   Battista Ariosti da Parma (AG, Lib. pat., 3, fol. 11: 1 Nov., 1 May; AG, b. 2453)

1499–1500 Francesco Tonsi da Parma (AG, Lib. pat., 3, fol. 11: 1 Nov., 1 May; AG, b. 2453)

Modena

(Vicini, "I podestà di Modena," 253–96)

May 1450–May 1451	Mastino Soardi da Bergamo
May–June 1451	Francesco Ariosti da Ferrara, "legum doctor"
June–Dec. 1451	Francesco Talloni da Ferrara
Jan. 1452–Dec. 1453	Ugolotto Facini da Vicenza
Jan. 1454–Aug. 1455	Pino Vernazzi da Cremona, "legum doctor"
Sept. 1455–Jan. 1457	Antonio Micheli da Siena
Feb. 1457–Jan. 1458	Giacomo Brocardi da Imola
Feb. 1458–Mar. 1459	Lodovico da Gatego da Mantova
Apr. 1459–Feb. 1461	Pietro Trotti da Alessandria, "legum doctor"
Mar.–July 1461	Antonio da Montecatino, "legum doctor, comes"
Aug. 1461–July 1462	Roberto de' Maschi da Rimini, "legum doctor, eques, comes"
Sept. 1462–July 1463	Giacomo da Castello da Brescia, "comes"
Aug. 1463–July 1464	Pietro Gian Paolo Scariotti de' Bernabuzzi da Faenza, "legum doctor, eques, comes"
Aug. 1464–June 1465	Bartolomeo Mezzaprili da Ferrara, "miles"
Aug. 1465–Apr. 1467	Azzo Lapi da Cesena
May 1467–Aug. 1468	Battista Bendedei (da Ferrara), "legum doctor"
Aug. 1468–Jan. 1470	Luchino Negri da Savona, "comes, miles, doctor"
Jan.–July 1470	Scipione Roberti da Borgo San Sepolcro, "miles, comes"
Aug. 1470–July 1471	Cristoforo Almerici da Pesaro, "comes, miles, doctor"
Aug. 1471–July 1472	Giovanni Calcetta da Ferrara, "legum doctor, comes"
Aug. 1472–Apr. 1473	Battista Bendedei
May 1474–Apr. 1475	Antonio da Montecatino
May 1475–Apr. 1476	Bartolomeo Cartari da Reggio, "legum doctor, comes"
May 1476–Apr. 1477	Francesco Stafani da Mercatello, "legum doctor, comes"
May 1477–Apr. 1478	Giovanni Marco de' Medici da Lucca, "eques, comes, legum doctor"

May 1478–Apr. 1479	Francesco Vimercati da Crema, "comes, eques, legum doctor"
May 1479–Apr. 1480	Giovanni Guerra da Castelnovo di Tortona, "legum doctor, comes"
May 1480–Apr. 1481	Marco Antonio Scalamonti da Ancona, "legum doctor, comes, eques"
May 1481–Apr. 1482	Bernardo Trotti da Alessandria, "legum doctor, comes"
May 1482–Dec. 1483	Niccolò Bonzagni da Reggio, "eques, comes, legum doctor"
1484	Pietro Vespucci da Firenze, "eques, comes"
1485	Girolamo Spolverini da Verona, "legum doctor"
1486	Antonio Gazzoli da Reggio, "legum doctor"
1487	Niccolò Coccapani da Carpi, "eques, legum doctor"
Jan. 1488–Apr. 1489	Giacomino Compagni da Ferrara, "comes, doctor"
May 1489–May 1490	Antonio Oldoini da Cremona, "eques, legum doctor"
May 1490–May 1493	Antonio dal Pozzo da Alessandria, "comes, eques, legum doctor"
May 1493–June 1495	Pietro Tigrini da Lucca, "comes, eques"
July 1495–June 1497	Branca Manfredi da Reggio, "comes, eques, legum doctor"
July 1497–Dec. 1499	Demetrio Vistarini da Lodi, "comes, eques"
Jan. 1500–Sept. 1501	Francesco Bosi da Reggio, "legum doctor, comes"

Reggio

1481	Gabriele Ginori (ASRe, Atti del podestà)
1482	Fabrizio Zucchi da Cremona (ibid.)
1487–88	Antonio Oldoini (RdS, Reggio 112, 11 Dec.)
1489–90	Giacomino Compagni (ibid., 23 Dec. 1489, 25 Dec. 1490; entered office 1 May 1489: ASRe, Provvigioni, reg. 98, fol. 131v)
1490–91	Domenico Boldrini da Mantova (entered office 1 May 1490: ASRe, Provvigioni, reg. 98, fol. 185; RdS, Reggio 112, 4 June, 23 July 1491)

1492–93   Giovanni Maria Guidoni (entered office 1 May 1492: ASRe, Provvigioni, reg. 100, fol. 24v; RdS, Reggio 112, 13 Feb. 1493)

1493–95   Paolo Prosperi da Lucca (entered office 2 June 1493: ASRe, Provvigioni, reg. 100, fol. 89; RdS, Reggio 112, 10 June 1494, 13 Jan., 3 Mar. 1495)

1495   Anselmo Folenghi da Mantova (entered office 1 June 1495: ASRe, Provvigioni 100, fol. 210)

1497   Alberto da Montecatino (RdS, Reggio 112, 16 Apr., 23 Nov.)

Glossary

arbitrium	arbitrary will or discretionary judgment
anziani	city elders; elected communal council. Also known as *savi* (wise men)
armigeri	soldiers (see also *balestrieri, fanti, provvisionati, stradiotti*)
arengario	podium or balcony for public announcements
attinentes	wider kin
balestrieri	archers (crossbowmen)
banco	judicial bench
bargello	rural law enforcer appointed by a prince
bataioli	street fights
beato	beatified figure, i.e., a cult figure but not canonized
ben vivere	the good and worthy life (in material and moral sense); to lead such a life
berlina	pillory
berroeri	constables
boia	public executioner
braccia	a unit of measurement (an arm's length)
capi di parte	gang or faction leaders
capitano	captain, i.e., title for civic (as well as military) leader
capitano del divieto	law enforcement officer (against

	contraband, immorality, etc.) Also known in Mantua as *deputato al divieto*
capitano della piazza	chief of a squad of soldiers detailed to guard the main square of a city
capitano di contrada	elected district official in a city
capitoli	terms of agreement; clauses in a legal contract
caporali	leaders, principals
cattivi	bad people, malefactors
cavalero	knight
cognati	in-laws
compadri	godfathers (also, more generally, close friends, accomplices)
contadini	country-dwellers, peasants
contado	territory surrounding and dependent on a city
collaterale	special military officer (e.g., with extraordinary powers to enforce plague quarantine)
consiglio di giustizia	advisory, nominated council with specific powers in judicial administration (especially in civil cases)
consiglio generale	assembly of all eligible citizens
consorti	kinsmen, partners
corda	instrument of torture (rope hoist)
corruptelae	abuses
crida	see *grida*
danni dati	criminal damage in countryside (to, e.g., crops, livestock)
domicelli	squires
dominio	lordship, dominion
estimo	system of assessing real property for tax; assessment resulting from this
exactores	public-debt collectors
famiglia	staff or household

famiglio	member of staff or household
fanti	foot soldiers, armed servants
fattore generale	president (one of two) of the ducal revenue office *(camera)* in Ferrara
gentiluomini	gentlemen, nobles
giotti, ghiotti; giottoni, ghiottoni	malefactors, rogues (cf. Eng. *glutton*)
giova	bridle, instrument of punishment that restrained the tongue
giudice del maleficio	criminal judge, subordinate to podesta
gratia	grace, pardon
grida, gride	proclamation(s), edict(s)
honoranze	visible signs of honor, tribute, gifts in kind
inimicitia	enmity (feud?)
iudex aggerum	judge to ensure maintenance of river defenses
iudex appellationum et datiorum	judge of appeals and fiscal matters
iudex malleficiorum	see *giudice del maleficio*
laesa maiestas	treason, lèse-majesté
lire in pizzoli	pounds paid in coins of reduced weight and small value
magister intratarum	senior revenue official (Mantua); also *maestro dell'entrate*
malabiati	the infamous, or "gone-bad"
malgoverno	bad government
manegoldo, manigoldo	public executioner
marchesato	dominion subject to a marquis
massaro	chief revenue official in city
mattinata	charivari, rough music
mezzadro	sharecropper
ministro di giustizia	public executioner
parentado/i	relationship or kinship (esp. by marriage); group of persons linked thus
parentella	kinship, family
parenti	relatives (esp. by marriage)

podesta	senior judge in most north Italian cities, a nonnative appointed for six months or a year
podestaria	the above office
provvisionati	stipendiary troops
provvigioni	stipends; enactments
raccomandati	allies, contracted adherents
ragione	right, law, lawful justice
reggimento	regime, government; in Modena and Reggio, the group of three senior officials (podesta, captain, *massaro*) who governed on behalf of the duke
republica	the public interest, civic government based on its preservation
ribaldi	ribalds
sbirro	police constable
seigneur	lord (nonsovereign and on limited territorial scale)
signore	lord (on unlimited scale)
signoria	lordship, dominion
sindicare	to investigate the record of an officeholder
sindico	fiscal auditor and investigator
stanghetta	instrument of torture (a sort of vice attached to the foot)
stradiotti	mercenary cavalry (from Greece, Albania, etc.)
tristi	wretches, malefactors
uomini da bene	respectable people
vice-podesta	temporary stand-in *or* long-term substitute for the podesta

Bibliography

Unpublished Primary Sources

Archivio di Stato, Bologna

Comune, Governo, Lettere del comune, regs. 1, 5
Comune, Governo, Riformatori dello Stato di libertà, Libri partitorum, reg. 1

Archivio di Stato, Ferrara

Archivio storico del comune, serie patrimoniale
   Libro delle commissioni ducali 1476–81
   Libro delle provvigioni statutarie 1457–91
Archivio notarile, Ferrara, Bartolomeo Goggi

Archivio di Stato, Mantua

Archivio Gonzaga
   (Divisioni degli stati) b. 20
   (Trattati d'alleanza) b. 44
   (Controversie . . . fra Mantova, Asola e Brescia) b. 92
   (Corrispondenza estera): Francia, b. 629; Savoia, b. 731; Roma, b. 844, 846;
     Firenze, b. 1101; Lucca, b. 1138; Bologna, b. 1141; Ferrara, b. 1183,
     1229–30; Modena and Reggio, b. 1289; Guastalla, b. 1390; Venezia, b.
     1431bis–1432; Verona, b. 1593; Brescia, b. 1599; b. Milano, b. 1626–27;
     Gazoldo, b. 1795.
   (Statuti) b. 2002–3
   (Gride) b. 2038–39
   Libri dei decreti, reg. 4, 14–22, 28–29 Libri delle patenti, 2–3
   (Lettere originali dei Gonzaga) b. 2096, 2096 bis, 2103
   (Lettere da Mantova e paesi dello stato) b. 2390–2455
   (Copialettere dei Gonzaga) b. 2885–2906, 2961
   (Procedure criminali) b. 3452–53

Archivio notarile
  Registrazioni notarili (1477, 1483, 1484)
  Registrazioni straordinari, reg. 19

Archivio di Stato, Modena

Archivio segreto estense: Cancelleria
  Archivio militare, b. 2
  Archivio per materie, Capitani di ventura, b. 2
  Carteggio, Ambasciatori
    Mantova, b. 1
    Roma, b. 6, 7, 8, 9
  Carteggio di referendari, consiglieri, cancellieri e secretari, b. 4, 166
  Carteggio di ufficiali camerali, b. 1
  Carteggio, Principi esteri, Roma, b. 9
  Consigli, b. 1a
  Gridario, B, Registri di gride, b. 1, vol. 1
  Gridario, Gride manoscritte, 1
  Leggi e decreti, ser. A, regs. 1, 3, 4, 6
  Leggi e decreti, ser. B, regs. I–VI
  Leggi e decreti, ser. C, regs. 3–5, 10–14
  Minutario, Lettere sciolte, b. 3, 4
  Particolari, b. 213, 453, 557, 58, 1087, 1155, 1157, 1159, 1160, 1164, 1166,
    1169, 1176
  Rettori dello stato, Ferrara, b. 1, 12, 13, 19, 32, 35, 40, 41, 43, 45a, 46, 56
    Modena, b. 1a, 2c, 2d, 2e, 2f
    Modenese, Campogalliano
    Modenese, Finale, b. 1
    Modenese, San Felice, b. 1
    Reggiano, Albinea
    Reggiano, Carpineti, b. 1
    Reggiano, Castellarano
    Reggiano, Castelnovo ne' Monti
    Reggiano, Felina
    Reggiano, Toano
    Reggio, b. 1, 2, 112, 152, 153, 166, 173
Archivio segreto estense: Casa e stato, b. 131, 132
Archivio notarile, Modena, Libri memoriali, 332
Camera ducale
  Amministrazione finanziaria dei paesi, Modena, Massaria, b. 40–44
  Mandati, vols. 28, 30, 31, 32, 39
  Memoriale del soldo, regs. 10, 11

Notai camerali ferraresi, reg. 52
Soppressioni napoleoniche, 2653

Archivio di Stato, Reggio Emilia

Comune, Carteggio del reggimento, b. 561
Comune, Provvigioni, regs. 98, 100
Curie della città, Libri delle denuncie

Archivio di Stato, Venice

Consiglio dei Dieci, Misto, reg. 18
Senato, Terra, reg. 3

Archivio storico comunale, Modena

Carte sciolte (Ex actis), b. 1
Vacchette 1487–88, 1489, 1490, 1491, 1496–97

Biblioteca apostolica vaticana

MS Chigi I.I.4, Ugo Caleffini, "Cronaca ferrarese"

Biblioteca comunale ariostea, Ferrara

MS Cl. I, 404, "Libro dei giustiziati"
MS Cl. II, 357, "Hieremie Cusatri cremensis seu mantuani carmina"

Biblioteca comunale, Crema

Archivio storico, Atti del consiglio, regs. 1, 4, 9
"Codice Zurla" (genealogies)

Biblioteca comunale, Mantua

MS 775, "Statuta Mantuae"
MS 1019, Andrea Schivenoglia, "Cronica"

British Library, London

Add. MS 22,345, "Cronaca originale di Reggio di Giovanni Fontanella"

Printed Primary Sources

Statutes

Statuta civitatis Ferrarie. Ferrara, 1476.
Statuta civitatis Mutine. Modena, 1487.
Statuta Pomposiae annis MCCXCV et MCCCXXXVIII–LXXXIII. Ed. A. Samaritani. Rovigo, 1958.
Statuti di Lendinara del 1321. Ed. M. Pozza. Rome, 1984.
"Statuti di Massafiscaglia." Ed. P. Antolini. *Atti e memorie della Deputazione ferrarese di storia patria* 5 (1893): 83–265.

Chronicles

Beliardi, L. *Cronaca della città di Modena (1512–1518).* Ed. A. Biondi and M. Oppi. Modena, 1981.
Cronaca modenese di Tommasino de' Bianchi. Ed. C. Borghi. Vol. 1. Parma, 1862.
"Cronica di Mantova di Andrea Schivenoglia dal 1445 al 1484." Ed. C. D'Arco. In *Raccolta di cronisti e documenti storici lombardi,* ed. G. Müller, vol. 2. Milan, 1857.
Cronica fratris Salimbene de Adam ordinis minorum. Ed. O. Holder-Egger. Monumenta Germaniae historica, Scriptores, vol. 23. Hannover, 1905–13.
Diario ferrarese dall'anno 1409 sino al 1502. Ed. G. Pardi. In *Rerum italicarum scriptores,* 2d ed., vol. 24, pt. 7. Bologna, 1928–33.
Istorie di Giovanni Cambi. Ed. I. di San Luigi. 4 vols. Florence, 1785.
Minuti, A. *Vita di Muzio Attendolo Sforza.* Ed. G. Porro Lambertenghi. *Miscellanea di storia italiana* 7 (1869): 95–306.
Panciroli, G. *Storia della città di Reggio.* 2 vols. Reggio, 1846–48.
Zambotti, B. *Diario ferrarese dall'anno 1476 sino al 1504.* Ed. G. Pardi. In *Rerum italicarum scriptores,* 2d ed., vol. 24, pt. 7. Bologna, 1934–37.

Other Printed Primary Sources

Bernardy, A.A. "Dall'archivio governativo della repubblica di San Marino. Il carteggio della reggenza: 1413–1465." *Atti e memorie della Deputazione di storia patria per le Marche,* n.s., 8 (1912): 129–235.
Campanini, N. "Lettere edite ed inedite di Matteo Maria Boiardo." In *Studi su Matteo Maria Boiardo.* Bologna, 1894.
Cappelli, A., and S. Ferrari, eds. *Rime edite ed inedite di Antonio Cammelli detto il Pistoia.* Livorno, 1884.

Codice diplomatico dell'università di Pavia. Vol. 2. Pt. 2, "1441–50." Pavia, 1915.

Fabris, G., ed. "La cronaca di Giovanni da Nono." *Bollettino del Museo civico di Padova*, n.s., 10–11 (1934–39): 1–30.

Ferrari, G. "Documenti particolari alle notizie della vita di Matteo Maria Boiardo." In *Studi su Matteo Maria Boiardo*, Bologna, 1894.

Grignani, M.A., et al., eds. *Mantova 1430: Pareri a Gian Francesco Gonzaga*. Mantua, 1990.

Natale, A.R., ed. "I Diari di Cicco Simonetta." *Archivio storico lombardo*, 8th ser., 2 (1950): 157–80; 6 (1956): 58–125.

———, ed. *Acta in Consilio Secreto in Castello Portae Jovis Mediolani*. 3 vols. Milan, 1963–69.

Platina [B. Sacchi]. *De principe*. Ed. G. Ferraù. Messina, 1979.

Venturi, G.B. "Relazioni dei governatori estensi di Reggio al duca Ercole I in Ferrara (1482–99)." *AMMo*, 3d ser., 2 (1883–84): 225–387.

Venturini, O. "Dei gradi accademici conferiti dallo studio ferrarese nel primo secolo di sua istituzione." *Atti e memorie della Deputazione ferrarese di storia patria* 4 (1892): 63–107.

Vicini, E.P. "I podestà di Modena: Serie cronologica dal 1336 al 1796." *AMMo*, 5th ser., 10 (1917): 127–297.

Vittani, G., ed. *Inventari e regesti dell'Archivio di Stato in Milano*, vol. 2, *Gli atti cancellereschi viscontei*. Milan, 1919–20.

Zaccaria, V. "Il *Memorandarum rerum liber* di Giovanni di Conversino da Ravenna." *Atti dell'Istituto veneto di scienze, lettere ed arti* 106 (1947–48): 221–50.

Secondary Sources

Antonelli, G. "La magistratura degli Otto di Guardia a Firenze." *Archivio storico italiano* 112 (1954): 3–39.

Artifoni, E. "I ribaldi: Immagini e istituzioni della marginalità nel tardo Medioevo piemontese." In *Piemonte medievale: Forme del potere e della società*. Turin, 1985.

Ascheri, M. "Statuti, legislazione e sovranità: Il caso di Siena." In Chittolini and Willoweit, *Statuti città territori*.

Bagli, G. "Bandi malatestiani." *AMRo*, 3d ser., 3 (1884–85): 76–94.

Balletti, A. *Storia di Reggio nell'Emilia*. Reggio, 1925.

Baracchi, O. "Volte a crociera e affreschi del Duomo: Nuovi documenti del '400 e '500." *AMMo*, 11th ser., 15 (1993): 131–56.

Basaglia, E. "Il controllo della criminalità nella Repubblica di Venezia. Il secolo XVI: Un momento di passaggio." In *Venezia e la Terraferma attraverso le relazioni dei rettori*. Milan, 1981.

Basini, G.L. *L'uomo e il pane: Risorse, consumi e carenze alimentari della popu-lazione modenese nel Cinque e Seicento.* Milan, 1970.

Bellamy, J.G. *Bastard Feudalism and the Law.* London, 1989.

Bertolotti, A. *Prigioni e prigionieri in Mantova dal secolo XIII al XIX.* 1888. Repr., Bologna, 1976.

Bizzocchi, R. "La dissoluzione di un clan familiare: I Buondelmonti di Firenze nei secoli XV e XVI." *Archivio storico italiano* 140 (1982): 3–45.

Blickle, P. "Peasant Revolts in the German Empire in the Late Middle Ages." *Social History* 4 (1979): 223–39.

Bonfiglio Dosio, G. "Criminalità ed emarginazione a Brescia nel primo Quattro-cento." *Archivio storico italiano* 136 (1978): 113–61.

Bongi, S. "Ingiurie, improperi, contumelie ecc. Saggio di lingua parlata del Tre-cento cavata dai libri criminali di Lucca." *Il propugnatore,* n.s., 3, no. 1 (1890): 75–134.

Botteghi, L.A. "Clero e comune in Padova nel secolo XIII." *Nuovo archivio veneto,* n.s., 9 (1905): 215–72.

Bowsky, W.M. "The Medieval Commune and Internal Violence: Police Power and Public Safety in Siena, 1287–1355." *American Historical Review* 73 (1967–68): 1–17.

Brackett, J. *Criminal Justice and Crime in Late Renaissance Florence, 1537–1609.* Cambridge, 1992.

Brown, R.G. "The Politics of Magnificence in Ferrara, 1450–1505." Ph.D. diss., University of Edinburgh, 1982.

Bueno de Mesquita, D.M. "Niccolò da Correggio at Milan." *Italian Studies* 20 (1965): 42–54.

———. "The Place of Despotism in Italian Politics." In *Europe in the Late Mid-dle Ages,* ed. J. Hale, R. Highfield, and B. Smalley. London, 1965.

Burckhardt, J. *The Civilization of the Renaissance in Italy.* London, 1955. First German ed. 1860.

Caduff, C. "I 'pubblici latrones' nella città e nel contado di Firenze a metà Tre-cento." *Ricerche storiche* 18 (1988): 497–521.

Camerali, L. *La tortura a Mantova e altri scritti.* Mantua, 1974.

Campori, G. *Memorie patrie.* Modena, 1881.

Capitani, O. "L'incompiuto 'tractatus de iustitia' di fra Remigio de' Girolami." *Bollettino dell'Istituto storico italiano per il medio evo* 72 (1960): 91–134.

Cappelli, A. "Fra Girolamo Savonarola e notizie intorno il suo tempo." *AMMo* 4 (1867): 321–406.

Carpeggiani, P. "La rinascita del '400." In *I secoli del Polirone,* ed. P. Piva. San Benedetto Po, 1981.

Carpenter, C. "Law, Justice, and Landowners in Late Medieval England." *Law and History Review* 1 (1983): 205–37.

Catalano, M. *Vita di Ludovico Ariosto.* 2 vols. Geneva, 1930.

Cavalcabò, A. "Le vicende storiche di Viadana." *Estratto* from *Bollettino storico cremonese* 18 (1952–53).

Cecchini, G. "Ghino di Tacco." *Archivio storico italiano* 115 (1957): 263–98.

Chambers, D.S. "Cardinal Francesco Gonzaga in Florence." In *Florence and Italy: Renaissance Studies in Honour of Nicolai Rubinstein,* ed. P. Denley and C. Elam. London, 1988.

———. *A Renaissance Cardinal and His Worldly Goods: The Will and Inventory of Francesco Gonzaga (1444–83).* London, 1992.

———. "The Visit to Mantua of Federico da Montefeltro in 1482." *Civiltà mantovana* 28 (1993): 5–15.

Cherubini, G. "Appunti sul brigantaggio in Italia alla fine del Medioevo." In *Studi di storia medievale e moderna per Ernesto Sestan.* Florence, 1980.

Chiappini, A., ed. *Palazzo Paradiso e la biblioteca ariostea.* Rome, 1993.

Chiappini, L. "Ercole I d'Este e Girolamo Savonarola." *Atti e memorie della Deputazione ferrarese di storia patria* 7 (1952): pt. 3, 43–53.

———. "Eleonora d'Aragona, prima duchessa di Ferrara." *Atti e memorie della Deputazione ferrarese di storia patria,* n.s., 16 (1956): 9–121.

Chittolini, G. "Il 'privato,' il 'pubblico,' lo Stato." In *Origini dello Stato: Processi di formazione statale in Italia fra medioevo ed età moderna,* ed. G. Chittolini, A. Molho, and P. Schiera. Bologna, 1994.

———. "Feudatari e comunità rurali nell'Italia centro-settentrionale (secoli XV–XVII)." *Studi storici Luigi Simeoni* 36 (1986): 11–28.

———. "Stati regionali e istituzioni ecclesiastiche nell'Italia centrosettentrionale del Quattrocento." In *La chiesa e il potere politico del medioevo all'età contemporanea,* ed. G. Chittolini and G. Miccoli. Einaudi *Storia d'Italia. Annali* vol. 9. Turin, 1986.

———. "Stati padani, 'Stato del rinascimento': Problemi di ricerca." In *Persistenze feudali e autonomie comunitative in stati urbani fra Cinque e Settecento,* ed. G. Tocci. Bologna, 1988.

———. "L'onore dell'officiale." *Quaderni milanesi* 17–18 (1989): 3–53.

———. "Civic Religion and the Countryside in Late Medieval Italy." In *City and Countryside in Late Medieval and Renaissance Italy: Essays Presented to Philip Jones,* ed. T. Dean and C. Wickham. London, 1990.

———. "Statuti e autonomie urbane: Introduzione." In Chittolini and Willoweit, *Statuti città territori.*

Chittolini, G., and D. Willoweit, eds. *Statuti città territori in Italia e Germania tra Medioevo ed Età moderna.* Annali dell'istituto storico italo-germanico, Quaderno 30. Bologna, 1991.

Cittadella, L.N. *Notizie relative a Ferrara per la maggior parte inedite.* Ferrara, 1864.

Clanchy, M. "Law, Government, and Society in Medieval England." *History* 59 (1974): 73–78.

Cognasso, F. *L'Italia nel rinascimento*. 2 vols. Turin, 1966.

Cohn, S. "Criminality and the State in Renaissance Florence, 1344–1466." *Journal of Social History* 14 (1980–81): 211–33.

———. *The Cult of Remembrance and the Black Death: Six Cities in Central Italy*. Baltimore, 1992.

Comani, F.E. "I denari per la dote di Valentina Visconti." *Archivio storico lombardo*, 3d ser., 15, *anno* 29 (1901): 37–82.

Comba, R. "Il progetto di una società coercitivamente cristiana: Gli Statuti di Amedeo VIII di Savoia." *Rivista storica italiana* 103 (1991): 33–56.

Connell, W.J. "Il commissario e lo stato territoriale fiorentino." *Ricerche storiche* 18 (1988): 591–617.

Cozzi, G. *Repubblica di Venezia e stati italiani: Politica e giustizia dal secolo XVI al secolo XVIII*. Turin, 1982.

D'Arco, C. *Studi intorno al municipio di Mantova*. Vols. 2 and 6. Mantua, 1871 and 1874.

Davari, S. *I palazzi dell'antico comune di Mantova e gli incendi da essi subiti*. 1888. Repr., Mantua, 1974.

Dean, T. "Venetian Economic Hegemony: The Case of Ferrara, 1200–1500." *Studi veneziani*, n.s., 12 (1986): 45–98.

———. *Land and Power in Late Medieval Ferrara: The Rule of the Este, 1350–1450*. Cambridge, 1987.

———. "After the War of Ferrara: Relations between Venice and Ercole d'Este, 1484–1505." In *War, Culture, and Society in Renaissance Venice*, ed. D.S. Chambers, C.H. Clough, and M.E. Mallett. London, 1993.

———. "Ercole I d'Este." *DBI* 43 (1993): 97–107.

———. "Criminal Justice in Mid-Fifteenth-Century Bologna." In Dean and Lowe, *Crime, Society, and the Law*.

Dean, T., and K. Lowe. "Writing the History of Crime in the Renaissance." In Dean and Lowe, *Crime, Society, and the Law*.

———, eds. *Crime, Society, and the Law in Renaissance Italy*. Cambridge, 1994.

De Caro, G. "Boschetti, Albertino." *DBI* 13 (1971): 170–74.

Fasano Guarini, E. "Gli stati dell'Italia centro-settentrionale tra Quattro e Cinquecento: Continuità e trasformazioni." *Società e storia* 21 (1983): 617–39.

———. "Gli statuti delle città soggette a Firenze tra '400 e '500: Riforme locali e interventi centrali." In Chittolini and Willoweit, *Statuti città territori*.

———. "The Prince, the Judges, and the Law: Cosimo I and Sexual Violence, 1558." In Dean and Lowe, *Crime, Society, and the Law*.

Fino, A. *Scielta degli huomini di pregio usciti da Crema*. Brescia, 1576.

Forti, F. "Boiardo Matteo Maria." *DBI* 11 (1969): 211–23.

Fossati, F. "Noterelle viscontee-sforzesche." *Archivio storico lombardo*, 8th ser., 4, *anno* 80 (1953): 218–27.

——. "Nuove spigolature d'archivio." *Archivio storico lombardo,* 8th ser., 7, *anno* 84 (1957): 357–91.

Franchini, L. *Simboli, emblemi, impresi nel castello di Vignola.* Vignola, 1977.

Frizzi, A. *Memorie per la storia di Ferrara.* 2d ed. 5 vols. Ferrara, 1847–48.

Gardner, E.G. *Dukes and Poets in Ferrara.* London, 1904.

Gazzola, P. *Il palazzo del podestà a Mantova.* Mantua, 1973.

Généstal, R. *Le privilegium fori en France du décret de Gratien à la fin du XIVe siècle.* Paris, 1921.

Gianandrea, A. "Della signoria di Francesco Sforza nella Marca." *Archivio storico italiano,* 5th ser., 2 (1888): 21–38, 166–92, 289–323.

Golinelli, P. "Il monastero, la città, il territorio." In *S. Pietro di Modena, mille anni di storia e di arte.* Milan, 1984.

Griffiths, R.A. *The Reign of King Henry VI: The Exercise of Royal Authority, 1422–1461.* London, 1981.

Grubb, J.S. *Firstborn of Venice: Vicenza in the Early Renaissance State.* Baltimore, 1988.

Gundersheimer. W. "Crime and Punishment in Ferrara, 1440–1500." In *Violence and Civil Disorder in Italian Cities, 1200–1500,* ed. L. Martines. Berkeley, 1972.

——. *Ferrara: The Style of a Renaissance Despotism* (Princeton, N.J., 1973).

Ilardi, V. "Crosses and Carets: Renaissance Patronage and Coded Letters of Recommendation." *American Historical Review* 92 (1987): 1127–49.

Jones, P.J. "Communes and Despots: The City State in Late-Medieval Italy." *Transactions of the Royal Historical Society,* 5th ser., 15 (1965): 71–96.

——. *The Malatesta of Rimini and the Papal State.* Cambridge, 1974.

Kent, F.W. "*Ottimati* families in Florentine politics and society, 1427–1530: The Rucellai, Capponi, and Ginori." Ph.D. diss., University of London, 1971.

——. *Household and Lineage in Renaissance Florence: The Family Life of the Capponi, Ginori, and Rucellai.* Princeton, 1977.

Klapisch-Zuber, C. "The Medieval Italian Mattinata." *Journal of Family History* 5 (1980): 2–27.

Kristeller, P. *Andrea Mantegna.* Berlin, 1902.

Labalme, P.H. "Sodomy and Venetian Justice in the Renaissance." *Tijdschrift voor rechtsgeschiedenis* 52 (1984): 217–54.

Larner, J. "Order and Disorder in Romagna, 1450–1500." In *Violence and Civil Disorder in Italian Cities, 1200–1500,* ed. L. Martines. Berkeley, 1972.

Laruelle, E., E.-R. Labande, and P. Ourliac. *L'Eglise au temps du Grand Schisme et de la crise conciliaire (1378–1449).* N.p., 1962.

Lazzarini, I. "Il diritto urbano in una signoria cittadina: Gli statuti mantovani dai Bonacolsi ai Gonzaga (1313–1404)." In Chittolini and Willoweit, *Statuti città territori.*

————. *Gerarchie sociali e spazi urbani a Mantova dal comune alla signoria gonzaghesca.* Pisa, 1994.

Lesnick, D.R. "Insults and Threats in Medieval Todi." *Journal of Medieval History* 17 (1991): 71–83.

Litta, P. *Famiglie celebri italiane.* Milan, 1819–74; Naples, 1902–23.

Luzio, A. "Il Platina e i Gonzaga." *Giornale storico della letteratura italiana* 13 (1889): 430–40.

————. "Una ghigliottina rudimentale nel Cinquecento." *Gazzetta di Mantova,* Mar. 1899, 12–13.

————. "Isabella d'Este e Francesco Gonzaga, promessi sposi." *Archivio storico lombardo,* 4th ser., 9, *anno* 35 (1908): 34–69.

————. *L'Archivio Gonzaga.* Vol. 2. Verona, 1922.

Maire Vigueur, J.-C. "Justice et politique dans l'Italie communale de la seconde moitié du XIIIe siècle: L'exemple de Pérouse." *Académie des inscriptions et belles-lettres, Comptes rendus,* 1986, 312–28.

Malacarne, G. "La stemma del podestà di Mantova Gabriel Ginori: un magistrato del XV secolo," *Civiltà mantovana* 30 (1995): 39–55.

Mallett, M. "Ambassadors and Their Audiences in Renaissance Italy." *Renaissance Studies* 8 (1994): 229–43.

Manikowska, H. "Polizia e servizi d'ordine a Firenze nella seconda metà del XIV secolo." *Ricerche storiche* 16 (1986): 17–38.

————. "'Accorr'uomo': Il popolo nell'amministrazione della giustizia a Firenze durante il XV secolo." *Ricerche storiche* 18 (1988): 523–49.

Marani, E. "Architettura." In *Mantova: Le arti,* vol. 2, ed. E. Marani and C. Perina, Mantua, 1961.

————. *Il Palazzo D'Arco a Mantova.* Mantua, 1980.

Marini, L. *Lo stato estense.* Turin, 1987.

Massetto, G.P. *Un magistrato e una città nella Lombardia spagnola: Giulio Claro pretore a Cremona.* Milan, 1985.

Mazzi, M.S. "Il mondo della prostituzione nella Firenze tardo medievale." *Ricerche storiche* 14 (1984): 337–63.

Mazzoldi, L. *Mantova: La storia.* Vol. 2. Mantua, 1960.

McFarlane, K.B. *The Nobility of Later Medieval England.* Oxford, 1973.

Molho, A. *Marriage Alliance in Late Medieval Florence.* Cambridge, Mass., 1994.

Mozzarelli, C. "Il Senato di Mantova: Origini e funzioni." In *Mantova e i Gonzaga nella civiltà del rinascimento.* Mantua, 1977.

————. *Mantova e i Gonzaga dal 1382 al 1707.* Turin, 1987.

Muchembled, R. *Le temps des supplices: De l'obéissance sous les roirs absolus, XV–XVIIIᵉ siècles.* Paris, 1992.

Muir, E. *Mad Blood Stirring: Vendetta and Factions in Friuli during the Renaissance.* Baltimore, 1993.

Mulazzani, G. "La fonte letteraria della Camera degli Sposi di Mantegna." *Arte lombarda,* n.s., 50 (1978): 33–46.

Navarrini, R. *Il principato e la città: Giulio Cesare da Bozzolo.* Quaderni di Civiltà mantovana, 2 (Mantua, 1994): 19–31.

Nicolini, U. "Principe e cittadini: Una consultazione popolare del 1430 nella Mantova dei Gonzaga." In *Mantova e i Gonzaga nella civiltà del rinascimento.* Mantua, 1977.

Osheim, D.J. "Countrymen and the Law in Late Medieval Tuscany." *Speculum* 64 (1989): 317–37.

Paccagnini, G. *Mantova: Le arti,* vol. 1, Mantua, 1960.

Passerini, L. *Genealogia e storia della famiglia Ginori.* Florence, 1876.

Pavan, E. "Recherches sur la nuit vénitienne à la fin du Moyen Age." *Journal of Medieval History* 7 (1981): 339–56.

Pavesi, B. *Relazioni sui delitti commessi nelle terre dei Gonzaga dal 1492 al 1722.* Suzzara, 1993.

Pene Vidari, G.S. "Sulla criminalità e sui banni del comune di Ivrea nei primi anni della dominazione sabauda (1313–1347)." *Bollettino storico-bibliografico subalpino* 68 (1970): 157–211.

Picotti, G.B. *La Dieta di Mantova e la politica de' Veneziani.* Venice, 1912.

Pini, A.I. "Bonfranceschi, Agostino." *DBI* 12 (1970): 32–34.

Pinto, G. "Un vagabondo, ladro e truffatore nella Toscana della seconda metà del '300: Sandro di Vanni detto Pescione." *Ricerche storiche,* n.s., 4 (1974): 328–45.

———. "Controllo politico e ordine pubblico nei primi vicariati fiorentini: Gli 'Atti criminali degli ufficiali forensi.'" *Quaderni storici* 49 (1982): 226–41.

Povolo, C. "Aspetti e problemi dell'amministrazione della giustizia penale nella repubblica di Venezia: Secoli XVI–XVII." In *Stato, società e giustizia nella repubblica veneta (sec. XV–XVIII),* ed. G. Cozzi. Rome, 1980.

———. "Contributi e ricerche in corso sull'amministrazione della giustizia nella repubblica di Venezia in età moderna." *Quaderni storici* 44 (1980): 614–26.

Prosperi, A. "Brocadelli, Lucia." *DBI* 14 (1972): 381–83.

Raggio, O. *Faide e parentele: Lo stato genovese visto dalla Fontanabuona.* Turin, 1990.

Rangoni Machiavelli, L. *I Rangoni.* Rome, 1908.

Rasi, P. "I rapporti tra l'autorità ecclesiastica e l'autorità civile in Feltre." *Archivio veneto,* 5th ser., 13 (1933): 82–127.

Reichenbach, G. *Matteo Maria Boiardo.* Bologna, 1929.

Ricciardi, R. "Cusadro, Geremia." *DBI* 31 (1985): 494–95.

Richmond, C. "An English Mafia?" *Nottingham Medieval Studies* 36 (1992): 235–43.

Rocke, M. "Il controllo dell'omosessualità a Firenze nel XV secolo: Gli Ufficiali di notte." *Quaderni storici* 66 (1987): 701–23.

Roia, P. "L'amministrazione finanziaria del comune di Ancona nel secolo XV." *Atti e memorie della Deputazione di storia patria per le Marche*, 4th ser., 1 (1924): 141–246.

Romano, D. "*Quod sibi fiat gratia*: Adjustment of Penalties and the Exercise of Influence in Early Renaissance Venice." *Journal of Medieval and Renaissance Studies* 13 (1983): 251–68.

Rombaldi, O. "La comunità reggiana nello stato estense nel secolo XV." *Annuario del Liceo-Ginnasio statale "L. Ariosto" di Reggio-Emilia*, 1965–67.

Roque Ferrer, P. "L'infrazione della legge a Cagliari dal 1340 al 1380." *Quaderni sardi di storia* 5 (1985–86): 3–26.

Rotelli, C. *Una campagna medievale: Storia agraria del Piemonte fra il 1250 e il 1450*. Turin, 1973.

Rubinstein, N. "Il 'De optimo cive' del Platina." In *Bartolomeo Sacchi il Platina*, ed. A. Campana and P. Medioli Masotti. Padua, 1986.

Ruggiero, G. *Violence in Early Renaissance Venice*. New Brunswick, 1980.

———. *The Boundaries of Eros: Sexual Crime and Sexuality in Renaissance Venice*. New York, 1985.

Ryder, A. *The Kingdom of Naples under Alfonso the Magnanimous*. Oxford, 1976.

———. "The Incidence of Crime in Sicily in the Mid-Fifteenth Century: The Evidence from Composition Records." In Dean and Lowe, *Crime, Society, and the Law*.

Sandonini, T. "Del palazzo comunale di Modena." *AMMo*, 4th ser., 9 (1899): 93–132.

Santini, E. "La *protestatio de iustitia* nella Firenze medicea del secolo XV." *Rinascimento* 11 (1959): 33–106.

Secco d'Aragona, F. "Francesco Secco, i Gonzaga e Paolo Erba." *Archivio storico lombardo*, 8th ser., 6, *anno* 83 (1956): 210–61.

Signorini, R. "*Opus hoc tenue*": *La Camera dipinta di Andrea Mantegna*. Mantua, 1985.

———. "Baldassare Soardi, Dedicatoria della 'Vita' di Vittorino da Feltre del Platina." In *Bartolomeo Sacchi il Platina*, ed. A. Campana and P. Meioli Masotti. Padua, 1986.

Soli, G. *Chiese di Modena*. 3 vols. Modena, 1974.

Spinelli, G. "Mille anni di vita monastica." In *S. Pietro di Modena, mille anni di storia e di arte*. Milan, 1984.

Terno, P. *Della historia di Crema*. Ed. M. Verga and C. Verga. Crema, 1964.

Thomson, J.A.F. *Popes and Princes, 1417–1517*. London, 1980.

Tiraboschi, G. *Memorie storiche modenesi*. 4 vols. Modena, 1793–94.

Torri, T. "'Allegrezze' e feste pubbliche: Modena fra '400 e '500." *Quaderni storici* 79 (1992): 215–29.

Trombetti Budriesi, A.L. "Sui rapporti tra i Pio e gli Estensi: Lo scambio Carpi-

Sassuolo." In *Società, politica e cultura a Carpi ai tempi di Alberto III Pio.*
Vol. 2. Padua, 1981.

Vaini, M. "Gli statuti di Francesco Gonzaga IV Capitano: Prime ricerche." *Atti e memorie dell'Accademia virgiliana di Mantova,* n.s., 56 (1988): 187–214.

———. *Ricerche gonzaghesche.* Florence, 1994.

Varanini, G.M. "Gli statuti delle città della Terraferma veneta nel Quattrocento." In Chittolini and Willoweit, *Statuti città territori.*

Verga, C. *Pietro Terni.* Crema, 1964.

Verga, E. "Le sentenze criminali dei podestà milanesi, 1385–1429." *Archivio storico lombardo,* 3d ser., 16, *anno* 28 (1901): 96–142.

Waquet, J.-C. *Corruption: Ethics and Power in Florence, 1600–1770.* Trans. L. McCall. Oxford, 1991.

Wedgwood, C.V. *Thomas Wentworth First Earl of Strafford 1593–1641: A Revaluation.* London, 1961.

Zorzi, A. "L'amministrazione della giustizia penale nella repubblica fiorentina: Aspetti e problemi." *Archivio storico italiano* 533–34 (1987): 391–453, 527–78.

———. "I fiorentini e gli uffici pubblici nel primo Quattrocento: Concorrenza, abusi, illegalità." *Quaderni storici* 66 (1987): 725–51.

———. "Giustizia criminale e criminalità nell'Italia del tardo medioevo: Studi e prospettive di ricerca." *Società e storia* 46 (1989): 923–65.

———. "Giusdicenti e operatori di giustizia nello stato territoriale fiorentino del XV secolo." *Ricerche storiche* 19 (1989): 517–52.

———. "Tradizioni storiografiche e studi recenti sulla giustizia nell'Italia del rinascimento." *Cheiron* 8 (1991): 27–78.

———. "La giustizia a Firenze in età Laurenziana." In *Lorenzo il Magnifico,* ed. F. Cardini. Rome, 1992.

———. "The Judicial System in Florence." In Dean and Lowe, *Crime, Society, and the Law.*

Index

PLATES

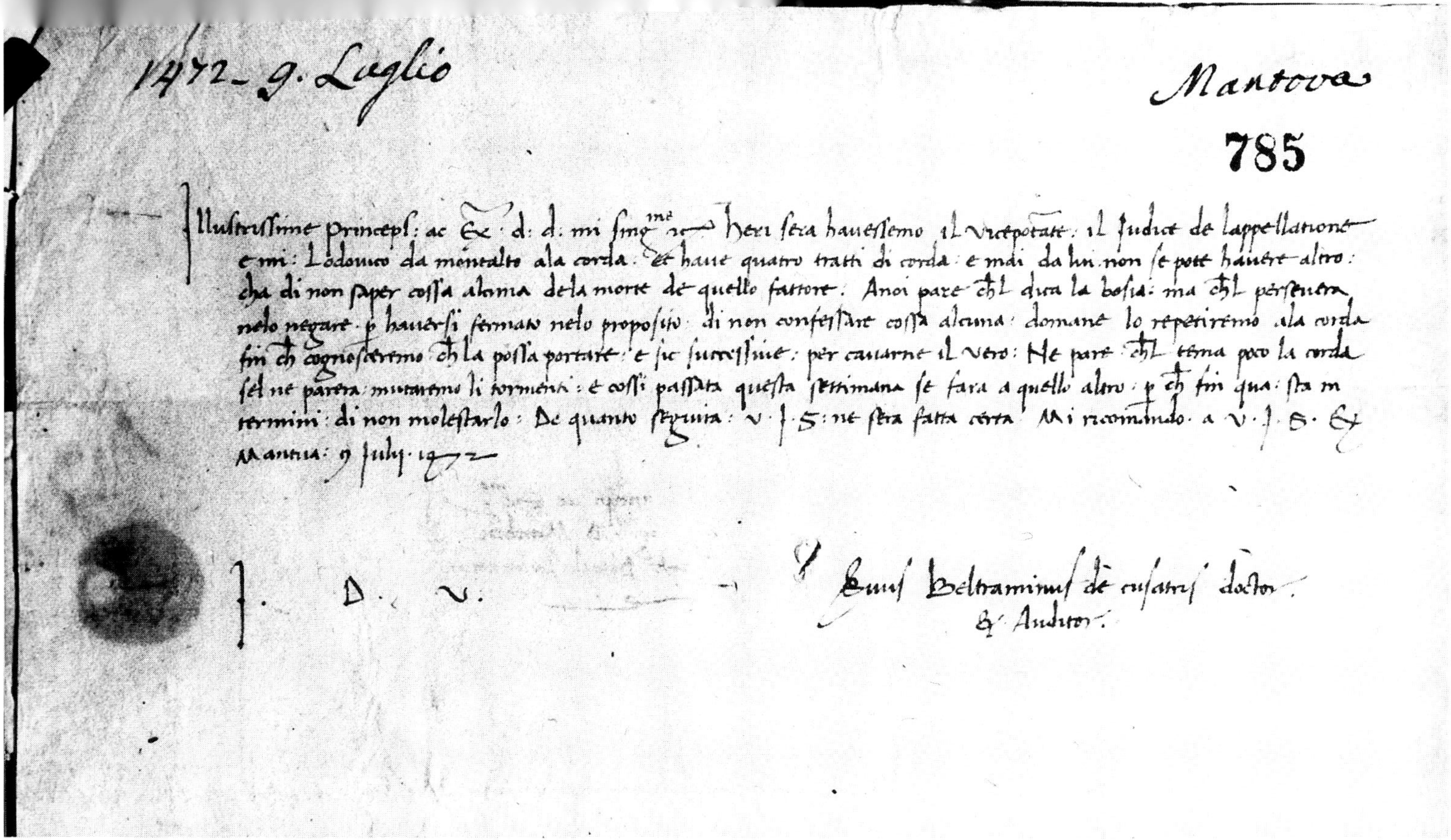
1472 - 9. Luglio

Mantova

785

Illustrissime princeps: ac Ex. d. d. mi sing.me etc. Heri sera havessemo il Vicepotate: il Judice de lappellatione e mi: Lodovico da monealto ala corda. et have quatro tratti di corda: e mai da lui non se pote havere altro: cha di non saper cossa alcuna dela morte de quello fattore. Anoi pare che dica la bosia: ma che persevera nelo negare. p haversi fermato nelo proposito di non confessare cossa alcuna: domane lo repetiremo ala corda fin ch cognosceremo ch la possa portare: e sic successive: per cavarne il vero: Ne pare che tema poco la corda sel ne parera mutaremo li tormenti: e cossi passata questa settimana se fara a quello altro: p ch fin qua: sta in termini: di non molestarlo: De quanto seguira: V. I. S. ne sera fatta certa. Mi recomando. a V. I. S. etc.

Mantue: 9 July. 1472

I. D. V.

Servus Beltraminus de cusatis doctor. et Auditor.

Plate 1. Beltramino's autograph (letter to Marquis Ludovico Gonzaga, 9 July 1472: AG, b. 2413, fol. 785r)

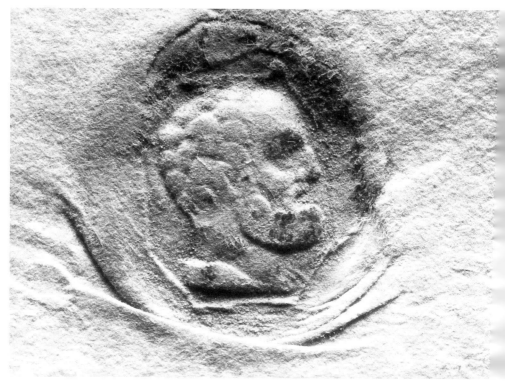

Plate 2. Beltramino's seal: impression from a gem, possibly representing Hercules, on a letter to Marquis Ludovico Gonzaga, 27 January 1473 (AG, b. 2413, fol. 783v)

Plate 3. The coat of arms of Gabriele Ginori, podesta of Mantua in 1493–94; formerly on the wall of the Palazzo del podestà (Museo del Palazzo ducale, Mantua)

Plate 4. Depiction of a public beheading in Ferrara (from "Libro dei giustiziati," Biblioteca comunale

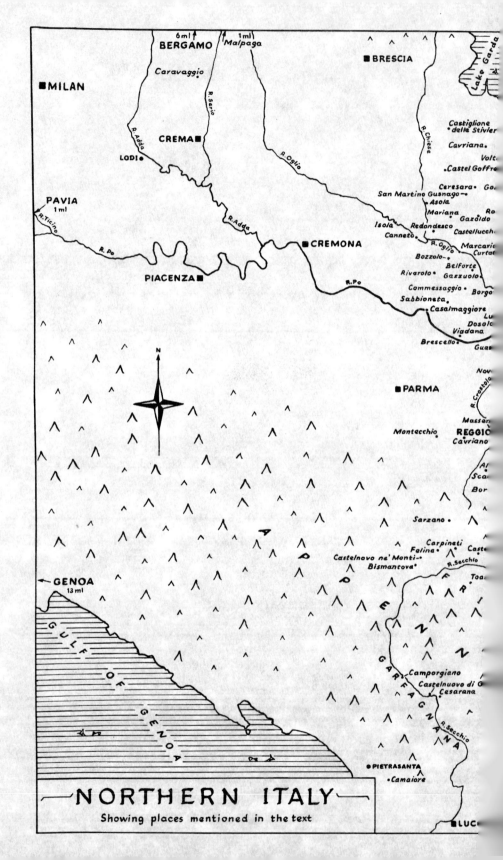

NORTHERN ITALY

Showing places mentioned in the text